Essays on the Theory of
Optimal Economic Growth

Essays on the Theory of Optimal Economic Growth

Edited by Karl Shell

THE M.I.T. PRESS
Massachusetts Institute of Technology
Cambridge, Massachusetts, and London, England

Preface

The fifteen essays that comprise this volume are based upon material that was presented, in one form or another, during 1965–1966 at an M.I.T. seminar on the theory of optimal economic growth. Most of the essays included in this volume can be thought of as elaborations of and extensions to the original 1928 contribution of Frank P. Ramsey.[1] In the context of the one-sector neoclassical model of production, Ramsey characterized the program of capital accumulation that maximizes the integral over time of utilities of per capita consumption. Essentially, Ramsey characterized the trajectory of capital accumulation that satisfies Euler's differential equation and the appropriate boundary conditions.[2] For a program to be a local interior extremal, it is necessary that Euler's equation be satisfied by the program. Under the usual curvature assumptions that are made in the theory of economic planning, a feasible program satisfying the Euler equation and the appropriate boundary conditions is a global interior maximum.[3]

Even in Ramsey's problem, there is the possibility that the optimal

---

[1] F. P. Ramsey, "A Mathematical Theory of Saving," *Economic Journal*, Vol. 38 (1928), pp. 543–549.

[2] A good introduction to the calculus of variations can be found in I. M. Gelfand and S. V. Fomin, *Calculus of Variations* (revised English edition translated and edited by R. A. Silverman), Englewood Cliffs, N.J.: Prentice-Hall, Inc., 1963.

[3] Economic problems in which there exist nonoptimal feasible programs satisfying the usual necessary conditions are encountered in Essays III and IV of this volume.

trajectory will not be interior to all constraints. If, for example, installed capital is not suitable for consumption, an economy that is capital rich must initially, for optimality, specialize to consumption. The maximum principle of L. S. Pontryagin *et al.*[4] does yield necessary conditions for a maximum (either interior or corner). For this reason and also for general convenience, several of the authors have chosen to employ this recent contribution to control theory rather than equivalent techniques from the classical calculus of variations.[5]

In the first essay, I treat the problem of maximizing the integral of discounted per capita consumption over a given (finite or infinite) planning period for neoclassical economies in which technical change is Hicks-neutral and proceeds at a fixed, exogenously given rate. Optimal programs, when they exist, possess a certain "modified golden rule turnpike property." For the one-sector model, the production possibility frontier is a straight-line segment in consumption-investment space. Therefore, since the maximand is linear in consumption, the infinite-horizon, zero-technical-change optimal program is "bang-bang." In the two-sector model, with differing efficient capital intensities between the sectors, the optimal consumption trajectory is continuous because of the curvature of the production possibility frontier.

In three of the essays (II–IV), the problem of optimal accumulation is studied for models in which technical change depends, in one way or another, upon economic variables. Eytan Sheshinski's essay (II) is based upon Arrow's theory of learning by doing. Sheshinski follows Arrow in making labor-augmenting technical progress dependent upon increases in cumulative investment. But unlike Arrow's model where technical change is embodied only in the latest vintage of capital, Sheshinski makes technical change disembodied. Disembodiment allows the analysis to be in terms of the standard variational techniques. Consumption-optimal programs are found together with a formula for optimal taxation to support investment for a decentralized

---

[4] L. S. Pontryagin, V. G. Boltyanskii, R. V. Gamkrelidze, and E. F. Mishchenko, *The Mathematical Theory of Optimal Processes* (translated by K. W. Trirogoff), New York: Interscience Publishers, Inc., 1962. Roughly, the maximum principle is to the ordinary calculus of variations as the Kuhn-Tucker conditions are to the ordinary (equality) first-order conditions of the differential calculus.

[5] I do not want to overstate the case for the application of the maximum principle to economic problems. I have encountered no economic problem that is amenable to solution by the maximum principle that could not have been solved by suitable extensions to the classical calculus of variations. Cf., e.g., F. A. Valentine, "The Problem of Lagrange with Differential Inequalities as Added Side Conditions," in G. A. Bliss (ed.), *Contributions to the Calculus of Variations, 1933–1937*, Chicago: University of Chicago Press, 1937, pp. 407–448. In fact, Richard Bellman in a book review for *Econometrica*, Vol. 33, No. 1 (January 1965), pp. 252–254, cites published and unpublished work in which the maximum principle has been derived from the classical calculus of variations and its extensions.

economy in which the benefits of learning by doing are not appropriated by the individual investor.

William Nordhaus in Essay III studies the properties of consumption-optimal programs for an economy that at any instant of time must choose rates of capital-augmenting and labor-augmenting technical change, rates that are constrained to lie within an innovation possibility set. If the elasticity of substitution between capital and labor is bounded below unity, then the only long-term equilibrium for the planning model is the Harrod point where technical change is purely labor augmenting. Nordhaus extends his analysis to consider the problem where the position of the innovation possibility frontier depends upon the current allocation of economic resources to inventive activity.

In Essay IV, I construct a model economy with three goods: consumption, investment, and invention. The economy can be efficiently decentralized so that the productive sector is competitive and the stock of technical knowledge enters each firm's production function as a pure public good. The inventive sector is assumed to maximize its output subject to revenue that is derived from taxation in the productive sector. The problem of optimal accumulation is briefly discussed. Long-run equilibrium in the economy with constant saving and tax rates is not globally stable.

Harl Ryder in Essay V characterizes optimal programs of accumulation for an open economy in which outputs are traded but in which there is no lending or borrowing. Ryder's moderate-sized economy faces a Marshallian offer curve that shifts at the same rate as growth of the home country labor force. This generalization of the problem of the small country in the large world seems to imply that the labor force of the rest of the world is expected to grow at the same rate as that in the home country and that the rest of the world seeks to maintain a constant capital-labor ratio. Pranab Bardhan in Essay VI treats the optimal accumulation problem in an economy with no international trade that faces a schedule of rates at which it can borrow foreign capital. His maximand is novel in that it is increasing in domestic per capita consumption but decreasing in foreign debt per capita.

In Essay VII, Mrinal Datta-Chaudhuri investigates a model economy divided into two regions having differing techniques of production and differing institutionally fixed savings ratios (out of profits). Transportation of investment goods between regions is allowed, but it is assumed that in the process a fixed fraction of the transported goods is lost to evaporation. Datta-Chaudhuri proceeds to characterize the program that achieves the given national target level of capital stock in the least time.

Stephen Marglin in Essay VIII studies an economy in which the supply of labor is infinitely elastic at an exogenously given wage rate (in terms of output) and in which all wage income is consumed. Marglin solves for the capital-labor ratio (chosen once and for all) that maximizes a Ramsey-like utility function.[6] An important consequence of the linkage between the capital-labor ratio and the savings rate is that the market price of capital and the market rate of interest are replaced by shadow values in the investment criteria that derive from utility maximization.

Nicholas Carter's contribution (Essay IX) is an empirical exercise in economic planning. Carter replaces the fixed-proportions market basket maximand in a model of Sandee with a maximand that allows for continuous substitution among consumption goods. An analysis of how such a maximand is derived from observed market data is included. Essay X, by Elizabeth Chase, is an extension of Ramsey's problem to the case where the maximand is an increasing, strictly concave function of per capita consumption and per capita leisure and where there is no satiation in production or consumption.

In Essay XI, Michael Bruno characterizes, for a variety of models of the discrete activity-analysis type, programs of capital accumulation that maximize the discounted integral of per capita consumption. Use of the "jump" (or "corner") conditions is intrinsic to planning models of this type. While the "jump" condition implies that the demand prices of the capital goods move continuously through time, the shadow wage and rentals rates are allowed to move in discrete steps. The two-sector, fixed-proportions model is studied in detail; the analysis is extended to allow choice of alternative production activities. Bruno also discusses the heterogeneous capital good model.[7]

In Essay XII, Paul Samuelson explores some problems recently raised by Frank Hahn. He considers a heterogeneous capital model in which a fixed fraction of income is saved. The assumption that expectations are always justified yields a system of differential equations obeyed by the demand prices of the capital goods. Even when momentary competitive equilibrium is unique, coupling the price differential equations with the capital-accumulation differential equations typically results in a long-run equilibrium that is a saddle point in the space of demand prices and capitals.[8] Thus for only one

---

[6] In as yet unpublished work growing out of the seminar, Marglin has extended the analysis to include economies in which labor supply is initially surplus (but not necessarily unlimited). In the unpublished work, the choice of programs has not been restricted to those with a constant capital-labor ratio.

[7] One cannot avoid comparing the qualitative aspects of optimal growth trajectories of the "blueprint" models with those of the neoclassical homogeneous capital models. In the latter case, I use the word "models" rather than "parables" because I do not think that there is a hierarchy of models—one being an "approximation," the other "true." It seems to me that there are many models and the appropriate model to use depends upon the problem being studied.

[8] One immediately notices that, unlike planning models, there are no boundary conditions accompanying the differential equations for prices. One's first instinct might be to look for these transversality conditions as the result of the behavior of firms engaged in production. Will the stipulation that producers maximize present value close

assignment of initial prices will the economy proceed to a golden age. Samuelson by thinking of consumption as necessitous reduces the model to a von Neumann system and finds that most of the paths of accumulation that are consistent with perfect foresight diverge from the golden-age turnpike. His heuristic argument is that a mixed economy may by trial, error, and speculative correction find its way back to the turnpike in the course of avoiding permanently inefficient programs.

David Cass and Menahem Yaari (Essay XIII) investigate the process of capital accumulation in a model in which production is neoclassical while aggregate saving is due to the desire of individuals to achieve an optimal lifetime consumption pattern. An example is presented in which a dynamic competitive equilibrium path is found on which the aggregate capital-labor ratio is forever bounded above the golden rule capital-labor ratio. By a theorem derived by Phelps and Koopmans, such a path is known to be inefficient in the sense that it is possible to raise consumption over some period without lowering it at any other point. For the Cass-Yaari model, if competitive equilibrium is efficient, then it is Pareto-optimal. The effects of a monetary system and a sector of accumulation-oriented firms are also analyzed; it is shown that such intermediation may preclude inefficiency.

In his second contribution to this volume (Essay XIV), Paul Samuelson examines the implications of the Phelps-Koopmans inefficiency theorem just discussed. He considers the one-sector model and adopts the Benthamite criterion of maximizing the sum of utilities of per capita consumption weighted by current population size over a given planning period.[9] If the planning period is finite and population is growing at a fixed positive rate, then the optimal program has a capital-labor ratio bounded above the golden rule level for a fraction of time that increases with the length of the planning period. This "paradox" is stated to highlight the limited applicability of the Phelps-Koopmans theorem; by this criterion no historically observed full-employment trajectory can be found to be inefficient.[10] The implication of the results for the Samuelson-Lerner-Diamond-Asimakopulos controversy is also discussed.

George Akerlof's contribution (Essay XV) is a proof of the stability of the long-run equilibrium in a putty-clay model fashioned after the model of

---

the model? The answer seems to be that in a closed economy in which economic actors mechanically consume a fraction of income independent of wealth there is no such boundary condition closing the model.

[9] Koopmans himself has found this maximand to be attractive. Cf., T. C. Koopmans, "On the Concept of Optimal Economic Growth," *Semaine d'Etude sur le Rôle de l'Analyse Econométrique dans la Formulation de Plans de Développement*, Vatican City: Pontifical Academy of Sciences, 1965, Vol. I, pp. 225–287.

[10] Like intuitionist mathematicians, Samuelson seems to be uncomfortable when contemplating infinity. Some economists, however, seem to be uncomfortable in choosing a finite planning horizon and the corresponding terminal requirements.

Johansen. Stability ensures that the long-run wage and the long-run marginal product of labor are well defined; when producers choose profit-maximizing machines, in the long run labor is paid its marginal product.

Eytan Sheshinski and I prepared the bibliography. We have attempted to include all contributions on the "Ramsey problem" and on "golden rules." Although a few papers from related fields have slipped in, we have not tried to cover such closely related topics as the von Neumann turnpike theory, empirical planning models, and inventory control theory. Nor have we included references on mathematical techniques.

My thanks go to Paul Samuelson, Robert Solow, and the members of the seminar for encouraging me to edit this volume.

Cambridge, Massachusetts   KARL SHELL
June 1966

CONTENTS

Preface   *Karl Shell*   v

ESSAY I   Optimal Programs of Capital Accumulation for an
           Economy in which there is Exogenous Technical Change   1
           Karl Shell

ESSAY II   Optimal Accumulation with Learning by Doing   31
           Eytan Sheshinski

ESSAY III The Optimal Rate and Direction of Technical Change   53
           William D. Nordhaus

ESSAY IV   A Model of Inventive Activity and Capital Accumulation 67
           Karl Shell

ESSAY V   Optimal Accumulation and Trade in an Open Economy of
           Moderate Size   87
           Harl E. Ryder, Jr.

ESSAY VI   Optimum Foreign Borrowing   117
           Pranab K. Bardhan

ESSAY VII Optimum Allocation of Investments and Transportation
           in a Two-Region Economy   129
           Mrinal Datta-Chaudhuri

ESSAY VIII The Rate of Interest and the Value of Capital with Un-
           limited Supplies of Labor   141
           Stephen A. Marglin

ESSAY IX   A New Look at the Sandee Model   165
           Nicholas G. Carter

ESSAY X   Leisure and Consumption   175
           Elizabeth S. Chase

xi

ESSAY XI   Optimal Accumulation in Discrete Capital Models   181
             Michael Bruno

ESSAY XII   Indeterminacy of Development in a Heterogeneous-Capital
             Model with Constant Saving Propensity   219
             Paul A. Samuelson

ESSAY XIII   Individual Saving, Aggregate Capital Accumulation, and
             Efficient Growth   233
             David Cass and Menahem E. Yaari

ESSAY XIV   A Turnpike Refutation of the Golden Rule in a Welfare-
             Maximizing Many-Year Plan   269
             Paul A. Samuelson

ESSAY XV   Stability, Marginal Products, Putty, and Clay   281
             George A. Akerlof

Selected Bibliography   295

Index   301

Essays on the Theory of
Optimal Economic Growth

I

Optimal Programs of Capital Accumulation for an Economy in which there is Exogenous Technical Change[1]

KARL SHELL

Massachusetts Institute of Technology

1. The One-Sector Model

Recall the aggregative economic growth model of Solow [13] and Swan [14]. In the model economy, there are two factors of production, capital and labor, that are combined to produce a single homogeneous output. At any instant in time a fraction of this homogeneous output may be allocated to consumption and the remaining fraction allocated to investment in capital accumulation. Once invested the capital stock is bolted down in the sense that in itself it is not a good that is fit for consumption.

If $K(t)$ and $L(t)$ denote the currently existing stocks of capital and labor, then the current rate of output $Y(t)$ can be expressed by

$$Y(t) = A(t)F[K(t), L(t)], \qquad (1)$$

where $A(t)$ is a measure of the current level of technical knowledge. Here $F[\cdot]$ is the neoclassical production function exhibiting constant returns to scale in capital and labor; that is,

$$\lambda Y = F[\lambda K, \lambda L] \qquad \text{for } K, L \geq 0 \text{ and } \lambda > 0. \qquad (2)$$

[1] Research for this paper was undertaken in 1963–1964 when I was Woodrow Wilson Dissertation Fellow at Stanford University. Preparation of the manuscript was supported in part by a Ford Foundation faculty research grant to the Department of Economics at Massachusetts Institute of Technology. I am indebted to K. J. Arrow, D. Cass, F. M. Fisher, P. A. Samuelson, R. M. Solow, and H. Uzawa for helpful suggestions.

1

Let $C(t)$ and $Z(t)$ denote the current rates of consumption and investment; let $0 \le s(t) \le 1$ denote the fraction of current output that is being saved (and invested). This yields the national income identities

$$Y \equiv C + Z \equiv (1 - s)Y + sY.$$

If capital is subject to evaporative decay at the constant rate $\mu > 0$, then growth of the capital stock is specified by the differential equation

$$\dot{K}(t) = s(t)A(t)F[K(t), L(t)] - \mu K(t). \tag{3}$$

Assume that $N(t)$ is the current size of the population for the entire society. Assume that population growth is independent of the economic variables, in particular that

$$\dot{N}(t) = nN(t),$$

where n is a constant. Assume further that the number of able-bodied workers is a stationary fraction $0 < \alpha < 1$ of the total population. If the central planning board requires all able-bodied citizens to be workers, $L(t) = \alpha N(t)$, and thus

$$\dot{L}(t) = nL(t). \tag{4}$$

Assume that technical change proceeds at an autonomous fixed relative rate ρ,[2]

$$\dot{A}(t) = \rho A(t). \tag{5}$$

The problem is to characterize the program of capital accumulation that is consistent with the system in Equations 1 through 5 and maximizes some suitable criterion (or welfare) functional while satisfying appropriate initial conditions and terminal requirements, if any. If $\delta > 0$ is the planning board's (constant) rate of time discount for per capita consumption, then the problem is equivalent to that of maximizing the expression

$$\int_0^T \frac{C(t)}{L(t)} e^{-\delta t} \, dt.$$

The maximand is constrained by the system of Equations 1 through 5 and by the given initial conditions $K(0) = K_0$, $L(0) = L_0$, and $A(0) = A_0$. It may also be required (for instance, for reasons of national prestige) that at the terminal planning date $0 < T \le \infty$, the capital-labor ratio is not less than some prescribed target, or that $K(T)/L(T) \ge k_T$.

---

[2] The model has three interpretations: (1) For $\rho = 0$, it is the one-sector model with an unchanging menu of techniques. (2) For $\rho > 0$, it is the model with positive technical progress. (3) For $\rho < 0$, it can be interpreted as a special case of my model [12]. Then A is interpreted as the stock of social capital. Under a libertarian administration (no support of social goods production), A declines following the equation $\dot{A} = \rho A$ where $(-\rho)$ is the instantaneous rate of depreciation of social capital.

First, define the usual per capita quantities:

> Output per worker: $y(t) = Y(t)/L(t)$.
> Aggregate capital-labor ratio: $k(t) = K(t)/L(t)$.
> Consumption per worker: $c(t) = C(t)/L(t)$.
> Investment per worker: $z(t) = Z(t)/L(t)$.

The problem reduces to the following problem in miniature form:

To maximize:

$$\int_0^T c(t)e^{-\delta t}\, dt \tag{6}$$

subject to the constraints:

$$\dot{k}(t) = s(t)y(t) - \lambda k(t), \tag{7}$$

$$y(t) = e^{\rho t}f[k(t)], \tag{8}$$

$$0 \le s(t) \le 1, \tag{9}$$

$$k(0) = k_0, \quad \text{and} \quad k(T) \ge k_T, \tag{10}$$

where δ, $\lambda \equiv n + \mu$, k_0, k_T are given constants, and $s(t)$ is some measurable control (or policy) variable to be chosen. Units of measurement have been chosen such that $A(0) = 1$ and therefore $A(t) = e^{\rho t}$.

The expression $F(k, 1)$ is replaced by the usual shorthand expression $f(k)$, which is assumed to be thrice continuously differentiable. Production satisfies the following neoclassical conditions:

$$f(k) > 0, \quad f'(k) > 0, \quad f''(k) < 0, \qquad \text{for } 0 < k < \infty,$$
$$f(0) = 0, \quad f'(0) = \infty, \quad f(\infty) = \infty, \quad f'(\infty) = 0. \tag{11}$$

The foregoing problem is solved by employing the "maximum principle" of Pontryagin *et al.* [8]. Introduce the Hamiltonian form

$$(1 - s)e^{(\rho - \delta)t}f(k) + qe^{-\delta t}[se^{\rho t}f(k) - \lambda k].$$

If a program $[k(t), s(t); 0 \le t \le T]$ is optimal,[3] then there exists a continuous function $q(t)$ such that

$$\dot{k}(t) = s(t)e^{\rho t}f[k(t)] - \lambda k(t), \tag{12}$$

with initial condition $k(0) = k_0$,

$$\dot{q}(t) = (\delta + \lambda)q(t) - \{[1 - s(t)] + q(t)s(t)\}e^{\rho t}f'[k(t)], \tag{13}$$

$$s(t) \text{ maximizes } [1 - s(t) + q(t)s(t)] \text{ subject to } 0 \le s(t) \le 1, \tag{14}$$

and s is a piecewise continuous function of t,

$$e^{-\delta T}q(T)[k(T) - k_T] = 0. \tag{15}$$

---

[3] Cf. [8], especially Theorem 3 (p. 50) and also pp. 108–114, 189–191.

For convenience set

$$\gamma = \max_{0 \le s \le 1} [(1 - s) + qs] = \max(1, q).$$

Notice that $q(t)$ has the interpretation of the social demand price of a unit of investment in terms of a currently forgone unit of consumption. Therefore, differential Equation 13 may be interpreted as the requirement of perfect foresight. In a competitive economy, for example, the change in the price of a unit of capital should compensate a *rentier* for loss due to depreciation and for "abstinence" net of any rewards from the employment of that unit of capital. Transversality Condition 15 states that at the target date the target requirement (Equation 10) must hold with equality or the present value of the target demand price of investment must be zero.

Next, it is required to study the singular solutions of differential Equation 13. Notice that $\dot{q} = 0$ if and only if

$$q = \frac{\gamma e^{\rho t} f'(k)}{\delta + \lambda}.$$ (16)

Equation 16 reduces to

$$e^{\rho t} f'(k_t) = \delta + \lambda \qquad \text{for case } q \ge 1,$$ (17)

and

$$q_t = \frac{e^{\rho t} f'(k_t)}{\delta + \lambda} \qquad \text{for case } q \le 1.$$ (18)

If the production function satisfies Conditions 11, it is well known that for any instant of time Equation 17 is uniquely solvable in k_t. Call the solution to Equation 17, k_t^*. Determination of k_t^* is shown in Figure 1. Here $\tilde{k}_t$ is the maximum sustainable capital-labor ratio when technology is held fixed.

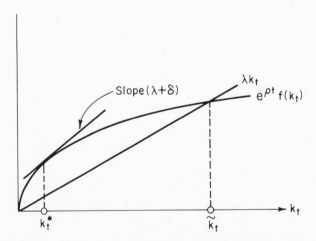

FIGURE 1. Determination of k_t^* and $\tilde{k}_t$.

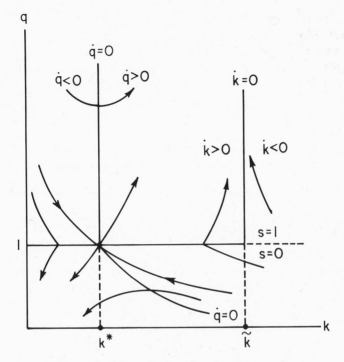

FIGURE 2. Phase diagram for the case $\rho = 0$.

It is easily shown that for fixed t, Equation 16 describes a continuous curve in the (k, q) plane with a kink at $(k = k^*, q = 1)$. Differentiating Equation 18 yields

$$\left.\frac{dq}{dk}\right|_{\dot{q}=0} = \frac{e^{\rho t} f''(k)}{\delta + \lambda} < 0 \qquad \text{for } q < 1. \tag{19}$$

2. The Case of $\rho = 0$

First we study the case of no technical change ($\rho = 0$). The appropriate phase diagram is given in Figure 2. Condition 14 implies that for optimality it is necessary for the following correspondence to hold:

$$s(q) = 1 \qquad \text{when } q > 1,$$
$$0 \le s(q) \le 1 \qquad \text{when } q = 1, \tag{20}$$
$$s(q) = 0 \qquad \text{when } q < 1.$$

Then, on any given trajectory not passing through the point $(k^*, 1)$, k can be written as a continuous function of q.[4] In fact a trajectory $[k(t), q(t): t \ge 0]$

---

[4] By assigning the value $s(q) = 1$, the right-hand sides of differential Equations 12 and 13 are seen to be twice continuously differentiable functions of their arguments, k, q,

not passing through $(k^*, 1)$ is uniquely determined by the specification of initial conditions $[k(t_0), q(t_0); t_0]$.

Assume for purposes of exposition that the initial capital-labor ratio is the balanced capital-labor ratio k^*; that is, $k(0) = k^*$. Assume that the planning period is infinite, $T = \infty$, and that the target capital-labor ratio is left free. Then, a program of capital accumulation satisfying the necessary conditions is that of fixing $q(t) = 1$ for $0 \le t \le \infty$ and maintaining the balanced capital-labor ratio $k(t) = k^*$ for $0 \le t \le \infty$.

As δ approaches zero, this program approaches the program

$$\left(k = k^*, s = \frac{\lambda k^*}{f(k^*)}; 0 \le t \le \infty \right)$$

which is what Phelps [6] and Robinson [10] have dubbed the golden rule of capital accumulation. For $\delta \ne 0$, this may be called the modified golden rule of capital accumulation.[5]

If $k(0) \ne k^*$, the planning board would assign initial price q_0 such that the point (k_0, q_0) lies on a trajectory passing through $(k^*, 1)$. Let $0 \le t^* < \infty$ be the time required for such a program to achieve $(k^*, 1)$. Then the optimal program is

$$\left(k = k^*, s = \frac{\lambda k^*}{f(k^*)}; t^* \le t \le \infty \right).$$

The initial savings ratio is zero or one, depending upon whether the initial capital-labor ratio is greater than or less than k^*.

The analysis is easily modified to handle the general case where $k(T) \ge$

---

and t, on the domain defined by $k > 0$, $q \ge 1$, $t \ge 0$. Further, by assigning the value $s(q) = 0$, the right-hand sides of Equations 12 and 13 are seen to be twice continuously differentiable functions of k, q, and t on the domain defined by $k > 0$, $q \le 1$, $t \ge 0$. Thus, when the control $s(t)$ is appropriately assigned, the system of Equations 12 and 13 is shown to be trivially Lipschitzian over the respective domains of definition. By classic theorems of ordinary differential equations (see, e.g., pp. 159–167 in [7]), we find that for a system satisfying Equations 12 through 14 and 20, specification of the parameters $[k(t_0), q(t_0); t_0]$ uniquely determines the entire trajectory for trajectories not passing through the locus of points defined by $\{(k, q, t) \mid k = k^*(t), q = 1, t \ge 0\}$. In fact, the solutions to the system of Equations 12 through 14 vary continuously when the initial parameters $[k(t_0), q(t_0); t_0]$ are allowed to vary. See, e.g., pp. 192–199 in [7].

[5] Or, perhaps, "the adulterated golden rule." For $\rho = 0$ and $T = \infty$, it is required that $\delta > 0$ in order that the value of the definite Integral 6 be finite for all feasible programs. For $T < \infty$, the requirement that δ be positive is too strong. Even for the case with nonzero technical change, if $\delta > f'(\tilde{k}_t) - \lambda$ for $t \ge 0$, then $\tilde{k}_t > k_t^*$. Koopmans [3] argues that if the ethical principle is held, that all men are to be treated equally (independently of the size of their generation or its "timing"), then δ should be chosen equal to $(-n) < 0$, for the case of positive population increase. As long as $T < \infty$, our analysis is congenial to this interpretation.

$k_T \geq 0$ and $T \leq \infty$. The initial point (k_0, q_0) is chosen on a trajectory leading to the point $(k^*, 1)$, if feasibility permits. The Pontryagin program

$$\left(k = k^*, s = \frac{\lambda k^*}{f(k^*)}; t^* \leq t \leq t^{**} \right)$$

is followed where t^{**} is the time at which the backward trajectory of the system of Equations 12 through 13 starting at $(k = k_T; t = T)$ passes through $(k = k^*, q = 1)$. If, however, $q(T) < 0$ for the backward trajectory to $(k^*, 1)$ starting at k_T, then t^{**} is defined to be the time at which a backward trajectory starting at time T and demand price $q(T) = 0$ intersects the point $(k^*, 1)$. Figure 3 illustrates a program satisfying Pontryagin's necessary conditions.

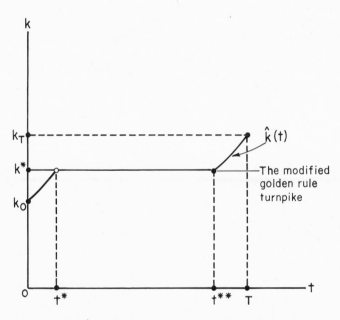

FIGURE 3. $\hat{k}(t)$, the Pontryagin path for the case $\rho = 0$.

Important assumptions are implicit in the construction of Figure 3. First, it is assumed that it is feasible for the economy with initial endowment $k(0) = k_0$ to achieve the target k_T in the specified time T. Even stronger, Figure 3 assumes that in fact

$$T > t^{**} > t^* > 0. \tag{21}$$

If it is feasible to achieve the target during the planning period but Inequality 21 fails to hold, then the Pontryagin path is the appropriate envelope of a forward trajectory from (k_0, q_0) to $(k^*, 1)$ and the backward trajectory from (k_T, q_T) to $(k^*, 1)$. In the degenerate case in which only one feasible path exists, the Pontryagin path is, of course, either a program of zero savings or a program of zero consumption. Since optimal programs do not permit the demand price of investment to become negative, if no trajectory is found with $k(T) = k_T$ and $q(T) \geq 0$, then the Pontryagin problem will yield $q(T) = 0$ and $k(T) > k_T$.

Some observations are in order. The linearity of the objective function (Integral 6) implies a kink in the graph of the stationary solutions to Equation 13. Extending the argument presented in footnote 4 on page 5, the backward solutions to the point $(k^*, 1)$ are unique. In general, however, $\hat{q}_0$ will not be uniquely determined by (k_0, k_T, T). For the degenerate Pontryagin paths that are everywhere specialized to production of the same good, there is a family of trajectories satisfying Equations 12 through 15. Nonetheless, the Pontryagin program of capital accumulation

$$[\hat{k}(t); 0 \leq t \leq T]$$

is uniquely determined by Equations 12 through 15 if a feasible program exists.

If t^* and $(T - t^{**})$ are finite this yields the following *turnpike property*: for the case of neoclassical production without technical change, the Pontryagin program of capital accumulation, if followed, requires the planning board to adopt the modified golden rule of capital accumulation for all but a finite amount of time. As the length of the planning period increases, the *fraction* of time spent on a program not satisfying the modified golden rule approaches zero.[6]

3. The Case of $\rho > 0$

Next, examine the case with positive technical progress $\rho > 0$. Notice that if ρ is nonzero, differential Equations 12 and 13 are nonautonomous, and thus the appropriate phase diagram must be drawn in three-dimensional space, (k, q, t). Time differentiation of Equation 17 yields

$$\dot{k}_t^* = \frac{-\rho(\delta + \lambda)e^{-\rho t}}{f''(k_t^*)} \gtrless 0 \qquad \text{as } \rho \gtrless 0. \tag{22}$$

In general, stationary solutions to the differential equation

$$\dot{q}(t) = (\delta + \lambda)q(t) - \gamma e^{\rho t}f'(k_t)$$

---

[6] If $\delta \leq f'(\tilde{k}) - \lambda$, then the Pontryagin program $[\hat{k}(t), 0 \leq t \leq T]$ is arbitrarily close to the ratio $\tilde{k}$ for all but a finite amount of time. The notion that the "turnpike property" arises in consumption-optimal programs is implicit in Cass [1], Ramsey [9], and Uzawa [16], among others, and is explicit in the recent contribution of Samuelson [11].

are shown to lie on a manifold embedded in (k, q, t) space. The manifold of solutions to $\dot{q} = 0$ is illustrated for ρ positive in Figure 4. Recalling that given t, Equation 17 has the unique solution k_t^*, suggests a program satisfying the necessary conditions of Equations 12 through 15. Consider for ease of exposition the case when the initial condition is $k(0) = k_0^*$ and the

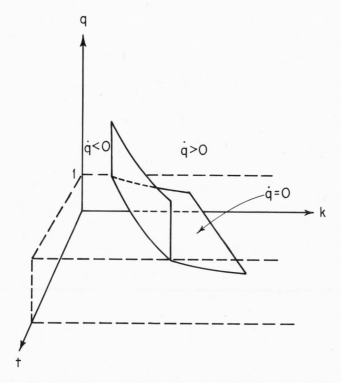

FIGURE 4. The manifold of solutions to $\dot{q} = 0$ for the case $\rho > 0$.

target requirement is $k(T) = k_T^*$. Clearly, a program of capital accumulation that follows the modified golden rule turnpike (illustrated in Figure 5) satisfies the necessary conditions of Equations 12, 13, and 15. But Equation 14 is not guaranteed. In other words, it is not guaranteed that a program of capital accumulation lying on the turnpike[7] of Figure 5 will have, for $0 \leq t \leq T$, a feasible savings ratio $0 \leq s_t \leq 1$.

---

[7] P. A. Samuelson has pointed out that "the turnpike" may be a misnomer for the curve $k^*(t)$ when $\rho \neq 0$. For example, in the Cobb-Douglas case with $\rho > 0$ and $s^* < 1$, if we require the target requirement to hold with equality, i.e., $k(T) = k_T$, then the fraction of time spent by the optimal program on the "turnpike" approaches $\lambda b/(\lambda b + \rho) < 1$ as T becomes large.

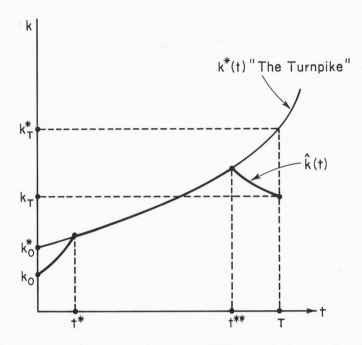

FIGURE 5. The turnpike when $\rho > 0$: the Pontryagin program of capital accumulation $\hat{k}(t)$ is shown by a heavy curve.

If $k_t = k_t^*$, Equation 12 becomes

$$\dot{k}_t = s_t e^{\rho t} f(k_t^*) - \lambda k_t^*. \tag{23}$$

The problem is to find $s_t = s_t^*$ such that, when $k_t = k_t^*$, $\dot{k} = \dot{k}_t^*$. Equating $\dot{k}_t$ to $\dot{k}_t^*$ yields

$$s^* e^{\rho t} f(k_t^*) - \lambda k_t^* = \frac{-\rho(\delta + \lambda)e^{-\rho t}}{f''(k_t^*)}$$

from Equations 22 and 23. Or rewriting

$$s_t^* = \frac{\lambda k_t^*}{e^{\rho t} f(k_t^*)} - \frac{\rho(\delta + \lambda)}{e^{2\rho t} f(k_t^*) f''(k_t^*)} > 0 \qquad \text{for } \rho > 0. \tag{24}$$

This is the common-sense result: to achieve a program of positive capital accumulation requires a positive savings fraction. However, Equation 24 does not guarantee $s_t^* \leq 1$ for $\rho > 0$. To see this, consider the case where the production function is linear-logarithmic in capital and labor, $y_t = e^{\rho t} k_t^a$. Let $0 < a < 1$ so that a is capital's share of output in a competitive economy and the production function is Cobb-Douglas. For the Cobb-Douglas case

$$k_t^* = \left(\frac{a e^{\rho t}}{\delta + \lambda}\right)^{1/b}$$

and

$$k_t^* = \frac{\rho}{b} \left(\frac{ae^{\rho t}}{\delta + \lambda} \right)^{1/b},$$

where b is defined by $b = 1 - a$. Therefore, for the Cobb-Douglas case,

$$s^* = \frac{a(\lambda b + \rho)}{b(\lambda + \delta)}.$$

For this special case, s^* is independent of time and greater than zero; but whether s^* is less than, equal to, or greater than unity depends upon the values of the parameters a, ρ, λ, δ.[8]

Returning to the case of general neoclassical production, an example of a Pontryagin program of capital accumulation is presented in Figure 5. In drawing this figure it is implicitly assumed that $0 < t^* < t^{**} < T$ and therefore that $s^*(t) \leq 1$ for $t^* < t < t^{**}$. It is further assumed that $\hat{q}(T) \geq 0$ when $\hat{k}(T) = k_T$.

The general case where s^* changes with time presents a sophisticated mathematical difficulty. If the number of switches from $s^* < 1$ to $s^* > 1$, and vice versa, is sufficiently large, it may be impossible to find a *piecewise continuous* control $\hat{s}(t)$ satisfying Equations 12 through 15. If no such control exists, then no maximum to Integral 6 exists.[9]

4. Optimality of the Pontryagin Program

In the previous sections, programs satisfying necessary Conditions 7–10 and 12–15 are referred to as Pontryagin programs. It remains to show that the necessary conditions are also sufficient, that such programs are indeed optimal.[10]

---

[8] Consider the "familiar economy" where $a = .30$, $\lambda = n + \mu = .10$, and $\rho = .03$. If the planning board's rate of discount $\delta = .05$, then $s^* = \frac{2}{7} < 1$. Hence if the "familiar economy" achieves the capital-labor ratio $k^*(t)$, at time t, then it can maintain the "turnpike" capital-labor ratio. It is not surprising that s^* is independent of t for Cobb-Douglas functions. Since technical change is labor augmenting in this case, to remain on the turnpike it is required that the capital-labor ratio *measured in efficiency units* be held constant. Indeed, if the parameters δ and λ are replaced by $\delta^0 = \delta + (\rho/b)$ and $\lambda^0 = \lambda + (\rho/b)$, respectively, then the analysis follows that of section 2. For example, the feasibility condition $s^* < 1$ simply reduces to the condition $\delta^0 > f'(\hat{k}) - \lambda^0$.

[9] If $T < \infty$ and the class of admissible controls $[0 \leq s(t) \leq 1; 0 \leq t \leq T]$ is restricted to piecewise continuous functions, then a maximum to Integral 6 exists if and only if the number of such switches in $[0, T]$ is finite. Therefore if s^* is an analytic function of t, then a maximum to Integral 6 exists.

[10] It is essential to impose some measurability requirement upon the set of admissible controls $[0 \leq s(t) \leq 1; 0 \leq t \leq T]$. If, as implied by Equation 14, attention is restricted to those controls that are piecewise continuous, then the integration performed in Expressions 6 and 25 through 30 is to be interpreted in the sense of Stieltjes. On the other hand, if attention is restricted to Lebesgue measurable controls, then the integration in Expressions 6 and 25 through 30 is to be interpreted in the sense of Lebesgue.

Let $[\hat{c}(t), \hat{z}(t), \hat{k}(t), \hat{q}(t), \cdots]$ be a program satisfying the conditions of Equations 7 through 10 and 12 through 15. Let $[c(t), z(t), k(t), q(t), \cdots]$ be any feasible program, that is, any program satisfying Conditions 7 through 10. It is necessary to show

$$\int_0^T (\hat{c} - c)e^{-\delta t}\, dt \geq 0. \tag{25}$$

The left-hand side of Inequality 25 can be rewritten in the form

$$\int_0^T e^{-\delta t}\, dt\{(\hat{c} - c) + \hat{\gamma}[(e^{\rho t}f(\hat{k}) - \hat{z} - \hat{c}) - (e^{\rho t}f(k) - z - c)]$$
$$+ \hat{q}[(\hat{z} - \lambda\hat{k} - \dot{\hat{k}}) - (z - \lambda k - k)]\},$$

which reduces to

$$\int_0^T e^{-\delta t}\, dt\{(1 - \hat{\gamma})(\hat{c} - c) + (\hat{q} - \hat{\gamma})(\hat{z} - z)$$
$$+ \hat{\gamma}e^{\rho t}[f(\hat{k}) - f(k)] + \hat{q}[\lambda(k - \hat{k}) + (k - \dot{\hat{k}})]\}. \tag{26}$$

Notice that

$$(1 - \hat{\gamma})(\hat{c} - c) \geq 0$$

and

$$(\hat{q} - \hat{\gamma})(\hat{z} - z) \geq 0.$$

Therefore Integral 26 is not less than the following expression

$$\int_0^T e^{-\delta t}\, dt\{\hat{\gamma}e^{\rho t}[f(\hat{k}) - f(k)] + \hat{q}[\lambda(k - \hat{k}) + (k - \dot{\hat{k}})]\}. \tag{27}$$

But since $f(\cdot)$ is a concave function, Integral 27 is not smaller than

$$\int_0^T e^{-\delta t}\, dt\{\hat{\gamma}e^{\rho t}[(\hat{k} - k)f'(\hat{k})] + \hat{q}[\lambda(k - \hat{k}) + (k - \dot{\hat{k}})]\}.$$

By collecting terms the previous expression yields

$$\int_0^T \hat{q}e^{-\delta t}(k - \dot{\hat{k}})\, dt + \int_0^T e^{-\delta t}\, dt(\hat{k} - k)[\hat{\gamma}e^{\rho t}f'(\hat{k}) - \hat{q}\lambda]. \tag{28}$$

Integrating the first term in Expression 28 by parts reduces to

$$\hat{q}(T)e^{-\delta T}[k(T) - \hat{k}(T)] - \hat{q}_0[k(0) - \hat{k}(0)]$$
$$- \int_0^T (k - \hat{k})(\dot{\hat{q}} - \delta\hat{q})e^{-\delta t}\, dt. \tag{29}$$

The transversality condition of Equation 15 says that the first term in Expression 29 is nonnegative. Since every feasible path must satisfy the given initial condition k_0, the second term in Expression 29 is identically zero. Hence

$$\int_0^T \hat{q}e^{-\delta t}(k - \hat{k})\, dt \geq - \int_0^T (k - \hat{k})(\dot{\hat{q}} - \delta\hat{q})e^{-\delta t}\, dt. \tag{30}$$

Hence Integral 28 is not smaller than

$$\int_0^T e^{-\delta t}\, dt\{(\hat{k} - k)[\hat{\gamma}e^{\rho t}f'(\hat{k}) - \lambda\hat{q}] + (\hat{k} - k)(\dot{\hat{q}} - \delta\hat{q})\}$$
$$= \int_0^T e^{-\delta t}\, dt(\hat{k} - k)[\dot{\hat{q}} - (\delta + \lambda)\hat{q} + \hat{\gamma}e^{\rho t}f'(\hat{k})],$$

which by Conditions 13 and 14 is identically zero. Hence the optimality requirement of Inequality 25 is established. In fact, if $k \neq \hat{k}$ on some interval, then Inequality 25 is strict.

5. The Two-Sector Model

Consider the two-sector model of economic growth that was introduced by Meade [4] and Uzawa [15]. The model economy consists of an investment-goods sector and a consumption-goods sector, labeled 1 and 2, respectively. In both sectors, production is subject to constant returns to scale, and marginal rates of substitution are positive. There are no external economies (diseconomies) and no joint products.

The quantity of the consumption goods $Y_2(t)$ currently produced depends upon the current allocation $K_2(t)$ and $L_2(t)$ of capital and labor to the consumption sector:

$$Y_2(t) = M(t)F_2[K_2(t), L_2(t)]. \tag{31}$$

Similarly, current production of the investment goods $Y_1(t)$ is dependent upon the current allocation of factors to the investment sector:

$$Y_1(t) = G(t)F_1[K_1(t), L_1(t)]. \tag{32}$$

We have $F_1[\cdot]$ and $F_2[\cdot]$ as neoclassical production functions, homogeneous of degree one in their respective arguments. Thus

$$F_j(\lambda K_j, \lambda L_j) = \lambda F_j(K_j, L_j) \qquad \text{for } j = 1, 2, \tag{33}$$

where $K_j, L_j \geq 0$ and $\lambda > 0$. Labor and capital can be freely shifted between the two sectors.[11] For an allocation of resources to be feasible at time t,

$$K_1(t) + K_2(t) \leq K(t),$$
$$L_1(t) + L_2(t) \leq L(t), \tag{34}$$

with $K_1(t)$, $K_2(t)$, $L_1(t)$, $L_2(t) \geq 0$, where $K(t) > 0$ and $L(t) > 0$ are the current stocks of available capital and labor.

If the capital stock is subject to evaporative decay at the constant rate $\mu > 0$, then growth of the capital stock is specified by the differential equation

$$\dot{K}(t) = Y_1(t) - \mu K(t). \tag{35}$$

---

[11] In the terminology of Meade [4], the factors of production are assumed to be perfectly malleable.

Assume that labor is inelastically supplied, that it is a stationary fraction of total population, and grows at the constant relative rate n,

$$\dot{L}(t) = nL(t). \tag{36}$$

In Equations 31 and 32 it is assumed that technical change in the two sectors is of the Hicks-neutral type. Assume further that change in the respective levels of technique is independent of other economic variables and proceeds at constant relative rates,

$$\dot{G}(t) = gG(t) \quad \text{and} \quad \dot{M}(t) = mM(t). \tag{37}$$

Formally the problem is to maximize

$$\int_0^T \frac{C(t)}{L(t)} e^{-\delta t} dt, \tag{38}$$

where δ is the social rate of time discount and T is the length of the planning period. The maximand of Expression 38 is constrained by the Conditions 31 through 37 and by the given initial conditions $K(0) = K_0$, $L(0) = L_0$, $G(0) = G_0$, $M(0) = M_0$, and subject to the requirement that the terminal capital-labor ratio be at least as great as some specified target, $k(T) \geq k_T$.

In order to facilitate the exposition, certain important constructions introduced in [15], [16], and [5] are reproduced in this section. Define the per capita quantities:

$$y_j(t) = \frac{Y_j(t)}{L(t)},$$

$$k_j(t) = \frac{K_j(t)}{L_j(t)},$$

$$l_j(t) = \frac{L_j(t)}{L(t)},$$

$$f_j(k_j) = F_j(k_j, 1) \qquad \text{for } j = 1, 2,$$

$$k(t) = \frac{K(t)}{L(t)}.$$

Assume that $f_j(k_j)$ is three times continuously differentiable and

$$f_j(k_j) > 0, \quad f_j'(k_j) > 0, \quad f_j''(k_j) < 0 \qquad \text{for } 0 < k_j < \infty,$$

$$\lim_{k_j \to 0} f_j(k_j) = 0, \quad \lim_{k_j \to \infty} f_j(k_j) = \infty, \tag{39}$$

$$\lim_{k_j \to 0} f_j'(k_j) = \infty, \quad \lim_{k_j \to \infty} f_j'(k_j) = 0.$$

Because positive marginal products are assumed, optimality requires that Inequalities 34 hold with equality. If ω is an arbitrarily given wage-rentals ratio, then efficient capital-labor ratios can be found by solving for k_j,

$$\omega = \frac{f_j(k_j)}{f_j'(k_j)} - k_j \quad \text{for } j = 1, 2. \tag{40}$$

From Conditions 39 and 40,

$$\frac{dk_j}{d\omega} = \frac{-[f_j'(k_j)]^2}{f_j(k_j)f_j''(k_j)} > 0. \tag{41}$$

Thus the efficient capital-labor ratio k_j is a uniquely determined, increasing function of the wage-rentals ratio ω.

Define $p(\omega, t)$ the supply price of a unit of investment goods at time t,

$$p(\omega, t) = \frac{M_0 e^{mt} f_2'[k_2(\omega)]}{G_0 e^{gt} f_1'[k_1(\omega)]}, \tag{42}$$

where a unit of consumption goods is the *numéraire*. Logarithmic differentiation of Equation 42 yields

$$\frac{1}{p} \frac{\partial p}{\partial \omega} = \frac{1}{k_1(\omega) + \omega} - \frac{1}{k_2(\omega) + \omega} \gtrless 0 \quad \text{as } k_2 \gtrless k_1. \tag{43}$$

The Conditions 34 and 39 imply that

$$k_1 l_1 + k_2 l_2 = k, \tag{44}$$

$$l_1 + l_2 = 1, \tag{45}$$

where $k_1, k_2, l_1, l_2 \geq 0$. Given k and t, Equations 44 and 45, together with Equations 40 and 42, define the range of p and ω. This is illustrated graphically for the case $k_2(\omega) > k_1(\omega)$ in Figure 6. In general, define the critical wage-rentals ratios by

$$\omega_{\min}(k) = \min [\omega_2(k), \omega_1(k)],$$
$$\omega_{\max}(k) = \max [\omega_2(k), \omega_1(k)], \tag{46}$$

and the critical supply prices by

$$p_{\min}(k, t) = p_2(k, t),$$
$$p_{\max}(k, t) = p_1(k, t), \tag{47}$$

where $k_j(\omega_j) = k$ and $p_j(k, t) = p[\omega_j(k), t]$ for $j = 1, 2$.

It is possible to choose units of measurement such that $G_0 = M_0 = 1$. From Equations 31, 32, 44, and 45, we have

$$y_1 = \frac{k_2 - k}{k_2 - k_1} e^{gt} f_1(k_1), \tag{48}$$

$$y_2 = \frac{k - k_1}{k_2 - k_1} e^{mt} f_2(k_2), \tag{49}$$

where the variables y_1, y_2, k, k_1, k_2 are understood to be functions of time.

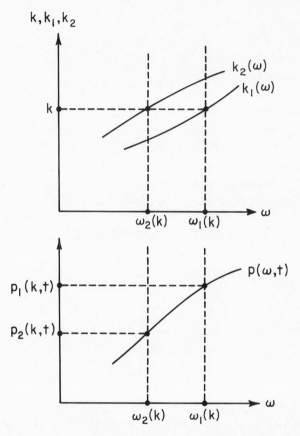

FigURE 6. Determination of critical wage-rentals ratios and critical price ratios.

Thus given k, ω, and t, Equations 40, 42, 48, and 49 uniquely determine the allocation of factors between the two sectors, the level of production in both sectors,[12] and the implicit price of a unit of the investment good in terms of a unit of the consumption good. Partial differentiation of Equations 48 and 49 yields

$$\frac{\partial y_1}{\partial k} = \frac{-e^{gt}f_1(k_1)}{k_2 - k_1}, \tag{50}$$

$$\frac{\partial y_2}{\partial k} = \frac{e^{mt}f_2(k_2)}{k_2 - k_1}, \tag{51}$$

---

[12] As long as $k_2(\omega) \neq k_1(\omega)$.

$$\frac{\partial y_1}{\partial \omega} = e^{gt}\left[\left(\frac{k_2 - k}{(k_2 - k_1)^2}\right)\left(\frac{f_1'^2}{f_1 f_1''}\left[-k_2 f_1' - (f_1 - k_1 f_1')\right]\right)\right.$$
$$\left. + \left(\frac{k_1 - k}{(k_2 - k_1)^2}\right)\left(\frac{f_2'^2 f_1}{f_2 f_2''}\right)\right], \tag{52}$$

$$\frac{\partial y_2}{\partial \omega} = e^{mt}\left[\left(\frac{k - k_1}{(k_2 - k_1)^2}\right)\left(\frac{f_2'^2}{f_2 f_2''}\left[k_1 f_2' + (f_2 - k_2 f_2')\right]\right)\right.$$
$$\left. + \left(\frac{k_2 - k}{(k_2 - k_1)^2}\right)\left(\frac{f_1'^2 f_2}{f_1 f_1''}\right)\right]. \tag{53}$$

The implicit value of gross national product per worker y is defined by

$$y = y_2 + p y_1. \tag{54}$$

It is useful to define s, the fraction of implicit gross national product assigned to investment,

$$s = \frac{p y_1}{y}. \tag{55}$$

6. Optimal Control in the Two-Sector Model

Maximization of Integral 38 is equivalent to maximization of

$$\int_0^T y_2 e^{-\delta t}\, dt. \tag{56}$$

Without loss in generality, the central planning board can consider $s(t)$ to be the control variable chosen from among all, say, piecewise continuous functions defined upon $0 \le t \le T$, such that $0 \le s(t) \le 1$ for $0 \le t \le T$.

The problem reduces to choosing $s(t)$ to maximize

$$\int_0^T [1 - s(t)] y(t) e^{-\delta t}\, dt, \tag{57}$$

subject to the constraints:

$$\dot{k}(t) = \frac{s(t) y(t)}{p(t)} - \lambda k \qquad \text{where } \lambda = \mu + n, \tag{58}$$

$$0 \le s(t) \le 1 \qquad \text{for } 0 \le t \le T \tag{59}$$

and $s(t)$ is a piecewise continuous function of t,

$$k(0) = k_0 \quad \text{and} \quad k(T) \ge k_T. \tag{60}$$

As stated, this problem is soluble as an application of Pontryagin's maximum principle. First form the Hamiltonian expression

$$H(k, q, s, t) = (1 - s)e^{-\delta t} y + q e^{-\delta t}\left(\frac{sy}{p} - \lambda k\right), \tag{61}$$

where $q(t)$ is the current social demand price of a unit of the investment good in terms of a unit of the consumption good. From Equations 40, 42, 48, 49, and 54, y and p are interpreted as functions of k, s, and t.

It is necessary for optimality that $s(t)$ be chosen in $[0, 1]$ to maximize the socially imputed value of gross national product at time t,

$$(1 - s)y + q\left(\frac{sy}{p}\right). \tag{62}$$

Thus it is necessary for optimality that

$$s = 1, \quad k_1 = k, \quad l_1 = 1; \tag{63}$$

or

$$s = 0, \quad k_2 = k, \quad l_2 = 1; \tag{64}$$

or

$$\frac{\partial(1 - s)y}{\partial s} + q\,\frac{\partial(sy/p)}{\partial s} = 0. \tag{65}$$

Observe that by employing Equations 48 and 49, Equation 65 can be rewritten as

$$\frac{\partial y_1}{\partial \omega}\frac{\partial \omega}{\partial s} = -q\,\frac{\partial y_2}{\partial \omega}\frac{\partial \omega}{\partial s}. \tag{66}$$

But from Equations 40, 42, 52, and 53,

$$\frac{\partial y_2/\partial \omega}{\partial y_1/\partial \omega} = -p. \tag{67}$$

Hence if the maximum to Expression 62 is interior and thus characterized by Equation 65, then with $q(t)$ given, s is chosen such that $p(k, s, t) = q(t)$. Similarly if Equations 63 apply, then s has been chosen such that $p(k, s, t) < q(t)$; if Equations 64 apply then s has been chosen such that $p(k, s, t) > q(t)$.

Pontryagin's second necessary condition is that the social demand price of investment change through time in a manner reflecting the planning board's perfect foresight of the imputed marginal value product of capital,

$$\dot{q} = (\delta + \lambda)q - \left[\frac{\partial(1 - s)y}{\partial k} + q\,\frac{\partial(sy/p)}{\partial k}\right]. \tag{68}$$

From Equations 40 through 42, 50 through 53, and 67, we have

$$\frac{\partial(sy/p)}{\partial k} = \frac{\partial y_1}{\partial k} + \frac{\partial y_1}{\partial \omega}\frac{\partial \omega}{\partial k} = -e^{gt}f_1{}'\left(\frac{k_1 + \omega}{k_2 - k_1}\right) + \frac{\partial y_1}{\partial \omega}\frac{\partial \omega}{\partial k}, \tag{69}$$

and

$$\frac{\partial(1 - s)y}{\partial k} = \frac{\partial y_2}{\partial k} + \frac{\partial y_2}{\partial \omega}\frac{\partial \omega}{\partial k} = p\left[e^{gt}f_1{}'\left(\frac{k_2 + \omega}{k_2 - k_1}\right) - \frac{\partial y_1}{\partial \omega}\frac{\partial \omega}{\partial k}\right]. \tag{70}$$

Therefore if Equation 65 applies, and hence $p(k, s, t) = q(t)$, then differential Equation 68 reduces to

$$\dot{q} = [\delta + \lambda - e^{gt}f_1{}'(k_1)]q. \tag{71}$$

Also observe that if Equations 63 apply, that is, $p(k, s, t) < q(t)$, then Equation 68 reduces to Equation 71. But if Equations 64 apply, that is, $p(k, s, t) > q(t)$, then Equation 68 reduces to

$$\dot{q} = (\delta + \lambda)q - e^{mt}f_2{}'(k). \tag{72}$$

7. The Case where Production of the Consumption Good is more Capital Intensive than Production of the Investment Good

It is convenient to treat the general problem posed in section 6 by separate cases depending upon certain attributes of the techniques of production implied by Equations 31 and 32. This section treats the case where Equations 31 and 32 are such that

$$k_2(\omega) > k_1(\omega) \qquad \text{for } \omega > 0. \tag{73}$$

It is necessary to study the behavior of the nonautonomous pair of differential Equations 58 and 68. Equations 47 divide the (k, q, t)-phase space into three mutually exclusive regions:

$$S_1 = \{(k, q, t) \mid q > p_{\max}(k, t)\}, \tag{74}$$

$$S_2 = \{(k, q, t) \mid q < p_{\min}(k, t)\}, \tag{75}$$

$$N = \{(k, q, t) \mid p_{\min}(k, t) \le q \le p_{\max}(k, t)\}. \tag{76}$$

In region S_1, maximization of the imputed value of gross national product of Expression 62 implies specialization to the production of the investment good. Therefore Equations 58 and 68 reduce to

$$\dot{k} = e^{gt}f_1(k) - \lambda k, \qquad \text{in } S_1, \tag{77}$$

and

$$\dot{q} = [(\delta + \lambda) - e^{gt}f_1{}'(k)]q \qquad \text{in } S_1. \tag{78}$$

Likewise, maximization of Expression 62 requires that in region S_2 the economy be specialized to the production of the consumption good. Thus Equations 58 and 68 reduce to

$$\dot{k} = -\lambda k \qquad \text{in } S_2, \tag{79}$$

and

$$\dot{q} = (\delta + \lambda)q - e^{mt}f_2{}'(k) \qquad \text{in } S_2. \tag{80}$$

In the region N (for nonspecialization), maximization of Expression 62 implies Equation 65 and therefore by Equations 66, 67, 69, and 70, Equations 58 and 68 reduce to

$$k = e^{gt}f_1[k_1(\omega)] \frac{k_2(\omega) - k}{k_2(\omega) - k_1(\omega)} - \lambda k \qquad \text{in } N, \qquad (81)$$

and

$$\dot{q} = \{(\delta + \lambda) - e^{gt}f_1'[k_1(\omega)]\}q \qquad \text{in } N, \qquad (82)$$

where

$$q(t) = p(\omega, t) \qquad \text{in } N. \qquad (83)$$

By assumption of Inequality 73 and Equations 43, p is a strictly increasing function of ω. Therefore specification of $q(t)$ and t uniquely determines ω, which in turn uniquely determines $k_1(\omega)$ and $k_2(\omega)$ by Equations 40 and 41. Thus by Equations 48 and 49 the right-hand sides of Equations 81 and 82 are uniquely determined by specification of $(k, q, t) \in N$.

The problem is to characterize the behavior of the system in Equations 77 through 83 in (k, q, t)-space. Notice that by Relations 43, 47, and 73, $p_{max}(k, t)$ and $p_{min}(k, t)$ are strictly increasing functions of k. From Equation 42,

$$\frac{\partial p(\omega, t)}{\partial t} = \frac{(m - g)e^{(m-g)t}f_2'[k_2(\omega)]}{f_1'[k_1(\omega)]}$$

and therefore

$$\text{sgn}\left(\frac{\partial p}{\partial t}\right) = \text{sgn}(m - g). \qquad (84)$$

In particular,

$$\text{sgn}\left(\frac{\partial p_{max}}{\partial t}\right) = \text{sgn}\left(\frac{\partial p_{min}}{\partial t}\right) = \text{sgn}(m - g).$$

It follows from Equation 78, that for $(k, q, t) \in S_1$, $\dot{q} = 0$ if and only if

$$e^{gt}f_1'(k) = \delta + \lambda. \qquad (85)$$

Conditions 39, together with the requirement that $\delta > 0$ and $\lambda > 0$, ensure that there exists a uniquely determined function of t, $k_1^*(t)$ that solves Equation 85. In fact, time differentiation of Equation 85 yields

$$\frac{dk_1^*(t)}{dt} = \frac{-ge^{-gt}}{f_1''[k_1^*(t)]},$$

Applying Conditions 39 yields

$$\text{sgn}\left(\frac{dk_1^*}{dt}\right) = \text{sgn}(g). \qquad (86)$$

Further define

$$q_t^* = p_{max}[k_1^*(t), t]. \tag{87}$$

Since p_{max} is an increasing function of k, Equation 87 is well defined. Further, consider the equation

$$q_t^* = p(\omega, t). \tag{88}$$

Given t, Equation 88 has a unique solution $\omega = \omega_t^*$. Since $k_1^* = k_1(\omega_t^*, t)$, from Equation 82 for $(k, q, t) \in N$, $\dot{q} = 0$ if and only if $q(t) = q_t^*$.

For $(k, q, t) \in S_2$, $\dot{q} = 0$ if and only if

$$q_t = \frac{e^{mt} f_2'(k_t)}{\delta + \lambda} \tag{89}$$

by Equation 80. Equation 89 gives q_t as a function of k_t and t with

$$\left(\frac{\partial q_t}{\partial k}\right)_{\dot{q}=0} = \frac{f_2''(k_t)}{\delta + \lambda} < 0 \qquad \text{for } (k, q, t) \in S_2.$$

Next it is required to describe the set of points that yield stationary solutions to the capital accumulation Equation 58. For $(k, q, t) \in S_1$, $\dot{k} = 0$ if and only if

$$e^{gt} f_1(k_t) = \lambda k_t. \tag{90}$$

Conditions 39 ensure that the solution to Equation 90, $\tilde{k}_t$, is a well-defined function of t. If there is no technical change in the production of the investment good, that is, $g = 0$, then $\tilde{k}$ has the interpretation of the maximum sustainable capital-labor ratio. Also when $\lambda > 0$ and $\delta \geq 0$, $\tilde{k}_t > k_1^*(t)$ for all t. Time differentiation of Equation 90 yields

$$\dot{\tilde{k}}_t = g\left[\frac{\lambda \tilde{k}_t}{\lambda - e^{gt} f_1'(\tilde{k}_t)}\right].$$

From Conditions 39, the average product of capital is always greater than the marginal product of capital, and thus

$$\text{sgn}(\dot{\tilde{k}}_t) = \text{sgn}(g).$$

For $(k, q, t) \in N$ and $k_t > \tilde{k}_t$, there are no stationary solutions to the capital accumulation Equation 81. However, for $(k, q, t) \in N$ and $k_t < \tilde{k}_t$ stationary solutions to Equation 81 are such that $p_{min}(k, t) < q_t < p_{max}(k, t)$. Of course, for $(k, q, t) \in S_2$, there are no stationary solutions to the capital accumulation Equation 79 with $k_t > 0$.

For purposes of exposition, first consider the case of no technical change, $m = g = 0$. For this special case, the system of differential Equations 58 and 68 is autonomous and thus can be characterized by the two-dimensional

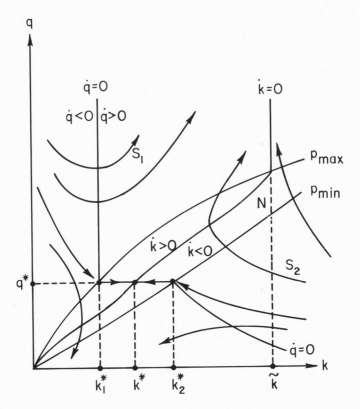

FIGURE 7. Phase diagram for the case where consumption goods production is more capital intensive and where there is no technical change.

phase diagram of Figure 7. The intersection of the locus $\dot{q} = 0$ with the locus $\dot{k} = 0$ is shown to be the point (k^*, q^*). To verify that (k^*, q^*) is a saddle point for the system of Equations 77 through 83, consider the linear Taylor approximations to Equations 81 and 82 evaluated at (k^*, q^*). The roots to the relevant characteristic equation are

$$\frac{1}{2} \left[\frac{\partial \dot{k}}{\partial k} + \frac{\partial \dot{q}}{\partial q} \pm \sqrt{\left(\frac{\partial \dot{k}}{\partial k} + \frac{\partial \dot{q}}{\partial q} \right)^2 - 4 \frac{\partial \dot{k}}{\partial k} \frac{\partial \dot{q}}{\partial q}} \right]_{(k^*, q^*)}.$$

But $(k^*, q^*) \in N$, thus

$$\frac{\partial \dot{q}}{\partial q} \bigg|_{(k^*, q^*)} = \left[-q f_1''(k_1) \frac{dk_1}{d\omega} \frac{\partial \omega}{\partial q} \right]_{(k^*, q^*)} > 0,$$

and

$$\frac{\partial \dot{k}}{\partial k} = \frac{-f_1(k_1)}{k_2 - k_1} - \lambda < 0,$$

since $k_2 > k_1$. The characteristic roots are real and opposite in sign and therefore the unique singular point (k^*, q^*) is a saddle point.[13]

If the length of the planning period is infinite, $T = \infty$, and the "terminal" capital-labor ratio $k(\infty)$ is allowed to be free, the optimal program of capital accumulation is such that $\lim_{t \to \infty} k(t) = k^*$. If $0 < k_0 < k_1^*$, then $\hat{q}(0)$ is chosen such that $[k_0, \hat{q}(0)]$ is on the unique backward solution from the point (k_1^*, q^*). Thus, for $0 \le t < t^*$, the savings fraction $\hat{s}(t) = 1$, where t^* is defined by

$$t^* = \int_{k_0}^{k_1^*} \frac{dk}{f_1(k) - \lambda k}.$$

For $t^* \le t \le \infty$, $\hat{\omega} = \omega^*$, which determines $\hat{k}_1 = k_1^*$ and $\hat{k}_2 = k_2^*$. Since $\lim_{t \to \infty} \hat{q}(t) = q^*$, the transversality condition is seen to hold.[14]

For $k_0 > k_2^*$, $q(0)$ is chosen such that $[k_0, q(0)]$ lies on the unique backward solution going through the point (k_2^*, q^*). For $0 \le t < t^{**}$, the optimal savings fraction $\hat{s}(t) = 0$, where t^{**} is defined by

$$t^{**} = \frac{\log (k_0/k_2^*)}{\lambda}.$$

For $t^{**} \le t \le \infty$, set $\hat{\omega} = \omega^*$ and thus $\hat{k}_1 = k_1^*$ and $\hat{k}_2 = k_2^*$. As in the previous case, the transversality conditions are seen to hold on such a path.

For the more general case when the planning period may be finite, $T \le \infty$, the optimal path (if feasible) is determined by specification of the vector (k_0, k_T, T). The program of capital accumulation thus determined is uniquely determined.[15] As in the one-sector case, the optimal paths of capital accumulation possess a certain "turnpike" property. Heuristically, it can be ascertained from Figure 7 that with (k_0, k_T) fixed, as $T \to \infty$, the optimal capital-labor ratio is arbitrarily close to the balanced capital-labor ratio k^* for all but a finite amount of time.[16]

Next, we extend these results to include the case of nonzero technical change. In order to guarantee that the value of the definite Integral 56 is finite on all feasible paths, we shall restrict our attention in what follows to

---

[13] Cf. pp. 246–254 in [7].

[14] Theorem 3, p. 50, in [8] requires for constrained optimality of Integral 56 that $e^{-\delta T} q(T)[k(T) - k_T] = 0$. That is, for optimality it is required that either the terminal target (Condition 60) hold with equality or that the terminal social demand price of investment be zero.

[15] See pp. 159–167 and pp. 192–199 in [7].

[16] In the one-sector model, the optimal program is such that the optimal capital-labor ratio is *equal* to the balanced capital-labor ratio for all but a finite amount of time. In the one-sector case, the production possibility set is an isosceles triangle. Thus $q(t)$ can be varied continuously while the optimal savings ratio jumps from one or zero to the balanced savings ratio. However, if $k_1(\omega) \ne k_2(\omega)$, then the production possibility frontier is *strictly* concave.

cases in which the length of the planning period is finite, $0 < T < \infty$. In general, the system of differential Equations 77 through 83 is nonautonomous and thus is appropriately characterized in the (k, q, t)-phase space. Since such figures are difficult to represent graphically, we shall present instead (k, q) "snapshots" of the basic (k, q, t)-phase space.

Consider, for example, the case where there is technical progress in both sectors, but progress in the production of the consumption good is more rapid than progress in the production of the investment good; that is,

$$m > g > 0. \tag{91}$$

From Equations 84, 86 through 90, and Inequality 91, we have

$$\frac{dk_1{}^*(t)}{dt} > 0,$$

$$\frac{\partial p_{\max}(k, t)}{\partial t} > 0, \quad \frac{\partial p_{\min}(k, t)}{\partial t} > 0, \tag{92}$$

$$\frac{d\tilde{k}(t)}{dt} > 0, \quad \text{and thus}$$

$$\frac{dq^*(t)}{dt} > 0 \quad \text{for } m > g > 0.$$

A "snapshot" of the relevant phase diagram for the case of Inequality 91 is given in Figure 8. The schedules $p_{\max}(k)$ and $p_{\min}(k)$ are shown for time t, thus dividing the space into the three regions S_1, S_2, and N. The region N is shown cross-hatched. The loci of points that satisfy $\dot{q} = 0$ and $\dot{k} = 0$ at time t are indicated by heavy solid lines. The direction of shifts of the respective loci as t increases are indicated by the heavy dashed arrows. Thus, for example, as t increases, the straight line $q_t{}^*$ generates a surface on which $dq^*(t)/dt$ is positive for all time $t \geq 0$.

The reader should use Figure 8 as an aid in visualizing the full three-dimensional phase diagram. Specification of the three boundary conditions (k_0, k_T, T) determines, if feasible, a path that satisfies Equations 77 through 83. The program of capital accumulation $\hat{k}(t)$ for $0 \leq t \leq T$, is thus uniquely determined. If on the path just chosen, the terminal value of the social demand price of investment is negative $q(T) < 0$, choose instead the path (yielding higher welfare) that is determined by the three boundary conditions $[k(0) = k_0, q(T) = 0, T]$.

The case where technical progress in the production of the investment good proceeds at a greater rate than technical progress in the production of the consumption good,

$$g > m > 0, \tag{93}$$

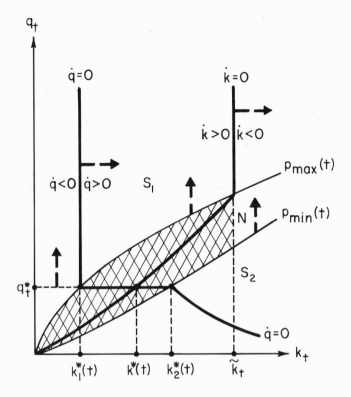

FIGURE 8. "Snapshot" at time t of the phase diagram for the case $m > g > 0$
and $k_2(\omega) > k_1(\omega)$.

is treated in similar fashion. The relevant phase diagram differs from that
suggested by Figure 8 in that

$$\frac{dk_1{}^*(t)}{dt} > 0, \quad \text{and}$$

$$\frac{d\tilde{k}(t)}{dt} > 0, \quad \text{but} \tag{94}$$

$$\frac{\partial p_{max}(k, t)}{\partial t} < 0, \quad \text{and} \quad \frac{\partial p_{min}(k, t)}{\partial t} < 0 \quad \text{for } m > g > 0.$$

The special case when the rates of technical change are identical, $g = m$,
is included as the final example. For this case

$$\text{sgn} \frac{dk_1{}^*(t)}{dt} = \text{sgn} \frac{d\tilde{k}(t)}{dt} = \text{sgn} (g),$$

$$\frac{\partial p_{max}(k, t)}{\partial t} = \frac{\partial p_{min}(k, t)}{\partial t} = 0, \quad \text{and thus} \tag{95}$$

$$\text{sgn} \frac{dq^*(t)}{dt} = \text{sgn} (g), \quad \text{for } g = m.$$

8. The Case where Production of the Investment Good is more Capital Intensive than Production of the Consumption Good

In this section, the problem posed in section 6 is treated for the case where the production functions of Equations 31 and 32 are such that

$$k_1(\omega) > k_2(\omega) \qquad \text{for } \omega > 0. \tag{96}$$

From Equations 41 through 43 and 47, the assumption of Inequality 96 implies that $p_{\max}(k, t)$ and $p_{\min}(k, t)$ are strictly decreasing functions of k. Since $p_{\max}(k, t) > p_{\min}(k, t)$, the (k, q, t)-space is thus divided into the three mutually distinct regions S_1, S_2, and N, defined in Equations 74 through 76. As in section 7, differential Equations 77 and 78 apply for $(k, q, t) \in S_1$; Equations 79 and 80 apply for $(k, q, t) \in S_2$; Equations 81 through 83 apply for $(k, q, t) \in N$.

Again, for purposes of exposition, first consider the case of no technical change, $m = g = 0$. Combining this assumption with the assumption of Inequality 96 yields the autonomous system of differential Equations 58 and 68, whose solutions are characterized in the phase diagram of Figure 9. The loci of points yielding a stationary solution to Equations 58 and 68 are shown with heavy solid curves. The unique value of k_1^* is determined by solving Equation 85. The unique value of q^* is found by solving

$$q^* = p_{\max}(k_1^*).$$

By Equation 83, q^* uniquely determines ω^*, which in turn uniquely determines $k_1^* = k_1(\omega^*)$ and $k_2^* = k_2(\omega^*)$. Call the intersection of the curves determined by $\dot{q} = 0$ and $\dot{k} = 0$, k^*. Assume that the backward solutions from the point (k^*, q^*) cross the curves $p_{\max}(k)$ and $p_{\min}(k)$ at k_1^{**} and k_2^{**} respectively.

If the length of the planning period is infinite, $T = \infty$, and the "terminal" capital-labor ratio $k(\infty)$ is left free, then the optimal program of capital accumulation is easy to characterize with the aid of Figure 9.

For example, given the initial capital-labor ratio $k(0) < k_1^{**}$, choose $\hat{q}(0)$ such that $[k_0, \hat{q}(0)]$ lies on the backward solution from (k^*, q^*). For this case, the optimal program is specialized to production of the investment good until the critical ratio k_1^{**} is achieved.

Consider the case where the planning period is finite and a terminal target must be met, that is,

$$0 < T < \infty \quad \text{and} \quad k(T) \geq k_T > 0.$$

The optimal program (if feasible) follows the path that traverses from k_0 to k_T in time T. For completeness, it should be remembered that if on the path so chosen $q(T) < 0$, the optimal path is instead the path that traverses from k_0 to $q(T) = 0$ in time T. If the boundary conditions k_0 and k_T are

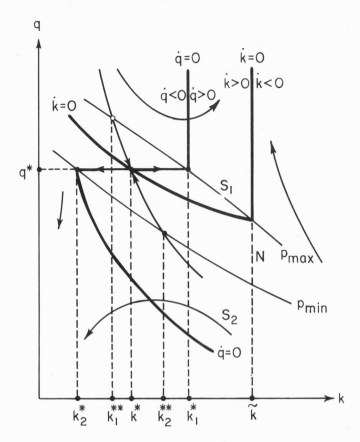

FIGURE 9. Phase diagram for the case where investment goods production is more capital intensive and where there is no technical change.

fixed as the length of the planning period is increased indefinitely, $T \rightarrow \infty$, it is seen that the optimal capital-labor profile will be arbitrarily close to the ratio k^* for all but a finite amount of time.

Next, let us turn to the case where g and m are not necessarily zero. We shall restrict our attention to the case where $T < \infty$ in order to guarantee that the value of Integral 56 is finite along all feasible paths.

As in section 7, it is convenient to suggest the appropriate three-dimensional phase diagram by a two-dimensional "snapshot" of the full diagram. The motion through time of $k_1^*(t)$ and $\tilde{k}(t)$ are given by Equations 86 and 90, respectively. Also $\partial p_{max}(k, t)/\partial t$, $\partial p_{min}(k, t)/\partial t$, and $(m - g)$ share the same sign.

In Figure 10, the phase diagram for the system of Equations 77 through 83 is characterized under the capital intensity assumption (Inequality 96) and under the assumption that technical progress is such that $m > g > 0$. The

loci of stationary solutions to Equations 58 and 68 are shown by the heavy
solid curves. Region N is indicated with crosshatching. The heavy broken
arrows indicate the direction of shift of the various schedules as t increases.
"Snapshots" for the various other cases may be constructed by the reader.
Given the appropriate phase diagram, the optimal path is chosen by a method
entirely analogous to that employed in section 7.

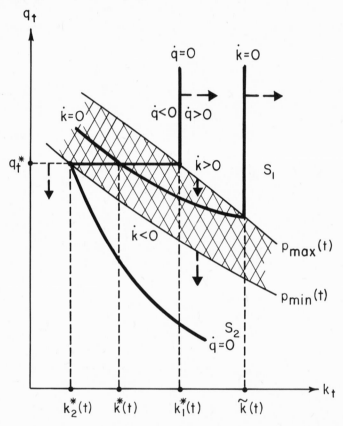

FIGURE 10. "Snapshot" at time t of the phase diagram for the case $g > m > 0$
and $k_1(\omega) > k_2(\omega)$.

9. Concluding Comments

The problem of this essay is to characterize programs of capital accumulation that maximize the discounted sum of per capita consumption over the
planning period subject to the available techniques of production, given
initial endowments and terminal requirements. Production is neoclassical,
and Hicks-neutral technical change is autonomous and proceeds at a constant
relative rate. Without too much difficulty the model can be extended to the

more general case where Hicks-neutral technical change proceeds at a given (but not necessarily constant) rate.

The case where techniques are such that the production of the consumption good is always more capital intensive than production of the investment good is treated in section 7. The opposite case is treated in section 8. The degenerate case where capital intensities are always equal (the one-sector model) is treated in sections 2 through 4. The remaining case is that of reversals in factor intensities: the case where $k_2(\omega^\dagger) > k_1(\omega^\dagger)$ for some $\omega^\dagger > 0$, but where $k_1(\omega^{\dagger\dagger}) > k_2(\omega^{\dagger\dagger})$ for some $\omega^{\dagger\dagger} > 0$, $\omega^{\dagger\dagger} \neq \omega^\dagger$. The general treatment of such cases is complicated, but at least in principle the method is easily explained. At any given instant $t_1 \geq 0$, Equations 85 and 90 uniquely determine the wage-rentals ratio $\omega^*(t_1)$. The snapshot at time t_1 is constructed by the method of section 7 or 8 depending upon whether $k_2[\omega^*(t_1)] \gtrless k_1[\omega^*(t_1)]$. At another instant $t_2 \geq 0$, $\omega^*(t_2)$ may be such that the factor intensities $k_2[\omega^*(t_2)]$ and $k_1[\omega^*(t_1)]$ are reversed from the situation at time t_1. In such a case the different snapshot applies.

References

1. Cass, D., "Optimum Growth in an Aggregative Model of Capital Accumulation," *Review of Economic Studies*, Vol. 32, No. 3 (July 1965).
2. Dorfman, R., P. A. Samuelson, and R. M. Solow, *Linear Programming and Economic Analysis*, New York: McGraw-Hill Book Company, 1958, Chapter 12.
3. Koopmans, T. C., "On the Concept of Optimal Economic Growth," *Semaine d'Etude sur le Rôle de l'Analyse Econométrique dans la Formulation de Plans de Développement*, Vatican City: Pontifical Academy of Sciences, 1965, Vol. I, pp. 225–287.
4. Meade, J. E., *A Neoclassical Theory of Economic Growth*, New York: Oxford University Press, 1961.
5. Oniki, H., and H. Uzawa, "Patterns of Trade and Investment in a Dynamic Model of International Trade," *Review of Economic Studies*, Vol. 32, No. 1 (January 1965).
6. Phelps, E. S., "The Golden Rule of Accumulation: A Fable for Growthmen," *American Economic Review*, Vol. 51, No. 4 (September 1961).
7. Pontryagin, L. S., *Ordinary Differential Equations* (translated from the Russian), Reading, Mass.: Addison-Wesley Publishing Company, 1962.
8. Pontryagin, L. S., V. G. Boltyanskii, R. V. Gamkrelidze, and E. F. Mishchenko, *The Mathematical Theory of Optimal Processes* (translated from the Russian), New York and London: Interscience Publishers, Inc., 1962.
9. Ramsey, F. P., "A Mathematical Theory of Saving," *Economic Journal*, Vol. 38 (1928), pp. 543–559.
10. Robinson, J., "A Neoclassical Theorem," *Review of Economic Studies*, Vol. 29, No. 3 (June 1962).
11. Samuelson, P. A., "A Catenary Turnpike Theorem Involving Consumption and the Golden Rule," *American Economic Review*, Vol. 55, No. 3 (June 1965).

12. Shell, K., "Toward a Theory of Inventive Activity and Capital Accumulation," *American Economic Review*, Vol. 56, No. 2 (May 1966).
13. Solow, R. M., "A Contribution to the Theory of Economic Growth," *Quarterly Journal of Economics*, Vol. 70, No. 1 (February 1956).
14. Swan, T., "Economic Growth and Capital Accumulation," *Economic Record*, Vol. 32 (November 1956).
15. Uzawa, H., "On a Two-Sector Model of Economic Growth II," *Review of Economic Studies*, Vol. 30, No. 2 (June 1963).
16. Uzawa, H., "Optimal Growth in a Two-Sector Model of Capital Accumulation," *Review of Economic Studies*, Vol. 31, No. 1 (January 1964).

II

Optimal Accumulation with Learning by Doing[1]

EYTAN SHESHINSKI

Massachusetts Institute of Technology

Even *so* time does not exist . . . apart
from the movement or quiet rest of things.
LUCRETIUS, *On the Nature of Things*

1. Introduction

In a recent paper [1] Arrow has analyzed a "learning by doing" model in which improvements in technique become available not from the passage of time as such but from the generation of "experience" within the production process itself. Consistent with the emphasis on investment as the vehicle of progress, Arrow takes experience as measured by cumulated gross investment. The consequences are then analogous to increasing returns to scale: the higher the investment, the greater will be the opportunities for learning, the faster the rate of technical progress, and thus the higher the level of production. Arrow assumes that in a competitive economy the investor cannot fully appropriate the extra knowledge that his investment produces. Investors thus receive less than the value of their marginal product, and therefore the amount of resources devoted to investment in a competitive economy will fall below the socially optimum level.

In this essay we are interested in developing a model that may exhibit in a clearer and more pronounced form the essential feature of Arrow's "learning by doing" model: the link between investment and technical progress. Our model is patterned after that of Arrow in that technical progress is taken to be measured by the integral of past gross investment. However, while Arrow

---

[1] I would like to thank, without implicating, Karl Shell and Robert Solow for helpful comments.

uses a vintage approach with fixed coefficients, in our model technical progress is disembodied and the production function is not restricted to fixed coefficients.[2] On the basis of this model we shall characterize the socially optimum path of capital accumulation by use of Pontryagin's "maximum principle" [4]. We shall also derive a formula for optimal taxation to support investment in a competitive economy.

In an economy with several sectors and foreign trade, if learning by doing is more pronounced in some industries than in others, the expansion of outputs and trade may radically change the comparative advantage situation. We shall illustrate this case with a two-sector model, a simple extension of the one-sector model, in which two goods are produced: an investment good and a consumption good. It is assumed that the production of the investment good alone is characterized by a dynamic learning process, and otherwise the two sectors are alike. Capital formation is taken as the source of the learning process. This assumption is meant to reflect the current tendency in the literature on economic development to think of external economies mainly as investment in the creation of a skilled labor force whose growth depends on the availability of capital and on the development of a manufacturing complex. The existence of such external infant economies provides a valid argument for government support aimed at the source of the learning process—capital formation.[3]

2. The Model

Consider the familiar one-good aggregative neoclassical model in which current output $Y(t)$ is divided between current consumption $C(t)$ and gross investment $Z(t)$. Output is produced by the currently existing stocks of capital $K(t)$ and labor $L(t)$. Thus,

$$Y(t) = C(t) + Z(t) = F[K(t), A(t)L(t)], \qquad (1)$$

where $F[\cdot]$ is the neoclassical production function exhibiting constant returns to scale and diminishing marginal rates of substitution. The current efficiency of labor is measured by $A(t)$.

Suppose that the rate of growth of labor is constant, say, n:

$$L(t) = e^{nt}. \qquad (2)$$

Define then the usual per capita quantities measured in terms of the efficiency of labor, so as to rewrite Equation 1 in the form

$$y(t) = c(t) + z(t) = f[k(t)], \qquad (3)$$

---

[2] The latter generalization is due to Levhari [3].

[3] Under our assumptions, there is no case for *direct* protection of any individual industry. To provide a valid argument for such protection, economies must be external to firms but internal to the industry in question. For a more detailed analysis see [6].

where

$$y(t) = \frac{Y(t)}{A(t)L(t)}, \quad c(t) = \frac{C(t)}{A(t)L(t)},$$

$$k(t) = \frac{K(t)}{A(t)L(t)}, \quad z(t) = \frac{Z(t)}{A(t)L(t)},$$

and the expression $F[k(t), 1]$ has been replaced by the shorthand notation $f[k(t)]$.

The function $f(\cdot)$ is assumed to satisfy the neoclassical conditions:

$f(k)$ is twice continuously differentiable, $\qquad\qquad$ (4)

$f(k) > 0, \quad f'(k) > 0, \quad f''(k) < 0 \qquad$ for all $0 < k < \infty,$ $\quad$ (5)

$f(0) = 0, \quad f(\infty) = \infty,$ $\qquad\qquad$ (6)

$f'(0) = \infty, \quad f'(\infty) = 0.$ $\qquad\qquad$ (7)

Now, technical progress $A(t)$, rather than proceeding at an externally given rate, is assumed to reflect cumulated experience in the production of investment goods. The hypothesis is that experience is measured by cumulated gross investment $G(t)$,

$$G(t) = \int_{-\infty}^{t} Z(v)\, dv.$$

Following Arrow's assumption (based on the experience of the airframe industry) let

$$A(t) = [G(t)]^{\alpha}, \qquad\qquad (8)$$

where α is a positive parameter, $0 < \alpha < 1$.

For simplicity, we assume that there is no capital depreciation.[4] In this case gross investment is equal to net capital formation $\dot{K}(t)$, so that cumulated past investments are equal to the current capital stock,

$$K(t) = G(t). \qquad\qquad (9)$$

It is noticed that the function $F[\cdot]$ is not homogeneous of degree one in K and L.[5] Rather, if K is multiplied by λ, and L is multiplied by $\lambda^{1-\alpha}(<\lambda)$, then[6]

---

[4] Simple depreciation formulas, like an evaporative decay, are easy to introduce.

[5] In general, the function $F[\cdot]$ is not homogeneous in K and L. The exception is the Cobb-Douglas, in which case learning by doing is identical with conventional homogeneity of a degree greater than one,

$$F(K, AL) = K^{\beta}(AL)^{1-\beta} = K^{\gamma}L^{(1-\beta)}, \qquad 0 < \beta < 1,$$

where $\gamma = \beta + \alpha(1 - \beta)$, and $\gamma + (1 - \beta) = 1 + \alpha(1 - \beta) > 1$ if $\alpha > 0$. In principle, however, learning by doing should be distinguished from the usual kind of increasing returns.

[6] All variables are understood to be functions of time.

$$F[\lambda K, (\lambda K)^\alpha(\lambda^{1-\alpha}L)] = F[\lambda K, \lambda(K^\alpha L)] = \lambda F(K, K^\alpha L) = \lambda F(K, AL). \quad (10)$$

Let w be the marginal product of labor, measured in efficiency units, and let ρ be the marginal product, or social rate of return of capital. In view of Equations 1, 3, 8, and 9, we have

$$w = w(k) = \frac{1}{A}\frac{\partial F}{\partial L} = F_2 = f(k) - kf'(k), \quad (11)$$

and

$$\rho = \rho(k) = \frac{\partial F}{\partial K} = F_1 + \alpha F_2 \frac{AL}{K} = f'(k) + \alpha\left[\frac{f(k)}{k} - f'(k)\right], \quad (12)$$

where subscripts denote partial differentiation with respect to the indicated argument. Since $F[\cdot]$ is not homogeneous of degree one in K and L, it would be impossible for both capital and labor to be paid their marginal products. In particular, if the labor market is perfectly competitive so that the wage rate equals w, then the private investor is paid a rental, denoted by r, that falls short of ρ:

$$r = r(k) = f'(k) = \rho - \alpha\frac{w}{k}. \quad (13)$$

It is seen that there is a gap between the social rate of return and the competitive rental on capital and that the gap is proportional to the wage bill per unit of capital.[7]

By implication, if labor were paid only a fraction $(1 - \alpha)$ of its marginal product by means, for instance, of a tax on wages, then the capital rental that includes the proceeds of the tax as a subsidy would be equal to the marginal product of capital.

3. Some Implications

Balanced growth. In view of Equations 1 through 7, it can be seen that there exists a unique positive number g,

$$g = \frac{n}{1 - \alpha}, \qquad 0 < \alpha < 1, \quad (14)$$

such that output and capital both grow at the constant rate g:

$$\dot{K}/K = \dot{Y}/Y = g.[8]$$

---

[7] The relation between what might be called the competitive and the social factor price frontiers can be seen by solving for w once in terms of r, from Equations 11 and 13, and once in terms of ρ, from Equations 11 and 12. Evidently, at any given wage rate, the social rate of return is proportionately higher than the private rental.

[8] Thus, substitute $Y(t) = Y_0 e^{gt}$ and $K(t) = K_0 e^{gt}$ in Equation 1, where Y_0 and K_0 are any positive numbers: $Y_0 e^{gt} = F[K_0 e^{gt}, K_0 e^{(\alpha g + n)t}]$ or $Y_0 e^{[g(1-\alpha)-n]t} = K_0 f\{e^{[g(1-\alpha)-n]t}\}$, which implies that $g(1 - \alpha) - n = 0$. The existence of g is guaranteed by Equations 4 through 7.

It is interesting to notice that in a state of balanced growth the undeflated wage rate increases at the rate $\alpha n/(1 - \alpha)$.[9] Thus, among balanced paths, the higher the labor-force growth the higher is the rate of growth of the wage rate. The reason for this seeming paradox is, as Arrow notes, that a higher growth rate of labor induces more investment, which in turn raises labor's efficiency and thus the wage rate.

Asymptotic growth with proportional savings. Using Equations 8 and 9, one derives from Equation 3 that[10]

$$\dot{k} = (1 - \alpha)[f(k) - c] - nk. \tag{15}$$

Suppose now that savings is a fixed fraction s, $0 \le s \le 1$, of output. Equation 15 then becomes a familiar differential equation

$$\dot{k} = s(1 - \alpha)f(k) - nk. \tag{16}$$

Let k^0 be the capital-labor ratio uniquely defined by

$$\frac{f(k^0)}{k^0} = \frac{n}{s(1 - \alpha)}. \tag{17}$$

Starting with any arbitrary initial stock of capital $k(0) = k_0$, it can be shown readily that the unique solution of Equation 16 has the property that $\lim_{t \to \infty} k(t) = k^0$, where k^0 is, of course, the balanced growth capital-labor ratio corresponding to a savings rate of s.[11]

The golden rule of capital accumulation. Consider the model in a state of balanced growth with fixed k and c. Observe first that by Equation 9,

$$\frac{\dot{A}}{A} = \alpha \frac{\dot{K}}{K} = \frac{\alpha}{1 - \alpha} \left(\frac{\dot{k}}{k} + n \right).$$

Integration of the foregoing expression, using Equation 2, yields that

$$A(t) = k(t)^{(\alpha/1 - \alpha)} e^{(\alpha n/1 - \alpha)t}. \tag{18}$$

Consumption per capita $C(t)/L(t)$ can thus be expressed as

$$\frac{C(t)}{L(t)} = \left[\frac{C(t)}{A(t)L(t)} \right] A(t) = c(t)k(t)^{(\alpha/1 - \alpha)} e^{(\alpha n/1 - \alpha)t}. \tag{19}$$

---

[9] Since k is fixed on the balanced growth path, it follows that

$$W(t) = [f(k) - kf'(k)]A(t) = [f(k) - kf'(k)]A_0 e^{(\alpha n/1 - \alpha)t}.$$

[10] By definition, $\dot{k}/k = (1 - \alpha)(\dot{K}/K) - n$, and $z = (1/1 - \alpha)(\dot{k} + nk)$.

[11] Analogous results hold for the case where a fixed fraction of profits is saved, or where wages and profits are saved in fixed, but different, proportions.

Hence, maximization of consumption per capita over all possible balanced growth configurations is equivalent to the maximization of $ck^{(\alpha/1-\alpha)}$. In view of Equation 15 we have, for $\dot{k} = 0$, that $c = f(k) - (n/1 - \alpha)k$. Now, maximization of the expression

$$ck^{(\alpha/1-\alpha)} = \left[f(k) - \frac{n}{1-\alpha}k \right]k^{(\alpha/1-\alpha)}$$

yields the following necessary condition for a maximum,[12]

$$(1-\alpha)f'(k) + \alpha\frac{f(k)}{k} = \frac{n}{1-\alpha}. \tag{20}$$

The solution to Equation 20, denoted by k^*, is called *the golden rule path of capital accumulation.* Here, as in other models, the rule requires that the steady-state capital-labor ratio k^* be determined by the equality of the social rate of return on capital (Equation 12) and the rate of growth: $\rho = n/(1-\alpha)$. The determination of k^* is illustrated in Figure 1.[13]

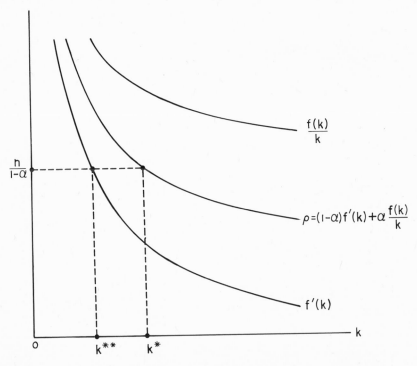

FIGURE 1. Private and social rates of return on capital.

---

[12] By the concavity (Equation 4) of f, Equation 20 is also sufficient.

[13] Let $\hat{k}$ be the maximal sustainable capital-labor ratio: $f(\hat{k})/\hat{k} = n/(1-\alpha)$. It should

4. The Optimal Program of Capital Accumulation

We address ourselves now to the problem of characterizing the program of capital accumulation that optimizes some suitable criterion (welfare) function subject to the assumptions about technology and given initial conditions.

We assume that there is a planning board whose objective is to maximize the sum of discounted future consumption per capita.[14] If $\delta' > 0$ is the planning board's constant rate of time discount, then the problem is to maximize the expression

$$\int_0^\infty \frac{C(t)}{L(t)} e^{-\delta' t} \, dt.$$

It is convenient to write the maximand in the equivalent form

$$\int_0^\infty \left[\frac{C(t)}{L(t)e^{(\alpha n/1 - \alpha)t}} \right] e^{-\delta t} \, dt,$$

where $\delta = \delta' - (n/1 - \alpha)$. In this form the objective appears to be the maximization of the sum of discounted future consumption per capita deflated by a time trend. This change is not essential so long as $\delta > 0$, so that an optimal plan can exist.

The maximand is constrained by the conditions

$$\dot{K}(t) = s(t)F[K(t), A(t)L(t)],$$

and given that $K(0) = K_0$,

$$A(t) = K(t)^\alpha,$$

where $0 \leq s(t) \leq 1$ denotes the fraction of output currently saved.

Using intensive variables, the previous problem can be reduced to the following form:

To maximize

$$\int_0^\infty [cx] e^{-\delta t} \, dt \tag{21}$$

from (18)

---

be clear that the solution k^* to Equation 20 is always lower than $\hat{k}$. To see this, observe that the social rate of return ρ is an average of the marginal and average products of capital:

$$f'(k) < \rho = (1 - \alpha)f'(k) + \alpha \frac{f(k)}{k} < \frac{f(k)}{k}.$$

Hence, at $k = k^*$, $\rho = n/(1 - \alpha) = f(\hat{k})/\hat{k} < f(k^*)/k^*$, which implies that $k^* < \hat{k}$.

[14] Modifications that are required when the objective function is not linear in consumption per capita are discussed in the appendix to this essay.

subject to the constraints:

$$\dot{k} = (1 - \alpha)sf(k) - nk, \tag{22}$$

$$c = (1 - s)f(k), \tag{23}$$

$$x = k^{(\alpha/1-\alpha)}, \tag{24}$$

$$0 \le s \le 1, \tag{25}$$

$$k(0) = k_0, \tag{26}$$

where s is, say, a piecewise continuous function of time that has to be chosen optimally.

This problem is solved by use of Pontryagin's "maximum principle" [4]. Application of his third theorem ([4] p. 63) shows that if a program $[k(t), s(t); 0 \le t \le \infty]$ is optimal, it is necessary to have a continuous function of time $q(t)$ such that

$$\dot{k} = (1 - \alpha)sf(k) - nk \tag{27}$$

with initial condition $k(0) = k_0$,

$$\dot{q} = -\frac{(1 - s)x}{1 - \alpha}\,\rho(k) - q[(1 - \alpha)sf'(k) - n] + \delta q, \tag{28}$$

$$s \text{ maximizes } [q(1 - \alpha) - x]s \qquad \text{subject to } 0 \le s \le 1, \tag{29}$$

and s is a piecewise continuous function of time, and

$$\lim_{t \to \infty} qe^{-\delta t} = 0. \tag{30}$$

By virtue of the assumptions of diminishing marginal rates of substitution in Equations 4 and 5, and the weak concavity of Equation 21, the necessary conditions just given are also sufficient and characterize a unique optimum growth path, whenever such a path exists.[15]

It is natural to look first whether there is any path that satisfies all the optimality conditions of Equations 27 through 30 save, probably, the initial conditions. One such path is the singular solution to the pair of differential Equations 27 through 28, given the allocation condition of Equation 29. The solution, denoted by (k^*, q^*) and s^*, is uniquely defined by

$$\rho(k^*) = (1 - \alpha)f'(k^*) + \alpha\frac{f(k^*)}{k^*} = \frac{n}{1 - \alpha} + \delta, \tag{31}$$

$$q^* = \frac{x^*}{1 - \alpha}, \qquad \text{where } x^* = k^{*(\alpha/1-\alpha)}, \tag{32}$$

$$s^* = \frac{n}{1 - \alpha}\frac{k^*}{f(k^*)}. \tag{33}$$

---

[15] The usual sufficiency proof for such problems can be applied to our case. See, e.g., [2] and [5].

Assume that the initial capital-labor ratio is k^*, that is, $k(0) = k^*$. Then a program of capital accumulation satisfying the necessary conditions is one that fixes $q(t) = q^*$ for $0 \le t \le \infty$, and maintains the capital-labor ratio $k(t) = k^*$, for $0 \le t \le \infty$. The savings ratio corresponding to this program is s^*. This unique program will be referred to as *the optimum balanced growth path*.

Note that the optimum balanced growth path is merely a modified golden rule path (Equation 20). The modification is that the social rate of return ρ is equated not to the rate of growth $n/(1 - \alpha)$ but to the latter plus the discount factor δ that reflects the community's rate of time preference.

Consider now the linear Taylor approximation of the system of differential Equations 27 and 28, evaluated at (k^*, q^*). In the domain $[k, q \mid x < q(1 - \alpha)]$, the roots λ_1, λ_2 of the characteristic equation of the linear system associated with Equations 27 and 28 are the solutions of

$$(a_1 - \lambda_1)(a_2 - \lambda_2) = 0,$$

where $a_1 = (1 - \alpha)f'(k^*) - n < 0$ and $a_2 = -(1 - \alpha)f'(k^*) + (n + \delta) > 0$. In the domain $[k, q \mid x > q(1 - \alpha)]$, the roots λ_1', λ_2' of the characteristic equation of the linear system associated with Equations 27 and 28 are the solutions of

$$(a_1' - \lambda_1')(a_2' - \lambda_2') = 0,$$

where $a_1' = -n < 0$ and $a_2' = n + \delta > 0$. In both cases, therefore, the roots are real and opposite in sign. This *saddle-point property* of the balanced-growth path (k^*, q^*) suggests that the stable branches form a unique optimal path for any initial $k(0) = k_0 \ne k^*$. A proof of this assertion follows.

We shall describe the solutions of the system of Equations 27 and 28, given the allocation rule of Expression 29, in the positive quadrant of the (k, q) plane. The appropriate phase diagram is given in Figure 2.

The conditions of Expression 29 imply that for optimality it is necessary that

$$
\begin{aligned}
s = 0 \quad &\text{when } x > q(1 - \alpha) \\
0 \le s \le 1 \quad &\text{when } x = q(1 - \alpha) \\
s = 1 \quad &\text{when } x < q(1 - \alpha).
\end{aligned}
\tag{34}
$$

The curve $x = q(1 - \alpha)$ is seen to divide the (k, q) plane into two separate domains. The solutions to Equations 27 and 28 will be studied separately for each domain.

The domain $\{k, q \mid 0 \le x < q(1 - \alpha)\}$. In this domain s is assigned a value of one. The differential Equations 27 and 28 thus become

$$k = (1 - \alpha)f(k) - nk, \tag{35}$$

$$\dot{q} = -q[(1 - \alpha)f'(k) - (n + \delta)]. \tag{36}$$

Consider then the two functions

$$\psi_1(k, q) = (1 - \alpha)f(k) - nk, \tag{37}$$

and

$$\psi_2(k, q) = (1 - \alpha)f'(k) - (n + \delta). \tag{38}$$

The locus of all the pairs (k, q) that yield $\dot{k} = 0$ is defined by $\psi_1(k, q) = 0$, while the locus of all the pairs (k, q) that yield $\dot{q} = 0$ is defined by $\psi_2(k, q) = 0$.

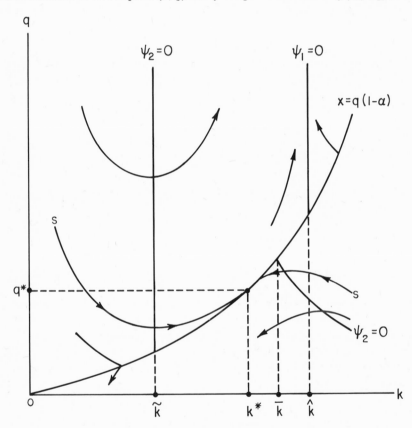

FIGURE 2. Phase diagram of the solutions (k, q) that satisfy Equations 27 through 30.

The locus $\psi_1 = 0$, being independent of q, defines a unique capital-labor ratio, denoted $\hat{k}$, given by

$$\frac{f(\hat{k})}{\hat{k}} = \frac{n}{1 - \alpha}. \tag{39}$$

Similarly, the locus $\psi_2 = 0$, being independent of q, defines a unique capital-labor ratio, denoted $\tilde{k}$, given by

$$f'(\tilde{k}) = \frac{n + \delta}{1 - \alpha}. \tag{40}$$

Typical trajectories can now be drawn using the fact that $\dot{k} > 0$ for all $k < \hat{k}$, while $\dot{k} < 0$ for all $k > \hat{k}$, and that $\dot{q} < 0$ for all $k < \tilde{k}$ and $\dot{q} > 0$ for all $k > \tilde{k}$.

The domain $\{k, q \mid x > q(1 - \alpha) \geq 0\}$. In this domain s is assigned a value of zero. The differential Equations 27 and 28 thus become

$$\dot{k} = -nk, \tag{41}$$

$$\dot{q} = -\frac{x}{1 - \alpha} \rho(k) + q(n + \delta). \tag{42}$$

Hence, $\dot{k} < 0$ in this domain. Define the function $\psi_2(k, q)$ in this domain as

$$\psi_2(k, q) = -\frac{x}{1 - \alpha} \rho(k) + q(n + \delta). \tag{43}$$

The locus of all the pairs (k, q) that yield $\dot{q} = 0$ is defined by $\psi_2(k, q) = 0$. Observe that since $x < q(1 - \alpha)$,

$$\psi_2(k, q) = -\frac{x}{1 - \alpha} \rho(k) + q(n + \delta) < -q[\rho(k) - (n + \delta)]. \tag{44}$$

Thus, if $\bar{k}$ is the capital-labor ratio defined by

$$\rho(\bar{k}) = (1 - \alpha)f'(\bar{k}) + \alpha \frac{f(\bar{k})}{\bar{k}} = n + \delta, \tag{45}$$

then from Equations 44 and 45 it is seen that for a nonnegative q, $\psi_2(k, q) < 0$ for all $k \leq \bar{k}$. In the positive quadrant, therefore, the locus $\psi_2(k, q) = 0$ is defined for all $\bar{k} < k \leq \infty$. To calculate the slope (dq/dk) along this locus, one first finds that

$$\frac{\partial \psi_2(k, q)}{\partial k}\bigg|_{\psi_2 = 0} = \frac{q}{k}\left(\frac{\alpha}{1 - \alpha} - \eta\right)(n + \delta),$$

and

$$\frac{\partial \psi_2(k, q)}{\partial q}\bigg|_{\psi_2 = 0} = n + \delta,$$

where $\eta = -[\rho'(k)k/\rho(k)]$ is the elasticity of ρ with respect to k. Thus

$$\frac{dq}{dk}\bigg|_{\psi_2 = 0} = -\frac{\partial \psi_2/\partial k}{(\partial \psi_2/\partial q)}\bigg|_{\psi_2 = 0} = \frac{q}{k}\left(\frac{\alpha}{1 - \alpha} - \eta\right) \gtrless 0 \qquad \text{as} \quad \frac{\alpha}{1 - \alpha} \gtrless \eta. \tag{46}$$

Without further assumptions about the relation between α and the elasticity η, the sign of Equation 46 is indeterminate.

Corresponding to $\bar{k}$, in Equation 45 define $\bar{q}$ by

$$\bar{q} = \frac{\bar{k}^{(\alpha/1-\alpha)}}{1-\alpha} = \frac{\bar{x}}{1-\alpha} \quad \text{where } \bar{x} = \bar{k}^{(\alpha/1-\alpha)}. \qquad (47)$$

By virtue of Equations 43 and 45, it is seen that $(\bar{k}, \bar{q})$ is a limit point of the locus $\psi_2(k, q) = 0$ and that there is no other common point to this locus and the curve $x = q(1 - \alpha)$.

Typical trajectories can now be drawn using the fact that $\dot{q} < 0$ for all q below the locus $\psi_2(k, q) = 0$, while $\dot{q} > 0$ for all q above $\psi_2(k, q) = 0$.

The optimal path. On any trajectory not passing through the point (k^*, q^*), k can be written as a continuous function of q. In fact, a trajectory not passing through (k^*, q^*) is uniquely determined by specification of the initial conditions (k_0, q_0). The existence of a unique optimal path satisfying the conditions of Equations 27 through 30 can be established.

If $k_0 = k(0) \neq k^*$, then the planning board would assign a price $q_0 = q(0)$, such that the point (k_0, q_0) lies on a trajectory that passes through (k^*, q^*). Let $0 \leq t^* < \infty$ be the time required for such a program to achieve (k^*, q^*). Then the optimal program is

$$[k(t) = k^*, s(t) = s^*; t^* \leq t \leq \infty].$$

It is seen that any other path leads ultimately to a violation of the condition of Equation 30 or of the nonnegativity of k. The saddle-point property of the unique optimal path, denoted SS, is illustrated in Figure 2.[16]

It is noticed that the savings ratio on the unique optimum path is either one or zero depending upon whether the initial capital-labor ratio is less or

---

[16] To see that in each of the domains there exists a trajectory, *wholly contained in the domain*, which leads to the point (k^*, q^*), calculate the slope of a typical trajectory. From Equations 32 and 33 we have, at any point (k, q) in the domain $\{k, q \mid 0 \leq x < q(1 - \alpha)\}$,

$$\frac{dq}{dk}\Big|_{(k,q)} = -\frac{q[(1 - \alpha)f'(k) - (n + \delta)]}{(1 - \alpha)f(k) - nk}.$$

Thus, in view of Conditions 34, at any point (k, q), $k < k^*$,

$$\frac{dq}{dk}\Big|_{(k,q)} < \frac{\alpha}{1-\alpha}\frac{q}{k} \quad \text{while} \quad \frac{dq}{dk}\Big|_{(k^*,q^*)} = \frac{\alpha}{1-\alpha}\frac{q^*}{k^*}.$$

On the other hand, the slope of the curve $x = q(1 - \alpha)$ is given by

$$\frac{dq}{dk}\Big|_{x = q(1-\alpha)} = \frac{\alpha}{1-\alpha}\frac{q}{k}.$$

This is sufficient to prove the existence of a trajectory that lies in the domain and leads to (k^*, q^*). A similar argument can be applied to the domain $\{k, q \mid x > q(1 - \alpha) \geq 0\}$.

greater than k^*, respectively. This follows from the linearity of instantaneous utility (of per capita consumption) assumed in Equation 21.

The behavior of the social demand price of investment q on the optimum path is also of some interest. In particular, the shadow price of investment is not a monotonic function of the capital-labor ratio, so that q, say, might fall and then rise while k is increasing. As we know from orthodox neoclassical models [2], this behavior would not be optimal if it were not for the returns to investment due to learning by doing.

5. The Competitive Solution and Corrective Fiscal Policy

Consider now the path of capital accumulation that would obtain if the economy were not centrally planned but under conditions of perfect competition with all the individuals having the same utility function of Integral 21.

In this case the supply of capital in the economy is infinitely elastic at a rental, or rate of interest, of $(n/1 - \alpha) + \delta$; that is, investors will take any investment with a (private) rate of return that exceeds or equals the rate of growth plus the time discount factor δ and will take no investment at lower rates of return. For an equilibrium in which some, but not all, of income is saved, we must have the equality $r = (n/1 - \alpha) + \delta$. In view of Equation 13, this condition defines the unique competitive balanced capital-labor ratio, denoted by k^{**},

$$r(k^{**}) = f'(k^{**}) = \frac{n}{1 - \alpha} + \delta, \tag{48}$$

which is to be compared with the socially optimum balanced capital-labor ratio k^* (Equation 31). It is readily seen that $k^* > k^{**}$, which implies that the competitive economy has a tendency to settle to a steady state in which investment is below the socially optimum level. The reason for this inefficiency is that under competitive conditions those responsible for technical progress, that is the private entrepreneurs, are not rewarded with their full marginal product, and consequently they tend to devote less resources to investment than is socially desirable.

Corrective fiscal policy should obviously be aimed to subsidize investment so as to equate the social and the competitive rates of return on investment. The exact amount of the subsidy per unit of capital is given by the difference between these rates

$$\rho - r = \alpha\left[\frac{f(k)}{k} - f'(k)\right] > 0. \tag{49}$$

One can calculate of course how the rate of subsidy changes along the optimal path. For example, in the Cobb-Douglas case where $f(k) = k^\beta$, $0 < \beta < 1$, Equation 49 becomes

$$\rho - r = \alpha(1 - \beta)k^{\beta - 1}.$$

Thus, as the capital-labor ratio increases (for all $k < k^*$) the rate of subsidy decreases, and vice versa, but this result is not necessary for other production functions.[17]

6. A Two-Sector Open Model

We shall now consider briefly a simple extension of the closed one-sector model to a case of two sectors with foreign trade.

The model economy consists of two sectors, an investment-good sector, labeled 1, and a consumption-good sector, labeled 2. The quantity of the currently produced consumption goods $Y_2(t)$ depends upon the allocation of capital $K_2(t)$ and labor $L_2(t)$ to the consumption sector

$$Y_2(t) = F[K_2(t), L_2(t)]. \tag{50}$$

Similarly, the quantity of investment goods currently produced $Y_1(t)$ depends upon the current allocation of factors to the investment sector

$$Y_1(t) = A[G(t)]F[k_1(t), L_1(t)], \tag{51}$$

where $A[G(t)]$, the productivity of the investment sector, depends on cumulated "experience" $G(t)$. As before, we adopt the particular form of Equation 8,

$$A[G(t)] = [G(t)]^\alpha, \qquad 0 < \alpha < 1.$$

Free shiftability of factors between sectors and Assumptions 4 through 7 guarantee that the resources of the economy are fully utilized:

$$K_1(t) + K_2(t) = K(t) \tag{52}$$

$$L_1(t) + L_2(t) = L(t). \tag{53}$$

The model assumes that capital formation is the source of the learning process in the investment sector. To provide for balanced growth, the index of experience will be expressed here by the per capita amount of capital

$$G(t) = k(t) = \frac{K(t)}{L(t)}. \tag{54}$$

---

[17] In general

$$\frac{d(\rho - r)}{dk} = \alpha f'' \left[\frac{\sigma}{\pi} - 1 \right] \gtrless 0,$$

where

$$\sigma = -\frac{f'(k)[f(k) - kf'(k)]}{f(k)f''(k)k} \quad \text{(elasticity of substitution),}$$

and

$$\pi = \frac{kf'(k)}{f(k)} \qquad \text{(relative share of capital).}$$

Since both sectors have the same production function (except for the neutral efficiency index), they are equally capital intensive. Thus, if s, $0 \leq s \leq 1$, is the proportion of resources allocated to the investment sector, then

$$\frac{K_1(t)}{K(t)} = \frac{L_1(t)}{L(t)} = s, \quad \text{and} \quad \frac{K_2(t)}{K(t)} = \frac{L_2(t)}{L(t)} = 1 - s. \tag{55}$$

Using small letters for per capita quantities, Equations 50 and 51 can now be written

$$y_1(t) = sk(t)^\alpha f[k(t)] \tag{56}$$

and

$$y_2(t) = (1 - s)f[k(t)]. \tag{57}$$

Given $k(t)$, one can use Equations 56 and 57 to trace out all the points on the (straight-line) production possibility curve between $y_1(t)$ and $y_2(t)$ by varying s from 0 to 1 (see Figure 3).

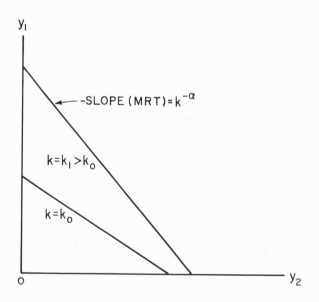

FIGURE 3. Production possibility curve.

The slope of the curve is equal to $-k^\alpha$; hence, the process of capital accumulation shifts the curve upwards and at the same time changes the production terms of trade in favor of the investment sector.

The economy is assumed to be sufficiently small so that the international price of the investment good in terms of the consumption good p is taken as given.

Let $z_1(t)$ and $z_2(t)$ be the per capita amounts imported of investment and consumption goods, respectively. It is required that the net value of imports be zero; that is,

$$pz_1(t) + z_2(t) = 0. \tag{58}$$

The per capita absorptions of investment $x_1(t)$ and consumption $x_2(t)$ can then be written

$$x_1(t) = y_1(t) + z_1(t), \tag{59}$$

$$x_2(t) = y_2(t) - pz_1(t). \tag{60}$$

Nonnegativity of absorptions requires that

$$-y_1(t) \le z_1 \le \frac{y_2(t)}{p}. \tag{61}$$

In the absence of depreciation, changes in the per capita stock of capital are given by

$$\dot{k}(t) = x_1(t) - nk(t). \tag{62}$$

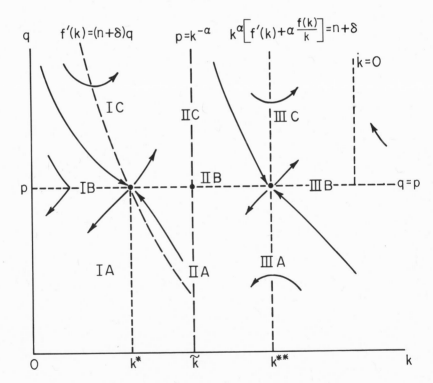

FIGURE 4. Phase diagram of solutions in Table 1.

Suppose that the objective of the economy is to maximize

$$\int_0^\infty x_1(t)e^{-\delta t}\,dt,$$

subject to Conditions 56 through 61 and $k(0) = k_0$. Necessary conditions for optimality can be obtained by use of Pontryagin's maximum principle.

Table 1. Necessary Conditions for Optimality

	I	II	III
A	$q < p$ $p < k^\alpha$ $s = 0$ $z = 0$	$q < p$ $p = k^{-\alpha}$ $0 \le s \le 1$ $-sk^\alpha f(k) = z$	$q < p$ $p > k^{-\alpha}$ $s = 1$ $z = -pk^\alpha f(k)$
B	$q = p$ $p < k^{-\alpha}$ $s = 0$ $0 \le z \le f$	$q = p$ $p = k^{-\alpha}$ $0 \le s \le 1$ $-psk^\alpha f \le z \le (1-s)f$	$q = p$ $p > k^{-\alpha}$ $s = 1$ $-pk^\alpha f(k) \le z \le 0$
C	$q > p$ $p < k^{-\alpha}$ $s = 0$ $z = f$	$q > p$ $p = k^{-\alpha}$ $0 \le s \le 1$ $z = (1-s)f$	$q = p$ $p > k^{-\alpha}$ $s = 1$ $z = 0$

Following the notation of Ryder,[18] we designate the pattern of production by roman numerals (I = specialized in consumption, III = specialized in investment) and the pattern of absorption by capital letters (A = specialized in consumption, C = specialized in investment). Nonspecialization is designated by II and B for production and absorption, respectively. The various solutions are summarized in Table 1 and illustrated in Figure 4.

It is seen that the optimum capital-labor ratio approaches asymptotically either k^* or k^{**}, depending on the initial ratio $k(0)$. In particular, if $k(0) < \tilde{k}$ (where $\tilde{k}^{-\alpha} = p$), two basic optimal patterns seem possible:(1) If $k(0) < k^*$ (defined by $f'(k^*) = (n + \delta)p$), the economy first specializes in the production of the consumption good and in the absorption of the investment good. Having reached k^* after a finite period of time, the economy entertains a positive absorption of consumption thereafter. This economy never invests sufficiently to gain comparative advantage in the production of the investment good. (2)A more interesting case is where, starting with $k^* < k(0) \le \tilde{k}$, the economy

---

[18] Essay V in this book.

first specializes in the production of consumption and absorption of investment, switching after a finite period to production, as well as absorption, of investment. Finally, having reached k^{**}, the economy invests just to keep k^{**} intact and enjoys a positive absorption of consumption. This case brings out the possibility of dramatic changes in comparative advantage due to learning by doing.

As before, under competitive conditions, there is need to raise investment to the socially optimum level, or else the economy will never realize its full potential in production of the investment good. The formula for the optimal subsidy can be shown to be

$$\rho - r = \alpha \frac{y_1(t)}{k(t)}.$$

APPENDIX

Let $U[\cdot]$ be a concave utility (welfare) function, defined over deflated consumption per capita:

$$U\left[\frac{C}{Le^{[\alpha n/(1-\alpha)]t}}\right] = U[cx]. \tag{A.1}$$

The deflator is a pure time trend that reflects the increase in labor productivity at given capital-labor ratios. The planning board's objective function is defined by the integral

$$\int_0^\infty U[cx]e^{-\delta t}\, dt, \tag{A.2}$$

where

$$c = (1 - s)f(k). \tag{A.3}$$

The problem is to choose a piecewise continuous function s so as to maximize Integral A.2, subject to the constraints of Equations 22 through 26.

It is assumed that

$$U'[cx] > 0, \quad U''[cx] < 0 \qquad \text{for all } 0 < cx < \infty. \tag{A.4}$$

Furthermore, in order to guarantee that the optimal consumption path is always positive, it is postulated that

$$U'[0] = \infty. \tag{A.5}$$

Application of the "maximum principle" (in particular Theorem 3 in [4], p. 63), yields that if a program $[k(t), s(t); 0 \le t \le \infty]$ is optimal then there exists a continuous function q, such that

$$k = (1 - \alpha)sf(k) - nk \tag{A.6}$$

with initial condition $k(0) = k_0$,

$$\dot{q} = -\frac{(1 - s)U'[cx]\cdot x}{1 - \alpha}\cdot\rho(k) - q[(1 - \alpha)sf'(k) - (n + \delta)], \tag{A.7}$$

s maximizes $[q(1 - \alpha) - U'(cx)x]s$ subject to $0 \leq s \leq 1$,   (A.8)

and s is a piecewise continuous function of t,

$$\lim_{t \to \infty} q \cdot e^{-\delta t} = 0.$$ (A.9)

It is immediately seen that the condition of Inequality A.4 guarantees that $0 \leq s < 1$ for all $0 \leq t \leq \infty$.

By virtue of the assumptions of diminishing marginal rates of substitution of Expressions 4 and 5, and diminishing marginal utility of Integral A.4, these necessary conditions are also sufficient and characterize a unique optimal growth path, whenever this exists.[19]

To start with, consider the singular solutions to the differential Equations A.5 and A.6, given Equation A.3 and the allocation rule of Expression A.8, denoted k^*, q^*, s^*, and c^*, and uniquely defined by

$$\rho(k^*) = \alpha \frac{f(k^*)}{k^*} + (1 - \alpha)f'(k^*) \frac{n}{1 - \alpha} + \delta,$$ (A.10)

$$s^* = \frac{n}{1 - \alpha} \frac{k^*}{f(k^*)},$$ (A.11)

$$c^* = (1 - s^*)f(k^*),$$ (A.12)

and

$$q^* = \frac{U'[c^*x^*]x^*}{1 - \alpha}, \quad \text{where } x^* = k^{*a/(1-a)}.$$ (A.13)

The path $k(t) = k^*$, $q(t) = q^*$, $s(t) = s^*$, and $c(t) = c^*$ for $0 \leq t \leq \infty$, is a unique *optimum balanced growth path* and it satisfies the conditions of Equations A.6 through A.9 provided $k(0) = k^*$. Notice that, unlike the balanced price of investment q^*, the balanced capital-labor ratio k^* (Equation A.10), is independent of the form of the utility function.

Expanding Equations A.6 and A.7 around (k^*, q^*), one can verify that the balanced growth path is a saddle point. To examine the behavior of the differential Equations A.6 and A.7 in the positive quadrant of the (k, q) plane, consider first the case where Expression A.8 gives an interior solution, that is,

$$q(1 - \alpha) = U'[(1 - s)f(k) \cdot x]x \quad \text{and} \quad 0 < s < 1.$$ (A.14)

Whenever satisfied, one can solve Equation A.14 for s in terms of k and q,

$$s = s(k, q).$$ (A.15)

Denoting $\sigma = -[U''(cx)cx]/U'(cx)$ and $\pi = [f'(k)k]/f(k)$, one can differentiate Equation A.14 implicitly and calculate that

$$\frac{\partial s}{\partial q} = \frac{1 - s}{\sigma} \cdot \frac{1}{q} > 0,$$

---

[19] Again, the usual sufficiency proof for such cases can be applied here. Cf., e.g., [2] or [5].

and $s(k, \infty) = 1$ for any $0 < k < \infty$,

$$\frac{\partial s}{\partial k} = \frac{1 - s}{k} \left[\pi - \left(\frac{\alpha}{1 - \alpha} \right) \left(\frac{1 - \sigma}{\sigma} \right) \right].$$

The sign of the last expression is in general indeterminate. Consider now the two functions ψ_1 and ψ_2:

$$\psi_1(k, q) = (1 - \alpha)s(k, q)f(k) - nk, \tag{A.16}$$

$$\psi_2(k, q) = [1 - s(k, q)]\rho(k) + (1 - \alpha)s(k, q)f'(k) - (n + \delta). \tag{A.17}$$

The locus of all the pairs (k, q) that yield $\dot{k} = 0$ is defined by $\psi_1(k, q) = 0$, while the locus of all the pairs (k, q) that yield $\dot{q} = 0$ is defined by $\psi_2(k, q) = 0$.

The curve $\psi_1(k, q) = 0$. Let $\hat{k}$ be the capital-labor ratio given by $f(\hat{k})/\hat{k} = n/(1 - \alpha)$. The locus $\psi_1(k, q) = 0$ is seen to be defined only for $k < \hat{k}$, and $\psi_1(\hat{k}, \infty) = 0$. In general, one can calculate that

$$\frac{dq}{dk}\bigg|_{\psi_1 = 0} = \frac{q}{k} \left(\frac{s}{1 - s} \right) \left[(1 - \pi) - \frac{k}{s} \frac{ds}{dk} \right] \sigma = \frac{q}{k} \left[\frac{s - \pi}{1 - s} + \left(\frac{\alpha}{1 - \alpha} \right) \left(\frac{1 - \sigma}{\sigma} \right) \right].$$

Without further restrictions, the sign of the last expression is indeterminate.

The curve $\psi_2(k, q) = 0$. Let $\tilde{k}$ be the capital-labor ratio given by $f'(\tilde{k}) = (n + \delta)/(1 - \alpha)$. It can be seen from Equation A.13 that the locus $\psi_2(k, q) = 0$ is defined only for $k > \tilde{k}$, and $\psi_2(\tilde{k}, \infty) = 0$. Implicit differentiation along $\psi_2 = 0$ gives

$$\frac{dq}{dk}\bigg|_{\psi_2 = 0} = \frac{q}{k} \left[\left(\frac{1 - \sigma}{\sigma} \right) \left(\frac{\alpha}{1 - \alpha} \right) - 1 - \frac{\xi f'(k)}{\frac{n + \delta}{1 - \alpha} - f'(k)} \right] \sigma,$$

where $\xi = -[f''(k)k/f'(k)]$. Again the assumptions that have been made so far are insufficient to determine the sign of the last expression.

Finally, let ψ_3 be the function,

$$\psi_3(k, q) = q(1 - \alpha) - U'[f(k)x]x. \tag{A.18}$$

The locus $\psi_3(k, q) = 0$ divides the (k, q) plane into two domains. Given any (k_0, q_0) such that $\psi_3(k_0, q_0) = 0$, we find that for any point (k_0, q), $q > q_0$, the allocation rule of Expression A.8 gives an interior solution, that is, $0 < s < 1$, while for any pair (k_0, q), $q \leq q_0$, Expression A.8 implies that $s = 0$. Differentiating Equation A.18 implicitly gives the expression

$$\frac{dq}{dk}\bigg|_{\psi_3 = 0} = -\frac{q}{k} \left[\pi - \left(\frac{1 - \sigma}{\sigma} \right) \left(\frac{\alpha}{1 - \alpha} \right) \right] \sigma,$$

the sign of which is indeterminate.

Since the shape of all the critical loci cannot be established without further assumptions, it is generally impossible to further characterize the optimal path (beyond uniqueness). For illustrative purposes, however, we shall consider now the special case where the utility function is logarithmic; that is,

$$U[cx] = \log(cx). \tag{A.19}$$

Equations A.15 through A.18 become, in this case

$$s(k, q) = 1 - \frac{1}{q(1 - \alpha)f(k)} \qquad \text{for all } q(1 - \alpha)f(k) > 1,$$

$$\psi_1(k, q) = (1 - \alpha)f(k) - nk - \frac{1}{q},$$

$$\psi_2(k, q) = \frac{\alpha}{1 - \alpha}\frac{1}{qk} + (1 - \alpha)f'(k) - (n + \delta), \tag{A.20}$$

$$\psi_3(k, q) = q(1 - \alpha) - \frac{1}{f(k)}.$$

The reader can easily verify that in this case the shape of the loci $\psi_i(k, q) = 0$, $i = 1, 2, 3$, is as illustrated in Figure 5.

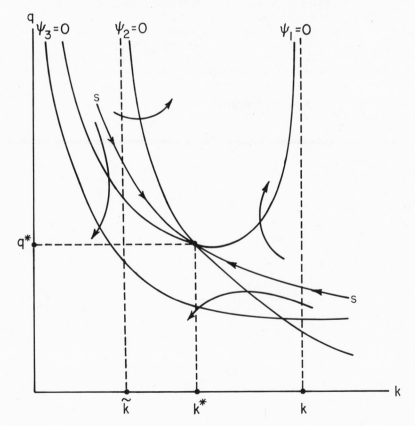

FIGURE 5. Phase diagram of the solutions (k, q) that satisfy Equations A.20.

We see that the stable branches of the saddle point (k^*, q^*) depict a unique optimal growth path. Any other path ultimately leads to a violation of the condition of Equation 40 or of a nonnegativity condition. In addition, for the particular case of Equation A.20 along the optimal path, q is strictly decreasing (increasing) with k if $k(0) < k^*[k(0) > k^*]$.

References

1. Arrow, K. J., "The Economic Implications of Learning by Doing," *Review of Economic Studies*, Vol. 29 (1962), pp. 155–174.
2. Cass, D., "Optimum Growth in an Aggregative Model of Capital Accumulation," *Review of Economic Studies*, Vol. 32 (1965), pp. 233–240.
3. Levhari, D., "Extensions of Arrow's Learning by Doing," *Review of Economic Studies*, Vol. 33 (1966), pp. 117–132.
4. Pontryagin, L. S., *et al.*, *The Mathematical Theory of Optimal Processes*, New York and London: Interscience Publishers, Inc., 1962.
5. Shell, K., "Optimal Programs of Capital Accumulation for an Economy in which there is Exogenous Technical Change," Essay I in this volume.
6. Sheshinski, E., "An 'Infant Industry' Growth Model," unpublished, Department of Economics, Massachusetts Institute of Technology, 1966.
7. Sheshinski, E., "Some Tests of the Learning by Doing Hypothesis," unpublished Ph.D. dissertation, Massachusetts Institute of Technology, 1966, Chapter 6.

III

The Optimal Rate
and Direction of Technical Change

WILLIAM D. NORDHAUS

Massachusetts Institute of Technology

Economists have long suspected that there is a bias in technical change.[1] Kennedy [4] allowed the entrepreneur to choose the desired bias by introducing the innovation possibility curve (IPC), which shows the trade-off between labor-augmenting and capital-augmenting technical change. The Kennedy model of induced innovation is the combination of the IPC with the neoclassical growth model.

Kennedy and others[2] have described the behavior of the model under the assumption that the economy is competitive and is composed of firms which maximize the instantaneous rate of cost reduction. The equilibrium of the model displays constant relative shares of the two factors, but the bias of technical change varies according to the savings assumption. When the savings rate is a constant and the elasticity of substitution is less than one, the long-run equilibrium has Harrod-neutral technical change.

A natural extension of the Kennedy model is to determine the optimal plan in an economy where the planning authorities choose the savings rate as well as the rate and direction of technical change. Sections 1 through 3 of this essay analyze the planned economy in which only the savings rate and

[1] This work was done during the tenure of a National Science Foundation Cooperative Fellowship. I should like to thank Karl Shell for his many comments.

[2] See the early verbal discussion of Hicks [3]. The IPC was first introduced in the published literature by Kennedy [4], with subsequent analysis by Samuelson [7] and Drandakis and Phelps [2].

the direction of technical change are controlled. Section 4 allows the planning authorities to control the rate of technical change. Finally, in section 5 it is argued that the descriptive model of the competitive economy labors under a theory of the firm that is so dubious as to vitiate the descriptive analysis.

1. The Kennedy Model of Induced Innovation

The economy that we are analyzing is identical to that of Samuelson [7]. There are two productive inputs, labor L and capital K, which are combined to produce a homogeneous output. Production is described by a constant returns to scale, neoclassical production function. Output can either be consumed or invested as capital. Thus, suppressing time subscripts where possible, we have

$$Y = F(K, L; t), \tag{1}$$

$$Y = I + C, \tag{2}$$

where Y, I, and C are instantaneous output, gross investment, and consumption. The function F is homogeneous of degree one in K and L, is twice differentiable, and has diminishing returns. The t parameter in F represents the shifts of the production function over time due to changes in technology. In particular, technical change is disembodied and takes the form of labor augmentation and capital augmentation. We can then rewrite Equation 1 with a time-invariant F as

$$Y = F(\lambda K, \mu L), \tag{3}$$

where λ and μ are the capital- and labor-augmentation factors, respectively.[3]

The augmentation factors are generated according to an innovation possibility curve (IPC) similar to that of Kennedy and Samuelson. Thus the rates of factor augmentation follow the rule:

$$\frac{\dot{\lambda}}{\lambda} = g\left(\frac{\dot{\mu}}{\mu}\right), \tag{4}$$

where $g' < 0$ and $g'' < 0$. A typical IPC is pictured by the solid line in Figure 1.[4]

---

[3] This characterization of technical change is general in the sense that in a competitive economy (where only one technique is used at a given point of time) one cannot use observed magnitudes to identify between factor-augmenting technological change and any other form of technical change. For planning purposes, however, we need to know more than just the local properties of technical change.

[4] It is assumed for convenience that the IPC extends into the second and fourth quadrants in Figure 1. This is not strictly necessary for the argument but it is necessary for the generality mentioned in footnote 3. In an early draft Drandakis and Phelps [2] argue that the IPC should remain in the first quadrant, because in any other case isoquants will cross giving the appearance of technical regress. Their argument overlooks

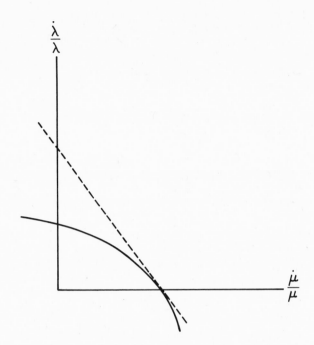

FIGURE 1. The innovation possibility curve.

Labor grows exponentially at rate n. Capital is accumulated according to the savings identity

$$\dot{K} = sY - \delta K, \tag{5}$$

where δ is the rate of depreciation of capital.

It will be helpful to put all variables in efficiency units. Thus, define new variables y, k, and x:

$$y = \frac{Y}{L}, \quad k = \frac{K}{L}, \quad x = \frac{\lambda K}{\mu L}.$$

Then rewrite Equations 3 and 5 as follows:

$$y = \mu f(x), \tag{6}$$

$$\dot{k} = s\mu f(x) - (\delta + n)k. \tag{7}$$

The planning authority of our stylized economy controls the aggregate savings rate s and the direction of technical change $\beta = \dot{\mu}/\mu$. It is assumed to maximize a utility function that is linear with respect to per capita consumption and that discriminates between generations by discounting future

---

the fact that for a strictly convex technology set the firm is concerned with only local changes in the production function. As long as the time path of λ and μ is efficient, the economy will never be in the region where isoquants are crossing.

consumption at the constant positive rate ρ. Thus, assuming the integral converges, the planning authority chooses the path that maximizes the integral:

$$J = \int_0^\infty \frac{C}{L} e^{-\rho t}\, dt = \int_0^\infty (1 - s)\mu f(x) e^{-\rho t}\, dt. \tag{8}$$

The problem of the planning authority can be solved by the "maximum principle" of Pontryagin and his associates.[5] By applying the maximum principle we can derive the necessary conditions for a maximum of our preference functional, Equation 8; these necessary conditions are described by Equations 9 through 21.

The state variables of the system are k, λ, and μ, whose motion is described by the following differential equations:

$$k = s\mu f\left(\frac{\lambda k}{\mu}\right) - (\delta + n)k, \tag{9}$$

$$\dot{\lambda} = g(\beta)\lambda, \tag{10}$$

$$\dot{\mu} = \beta\mu. \tag{11}$$

The control variables are s and β. We can form the Hamiltonian of the system:[6]

$$H = e^{-\rho t}\left\{(1 - s)\mu f\left(\frac{k\lambda}{\mu}\right) + p_1\left[s\mu f\left(\frac{k\lambda}{\mu}\right) - (\delta + n)k\right] + p_2 e^{ht}g(\beta)\lambda + p_3\beta\mu\right\}, \tag{12}$$

where the p_i are the conjugate (or Lagrange) variables of the system, and h is the rate of Harrod neutral technical change; that is, h is the solution to the equation $g(\beta) = 0$.

From Theorem 3 in [6] we know that if a program $[s(t), \beta(t)]$ is optimal, then there exist continuous functions $p_1(t)$, $p_2(t)$, and $p_3(t)$ that satisfy

$$\dot{p}_1 = (\rho + \delta + n)p_1 - f'(x)\gamma\lambda, \tag{13}$$

$$\dot{p}_2 = [\rho - h - g(\beta)]p_2 - f'(x)k\gamma e^{-ht}, \tag{14}$$

$$\dot{p}_3 = (\rho - \beta)p_3 - \gamma[f(x) - xf'(x)], \tag{15}$$

where $\gamma = (1 - s + sp_1)$.

The analogous conditions to the first-order conditions in the ordinary calculus are that $[s(t), \beta(t)]$ maximizes H at every point of time. This implies that

$$s(t) \text{ maximizes } (1 - s + p_1 s)$$

or

$$\gamma = \max (1, p_1). \tag{16}$$

---

[5] See Pontryagin *et al.* [6] and the discussion of the maximum principle by Shell [8].

[6] Note that the original conjugate variable of λ is now $p_2 e^{ht}$, which explains the appearance of e^{ht} in Equations 12 and 14, as well as the h in the first term of Equation 14.

In addition, $\beta(t)$ satisfies the equation

$$\frac{\partial H}{\partial \beta} = 0 = p_2 g'(\beta)\lambda e^{ht} + p_3 \mu. \tag{17}$$

The concavity of g and the requirement that prices be nonnegative imply that $\partial^2 H/\partial \beta^2 \leq 0$, which ensures that the solution to Equations 16 and 17 is maximum.

Finally, it is necessary that the system satisfy the initial conditions:

$$k(0) = k_0, \tag{18}$$

$$\lambda(0) = \lambda_0, \tag{19}$$

$$\mu(0) = \mu_0, \tag{20}$$

and that it meet the transversality conditions:

$$\lim_{t \to \infty} e^{-\rho t}p_1(t) = \lim_{t \to \infty} e^{(h-\rho)t}p_2(t) = \lim_{t \to \infty} e^{-\rho t}p_3(t) = 0. \tag{21}$$

The only parts of the system that need interpretation are Equations 13 through 15. The p_i represent shadow prices of the state variables. Equation 13 has the market interpretation that there must exist a price for capital such that all assets have a real rate of return equal to the social rate of return, ρ. Equations 14 and 15 have the usual dynamic programming interpretation of shadow prices, but (for reasons that will become apparent in section 5) they do not have market interpretations since technical change is not a marketable commodity.

2. The Optimal Direction of Technical Change

The first step of the analysis is to determine whether there is a long-run equilibrium of the system of necessary conditions of Equations 9 through 21. Assume that the shadow price of capital p_1 is constant. Using the definition that $x = \lambda k/\mu$, constancy of p_1 implies from Equation 13 that

$$\lambda f'(x) = \frac{p_1}{\gamma} (\rho + \delta + n). \tag{22}$$

Differentiating Equation 22 totally with respect to time we have

$$0 = f''(x)\lambda \dot{x} + f'(x)\dot{\lambda} = \frac{f''(x)\dot{x}}{f'(x)} + \frac{\dot{\lambda}}{\lambda}$$

$$= \frac{f''(x)xf(x)}{f'(x)[f(x) - xf'(x)]} \frac{[f(x) - xf'(x)]}{f(x)} \frac{\dot{x}}{x} + \frac{\dot{\lambda}}{\lambda}$$

$$= -\frac{1 - \alpha}{\sigma} \frac{\dot{x}}{x} + g(\beta)$$

or

$$\frac{\dot{x}}{x} = \frac{\sigma g(\beta)}{1 - \alpha}, \tag{23}$$

where σ = the elasticity of substitution = $-f'(x)[f(x) - xf'(x)]/[xf(x)f''(x)]$ and α = the share of capital = $f'(x)x/f(x)$. The constancy of the effective capital-labor ratio x implies from Equation 23 that

$$g(\beta^*) = 0, \tag{24}$$

$$\beta^* = h, \tag{25}$$

where asterisks represent long-run equilibrium values of the variables.

Similarly, using Equations 24 and 25, we can determine the stationary values of Equations 14 and 15:

$$p_2^* = \frac{\gamma f'(x)x\mu e^{-ht}}{\lambda(\rho - h)},$$

$$p_3^* = \frac{\gamma(1 - \alpha)f(x)}{\rho - h}.$$

Putting these into the maximum condition (Equation 17) we have

$$g'(\beta^*) = g'(h) = -\frac{1 - \alpha(x^*)}{\alpha(x^*)}, \tag{26}$$

which defines the equilibrium value of x^*. Thus the only equilibrium of the system is the equilibrium where technical change is purely labor augmenting. If σ is bounded away from unity, we know the equilibrium in Equation 26 exists and is unique, since α ranges from 0 to 1 and $[-(1 - \alpha)/\alpha]$ ranges from 0 to $-\infty$.

In this equilibrium it is easily seen that $p_1 = 1$, since if $p_1 > 1$, then $s = 1$, consumption is 0, and we have a minimum of Equation 8; while if $p_1 < 1$ then $\dot{x} = -(\delta + n + h)x < 0$, violating the stationarity of x.

From Equation 22, since $p_1 = \gamma = 1$, we know:

$$\lambda^* = \frac{\rho + \delta + n}{f'(x^*)}. \tag{27}$$

From Equation 9 we know that $\dot{x} = 0$ implies that

$$s = \frac{\delta + n + h}{\lambda f(x)} x$$

or, using Equation 27 and the definition of α,

$$s^* = \frac{\delta + n + h}{\lambda f'(x)} \frac{f'(x)x}{f(x)} = \frac{\delta + n + h}{\delta + n + \rho} \alpha^*. \tag{28}$$

Since $\rho > h$ is a necessary condition for convergence of the integral in Equation 8, we know that $0 < s^* < 1$. Finally, $\mu(t) = \mu^* e^{ht}$, where μ^* is determined by initial conditions.

Bringing all results together we have

$$g'(\beta^*) = -\frac{1 - \alpha^*}{\alpha^*},$$

$$\lambda^* f'(x^*) = \rho + \delta + n,$$

$$\beta^* = h, \tag{29}$$

$$s^* = \frac{\delta + n + h}{\delta + n + \rho} \alpha^*.$$

The equilibrium exists and is unique if $\sigma(x) \neq 1$.

We can call Equations 29 the *Harrod equilibrium*, which is the unique long-run equilibrium with a constant effective capital-labor ratio. Unlike most models of optimal accumulation, the equilibrium effective capital-labor ratio is independent of tastes, depending only on technology. When there is no technical change ($h = 0$), the savings rate is exactly that of the usual model (cf. [8]); and as a limit for $h = \rho = 0$ we get the golden rule savings rate of $s^* = \alpha^*$.

3. Optimality of the Harrod Equilibrium

It was shown in section 2 that for $\sigma \neq 1$ there is a unique stationary equilibrium satisfying the necessary conditions. We called this the Harrod equilibrium. If we stay forever in the Harrod equilibrium, then the necessary conditions of Equations 9 through 21 are satisfied irrespective of the value of σ.

We can prove the rather remarkable result that if $\sigma < 1$, then an economy that remains in the Harrod equilibrium maximizes the preference functional in Equation 8; while, if $\sigma > 1$, the Harrod equilibrium is certainly not the optimal path.[7]

Before proving the proposition, we introduce some additional notation. Let $z = (x, \lambda, \mu, \beta, s)$. When $z = z^* = (x^*, \lambda^*, \mu^*, \beta^*, s^*)$, the system is in

---

[7] This surprising result is due to the effect of capital deepening on capital's productivity. If $\sigma < 1$ then the elasticity of output with respect to effective capital (α) approaches zero as capital deepens. Under this condition it does not pay to continue to deepen capital past x^*. Rather, it is optimal to expand effective labor. On the other hand, if $\sigma > 1$, then α approaches unity as effective capital is deepened, and it is possible to have very large growth rates by further capital deepening. Thus in the case where $\sigma > 1$ it is suboptimal to limit the system's growth rate to the pedestrian $n + h$ associated with the Harrod equilibrium.

Harrod equilibrium as described by Equations 29. The condition $z_0 = z^*$ implies that the system starts in Harrod equilibrium.

The proof of the proposition requires a slight modification of the original system outlined in section 1. We modify by linearizing $g(\beta)$ at $\beta = h$, thereby replacing Equation 4 with

$$\frac{\dot{\lambda}}{\lambda} = Ah - \beta A, \tag{30}$$

where $g'(h) = -A$. The linearized function in Equation 30 is depicted by the broken line in Figure 1. All other equations remain unchanged. We call the new system, including Equation 30, the "modified system."

We can without loss of generality normalize by setting $\lambda^* = \mu^* = 1$. Define $B(t)$ by

$$B(t) = \int_0^t \beta(v) \, dv - ht. \tag{31}$$

We know from Equation 30 that

$$\mu = e^{ht}e^B,$$
$$\lambda = e^{-AB}. \tag{32}$$

Now consider an optimal path in the modified system with control variables $s(t)$ and $B(t)$. The Hamiltonian of the system is

$$H = e^{-\rho t}\{(1 - s)e^{ht+B}f(x) + q[se^{ht+B}f(x) - (\delta + n)k]\}, \tag{33}$$

where for simplicity we make use of the equality $x = ke^{-B(A+1)-ht}$. The necessary conditions for a maximum of the modified system are that there exists a continuous function $q(t)$ such that

$$\dot{q} = (\rho + \delta + n)q - e^{-AB}f'(x)\gamma, \tag{34}$$

$$\dot{k} = se^{ht+B}f(x) - (\delta + n)k, \tag{35}$$

$$\lim_{t \to \infty} e^{-\rho t}q(t) = 0. \tag{36}$$

Further, the control variables s and B must maximize H at every point of time. This implies that $\gamma = \max(1, q)$ as in the original system. To determine the maximum with respect to B, take the partial derivative of H:

$$\frac{\partial H}{\partial B} = \gamma e^{(h-\rho)t+B}f(x)(A + 1)\left[\frac{1}{1 + A} - \alpha(k, B)\right], \tag{37}$$

where $\alpha(k, B) = \alpha(x)$. If $\sigma < 1$, then H is maximized when $\alpha = 1/(1 + A)$. Similarly if $\sigma > 1$, then H is minimized for $\alpha = 1/(1 + A)$.

We can now show that for initial conditions $z(0) = z^*$, when $\sigma < 1$, the optimal path in the modified system is [$z(t) = z^*$ for all t]. If $z(t) = z^*$,

$q(t) = 1$, $B(t) = 0$, and $s(t) = s^*$, then $\alpha = 1/(1 + A)$ and all the necessary conditions of the modified problem are satisfied. Since both terms in Equation 33 are concave in the state variable k and control variables s and B—when the maximizing condition in Equation 37 and $\gamma = \max(1, q)$ are taken into account—the necessary conditions are sufficient. Therefore, if $\sigma < 1$, then $[z(t) = z^*]$ is the optimal path in the modified system.[8]

Given that z^* is optimal in the modified system, we can deduce, for $z_0 = z^*$ and for $\sigma < 1$, that $[z(t) = z^*$ for all $t]$ is optimal in the original system. Let $g(\beta)$ be the innovation possibility curve (IPC) in Equation 4 and $\tilde{g}(\beta)$ the linearized system in Equation 30. Assume that the closed sets to the southwest of g and $\tilde{g}$ are feasible regions. Denote U as the control region $[s(t), \beta(t)]$ for g, and $\tilde{U}$ the control region for $\tilde{g}$. The optimal path is seen to lie on the frontier in each region. Now for $z_0 = z^*$, the path $[z(t) = z^*]$ is the optimal path in $\tilde{U}$. Therefore $[z(t) = z^*]$ is the optimal path in any subset of $\tilde{U}$ that includes z^*. But since $z^* \in U \subset \tilde{U}$, then z^* is optimal in U.

Therefore, in the original system, if $\sigma < 1$ and if the system starts out in Harrod equilibrium, then the optimal path is to remain in Harrod equilibrium for all time.

If $\sigma > 1$, the result does not hold. Examining Equation 37, we see that since $\partial H/\partial B$ has the sign of $(\alpha - \alpha^*)$, the Harrod equilibrium is a minimum with respect to B in the modified system. Application of l'Hôpital's rule shows that $J \to \infty$ as $B \to -\infty$ and $\alpha \to 1$. We cannot, however, use this result to prove the inferiority of the Harrod equilibrium in the original system, since (using the notation of the previous paragraphs) the optimal path in $\tilde{U}$ will not be in U.

We can use a constructive approach to show the inferiority of the Harrod equilibrium in the original system. If $\sigma > 1$, pick the path that has Hicks-neutral technical change and a constant, positive savings rate. Then, as is shown in [1], the growth rate of output and consumption is unbounded. For long horizons the Hicks path will dominate the Harrod path, according to the criterion function of Equation 8.

The economic interpretation of the result for $\sigma > 1$ is that, as substitution of capital for labor occurs, the productivity of capital is so high that growth is unbounded. Robots are making robots at an ever increasing rate.

There are certain questions open at this point. We have shown only that for $\sigma < 1$ and for $z_0 = z^*$ the optimal path is to remain in Harrod equilibrium. We have not shown that in the general case (that is, for other initial conditions) the optimal path is to go to the Harrod equilibrium.

---

[8] This sufficiency condition is similar to the strengthened Legendre condition in the calculus of variations. This result can also be seen by showing that all other paths except $z(t) = z^*$ violate the transversality condition in Equation 36. It can be shown that for all initial conditions in the modified system the optimal path will go to z^* in finite time.

4. The Optimal Rate of Technical Change

We have considered an economy that controls only the direction of technical change. It is not clear what is generating this technical change, although some authors have suggested that a fixed quantum of research activity or exogenously supplied inventors determines the IPC. How an economy or a firm might change the direction of technical change is not specified. A more natural formulation of the problem from the point of view of actual policy is to allow the rate or intensity of technical change to be controlled explicitly by varying the amount of resources devoted to technical change.

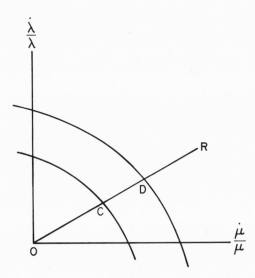

FIGURE 2. The IPC with variable rate of technical change.

In this section we follow Uzawa [9] in assuming that the central planners determine the intensity of technical change by allocating a percentage of the labor force to the research or educational sector.[9] A higher percentage of the labor force thus allocated pushes out the IPC in a homogeneous fashion, as in Figure 2. Thus all the IPC have the same shape but are blown up by a scale factor; in Figure 2, on an arbitrary ray from the origin, OC/OD is constant for any two IPC. Using Uzawa's notation, let researchers $= L_e = (1 - u)L$. We can rewrite Equation 4 as

---

[9] The assumption that technical change is a function of the relative size (either of the labor force or of production) devoted to research is not satisfactory. Empirical studies such as [5] indicate that the absolute amount of resources devoted to research is the appropriate variable. Unfortunately, the correct formulation does not allow a steady state equilibrium.

$$\dot{\mu} = \beta\phi(1 - u)\mu, \tag{38}$$

$$\dot{\lambda} = g(\beta)\phi(1 - u)\lambda, \tag{39}$$

where the function $\phi(1 - u)$ is the intensity of technical change that blows up the IPC in Figure 2. Normalize the system by setting $\beta = h$ when $g(\beta) = 0$. We assume that ϕ is sufficiently concave in u to ensure that the integral converges; thus $\phi(1) < \rho < \phi(0) + \phi'(0)$ with $\phi''(1 - u) < 0$.

To determine the optimal policy, we can use the same system as Equations 9 through 21 in section 1. We have control variables $s(t)$, $\beta(t)$, and $u(t)$. The Hamiltonian form is

$$H = e^{-\rho t}\left\{(1 - s)\mu u f\left(\frac{x}{u}\right) + p_1\left[s\mu u f\left(\frac{x}{u}\right) - (\delta + n)\frac{x\mu}{\lambda}\right]\right.$$
$$\left. + p_2 e^{ht}g(\beta)\phi\lambda + p_3\beta\phi\mu\right\}. \tag{40}$$

When ϕ is constant and equal to 1, it is seen that the problem is identical to that in Equation 12. Necessary conditions for a maximum include Equations 9 through 11 and 16 through 21, making the modifications that the right-hand sides of Equations 10, 11, and 17 are multiplied by $\phi(1 - u)$ and that x/u replaces x. In addition, the price equations become

$$\dot{p}_1 = (\rho + \delta + n)p_1 + f'\left(\frac{x}{u}\right)\lambda\gamma, \tag{41}$$

$$\dot{p}_2 = [\rho - h - g(\beta)\phi]p_2 - \frac{f'(x/u)x\gamma\mu e^{-ht}}{\lambda}, \tag{42}$$

$$\dot{p}_3 = (\rho - \beta\phi)p_3 - \gamma\left[uf\left(\frac{x}{u}\right) - xf'\left(\frac{x}{u}\right)\right], \tag{43}$$

and we need the condition that u maximizes H, which is

$$\frac{\partial H}{\partial u} = \gamma(1 - s)\mu\left[f - \frac{x}{u}f'\right] - p_2 e^{ht}g(\beta)\phi'\lambda - p_3\beta\phi'\mu = 0. \tag{44}$$

To find the stationary equilibrium, note that for $u = u^*$ the Equations 9 through 11 and 16 through 21, with Equations 41 through 43, have the same equilibrium as Equation 29, with the modifications that x^*/u^* replace x^* and $\beta^*\phi(1 - u)$ replaces β^*. The equilibrium condition for the amount of resources allocated to the research sector is, from Equation 44,

$$\rho - \phi(1 - u^*) = \rho - h = u^*\phi'(1 - u^*), \tag{45}$$

which is exactly Equation 36 in Uzawa.

We have thus shown that the only long-run equilibrium in the economy where the rate and direction of technical change are controlled is the Harrod equilibrium with the rate of technical change given by Equation 45.

To prove that this new Harrod equilibrium is a maximum for $\sigma < 1$, we use essentially the same technique as in section 3. Call the new equilibrium $z^{**} = (z^*, u^*)$. By linearizing Equations 38 and 39 exactly as in Equation 30, we see that in this modified system the z^{**} equilibrium satisfies all the necessary conditions. Since the terms of the Hamiltonian are concave when $\sigma < 1$, the necessary conditions are sufficient. Thus, if $z_0 = z^{**}$, then $[z(t) = z^{**}$ for all $t]$ is the optimal path for the modified system. By exactly the same reasoning as in section 3, for $z_0 = z^{**}$ in the original system, the Harrod equilibrium z^{**} is the optimal path.

Similarly, for $\sigma > 1$, the new Harrod equilibrium z^{**} will be dominated by other paths and is therefore not the optimum.

5. Competitive Markets and Induced Technical Change

The results of this analysis are applicable to economies in which planning authorities direct capital accumulation and the rate and direction of technical change. They have a more limited application to competitive capitalistic economies than do most models of optimal growth. In most models a government pursuing the correct monetary and fiscal policy can make a competitive economy parrot the optimal plan of a centrally planned economy. Whether such mimicry can occur in the Kennedy model depends on the microeconomic framework.

Since the possibility of parallelism between a market economy and a planned economy depends chiefly on the existence of a competitive equilibrium, the logical question to ask is whether a Kennedy economy is compatible with competition. The answer depends on where the technical change comes from and whether it is costless. Suppose, to follow most writers,[10] that the IPC is generated by a fixed amount of research expenditures. There are a number of possible techniques that it is possible to invent through research, and the bias of the change in techniques is dictated by the IPC. It is implicitly assumed that the level of research is independent of the size of the firm, for otherwise the size of the firm would enter the maximum problem. But since constant returns to K and L are assumed by all authors, cost per unit output, or $(wL + rK + R \& D)/Y$, will be a decreasing function of output of the firm. Competition will break down.[11] One could, it is true, dream up ways to preserve constant costs and competition, but this would only come at the

---

[10] Kennedy [4] gives no microeconomic interpretation. Samuelson ([7], p. 343) states, "Presumably a limited amount of resources available for research and development can be used to get a larger [increase in λ] only at the expense of a slower [increase in μ]." Drandakis and Phelps ([2], p. 11) explain that "firms can contrive to increase [λ] and [μ] or both by employing exogenously supplied inventors."

[11] The fact that competition breaks down should not come as a surprise at this point. The difficulty originates in the same place as our difficulties in showing sufficiency: the lack of convexity in the production set or increasing returns.

expense of realism, since technical change is endogenous and is produced by the firm.

In fact, about the only microeconomic framework that preserves competition is one in which a book of new blueprints falls from the sky every period—the new techniques given according to the IPC—and the entrepreneur chooses the best technique. In this case it would be quite misleading to say that technical change is induced. Rather, the IPC gives the technical possibilities at a point of time. The model is then just a disguised version of the neoclassical model with exogenous technical change.

The next step is to realize that if we cannot sustain competition, except in what is equivalent to the exogenous case, the behavior equations of the descriptive model are incorrect. A monopolist would minimize cost according to actual relative shares, not competitively determined relative shares that add up to greater than unity. He must then consider the elasticity of supply and demand. The theory becomes much more complicated, and the hope of getting some kind of steady state is dim.

There is one further reason to believe that in such a world a centrally planned economy would have certain advantages over a capitalistic economy. It is usually the case that a competitive economy economizes on the use of information. Sufficient information for a competitor to behave efficiently is the knowledge of current prices and of prices one period ahead. In the Kennedy model the firm needs to know all future prices over the infinite horizon to perform efficiently, since the firm cannot sell its investment in technology as it can its capital. Redundant information is worthless. The firm must make sure the infinite stream of quasi-rents on technical change covers costs. Each firm must assume a heavy computational burden.

None of these complications that burden a capitalistic economy with a Kennedy technology causes any additional burdens to the centrally planned economy.

References

1. Akerlof, G., and W. Nordhaus, "Balanced Growth: A Razor's Edge?" *International Economic Review*, forthcoming.
2. Drandakis, E. M., and E. S. Phelps, "A Model of Induced Invention, Growth and Distribution," Cowles Foundation Discussion Paper No. 186, Yale University, New Haven, Conn., July 1965.
3. Hicks, J. R., *The Theory of Wages*, London: Macmillan and Company, 1932.
4. Kennedy, C., "Induced Bias in Innovation and the Theory of Distribution," *Economic Journal*, Vol. 74 (September 1964).
5. Freeman, C., "Research and Development in the Electronics Capital Goods Industry," *National Institute Economic Review*, No. 34 (November 1965).
6. Pontryagin, L. S., *et al.*, *The Mathematical Theory of Optimal Processes*, New York and London: Interscience Publishers, Inc., 1962.

7. Samuelson, P. A., "A Theory of Induced Innovation along Kennedy–Weizsäcker Lines," *Review of Economics and Statistics*, Vol. 47, No. 4 (November 1965).
8. Shell, K., "Optimal Programs of Capital Accumulation for an Economy in which there is Exogenous Technical Change," Essay I in this volume.
9. Uzawa, H., "Optimal Technical Change in an Aggregative Model of Economic Growth," *International Economic Review*, Vol. 6, No. 1 (January 1965).

IV

A Model of Inventive Activity and Capital Accumulation[1]

KARL SHELL

Massachusetts Institute of Technology

1. Introduction

In the contemporary revival of the theory of economic growth, the implications of capital accumulation and population growth have been investigated by several authors, for example, [17,18]. However, technical change has been introduced into these models by means of a continuous secular shift in the aggregate production function—the rate and nature of which are exogenous to the policy variables of the model.

In two models, however, the rate of technical change is related to economic variables. The first is a model introduced by Kaldor in a series of papers [8, 9, 10]. Kaldor posits a positive relation (the technical progress function) between relative changes in per capita productivity and relative changes in gross investment. The technical progress function is an eclectic amalgam of basic technical and institutional forces in a free-enterprise economy. Kaldor takes the Schumpeterian view that the creation of new ideas largely occurs at an autonomous rate but that the implementation of these new techniques by entrepreneurs can be explained by economic phenomena. Obviously, if the implementation of a new technique requires new capital equipment, as opposed to mere organizational change, increased productivity can be

[1] Preparation of an earlier draft of this essay was supported in part by the National Science Foundation under Grant GS-420 to the University of Chicago. K. J. Arrow, D. Cass, L. Hurwicz, and H. Uzawa contributed valuable comments and criticism.

transmitted only through new gross investment. In addition, Kaldor argues that for a capitalist economy the higher the relative rate of gross investment the higher is the degree of "technical dynamism." Technical dynamism is a mass measure of entrepreneurial psychology including the readiness to adopt new methods of production.

In the second model with endogenous technical change [3], Arrow concentrates upon the relation between learning and experience. Economic learning results in higher productivity; and cumulative gross investment is the measure of such economic experience. Therefore, in refining the technical progress function, Arrow explicitly postulates that per capita productivity is determined by accumulated gross investment. In this model, then, the production of new technical knowledge (invention) and the transmission and application of that knowledge (innovation) are treated as by-products in the production and adoption of new capital goods.

While it is doubtlessly true that technical change is related to gross investment both as a by-product of capital-goods production and as a vehicle for embodying new techniques in new capital equipment, it is also true that the rate of production of technical knowledge can be increased by increasing the allocation of economic resources explicitly devoted to inventive activity. In fact, much attention has been focused recently upon the economic aspects of invention or the process of creation of new technical knowledge.[2]

At least two peculiar properties of technical knowledge require special study. First, technical knowledge can be used by many economic units without altering its character. Thus, for the economy in which technical knowledge is a commodity, the basic premises of classical welfare economics are violated, and the optimality of the competitive mechanism is not assured. Typically, technical knowledge is very durable and the cost of transmission is small in comparison to the cost of production. Second, at least on the microeconomic level, the inventive process is characterized by extreme riskiness.

2. The Model

It has been argued that for an organized economy increases in technical knowledge are fundamentally related to the amount of resources devoted to inventive activity. In order to study the role of invention in economic growth, the model economy is divided into two sectors: a productive sector and an inventive sector.[3]

The homogeneous output of the productive sector $Y_2(t)$ is dependent upon

---

[2] Cf. [12], especially Arrow's contribution on pp. 609–625.

[3] This model is a two-sector extension of the one-sector model treated in [16]. In [16] I restricted myself to the special case where the production possibility frontier is a plane surface in the nonnegative orthant of the consumption-investment-invention space.

the amount of capital $K_2(t)$ and labor $L_2(t)$ currently devoted to that sector and upon the current level of technical knowledge $A(t)$.[4] Thus

$$Y_2(t) = \Phi_2[K_2(t), L_2(t), A(t)]. \tag{1}$$

The output of the productive sector either can be consumed or can be added to the existing capital stock. If capital is subject to evaporative decay at the given technical rate $\mu > 0$, then

$$\dot{K}(t) = s(t)Y_2(t) - \mu K(t), \tag{2}$$

where $K(t)$ is the current level of the capital stock, and $0 \le s(t) \le 1$ is the fraction of the productive output saved (and invested) at time t.

Abstracting from problems posed by uncertainty in aggregative invention, a deterministic relationship between the output of the inventive (or research) sector $Y_1(t)$ and the resources currently devoted to that sector is posited:

$$Y_1(t) = \Phi_1[K_1(t), L_1(t), A(t)]. \tag{3}$$

Of course, if $A(t)$ is interpreted as the current level of the stock of "social capital," then $Y_1(t)$ is current output of social capital. The stock of technical knowledge is considered to be subject to some rate $\rho \ge 0$ of instantaneous decay,

$$A(t) = Y_1(t) - \rho A(t). \tag{4}$$

For the case of positive ρ, Equation 4 should be understood as a long-run approximation to processes not explicitly treated in this model. For example, decay in technical knowledge is observed because of imperfect transmission of technical information from one generation of the labor force to the next.

It is assumed that the production functions defined in Equations 1 and 3 exhibit neoclassical constant returns to scale in capital and labor. That is, given A,

$$\lambda Y_j = \Phi_j(\lambda K_j, \lambda L_j, A) \qquad \text{for } K_j, L_j \ge 0, \lambda > 0; \qquad j = 1, 2.$$

In particular, assume that the production relations are multiplicative and of the homogeneous form

$$Y_j = AF_j(K_j, L_j) = \Phi_j(K_j, L_j, A) \qquad \text{for } j = 1, 2, \tag{5}$$

so that $F_j(\cdot)$ is positively linear-homogeneous in K_j and L_j.[5] Define $L(t)$ to

---

[4] Increases in efficiency are shared by all vintages of capital and labor; the embodiment problem is ignored.

[5] Thus, if $F_j(\cdot)$ is concave and increasing, $\Phi_j(\cdot)$ is an increasing semistrictly, quasi-concave function that is positively homogeneous of second degree. The specification of the production function given in Equation 5 is not crucial for the treatment of long-run behavior developed in section 5. However, specification of Equation 5 does

be the labor force inelastically offered for employment at time t. For an allocation of resources to be feasible at time t, it is required that

$$K_1(t) + K_2(t) \leq K(t)$$

where $K_1(t), K_2(t), L_1(t), L_2(t) \geq 0$.   (6)

$$L_1(t) + L_2(t) \leq L(t)$$

3. A Decentralized Economy

It is assumed that the productive sector is composed of many individual firms. The level of technical knowledge enters the firms' production functions as a pure public good of production. Hence, the competitive price of the output of the research sector is zero. This suggests the desirability of intervention in the market process.

Historically, intervention in behalf of inventive activity has taken two basic forms: first, the establishment of a legal device, the patent, designed to bestow property rights on certain of the outputs of the inventive process. The second form of intervention is that of direct nonmarket support of research and development. Universities have long played such a role in Western economies. In the United States, the Department of Agriculture has undertaken research activities since its inception. The Department of Commerce has initiated industrial research programs modeled after the agricultural research stations. The Department of Defense often uses the device of contracting research to private enterprises on a cost-plus-fixed-fee basis.

In the model decentralized economy, the rewards to capital and labor are paid in units of the output of the productive sector. The only form of intervention in the market process is an excise tax rate, $0 \leq \alpha < 1$, imposed upon the output of the productive sector. The revenue from the tax αY_2 is used for payment to the factors employed in the inventive sector. The research manager is assumed to maximize output of the inventive sector subject to this budget constraint.

Profits (after taxes) for the productive sector are

$$(1 - \alpha)Y_2 - wL_2 - rK_2,$$

where w is the wage rate of labor, and r is the rental rate of capital. If the individual production functions are identical and linear-homogeneous in capital and labor, then the result of the profit-maximization hypothesis is that

---

allow a simple aggregation in the productive sector that is congenial to the competitive hypothesis:

$$Y_2 \equiv \sum_i Y_2{}^i = A \sum_i F_2(K_2{}^i, L_2{}^i),$$

where, for example, $K_2{}^i$ is the quantity of capital employed by the ith firm.

$$\frac{\partial Y_2}{\partial K_2} \leq \frac{r}{1 - \alpha}$$

with equality if $F_2(K_2, L_2) > 0$. (7)

$$\frac{\partial Y_2}{\partial L_2} \leq \frac{w}{1 - \alpha}$$

To maximize output in the inventive sector, consider the Lagrangian form:

$$Y_1 + \theta(\alpha Y_2 - wL_1 - rK_1),$$

when $\theta \geq 0$ is a Lagrange multiplier. The conditions for maximization are

$$\frac{\partial Y_1}{\partial K_1} \leq \theta r$$

with equality if $F_1(K_1, L_1) > 0$. (8)

$$\frac{\partial Y_1}{\partial L_1} \leq \theta w$$

Notice that if ω is defined to be the wage-rentals ratio (w/r), then if $F_j(K_j, L_j) > 0$,

$$\omega = \left(\frac{\partial F_j/\partial L_j}{\partial F_j/\partial K_j}\right) \quad \text{for } j = 1, 2.$$

Define the usual per capita quantities:

$$k = \frac{K}{L}$$

and

$$k_j = \frac{K_j}{L_j}, \quad y_j = \frac{Y_j}{L}, \quad l_j = \frac{L_j}{L} \quad \text{for } j = 1, 2.$$

The conditions for static equilibrium reduce to

$$wl_2 + rk_2l_2 = (1 - \alpha)y_2, \tag{9}$$

$$wl_1 + rk_1l_1 = \alpha y_2, \tag{10}$$

$$y_j = Af_j(k_j)l_j \quad \text{for } j = 1, 2, \text{ where } f_j(k_j) = F_j(k_j, 1), \tag{11}$$

$$l_1 + l_2 = 1, \tag{12}$$

$$k_1l_1 + k_2l_2 = k, \tag{13}$$

$$\omega = \frac{f_j(k_j)}{f_j'(k_j)} - k_j \quad \text{for } j = 1, 2. \tag{14}$$

Also assume that for each j, the function $f_j(k_j)$ is twice continuously differentiable for all k_j, and

$$f_j(k_j) > 0, \quad f_j'(k_j) > 0, \quad f_j''(k_j) < 0 \quad \text{for } 0 < k_j < \infty;$$

$$f_j(0) = 0, \quad f_j(\infty) = \infty, \tag{15}$$

$$f_j'(0) = \infty, \quad f_j'(\infty) = 0.$$

Then, the implicit relations $k_j(\omega)$ are well defined because

$$\frac{dk_j}{d\omega} = \frac{-[f_j'(k_j)]^2}{f_j(k_j)f_j''(k_j)} > 0, \qquad j = 1, 2. \tag{16}$$

Adding Equation 9 to Equation 10 and substituting in Equation 11,

$$Al_2 f_2(k_2) = w + rk.$$

But solving Equations 12 and 13 for l_2 yields

$$w + rk = \left(\frac{k - k_1}{k_2 - k_1}\right) Af_2(k_2).$$

However, from Equations 9 and 11,

$$f_2(k_2) = \frac{w + rk_2}{(1 - \alpha)A}.$$

Thus

$$w + rk = \left(\frac{w + rk_2}{1 - \alpha}\right)\left(\frac{k - k_1}{k_2 - k_1}\right).$$

Dividing by r yields

$$\omega + k = \left(\frac{\omega + k_2}{1 - \alpha}\right)\left(\frac{k - k_1}{k_2 - k_1}\right).$$

Let $Z = k + \omega$ and $Z_j = k_j + \omega$ for $j = 1, 2$.

$$Z(\omega) = \frac{Z_2 Z_1}{\alpha Z_2 + (1 - \alpha)Z_1} \qquad \text{where } 0 \leq \alpha < 1. \tag{17}$$

The right-hand side of Equation 17 takes all positive values and has a derivative everywhere greater than unity. Here $Z'(\omega)$ is identically unity, and hence, for given positive k, Equation 17 is uniquely solvable for ω, and *the greater the value of k, the greater the equilibrium value of ω.*[6]

Manipulation of Equation 17 yields theorems in comparative statics. For example, if the productive sector is always more (less) capital intensive than the inventive sector, (1) the higher the wage-rentals ratio, the higher (lower) is the equilibrium level of output of the inventive sector; (2) the higher the excise tax rate α, the higher (lower) is the wage-rentals ratio ω.

4. Static Efficiency and Optimal Taxation

Suppose that at a given moment in time the central planning board desires to maximize the expression

$$Y_2 + \lambda Y_1 \tag{18}$$

---

[6] My Equation 17 is formally equivalent to Equation 23 in [19]. Thus determination of static equilibrium in the model just outlined is equivalent to determination of static equilibrium in [19] with my excise tax rate playing the same role as Uzawa's average propensity to save.

subject to the resource constraint of Inequalities 6. Here λ is the social demand price of inventive output in terms of productive output.[7] By Conditions 15, maximization of Expression 18 requires full employment of resources; that is, Inequalities 6 must hold with equality. The maximum is achieved when $K_1 = K$, $L_1 = L$, *or* when $K_2 = K$, $L_2 = L$, *or* by solving the system

$$\frac{\partial Y_2}{\partial K_2} = \lambda \frac{\partial Y_1}{\partial K_1}, \quad K_1 + K_2 = K,$$

$$\frac{\partial Y_2}{\partial L_2} = \lambda \frac{\partial Y_1}{\partial L_1}, \quad L_1 + L_2 = L. \tag{19}$$

Oniki and Uzawa [13] show that if the production functions satisfy Conditions 15, then there exist positive finite prices $\underline{\lambda}$ and $\bar{\lambda}$, with $0 < \underline{\lambda} \leq \bar{\lambda} < \infty$, such that for $\lambda \leq \underline{\lambda}$, maximization of Expression 18 requires specialization to production, and for $\lambda \geq \bar{\lambda}$, maximization of Expression 18 requires specialization to invention. For $\underline{\lambda} \leq \lambda \leq \bar{\lambda}$, first-order conditions of Equations 19 apply. By varying λ we obtain optimal outputs

$$Y_1 = Y_1(\lambda) \quad \text{and} \quad Y_2 = Y_2(\lambda),$$

---

[7] Suppose, for example, that the criterion of the planning board is to maximize the integral of discounted per capita consumption over some planning period $T > 0$,

$$\int_0^T (1 - s)AF_2(K_2, L_2)e^{-(n+\delta)t}\, dt,$$

where δ is the (constant) social discount rate, subject to initial conditions and terminal requirements. It is necessary for intertemporal optimality that the imputed value of gross national product

$$[(1 - s) + qs]Y_2 + vY_1$$

be maximized at every point in time. Here q is the social demand price of investment and v is the social demand price of invention. Thus for Expression 18,

$$\lambda = \frac{v}{(1 - s) + qs}.$$

Determination of the optimal trajectories for $q(t)$, $v(t)$, $s(t)$, and thus $\lambda(t)$, follows from the techniques of [14], and a treatment of the case where $k_1(\omega) = k_2(\omega)$ for all positive ω appears in [16]. In [16] the maximand was assumed to be a strictly concave function of per capita consumption and the production function was assumed to be strictly concave in its arguments. Under such conditions a long-run turnpike is found where A, k, q, and v are stationary and the net (of depreciation) socially valued marginal product of capital is equal to the net socially valued marginal product of technical knowledge. In the partially controlled economy, if long-run capital formation is lower (higher) than called for in the fully controlled economy, then long-run inventive activity should be higher (lower) in the partially controlled economy. It should be remarked that quasi-concavity of the $\Phi_j(\cdot)$ is not enough to ensure that Pontryagin's necessary conditions are sufficient. In fact, for $\Phi_j(\cdot)$ quasi-concave but not concave, I have found clearly nonoptimal programs satisfying the necessary conditions.

as nondecreasing and nonincreasing (respectively) upper-semicontinuous correspondences in λ.[8]

This is shown by simple construction. Choose social demand price λ^1 such that

$$Y_2{}^1 \in Y_2(\lambda^1) \quad \text{and} \quad Y_1{}^1 \in Y_1(\lambda^1).$$

Also choose social demand price λ^2 such that

$$Y_2{}^2 \in Y_2(\lambda^2) \quad \text{and} \quad Y_1{}^2 \in Y_1(\lambda^2).$$

Since Expression 18 is to be maximized,

$$Y_2{}^1 + \lambda^1 Y_1{}^1 \geq Y_2{}^2 + \lambda^1 Y_1{}^2, \tag{20}$$

and

$$Y_2{}^1 + \lambda^2 Y_1{}^1 \leq Y_2{}^2 + \lambda^2 Y_1{}^2. \tag{21}$$

Subtracting Inequality 21 from 20 yields

$$(\lambda^1 - \lambda^2)(Y_1{}^1 - Y_1{}^2) \geq 0,$$

which can be written as

$$\frac{\Delta Y_1}{\Delta \lambda} \geq 0, \quad \text{and similarly} \frac{\Delta Y_2}{\Delta \lambda} \leq 0, \tag{22}$$

where Δ is the finite difference operator.

Notice that for $0 < \alpha < 1$, the system of Equations 7 and 8 reduces to the system of Equations 19 when

$$\lambda = \frac{1}{\theta(1 - \alpha)}, \tag{23}$$

that is, if the social demand price of inventive output is equal to the implicit (supply) valuation of inventive output. If Equation 23 holds, factor payments in the inventive sector are

$$\lambda(1 - \alpha)L_1 \frac{\partial Y_1}{\partial L_1} + \lambda(1 - \alpha)K_1 \frac{\partial Y_1}{\partial K_1}.$$

When the inventive sector equates factor payments to revenues

$$\frac{\alpha}{1 - \alpha} = \frac{\lambda L_1(\partial Y_1/\partial L_1) + \lambda K_1(\partial Y_1/\partial K_1)}{Y_2}.$$

But by Euler's theorem

$$\frac{\alpha}{1 - \alpha} = \frac{\lambda Y_1(\lambda)}{Y_2(\lambda)}. \tag{24}$$

For $0 < \alpha < 1$, the left-hand side of Equation 24 is a strictly increasing function of α with range $(0, \infty)$. For $\underline{\lambda} < \lambda < \bar{\lambda}$, the right-hand side of

---

[8] Cf. p. 17 in [5].

Equation 24 is a nondecreasing correspondence of λ with range $(0, \infty)$. Given $\alpha \in (0, 1)$, Equation 24 is solvable for $\lambda \in (\underline{\lambda}, \bar{\lambda})$.

Thus *for any tax rate* $0 < \alpha < 1$, *the decentralized economy is efficient.* The trivial case $\alpha = 0$ corresponds to maximization of Expression 18 for the case $\lambda \leq \underline{\lambda}$. For $\alpha = 1$, allocation of resources between the two sectors is not uniquely determined.

Next define the implicit (supply) price of invention by

$$p(\alpha) = \frac{f_2'\{k_2[\omega(\alpha)]\}}{f_1'\{k_1[\omega(\alpha)]\}} = \frac{1}{\theta(1 - \alpha)} \qquad \text{for } 0 < \alpha < 1. \tag{25}$$

But notice by Equation 17,

$$\lim_{\alpha \to 0} k_2[\omega(\alpha)] = k, \quad \lim_{\alpha \to 1} k_1[\omega(\alpha)] = k,$$

and thus

$$\lim_{\alpha \to 0} p(\alpha) = \bar{\lambda}, \quad \lim_{\alpha \to 1} p(\alpha) = \underline{\lambda}.$$

Logarithmic differentiation of Equation 25 yields

$$\frac{1}{p}\frac{dp}{d\omega} = \frac{1}{k_1 + \omega} - \frac{1}{k_2 + \omega} \gtreqless 0 \qquad \text{as } k_2 \gtreqless k_1,$$

and differentiation of Equation 17 yields

$$\frac{\partial \omega}{\partial \alpha} = \frac{(1/Z_1) - (1/Z_2)}{(\alpha Z_1'/Z_1^2) + [(1 - \alpha)Z_2'/Z_2^2] - (1/Z^2)} \gtreqless 0 \qquad \text{as } k_2 \gtreqless k_1.$$

Thus

$$\frac{\partial p}{\partial \alpha} > 0 \qquad \text{for } 0 < \alpha < 1.$$

Hence, *given the social demand price for inventive output in terms of productive output,* $\underline{\lambda} < \lambda < \bar{\lambda}$, *the optimum excise tax rate* $0 < \alpha < 1$ *can be determined by solving Equation 24.* For $\lambda \leq \underline{\lambda}$, optimality requires that in the decentralized economy the excise tax rate be set equal to zero. For $\lambda \geq \bar{\lambda}$, optimality requires the economy to be centralized with all factors of production to be allocated to the research manager.

5. Long-Run Behavior of the Economy with Constant Rates of Savings and Taxation

Consider the stylized Western economy in which static equilibrium is determined by Equations 9 through 14. Assume that the excise tax rate α and the savings fraction s are institutionally given and fixed through time with $0 < \alpha < 1$ and $0 < s < 1$. Capital accumulation is determined by Equation 2 and the change over time of the stock of technical knowledge proceeds in accordance with Equation 4. In order to simplify the analysis, assume that the working population is stationary so that we can set $L = 1$ without loss in generality. Initial endowments of resources $A(0)$, $K(0)$, and $L(0) = 1$ are given.

Rewriting Equation 2 in per capita terms yields

$$\dot{k} = sAl_2 f_2(k_2) - \mu k. \tag{26}$$

The capital stock is stationary ($\dot{k} = 0$) if and only if

$$A = \frac{\mu k}{sl_2 f_2(k_2)}. \tag{27}$$

Equation 27 defines a curve in the positive quadrant of the $k - A$ plane.[9]

Rewriting Equation 4 yields

$$\dot{A} = A[l_1 f_1(k_1) - \rho]. \tag{28}$$

With $A > 0$, the stock of technical knowledge is stationary only if the stock of physical capital is such that

$$l_1 f_1(k_1) = \rho \tag{29}$$

is satisfied. By Equations 15 the left-hand side of Equation 29 tends to zero as k tends to zero. Assume, for example, that the left-hand side of Equation 29 is an analytic function of k and tends to infinity as k tends to infinity. Then there exists $0 < \bar{k} < \infty$ such that

$$l_1 f_1(k_1) > \rho \qquad \text{for } k > \bar{k}.$$

By a classic theorem of analytic function theory,[10] solutions to Equation 29 cannot be dense. Therefore by the Bolzano-Weierstrass theorem, the number of distinct solutions to Equation 29 is finite and odd.

The phase diagram (Figure 1) depicts the long-run behavior of the system of differential Equations 26 and 28 for the case when there are exactly three solutions k^*, k^{**}, k^{***} to Equation 29. Let

$$0 < k^* < k^{**} < k^{***} < \infty.$$

There are then exactly three equilibrium points. The points (k^*, A^*) and

---

[9] In fact, if the elasticity of substitution between capital and labor is never less than unity in the inventive sector *or* if invention is always more capital intensive than production, then

$$\frac{dA}{dk}\bigg|_{\dot{k}=0} = \frac{A\mu}{s}\left[\frac{y_2 - k(dy_2/dk)}{y_2^2}\right] > 0.$$

The proof of this proposition is in the appendix to this essay.

[10] Here $l_1 f_1$ is assumed to be an analytic function of k and the constant ρ is a trivial analytic function of k. Hence, if $l_1 f_1$ equals ρ on a set that has an accumulation point in $k \geq 0$, then $l_1 f_1$ must be identical to ρ for $k \geq 0$. Cf. p. 102 in [1].

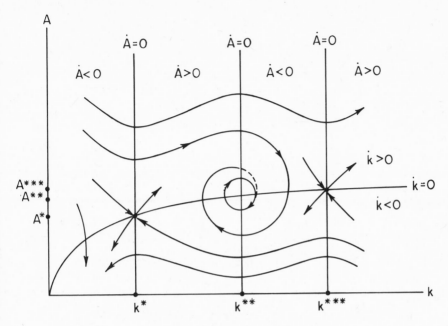

FIGURE 1. Multiple equilibriums.

(k^{***}, A^{***}) are saddle points.[11] Locally, the point (k^{**}, A^{**}) is either stable or (by the Poincaré-Bendixon theorem) there exists a limit cycle forming a periodic orbit about (k^{**}, A^{**}). The limit cycle case is illustrated in Figure 1.

The case where

$$\frac{dy_1}{dk} > 0 \qquad \text{for } k > 0 \tag{30}$$

is of special interest.[12] If Inequality 30 holds, the solution to Equation 29 is unique, and therefore there is a unique equilibrium for the system of differential Equations 26 and 28. This case is illustrated in the phase diagram of Figure 2. The unique equilibrium (k^*, A^*) is a saddle point. Thus the $k–A$ plane is divided by a "razor's edge." For initial endowments of physical capital and technical knowledge below this line, the economy "decays." For initial endowments above this line, the economy "explodes." In the general case, there exists the possibility that the economy tends to a technological trap or periodic orbit,[13] for example, the point (k^{**}, A^{**}) in Figure 1.

---

[11] Remembering that $f_j(\cdot)$ is twice continuously differentiable.

[12] A sufficient condition for Inequality 30 to hold is (1) invention is always more capital intensive than production, or (2) the elasticity of substitution in production is never less than unity. Again, the proof of this proposition appears in the appendix to this essay.

[13] In the recent literature of economic growth theory it is usual to examine a model for global stability. It has been found for certain models that their ultimate long-run behavior

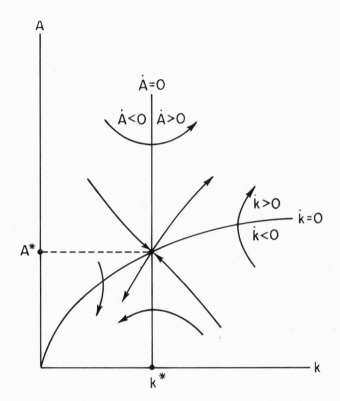

FIGURE 2. Unique equilibriums.

6. Concluding Comments

The model just discussed focuses upon the role of invention in economic growth. In order to simplify the analysis, certain important phenomena are ignored. Among other things, the effects of a growing labor force and the process of transmission of knowledge within the economy are ignored. Nonetheless, the model is sufficiently rich at least to suggest explanations for some economic problems.

The post-World War II experience of Germany and Japan provides an instructive example from recent economic history. It could be argued that although large amounts of their physical capital were destroyed during the

is independent of initial endowments. See, e.g., [17] and [19]. While such stability (if it exists) is certainly an interesting property of any model, it should not be considered an essential property for a growth model. In fact, Maruyama [11] argues just the opposite: that social systems are basically morphogenetic rather than morphostatic. The notion and the usefulness of the concept of stability in the engineering sciences is treated in [4].

war, their stocks of technical knowledge remained large enough with respect to the remaining stocks of physical capital to ensure the sustenance of explosive growth.[14] Thus the war-torn economies staged "miraculous" recoveries while certain nonbelligerent but impoverished economies remained impoverished.

This example raises an important question: Why do not technically backward economies freely adopt the techniques developed in the advanced economies? A certain amount of such "copying" does occur, but, contrary to the model presented here, in real life endowments of productive factors are not homogeneous, and knowledge that is useful to one country may not be useful for production in another country. Even then, transmission of technical information (education, innovation, and so on) is certainly not a costless activity. The role of transmission of technical information in the process of economic development is a topic that is worthy of further investigation.

APPENDIX: COMPARATIVE STATICS FOR THE TWO-SECTOR MODEL

In this appendix, certain simple propositions in comparative statics are developed for the two-sector model. I was led to the study of these propositions because of their relevance to the direction and stability of long-run growth in the model of inventive activity and capital accumulation. These propositions are of some independent interest and therefore a separate treatment is warranted.[15]

Consider the miniature two-sector Walrasian equilibrium system given by Equations 9 through 14. Using the supply price p defined in Equation 25, gross national income per capita y is given by

$$y = y_2 + py_1. \tag{A.1}$$

Demand for output can be rewritten as

$$py_1 = \alpha y. \tag{A.2}$$

---

[14] My colleague P. N. Rosenstein-Rodan stresses also the importance in the recovery process of the remaining stocks of *physical* social capital. He has told me that because of exceptional circumstances the Neapolitan sewers were devastated by Allied bombing. This, he argues, was sufficient to cause Naples to require enormous outside aid in order to "get back on its feet."

[15] The pioneer work in two-sector comparative statics seems to be that of Rybczynski [15] whose analysis is in terms of the Samuelson-Stolper box diagram. I am indebted to J. Wise for the reference to Rybczynski's note.

Setting $A = 1$ for convenience, and combining Equations A.1 and A.2 with Equation 11 yields the basic equation

$$\left(\frac{1-\alpha}{\alpha}\right)\frac{f_2'(k_2)}{f_1'(k_1)} = \left(\frac{k-k_1}{k_2-k}\right)\frac{f_2(k_2)}{f_1(k_1)}. \tag{A.3}$$

Logarithmically differentiating both sides of Equation A.3 with respect to k, yields the total derivative

$$\frac{d\omega}{dk} = \frac{\dfrac{k_2-k_1}{(k-k_1)(k_2-k)}}{\dfrac{dk_2}{d\omega}\left(\dfrac{f_2''}{f_2'} - \dfrac{f_2'}{f_2} + \dfrac{1}{k_2-k}\right) + \dfrac{dk_1}{d\omega}\left(\dfrac{f_1'}{f_1} - \dfrac{f_1''}{f_1'} + \dfrac{1}{k-k_1}\right)}. \tag{A.4}$$

Because of Equations 14 and 16, Equation A.4 can be rewritten as

$$\frac{d\omega}{dk} =$$

$$\frac{\dfrac{k_2-k_1}{(k-k_1)(k_2-k)}}{\dfrac{dk_2}{d\omega}\left[\dfrac{k+\omega}{(k_2-k)(k_2+\omega)}\right] + \dfrac{dk_1}{d\omega}\left[\dfrac{k+\omega}{(k-k_1)(k_1+\omega)}\right] + \left[\dfrac{k_2-k_1}{(k_2+\omega)(k_1+\omega)}\right]}. \tag{A.5}$$

For $k_2 \neq k \neq k_1$, the numerator and the denominator of the right-hand side of Equation A.5 are seen to agree in sign, and therefore $(d\omega/dk) > 0$ for $0 < k < \infty$. This is the proposition (Uzawa) that if the demand for output is such that the marginal propensity to consume equals the average propensity to consume, then *the higher the endowment of a factor of production, the lower is the equilibrium level of the relative reward to that factor.* Also given $0 < k < \infty$, the equilibrium value of ω is uniquely determined.

Next, observe the *direct* effect of differing factor endowments upon the equilibrium composition of output. From Equation 11,

$$\frac{\partial y_1}{\partial k} = \frac{-f_1(k_1)}{k_2-k_1},$$

$$\frac{\partial y_2}{\partial k} = \frac{f_2(k_2)}{k_2-k_1}. \tag{A.6}$$

The partial derivatives in Equations A.6 are independent of demand, and thus we have the proposition (Rybczynski): *If the rates of substitution in production are fixed, that is, $(d\omega/dk) = 0$, then the higher the endowment of a factor of production, the higher (lower) is the equilibrium level of production of the commodity using relatively much (little) of that factor.*

Logarithmic differentiation of Equation 11 yields

$$\frac{1}{y_1}\frac{dy_1}{d\omega} = \frac{dk_2}{d\omega}\left[\frac{k - k_1}{(k_2 - k)(k_2 - k_1)}\right] + \frac{dk_1}{d\omega}\left[\frac{k_2 + \omega}{(k_1 + \omega)(k_2 - k_1)}\right] \gtrless 0 \quad (A.7)$$

as $k_2 \gtrless k \gtrless k_1$. Similarly $(1/y_2)(dy_2/d\omega) \lessgtr 0$ as $k_2 \gtrless k \gtrless k_1$.

Since $(d\omega/dk) > 0$, we have for the system of Equations 9 through 14 that *the direct effect (Equation A.6) of varying factor endowment upon equilibrium levels of output is opposite in sign to the indirect effect (Equation A.7).*

The *total effect* is the sum of the direct effect and the indirect effect:

$$\frac{dy_1}{dk} = \frac{\partial y_1}{\partial k} + \frac{dy_1}{d\omega}\frac{d\omega}{dk},$$
$$\frac{dy_2}{dk} = \frac{\partial y_2}{\partial k} + \frac{dy_2}{d\omega}\frac{d\omega}{dk}. \quad (A.8)$$

Because of Equations A.6 and A.7, the first of Equations A.8 can be rewritten as

$$\frac{dy_1}{dk} = \frac{\partial y_1}{\partial k}\left(1 - \frac{N}{D}\right), \quad (A.9)$$

where N is defined by

$$N = \frac{dk_2}{d\omega}\left(\frac{k - k_1}{k_2 - k_1}\right) + \frac{dk_1}{d\omega}\left(\frac{k_2 - k}{k_2 - k_1}\right)\left(\frac{k_2 + \omega}{k_1 + \omega}\right) > 0, \quad (A.10)$$

and D is defined by

$$D = \frac{dk_2}{d\omega}\left(\frac{k - k_1}{k_2 - k_1}\right) + \frac{dk_1}{d\omega}\left(\frac{k_2 - k}{k_2 - k_1}\right)\left(\frac{k + \omega}{k_1 + \omega}\right)$$
$$+ \frac{(k - k_1)(k_2 - k)}{k_2 - k_1}\left[\left(\frac{f_2''}{f_2'} - \frac{f_2'}{f_2}\right)\frac{dk_2}{d\omega} - \frac{f_1''}{f_1'}\frac{dk_1}{d\omega}\right]. \quad (A.11)$$

Applying Equations 14 and 16 to Equation A.11 gives

$$D = \frac{dk_2}{d\omega}\left(\frac{k - k_1}{k_2 - k_1}\right) + \frac{dk_1}{d\omega}\left(\frac{k_2 - k}{k_2 - k_1}\right)\left(\frac{k + \omega}{k_1 + \omega}\right)$$
$$+ \frac{(k - k_1)(k_2 - k)}{k_2 - k_1}\left[\frac{1}{k_1 + \omega} - \frac{1 + (dk_2/d\omega)}{k_2 + \omega}\right] > 0. \quad (A.12)$$

Consider the case where $k_1 > k > k_2$. From Equations A.6 we have $(\partial y_1/\partial k) > 0$ and therefore $(dy_1/dk) > 0$ if and only if $D > N$. Examine the right-hand sides of Equations A.10 and A.12. The first terms are identical; for $k > k_2$ the second term in Equation A.12 is greater than the second term in Equation A.10. For $k_1 > k_2$, the third term in Equation A.12 is positive. Hence, when $k_1 > k > k_2$, then $D > N > 0$ or $0 < (N/D) < 1$.

For the two-sector economy (Equations 9 through 14), *the higher the endowment of a factor of production, the higher is the equilibrium level of output of the commodity using relatively much of that factor.*

Consider the reverse factor-intensity case, $k_2 > k > k_1$. Here (dy_1/dk) is positive if and only if $(D - N) < 0$, or subtracting Equation A.10 from Equation A.11,

$$(k - k_1)\frac{dk_2}{d\omega}\left(\frac{f_2''}{f_2'} - \frac{f_2'}{f_2}\right) - \frac{dk_1}{d\omega}\left[\frac{(k_2 - k)f_1'}{f_1} + \frac{(k - k_1)f_1''}{f_1'}\right] < 0. \quad \text{(A.13)}$$

Multiplying both sides of Inequality A.13 by $(\omega/k_1 k_2)$ and substituting from Equations 14 and 16 yields

$$\frac{(k - k_1)\sigma_2}{k_1(k_2 + \omega)} + \left(\frac{\omega}{k_1 k_2}\right)\left(\frac{k - k_1}{k_2 + \omega}\right) + \frac{(k_2 - k)\sigma_1}{k_2(k_1 + \omega)} > \left(\frac{\omega}{k_1 k_2}\right)\left(\frac{k - k_1}{k_1 + \omega}\right), \quad \text{(A.14)}$$

where σ_j $(j = 1, 2)$ is the elasticity of substitution between factors in the jth sector. This basic property of production functions was introduced by Hicks and refined by Allen.[16] The elasticity of substitution can be written as

$$\sigma_j(\omega) = \frac{\omega}{k_j}\frac{dk_j}{d\omega} \qquad \text{for } j = 1, 2.$$

Rearranging Inequality A.14 gives

$$\sigma_2 > \frac{\omega}{k_1 + \omega} - \frac{\omega k_1}{\omega k_2 + k_1 k_2} - \frac{k_1(k_2 + \omega)(k_2 - k)\sigma_1}{k_2(k_1 + \omega)(k - k_1)}. \quad \text{(A.15)}$$

From Inequality A.15 a simple *sufficient* condition for (dy_1/dk) to be positive is that $\sigma_2 \geq 1$. Thus, *if the elasticity of substitution in the production of commodity two (one) is greater than or equal to unity, then the higher the endowment of either factor of production, the higher is the equilibrium level of output of commodity one (two).*

It is instructive to study the special case where the production functions (Equations 1 and 3) are linear in logarithms. For this case, we can write

$$f_1(k_1) = k_1{}^a \qquad \text{where } 0 < a < 1,$$
$$f_2(k_2) = k_2{}^b \qquad \text{where } 0 < b < 1. \quad \text{(A.16)}$$

Applying Equation 14 to Equations A.16 yields

$$k_1 = \frac{a\omega}{1 - a} \quad \text{and} \quad k_2 = \frac{b\omega}{1 - b}. \quad \text{(A.17)}$$

---

[16] Cf. pp. 117, 245 in [6], pp. 341–343 in [2], and [7].

Substituting Equations A.16 and A.17 in Equation A.3 yields

$$\omega = \left[\frac{\alpha(1 - a) + (1 - \alpha)(1 - b)}{\alpha a + (1 - \alpha)b}\right]k. \tag{A.18}$$

From Equations A.17 and A.18,

$$k_1 = \gamma_1 k \quad \text{and} \quad k_2 = \gamma_2 k,$$

where $\gamma_1 > 0$ and $\gamma_2 > 0$ are constants fixed upon specification of the parameters α, a, b. Notice also that

$$l_1 = \frac{k_2 - k}{k_2 - k_1} = \frac{\gamma_2 - 1}{\gamma_2 - \gamma_1}$$

and

$$l_2 = \frac{k - k_1}{k_2 - k_1} = \frac{1 - \gamma_1}{\gamma_2 - \gamma_1}.$$

Therefore $0 < l_1 < 1$ and $0 < l_2 < 1$ are, in the Cobb-Douglas case, fixed constants. Hence if production satisfies Equations 11 through 14 and Equations A.16, and if demand satisfies Equations A.1 and A.2, then (dy_1/dk) and (dy_2/dk) are positive for all $k > 0$.

In the study of the model of inventive activity and capital accumulation,[17] one is interested in the sign of an expression that is equivalent to

$$y_2 - k\frac{dy_2}{dk}, \tag{A.19}$$

which can be rewritten as

$$\frac{f_2(k_2)}{D(k_2 - k_1)}(k\tilde{N} - k_1 D), \tag{A.20}$$

where by Equation 14, $\tilde{N}$ is given by

$$\tilde{N} = \frac{dk_2}{d\omega}\left(\frac{k_1 + \omega}{k_2 + \omega}\right)\left(\frac{k - k_1}{k_2 - k_1}\right) + \frac{dk_1}{d\omega}\left(\frac{k_2 - k}{k_2 - k_1}\right) > 0 \qquad \text{for } k_2 \neq k \neq k_1,$$

and where $D > 0$ is defined by Equation A.11.

Form the expression

$$
\begin{aligned}
k\tilde{N} - k_1 D = \frac{k - k_1}{k_2 - k_1}\Bigg\{ &\frac{dk_2}{d\omega}\left[k - k_1 - \frac{k(k_2 - k_1)}{k_2 + \omega} + \frac{k_1(k_2 - k)}{k_2 + \omega}\right] \\
&+ \frac{dk_1}{d\omega}\left(\frac{k_2 - k}{k - k_1}\right)\left[k - k_1 - \frac{k_1(k - k_1)}{k_1 + \omega}\right] \\
&+ \frac{k_1(k_2 - k)}{k_2 + \omega} - \frac{k_1(k_2 - k)}{k_1 + \omega}\Bigg\}.
\end{aligned} \tag{A.21}
$$

---

[17] Cf., e.g., p. 76 of the text.

The right-hand side of Equation A.21 can be rewritten as

$$\frac{(k - k_1)(k_2 - k)}{k_2 - k_1} \left[\frac{dk_2}{d\omega} \left(\frac{k - k_1}{k_2 - k} \right) \left(1 - \frac{k_2}{k_2 + \omega} \right) \right.$$

$$\left. + \frac{dk_1}{d\omega} \left(1 - \frac{k_1}{k_1 + \omega} \right) + k_1 \left(\frac{1}{k_2 + \omega} - \frac{1}{k_1 + \omega} \right) \right]. \tag{A.22}$$

Notice that for the case $k_1 > k > k_2$, Expression A.22 is negative. Therefore, if $k_1 > k > k_2$, then Expressions A.19 and A.20 are positive.

For the reverse case $k_2 > k > k_1$, Expression A.22 tells us that $k\tilde{N} > k_1 D$ if and only if

$$\frac{dk_2}{d\omega} \left(\frac{k - k_1}{k_2 - k} \right) \left(\frac{\omega}{k_2 + \omega} \right) + \frac{dk_1}{d\omega} \left(\frac{\omega}{k_1 + \omega} \right) > \frac{k_1(k_2 - k_1)}{(k_1 + \omega)(k_2 + \omega)}. \tag{A.23}$$

Dividing Inequality A.23 by $k_1 k_2$ yields

$$\sigma_1 > \frac{k_2}{k_2 + \omega} - \frac{k_1}{k_2 + \omega} - \left(\frac{k - k_1}{k_2 - k} \right) \left(\frac{k_1 + \omega}{k_2 + \omega} \right) \frac{k_2}{k_1} \sigma_2. \tag{A.24}$$

Therefore, a simple *sufficient* condition for Expression A.19 to be positive is for $k_1 > k_2$ or $\sigma_1 \geq 1$.

References

1. Ahlfors, L. V., *Complex Analysis*, New York: McGraw-Hill Book Company, 1953.
2. Allen, R. G. D., *Mathematical Analysis for Economists*, New York: St. Martin's Press, Inc., 1962.
3. Arrow, K. J., "The Economic Implications of Learning by Doing," *Review of Economic Studies*, Vol. 29 (June 1962), pp. 155–173.
4. Cunningham, W. J., "The Concept of Stability," *The American Scientist*, Vol. 51 (December 1963), pp. 425–436.
5. Debreu, G., *Theory of Value*, New York: John Wiley & Sons, Inc., 1959.
6. Hicks, J. R., *The Theory of Wages*, London: Macmillan and Company, 1932.
7. Hicks, J. R., and R. G. D. Allen, "A Reconsideration of the Theory of Value," *Economica* (N.S.), Vol. 1 (May 1934), pp. 196–217.
8. Kaldor, N., "A Model of Economic Growth," *Economic Journal*, Vol. 67 (December 1957). Reprinted in *Essays on Economic Stability and Growth*, New York: Free Press of Glencoe, Inc., 1960, pp. 256–300.
9. Kaldor, N., "Capital Accumulation and Economic Growth," in F. A. Lutz and D. C. Hague (eds.), *The Theory of Capital*, New York: St. Martin's Press, Inc., 1961, pp. 177–222.
10. Kaldor, N., and J. A. Mirrlees, "A New Model of Economic Growth," *Review of Economic Studies*, Vol. 29 (June 1962), pp. 174–192.
11. Maruyama, M., "Morphogenesis and Morphostasis," *Methodos*, Vol. 12, No. 48 (1960).

12. National Bureau of Economic Research, *The Rate and Direction of Inventive Activity*, Princeton: Princeton University Press, 1962.
13. Oniki, H., and H. Uzawa, "Patterns of Trade and Investment in a Dynamic Model of International Trade," *Review of Economic Studies*, Vol. 32, No. 1 (January 1965), pp. 15–38.
14. Pontryagin, L. S., *et al.*, *The Mathematical Theory of Optimal Processes*, New York and London: Interscience Publishers, Inc., 1962.
15. Rybczynski, T. N., "Factor Endowment and Relative Commodity Prices," *Economica* (N.S.), Vol. 22 (November 1955), pp. 336–341.
16. Shell, K., "Toward a Theory of Inventive Activity and Capital Accumulation," *American Economic Review*, Vol. 56, No. 2 (May 1966), pp. 62–68.
17. Solow, R. M., "A Contribution to the Theory of Economic Growth," *Quarterly Journal of Economics*, Vol. 32 (1956), pp. 65–94.
18. Swan, T., "Economic Growth and Capital Accumulation," *Economic Record*, Vol. 66 (1956), pp. 334–361.
19. Uzawa, H., "On a Two-Sector Model of Economic Growth II," *Review of Economic Studies*, Vol. 30 (June 1963), pp. 105–118.

V

Optimal Accumulation and Trade in an Open Economy of Moderate Size[1]

HARL E. RYDER, Jr.

Brown University

It has long been recognized that a complete analysis of the benefits of foreign trade must take into account not only a static concept of comparative advantage but also the intertemporal pattern of the allocation of all resources available to an economy—both foreign and domestic. The recently developed analysis by Uzawa [12] and Srinivasan [10] of optimal paths of capital accumulation in a two-sector neoclassical model gives an excellent context for the study of optimal intertemporal decisions as they affect foreign trade.

In this essay we extend the Uzawa-Srinivasan model by allowing the country to trade at terms dependent on the amount of trading done. So as not to complicate the analysis unduly we abstract from international lending and changes in the offer curve. The internal analysis of the rest of the world is excluded as being beyond the scope of our problem. Disembodied Harrod-neutral technical progress will be introduced after the basic model and its implications have been set forth. In the context of such a model we show that the introduction of dynamic optimization does not alter the nature of static allocation but merely generates a shadow price for the guidance of essentially static decisions.

This essay is a revision and extension of an earlier unpublished paper [9]. A model virtually identical to ours has been discussed briefly by Bardhan [1]

[1] I wish to express my appreciation for the valuable comments and suggestions of H. Uzawa and K. J. Arrow.

87

and with a different emphasis by Canitrot [2]. Here we give a more complete analysis of the patterns of production, trade, and absorption that may occur and trace their effect on the optimal plan. Goldman [4] has developed a similar model with three sectors—an export good, an investment good, and a consumption good.

We set forth the basic model in section 1 and formulate the optimization problem in section 2. The resulting patterns of specialization are analyzed in section 3 and their economic implications discussed in section 4. Sections 5 and 7 discuss the dynamic nature of the optimal path, while section 6 contains a formal proof of its optimality. In sections 8 and 9 we modify some of the assumptions of the previous analysis.

1. Definitions and Assumptions

Let us consider a two-sector neoclassical production model. There are two homogeneous commodities, an investment good I and a consumption good C, and two homogeneous factors, capital K and labor L. The allocation of resources between the investment- and consumption-good sectors is assumed to be controlled by the planning authority, either directly or by means of the price ratio to which competitive behavior of firms is adapted. Capital and labor are fully employed at all times, and if not directly controlled are paid their respective marginal products. Let

$K(t)$ = the capital stock in the economy at time t.

$K_i(t)$ = the capital employed in the i-sector at time t $(i = I, C)$.

$L(t)$ = the labor force in the economy at time t.

$L_i(t)$ = the labor force employed in the i-sector at time t $(i = I, C)$.

$q(t)$ = the accounting price of investment goods in terms of consumption goods at time t.

$Y(t)$ = the total production of the economy at time t, evaluated in terms of consumption goods.

$Y_i(t)$ = the production of the i-sector at time t $(i = I, C)$.

$Z_i(t)$ = the amount of the i-good imported (exported if $Z_i(t)$ is negative) at time t $(i = I, C)$.

$X_I(t)$ = the absorption of the investment good, that is, gross investment at time t.

$X_C(t)$ = the absorption of the consumption good, that is, consumption at time t.

$X(t)$ = the total absorption of the economy at time t, evaluated in terms of consumption goods.

n = the rate of growth of the labor force.

μ = the rate of depreciation of capital stock.

λ = $\mu + n$.

δ = the planner's subjective rate of discount.

$F_i(K_i, L_i)$ = the production function of the *i*-sector ($i = I, C$),

where $F_i(0, L_i) = F_i(K_i, 0) = 0$,

$$\frac{\partial F_i}{\partial K_i} > 0, \quad \frac{\partial F_i}{\partial L_i} > 0, \quad \frac{\partial^2 F_i}{\partial K_i \partial L_i} > 0,$$

and F_i is homogeneous of degree one in K_i and L_i.

Then the following relationships hold:

$$K_I(t) + K_C(t) = K(t), \tag{1}$$

$$L_I(t) + L_C(t) = L(t), \tag{2}$$

$$Y_i(t) = F_i[K_i(t), L_i(t)], \quad i = I, C, \tag{3}$$

$$Y(t) = Y_C(t) + q(t)Y_I(t), \tag{4}$$

$$X_i(t) = Y_i(t) + Z_i(t), \quad i = I, C, \tag{5}$$

$$X(t) = X_C(t) + q(t)X_I(t), \tag{6}$$

$$\dot{L}(t) = nL(t), \tag{7}$$

$$\dot{K}(t) = X_I(t) - \mu K(t). \tag{8}$$

Let us define per capita quantities as follows:

$$k(t) = \frac{K(t)}{L(t)}, \quad k_i(t) = \frac{K_i(t)}{L_i(t)}, \quad y(t) = \frac{Y(t)}{L(t)}, \quad y_i(t) = \frac{Y_i(t)}{L(t)},$$

$$x(t) = \frac{X(t)}{L(t)}, \quad x_i(t) = \frac{X_i(t)}{L(t)}, \quad z_i(t) = \frac{Z_i(t)}{L(t)}, \quad i = I, C. \tag{9}$$

Since F_i is homogeneous, we may define

$$f_i(k_i) = F_i(k_i, 1), \tag{10}$$

where

$$f_i(0) = 0, \quad f_i(\infty) = \infty, \quad f_i'(0) = \infty, \quad f_i'(\infty) = 0,$$

$$f_i(k_i) > 0, \quad f_i'(k_i) > 0, \quad f_i''(k_i) < 0 \quad \text{for } k_i > 0.^2$$

Then

$$F_i(K_i, L_i) = L_i f_i(k_i), \quad i = I, C.$$

Assuming that $k_I(t) \neq k_C(t)$, we may rewrite the system of Equations 1 through 8 as

$$y_I(t) = \frac{k_C(t) - k(t)}{k_C(t) - k_I(t)} f_I[k_I(t)] \geq 0, \tag{11}$$

$$y_C(t) = \frac{k(t) - k_I(t)}{k_C(t) - k_I(t)} f_C[k_C(t)] \geq 0, \tag{12}$$

---

² When no ambiguity results, we shall use the notation $f(a) = \infty, f(\infty) = b, f(a_+) = b$ to denote the corresponding limits $\lim_{x \to a} f(x) = \infty$, $\lim_{x \to \infty} f(x) = b$, $\lim_{x \to a_+} f(x) = b$.

$$y(t) = y_C(t) + q(t)y_I(t), \tag{13}$$

$$x_i(t) = y_i(t) + z_i(t) \geq 0, \qquad i = I, C, \tag{14}$$

$$k(t) = x_I(t) - \lambda k(t). \tag{15}$$

We shall assume that the economy under study is intermediate in size between the limiting cases of a "small country in a large world," which can trade in unlimited quantities at fixed terms, and a "large country in a small world," which cannot trade at all without a drastically unfavorable shift in the terms of trade. The latter case is identical to that of an isolated country and has been analyzed by Uzawa [12] and Srinivasan [10]. The former case has been analyzed by Goldman, Ryder, and Uzawa [5]. Here we assume that at any terms of trade set by the home country, a definite quantity of trade will be forthcoming from the rest of the world. To avoid approaching one or the other of the limiting cases, we shall assume that the Marshallian offer curve is growing exponentially at the same rate n as the labor force of the home country. Thus, we can write

$$z_C(t) = \theta[z_I(t)], \tag{16}$$

where θ is defined for $0 > z_{I\,\text{min}} \leq z_I \leq z_{I\,\text{max}} > 0$.

$$\theta(0) = 0, \quad \theta'(z_I) < 0, \quad \theta''(z_I) < 0,$$

$$0 \geq \theta'(z_{I\,\text{min}}) > \theta'(z_{I\,\text{max}}) \geq -\infty.$$

The general form of the offer curve θ is shown in Figure 1.

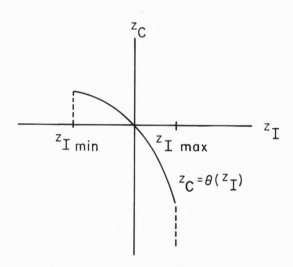

FIGURE 1. Offer curve.

The primary advantage of this assumption is its simplicity. It enables us to analyze the home country's trade policy without requiring a detailed study of the rest of the world's economy. Its greatest weakness is that it assumes the offer curve is fixed over the entire future regardless of the policy followed by the home country in the meanwhile. Even this, however, could be justified if we assume that the rest of the world has a labor force growing exponentially at the rate n, has stable, constant-returns production functions, and maximizes its consumption subject to the maintenance of a constant capital-labor ratio.

2. Statement of the Problem

Equations 11, 12, 14, 15, and 16 give the structure of the economy. Any function $k(t)$ that satisfies these equations and $k(0) = k_0$, where k_0 is the historically given capital-labor ratio at the beginning of the plan, is called a *feasible path*.

The task of optimal planning is to establish a preference ordering among feasible paths and to find a feasible path that is preferred to every other feasible path.

In recent years, the problem of evaluating alternative infinite income streams has received considerable attention. Koopmans [6], Diamond [3], and Williamson [7] have shown, under reasonable assumptions, that if a preference ordering exists it must have some degree of time preference. A convenient way of achieving time preference is to include some sort of discount factor in the criterion. Strotz [11] has shown that only an exponential discount factor avoids inconsistency when constant replanning is permitted. We shall include an exponential discount factor $e^{-\delta t}$ in our criterion.

There is general agreement that the appropriate comparison is between consumption streams rather than the streams of total income, since only consumption contributes directly to economic welfare. The true benefits of investment lie in the increased consumption that it facilitates. To incorporate investment directly into the criterion would be redundant. At any point in time, the social welfare function will depend on per capita consumption, abstracting from distribution problems. Thus, we have $u[x_C(t)]$ where $u'(x_C) > 0$, $u''(x_C) \leq 0$. Discounting and summing over all future time gives the criterion functional

$$V[k(\cdot)] = \int_0^\infty e^{-\delta t} u[x_C(t)] \, dt. \tag{17}$$

In the first analysis, we shall consider the special case where $u''(x_C) = 0$, so that instead of Equation 17 we have

$$V_0[k(\cdot)] = \int_0^\infty e^{-\delta t} x_C(t) \, dt. \tag{18}$$

Because of the linear utility function, the optimal policy will have an exaggerated form that may include an initial period of extreme austerity with consumption held to a minimum, followed by a period of consumption gradually rising until it reaches a stationary level.

Formally, then, we wish to maximize Expression 18 subject to Conditions 11, 12, 14, 15, and 16. This can be considered a problem in optimal control, where $k_I(t) \geq 0$, $k_C(t) \geq 0$, $z_{I\ min} \leq z_I(t) \leq z_{I\ max}$ are the control variables. Such problems can be solved by the Pontryagin maximum principle.[3]

Let

$$\Pi(k_I, k_C, z_I; k, q) = y_C + z_C + q(y_I + z_I - \lambda k) = x - q\lambda k,$$

$$H(k, q) = \max_{k_I, k_C, z_I} \Pi(k_I, k_C, z_I; k, q), \tag{19}$$

where y_I, y_C, and z_C satisfy Conditions 11, 12, and 16. For an optimal path $k(t)$, there must exist a function $q(t)$, for which the following necessary conditions hold:

$$\Pi[k_I(t), k_C(t), z_I(t); k(t), q(t)] = H[k(t), q(t)] \qquad \text{for all } t \geq 0. \tag{20}$$

$$k = \frac{\partial \Pi}{\partial q} = x_I(k, q) - \lambda k. \tag{21}$$

$$\dot{q} = \delta q - \frac{\partial H}{\partial k} = (\lambda + \delta)q - \frac{\partial}{\partial k} x(k, q). \tag{22}$$

$$k(0) = k_0, \quad \lim_{t \to \infty} e^{-\delta t} q(t) = 0. \tag{23}$$

Condition 20 means that resources are allocated at every point of time so as to maximize the value of absorption. Condition 21 is a simple repetition of the technical relation of Equation 15. Condition 22 has a simple interpretation in terms of the profitability of holding a unit of physical capital for a period of time. The term $(\partial/\partial k)x(k, q)$ represents its rental value (marginal product), $\dot{q}$ represents the capital gain resulting from the change in its price, δq represents interest, μq represents loss through physical depreciation, and nq represents dilution of equity by population growth. Their sum

$$\frac{\partial}{\partial k} x(k, q) + \dot{q} - \delta q - \mu q - nq$$

is the net profit, and will be zero when Condition 22 holds. Condition 23 gives initial and terminal conditions to identify a particular solution to the differential Equations 21 and 22. The particular solution, in fact, must start from the historically given initial capital-labor ratio k_0, and must not impute any value to capital in the terminal state ($t \to \infty$).

We shall show the existence of a unique path satisfying Conditions 20 through 23 for any initial k_0 and shall prove that this path is indeed optimal.

---

[3] See [8], especially pp. 69, 298.

3. Instantaneous Maximization

First, let us examine Conditions 20. At any point of time along the optimal path, k and q are given; hence, we must find the maximum of Π for all combinations of $k, q \geq 0$. If we ignore the nonnegativity constraints of Equations 11, 12, and 14, we obtain the following maximum conditions:

$$\frac{\partial \Pi}{\partial z_I} = \theta'(z_I) + q = 0, \tag{24}$$

$$\frac{\partial \Pi}{\partial k_I} = \frac{(k_C - k)}{(k_C - k_I)^2} \{-f_C(k_C) + q[f_I(k_I) + (k_C - k_I)f_I'(k_I)]\} = 0, \tag{25}$$

$$\frac{\partial \Pi}{\partial k_C} = \frac{(k - k_I)}{(k_C - k_I)^2} \{[-f_C(k_C) + (k_C - k_I)f_C'(k_C)] + qf_I(k_I)\} = 0. \tag{26}$$

If one or two of the nonnegativity constraints are effective, then we must be in some pattern of specialization, either in production (Equations 11 and 12) or in absorption (Equation 14). The nine patterns that may occur are classified in Table 1.

Table 1. Patterns of Specialization

	Production					
	I		II		III	
Absorption	Consumption Good		Nonspecialized		Investment Good	
A. Consumption	$y_I=0$	$y_C>0$	$y_I>0$	$y_C>0$	$y_I>0$	$y_C=0$
	$z_I=0$	$z_C=0$	$z_I=-y_I$	$z_C>0$	$z_I=-y_I$	$z_C>0$
	$x_I=0$	$x_C=y_C$	$x_I=0$	$x_C>0$	$x_I=0$	$x_C=z_C$
B. Non-specialized	$y_I=0$	$y_C>0$	$y_I>0$	$y_C>0$	$y_I>0$	$y_C=0$
	$z_I>0$	$-y_C<z_C<0$	$z_I>-y_I$	$z_C>-y_C$	$-y_I<z_I<0$	$z_C>0$
	$x_I=z_I$	$x_C>0$	$x_I>0$	$x_C>0$	$x_I>0$	$x_C=z_C$
C. Investment	$y_I=0$	$y_C>0$	$y_I>0$	$y_C>0$	$y_I>0$	$y_C=0$
	$z_I>0$	$z_C=-y_C$	$z_I>0$	$z_C=-y_C$	$z_I=0$	$z_C=0$
	$x_I=z_I$	$x_C=0$	$x_I>0$	$x_C=0$	$x_I=y_I$	$x_C=0$

Equation 24 gives us $\theta'(z_I) = -q$. Since $\theta''(z_I) < 0$, the function $\theta'(z_I)$ can be inverted. Let

$$\check{z}_I(q) \equiv \begin{cases} \theta'^{-1}(-q) & \text{for } -\theta'(z_{I\,\text{min}}) < q < -\theta'(z_{I\,\text{max}}) \\ z_{I\,\text{min}} & \text{for } q < -\theta'(z_{I\,\text{min}}) \\ z_{I\,\text{max}} & \text{for } q > -\theta'(z_{I\,\text{max}}) \end{cases} \tag{27}$$

$$\check{z}_C(q) \equiv \theta[\check{z}_I(q)]. \tag{28}$$

From these definitions it follows that

$$\check{z}_I'(q) = -\frac{1}{\theta''(\check{z}_I)} > 0, \quad \check{z}_C'(q) = \theta'(\check{z}_I)\check{z}_I'(q) < 0 \tag{29}$$

for $-\theta'(z_{I\ min}) < q < -\theta'(z_{I\ max})$.

As long as the inequalities of Equation 14 are satisfied, we are in pattern B where Equation 24 holds. Hence,

$$z_i = \check{z}_i(q), \quad i = I, C, \tag{30}$$

holds in pattern B.

In what follows, we shall assume for simplicity that

$$\theta'(z_{I\ max}) = -\infty, \quad \theta'(z_{I\ min}) = 0.$$

This assumption is not crucial to any of our results.

Solving Equations 25 and 26 for q gives us

$$\frac{f_C(k_C)}{f_I(k_I) + (k_C - k_I)f_I'(k_I)} = q = \frac{f_C(k_C) - (k_C - k_I)f_C'(k_C)}{f_I(k_I)}, \tag{31}$$

from which

$$\frac{f_C(k_C)}{f_C'(k_C)} - k_C = \frac{f_I(k_I)}{f_I'(k_I)} - k_I. \tag{32}$$

If we define

$$\omega_i(k_i) \equiv \frac{f_i(k_i)}{f_i'(k_i)} - k_i, \quad i = I, C, \tag{33}$$

then

$$\omega_i'(k_i) = -\frac{f_i(k_i)f_i''(k_i)}{[f_i'(k_i)]^2} > 0, \quad \omega_i(0) = 0, \quad \omega_i(\infty) = \infty.$$

Since $\omega_i(k_i)$ is monotonic, we can take its inverse

$$k_i(\omega) \equiv \omega_i^{-1}(\omega), \quad i = I, C. \tag{34}$$

Then

$$k_i'(\omega) = \frac{1}{\omega_i'(k_i)} > 0, \quad k_i(0) = 0, \quad k_i(\infty) = \infty. \tag{34a}$$

Now we seek to define $\omega(q)$ so that the substitution $k_i = k_i[\omega(q)]$ with $i = I, C$, into Equation 31 yields an identity. By Equations 31 and 32 we have

$$q = p(\omega) \equiv \frac{f_C'[k_C(\omega)]}{f_I'[k_I(\omega)]} > 0. \tag{35}$$

Differentiating $\log p(\omega)$,

$$\frac{p'(\omega)}{p(\omega)} = \frac{k_C(\omega) - k_I(\omega)}{[k_I(\omega) + \omega][k_C(\omega) + \omega]} \sim k_C(\omega) - k_I(\omega).[4] \tag{36}$$

---

[4] We shall use the symbol $\sim$ to mean "has the same sign as."

For convenience we assume that $k_C(\omega) - k_I(\omega)$ is of constant sign for all ω. This assumption is not crucial to results and is relaxed in section 8.

Since $p(\omega)$ is monotonic, we can invert it to obtain the desired function:

$$\omega(q) \equiv p^{-1}(q) \quad \text{for } q \text{ between } p(0) \text{ and } p(\infty). \tag{37}$$

Then

$$\omega'(q) = \frac{1}{p'(\omega)} \sim k_C(\omega) - k_I(\omega). \tag{37a}$$

Define

$$\check{y}_I(k, q) \equiv \frac{k_C[\omega(q)] - k}{k_C[\omega(q)] - k_I[\omega(q)]} f_I\{k_I[\omega(q)]\},$$

$$\check{y}_C(k, q) \equiv \frac{k - k_I[\omega(q)]}{k_C[\omega(q)] - k_I[\omega(q)]} f_C\{k_C[\omega(q)]\}. \tag{38}$$

Differentiating,

$$\frac{\partial \check{y}_I}{\partial k} = -\frac{f_I(k_I)}{k_C - k_I} = -\frac{(k_I + \omega)f_I'(k_I)}{k_C - k_I} \sim -(k_C - k_I),$$

$$\frac{\partial \check{y}_C}{\partial k} = \frac{f_C(k_C)}{k_C - k_I} = \frac{(k_C + \omega)f_C'(k_C)}{k_C - k_I} \sim k_C - k_I,$$

$$\frac{\partial \check{y}_I}{\partial q} = \frac{(k_C - k)(k_C + \omega)k_I'(\omega) + (k - k_I)(k_I + \omega)k_C'(\omega)}{(k_C - k_I)^2} \omega'(q)f_I'(k_I) > 0,$$

$$\frac{\partial \check{y}_C}{\partial q} = -\frac{(k_C - k)(k_C + \omega)k_I'(\omega) + (k - k_I)(k_I + \omega)k_C'(\omega)}{(k_C - k_I)^2} \omega'(q)f_C'(k_C) < 0. \tag{39}$$

As long as Inequalities 11, 12, and 14 are satisfied, we are in pattern IIB where Equations 25 and 26 hold. Hence,

$$k_i = k_i[\omega(q)], \quad y_i = \check{y}_i(k, q), \quad i = I, C, \tag{40}$$

hold in pattern IIB.

By Equations 30 and 40 and Table 1 the four boundaries of pattern IIB are given by

$$\check{y}_I(k, q) = 0 \quad \text{for the boundary with pattern IB}, \tag{41}$$

$$\check{y}_C(k, q) = 0 \quad \text{for the boundary with pattern IIIB}, \tag{42}$$

$$\check{z}_I(q) = -\check{y}_I(k, q) \quad \text{for the boundary with pattern IIA}, \tag{43}$$

and

$$\check{z}_C(q) = -\check{y}_C(k, q) \quad \text{for the boundary with pattern IIC}. \tag{44}$$

(See Figures 2 and 3.)

By Equation 38 we see that Equation 41 holds when $k_C[\omega(q)] = k$, or

$$q = p[\omega_C(k)]. \tag{41a}$$

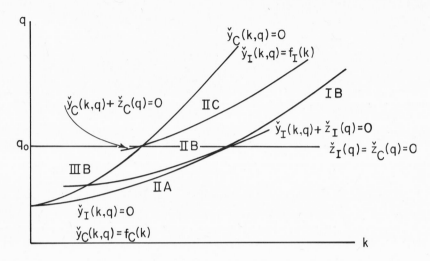

FIGURE 2. Pattern II when $k_C(\omega) > k_I(\omega)$.

Similarly, Equation 42 holds when $k_I[\omega(q)] = k$, or

$$q = p[\omega_I(k)].\tag{42a}$$

By Equation 36,

$$\frac{d}{dk}p[\omega_i(k)] \sim k_C(\omega) - k_I(\omega), \qquad i = I, C.$$

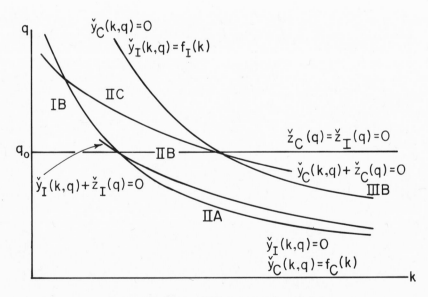

FIGURE 3. Pattern II when $k_C(\omega) < k_I(\omega)$.

From the signs of the derivatives in Equations 39 we see that

$$p[\omega_C(k)] \leq q \leq p[\omega_I(k)] \tag{45}$$

in pattern IIB. As long as Inequalities 14 hold, we shall have

$$y_I = 0, \quad y_C = f_C(k), \quad z_I = \check{z}_I(q), \quad z_C = \check{z}_C(q), \quad q \leq p[\omega_C(k)] \tag{46}$$

in pattern IB and

$$y_I = f_I(k), \quad y_C = 0, \quad z_I = \check{z}_I(q), \quad z_C = \check{z}_C(q), \quad q \geq p[\omega_I(k)] \tag{47}$$

in pattern IIIB.

Equations 43 and 44 define implicitly the functions

$$q = \check{q}_i(k), \qquad i = I, C, \tag{48}$$

where $\check{z}_i[\check{q}_i(k)] + \check{y}_i[k, \check{q}_i(k)] \equiv 0, i = I, C$. Then

$$\check{q}_i'(k) = -\frac{(\partial \check{y}_i/\partial k)}{(d\check{z}_i/dq) + (\partial \check{y}_i/\partial q)} \sim k_C - k_I, \qquad i = I, C, \tag{49}$$

by Equations 29 and 39. From the signs of the derivatives of Equation 49 we see that

$$\check{q}_I(k) \leq q \leq \check{q}_C(k) \tag{50}$$

in pattern IIB. As long as inequalities 11 and 12 hold, we shall have

$$y_i = \check{y}_i[k, \check{q}_I(k)], \quad z_i = \check{z}_i[\check{q}_I(k)], \quad q \leq \check{q}_I(k), \qquad i = I, C, \tag{51}$$

in pattern IIA and

$$y_i = \check{y}_i[k, \check{q}_C(k)], \quad z_i = \check{z}_i[\check{q}_C(k)], \quad q \geq \check{q}_C(k), \qquad i = I, C, \tag{52}$$

in pattern IIC. In pattern IB, substituting Equations 46 into 14 gives us

$$-f_C(k) \leq \check{z}_C(q) \leq 0. \tag{53}$$

Let us define q_0 and $\hat{q}_C(k)$ by

$$q_0 \equiv -\theta'(0), \tag{54}$$

$$\check{z}_C[\hat{q}_C(k)] + f_C(k) \equiv 0. \tag{55}$$

Then

$$\hat{q}_C'(k) = -\frac{f_C'(k)}{\check{z}_C'(q)} > 0, \quad \hat{q}_C(0) = q_0. \tag{55a}$$

Now Inequality 53 is equivalent to

$$q_0 \leq q \leq \hat{q}_C(k). \tag{56}$$

(See Figure 4.) In pattern IA, we have

$$y_I = z_I = z_C = 0, \quad y_C = f_C(k), \quad q \leq q_0 \leq p[\omega_C(k)]. \tag{57}$$

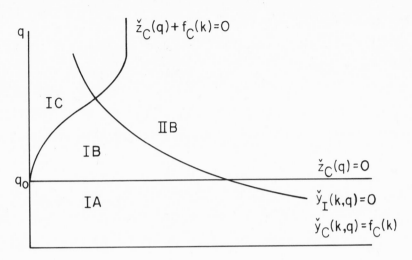

FIGURE 4. Pattern I when $k_C(\omega) < k_I(\omega)$.

In pattern IC, we have

$$y_I = 0, \quad y_C = f_C(k), \quad z_I = \check{z}_I[\hat{q}_C(k)], \quad z_C = -f_C(k),$$
$$q \geq \hat{q}_C(k) \leq p[\omega_C(k)]. \tag{58}$$

In pattern IIIB, substituting Equations 47 into 14 gives us

$$-f_I(k) \leq \check{z}_I(q) \leq 0. \tag{59}$$

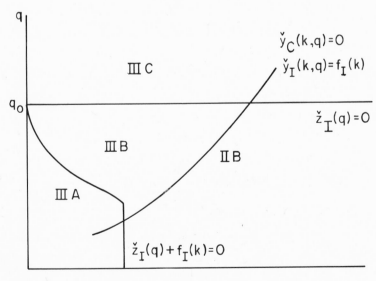

FIGURE 5. Pattern III when $k_C(\omega) > k_I(\omega)$.

Let us define $\hat{q}_I(k)$ by

$$\check{z}_I[\hat{q}_I(k)] + f_I(k) \equiv 0. \tag{60}$$

Then

$$\hat{q}_I'(k) = -\frac{f_I'(k)}{\check{z}_I'(q)} < 0, \quad \hat{q}_I(0) = q_0. \tag{60a}$$

Now Inequality 59 is equivalent to

$$\hat{q}_I(k) \leq q \leq q_0. \tag{61}$$

(See Figure 5.) In pattern IIIA, we have

$$y_I = f_I(k), \quad y_C = 0, \quad z_I = -f_I(k), \quad z_C = \check{z}_C[\hat{q}_I(k)], \tag{62}$$
$$q \leq \hat{q}_I(k) \geq p[\omega_I(k)].$$

In pattern IIIC, we have

$$y_I = f_I(k), \quad y_C = z_I = z_C = 0, \quad q \geq q_0 \geq p[\omega_I(k)]. \tag{63}$$

These relations are summarized in Tables 2 through 5.

It is not difficult to show that these functions are continuous across all pattern boundaries.

Table 2. Values of $y_I(k, q)$

$y_I(k, q) =$	I	II	III
A	0	$\check{y}_I[k, \check{q}_I(k)]$	$f_I(k)$
B	0	$\check{y}_I(k, q)$	$f_I(k)$
C	0	$\check{y}_I[k, \check{q}_C(k)]$	$f_I(k)$

Table 3. Values of $y_C(k, q)$

$y_C(k, q) =$	I	II	III
A	$f_C(k)$	$\check{y}_C[k, \check{q}_I(k)]$	0
B	$f_C(k)$	$\check{y}_C(k, q)$	0
C	$f_C(k)$	$\check{y}_C[k, \check{q}_C(k)]$	0

Table 4. Values of $z_I(k, q)$

$z_I(k, q) =$	I	II	III
A	0	$\check{z}_I[\check{q}_I(k)] \equiv -\check{y}_I[k, \check{q}_I(k)]$	$\check{z}_I[\hat{q}_I(k)] \equiv -f_I(k)$
B	$\check{z}_I(q)$	$\check{z}_I(q)$	$\check{z}_I(q)$
C	$\check{z}_I[\check{q}_C(k)]$	$\check{z}_I[\check{q}_C(k)]$	0

Table 5. Values of $z_C(k, q)$

$z_C(k, q) =$	I	II	III
A	0	$\check{z}_C[\check{q}_I(k)]$	$\check{z}_C[\check{q}_I(k)]$
B	$\check{z}_C(q)$	$\check{z}_C(q)$	$\check{z}_C(q)$
C	$\check{z}_C[\check{q}_C(k)] \equiv -f_C(k)$	$\check{z}_C[\check{q}_C(k)] \equiv -\check{y}_C[k, \check{q}_C(k)]$	0

4. Decentralized Decisions

We have been analyzing how the resources of the economy—capital, labor, and trade—should be allocated in order to maximize the value of absorption. In the process, we have implicitly assumed that these allocations are directly controlled by the planner. This, however, need not be the case. The same result can be obtained if the firms producing investment and consumption goods behave competitively subject to the price q established by the planner. In this case the wage rate of labor w and the quasi-rental rate of capital goods r will be equal to their respective marginal products.

$$w \geq \frac{\partial F_C}{\partial L} = f_C(k_C) - k_C f_C'(k_C) \qquad \text{with equality if } y_C > 0.$$

$$w \geq \frac{\partial F_I}{\partial L} = q[f_I(k_I) - k_I f_I'(k_I)] \qquad \text{with equality if } y_I > 0. \tag{64}$$

$$r \geq \frac{\partial F_C}{\partial K} = f_C'(k_C) \qquad \text{with equality if } y_C > 0.$$

$$r \geq \frac{\partial F_I}{\partial K} = q f_I'(k_I) \qquad \text{with equality if } y_I > 0. \tag{65}$$

Comparing these equations with Equation 33 we see that $(w/r) = \omega$.

International trade, however, cannot be handled so simply. The world price will be $-(z_C/z_I)$ while the domestic price is $q = -(dz_C/dz_I)$. The fact that the home country is large enough to affect the world price by its trade policy gives it some degree of monopoly power that cannot be exploited by competitive behavior. There are essentially three ways to handle this sector:

1. The government may control trade directly.
2. The privilege of trading may be granted as a monopoly concession to a single firm (its profits can be appropriated by taxation if desired).
3. The government may establish and constantly adjust a tariff, to which competitive trading firms are subject.

5. Dynamic Behavior

Now let us examine the solutions of the differential equations

$$\dot{k} = x_I(k, q) - \lambda k$$
$$= y_I(k, q) + z_I(k, q) - \lambda k, \tag{21}$$

$$\dot{q} = (\lambda + \delta)q - \frac{\partial}{\partial k} x(k, q)$$
$$= (\lambda + \delta)q - \frac{\partial y_C}{\partial k} - \frac{\partial z_C}{\partial k} - q\frac{\partial y_I}{\partial k} - q\frac{\partial z_I}{\partial k}, \tag{22}$$

where y_I, z_I, y_C, z_C are defined as in Tables 2 through 5. From Tables 2 through 5, and from Equations 29, 35, 37a, 39, 49, 55a, and 60a, we can determine the values of $(\partial x/\partial k)$ and $(\partial^2 x/\partial k^2)$ as shown in Tables 6 and 7.

Table 6. Values of $\dfrac{\partial x}{\partial k}(k, q)$

$\dfrac{\partial x}{\partial k} =$	I	II	III
A	$f_C'(k) > 0$	$f_C'(k_C) = \breve{q}_I(k)f_I'(k_I) > 0$	$\hat{q}_I(k)f_I'(k) > 0$
B	$f_C'(k) > 0$	$f_C'(k_C) = qf_I'(k_I) > 0$	$qf_I'(k) > 0$
C	$\dfrac{qf_C'(k)}{\hat{q}_C(k)} > 0$	$\dfrac{qf_C'(k_C)}{\breve{q}_C(k)} = qf_I'(k_I) > 0$	$qf_I'(k) > 0$

Table 7. Values of $\dfrac{\partial^2 x}{\partial k^2}(k, q)$

$\dfrac{\partial^2 x}{\partial k^2} =$	I	II	III
A	$f_C''(k) < 0$	$f_C''(k_C)k_C'(\omega)\omega'(q)\breve{q}_I'(k) < 0$	$\hat{q}_I(k)f_I''(k) + \hat{q}_I'(k)f_I'(k) < 0$
B	$f_C''(k) < 0$	0	$qf_I''(k) < 0$
C	$q\dfrac{\hat{q}_C(k)f_C''(k) - \hat{q}_C'(k)f_C'(k)}{[\hat{q}_C(k)]^2} < 0$	$qf_I''(k_I)k_I'(\omega)\omega'(q)\breve{q}_C'(k) < 0$	$qf_I''(k) < 0$

It is clear from Table 6 that $(\partial x/\partial k)$ is continuous across all pattern boundaries. From Table 7 we see that $(\partial^2 x/\partial k^2) \leq 0$ in all patterns with equality only in pattern IIB. Recalling Equation 34a and that k must lie between k_C and k_I in pattern II, we see that k_I and k_C must approach 0 or ∞

as k approaches 0 or ∞ if pattern II holds. Thus, we see from Table 6 and Equations 10, 55*a*, and 60*a* that

$$\lim_{k \to 0} \frac{\partial x}{\partial k} = \infty, \quad \lim_{k \to \infty} \frac{\partial x}{\partial k} = 0 \tag{66}$$

regardless of which pattern holds. Therefore,

$$\lim_{k \to 0} \dot{q} = -\infty, \quad \lim_{k \to \infty} \dot{q} = (\lambda + \delta)q > 0,$$

$$\frac{\partial}{\partial k} \dot{q} \geq 0 \tag{67}$$

with equality only in pattern IIB. From Equation 22 and Table 6 we see that

$$\frac{\partial}{\partial q} \left(\frac{\dot{q}}{q} \right) = 0 \quad \text{for patterns IC, IIC, IIIC, IIIB,}$$

$$\frac{\partial}{\partial q} \dot{q} = \lambda + \delta > 0 \quad \text{for patterns IB, IA, IIA, IIIA,} \tag{68}$$

$$\frac{\partial}{\partial q} \left(\frac{\dot{q}}{q} \right) = -f_I''(k_I)k_I'(\omega)\omega'(q) \sim (k_C - k_I) \quad \text{in pattern IIB.}$$

Because of these considerations, there will be a continuous, piecewise smooth curve in the (k, q)-plane along which $\dot{q} = 0$. This curve will be

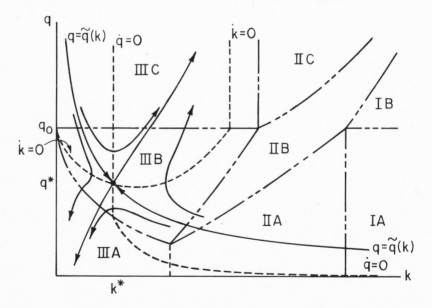

FIGURE 6. Optimal paths when the stationary point is in pattern IIIB and $k_C(\omega) > k_I(\omega)$.

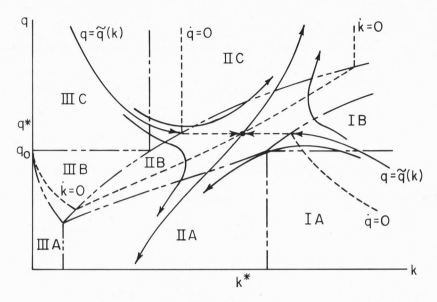

FIGURE 7. Optimal paths when the stationary point is in pattern IIB and
$k_C(\omega) > k_I(\omega)$.

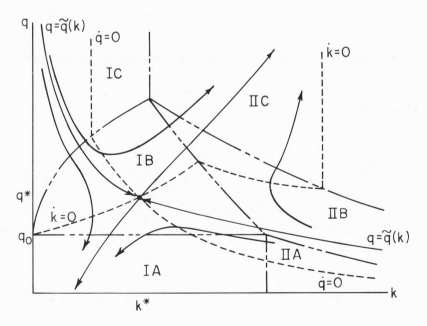

FIGURE 8. Optimal paths when the stationary point is in pattern IB and
$k_C(\omega) < k_I(\omega)$.

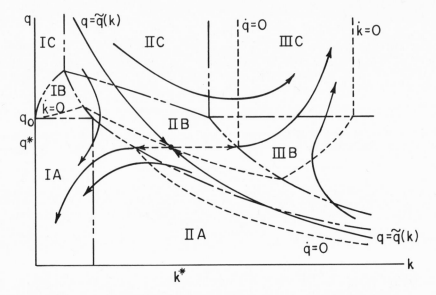

FIGURE 9. Optimal paths when the stationary point is in pattern IIB and $k_C(\omega) < k_I(\omega)$.

vertical in patterns IC, IIC, IIIC, IIIB, horizontal in pattern IIB, and negatively sloped in patterns IB, IA, IIA, IIIA. To the left of the curve, $\dot{q} < 0$; to the right, $\dot{q} > 0$. (See Figures 6 through 9.)

Next, let us consider Equation 21. In patterns IA, IIA, IIIA, we have $x_I = 0$, so that

$$\dot{k} = -\lambda k < 0 \qquad \text{for all } k > 0. \tag{69}$$

In patterns IC, IIC, IIIC, we have $x_I = x/q$. Here

$$\frac{\partial}{\partial k}\dot{k} = \frac{1}{q}\frac{\partial x}{\partial k} - \lambda = \delta - \frac{\dot{q}}{q}, \quad \text{with} \quad \dot{k} = 0 \qquad \text{when } k = 0.$$

$$\frac{\partial}{\partial q}\dot{k} = 0. \tag{70}$$

We have $(\partial/\partial k)\dot{k} > 0$ as long as $(\dot{q}/q) < \delta$, so $\dot{k} > 0$ when $\dot{q} = 0$ and $(\dot{q}/q) > \delta$ when $\dot{k} = 0$. From these considerations we see that there can be no intersection of $\dot{q} = 0$ with $\dot{k} = 0$ in patterns A or C. From Equation 10 and the fact that k is between k_c and k_I in pattern II, we conclude that $\lim_{k \to \infty} (\dot{k}/k) = -\lambda < 0$ in all patterns. Hence, there is some $\tilde{k}$ for which $\dot{k} = 0$ in pattern C. Then $\tilde{k}$ is the maximum sustainable capital-labor ratio. In pattern IB,

$$\frac{\partial \dot{k}}{\partial k} = -\lambda < 0, \quad \frac{\partial \dot{k}}{\partial q} = \check{z}_I'(q) > 0. \tag{71}$$

In pattern IIB,

$$\frac{\partial \dot{k}}{\partial k} = \frac{\partial \ddot{y}_I}{\partial k} - \lambda, \quad \frac{\partial \dot{k}}{\partial q} = \ddot{z}_I'(q) + \frac{\partial \ddot{y}_I}{\partial q} > 0. \tag{72}$$

By Equation 22 and Table 6 we have $f_I'(k_I) - \lambda = \delta$ when $\dot{q} = 0$. Substituting this and Equation 39 into Equations 72 gives

$$\frac{\partial \dot{k}}{\partial k} = - \frac{\delta(\omega + k_I) + \lambda(\omega + k_C)}{k_C - k_I} \sim -(k_C - k_I) \quad \text{when } \dot{q} = 0. \tag{73}$$

In pattern IIIB,

$$\frac{\partial \dot{k}}{\partial k} = f_I'(k) - \lambda, \quad \frac{\partial \dot{k}}{\partial q} = \ddot{z}_I'(q) > 0. \tag{74}$$

Again we have $f_I'(k) - \lambda = \delta$ when $\dot{q} = 0$, so that

$$\frac{\partial \dot{k}}{\partial k} = \delta > 0 \quad \text{when } \dot{q} = 0. \tag{75}$$

Drawing these considerations together, we find that the locus $\dot{k} = 0$ consists of the q axis and a continuous, piecewise smooth curve with an end point at $k = 0$, $q = q_0$. This curve will be vertical in patterns IC, IIC, IIIC, and positively sloped in pattern IB. In patterns IIB and IIIB, the slope may change sign, but when $\dot{q} = 0$ it is negative in pattern IIIB and has the same sign as $k_C - k_I$ in pattern IIB. Above this curve and to the left of its vertical section, $\dot{k} > 0$, below and to the right, $\dot{k} < 0$. (See Figures 6 through 9.)

In all possible cases, there exists a unique intersection of $\dot{k} = 0$ and $\dot{q} = 0$. Let us denote it by $k = k^*$, $q = q^*$. Regardless of whether this intersection is in pattern IB, IIB, or IIIB, it is a saddle point. Thus, there are two trajectories that converge to (k^*, q^*); one from $k < k^*$, $q \geq q^*$, and the other from $k > k^*$, $q \leq q^*$. These two trajectories form a monotonic nonincreasing curve $q = \tilde{q}(k)$.

It is easy to show that $\tilde{q}(k)$ is positive and finite for all $k > 0$. Any trajectory above $\tilde{q}(k)$ approaches the maximum sustainable capital-labor ratio $\bar{k}$, where $(\dot{q}/q) > \delta$. Along such a trajectory, $\lim_{t \to \infty} e^{-\delta t} q(t) = \infty$, which violates Equation 23. Along any trajectory below $\tilde{q}(k)$, $k \to 0$, $q \to -\infty$. In particular, once q becomes negative, $(\dot{q}/q) > \lambda + \delta$ so that $\lim_{t \to \infty} e^{-\delta t} q(t) = -\infty$, again violating Equation 23. Along the trajectory $q = \tilde{q}(k)$, $q \to q^*$, so that $\lim_{t \to \infty} e^{-\delta t} q(t) = 0$. Thus, $q = \tilde{q}(k)$ is the only trajectory satisfying the terminal condition of Equation 23. Applying the initial condition of Equation 23, we determine a unique time path $k(t)$, $q(t)$ for which

$$\begin{aligned} k(0) &= k_0, \quad q(0) = \tilde{q}(k_0), \\ \dot{k}(t) &= x_I[k(t), q(t)] - \lambda k(t), \\ q(t) &= \tilde{q}[k(t)], \\ k(\infty) &= k^*, \quad q(\infty) = q^*. \end{aligned} \tag{76}$$

6. Proof of Optimality

We have shown that the Pontryagin necessary conditions determine a unique time path $k(t)$ for any initial condition $k(0) = k_0$. It remains to prove that this solution is indeed optimal. Let us denote by $k^0(t)$, $q^0(t)$, $x_I^0(t)$, $x_C^0(t)$ the trajectory satisfying Equations 76 where $x_I^0(t) = x_I[k^0(t), q^0(t)]$, $x_C^0(t) = x_C[k^0(t), q^0(t)]$. Let $k^1(t)$, $x_I^1(t)$, $x_C^1(t)$ be an arbitrary trajectory satisfying Equations 11, 12, 14, 16, and

$$k^1(0) = k_0, \quad k^1(t) \leq \max(k_0, \tilde{k}) \qquad \text{for all } t \geq 0. \tag{77}$$

Let us define

$$\psi[k, x_I, x_C, q, t] \equiv e^{-\delta t}[x_C + q(x_I - \lambda k - \dot{k})]. \tag{78}$$

First, we shall prove the following *lemma*.

For all trajectories $k^1(t)$, $x_I^1(t)$, $x_C^1(t)$ satisfying the above conditions,

$$\int_0^\infty \psi[k^0(t), x_I^0(t), x_C^0(t), q^0(t), t] \, dt$$
$$\geq \int_0^\infty \psi[k^1(t), x_I^1(t), x_C^1(t), q^0(t), t] \, dt. \tag{79}$$

Proof: Since $x_C(k, q) + qx_I(k, q)$ maximizes $x_C + qx_I$ with respect to k_I, k_C, z_I for all k, q, we have

$$\psi[k^1, x_I(k^1, q^0), x_C(k^1, q^0), q^0, t] \geq \psi(k^1, x_I^1, x_C^1, q^0, t)$$

for all $t \geq 0$. Thus,

$$\int_0^\infty \psi[k^1, x_I(k^1, q^0), x_C(k^1, q^0), q^0, t] \, dt \geq \int_0^\infty \psi(k^1, x_I^1, x_C^1, q^0, t) \, dt.$$

Now it suffices to show that

$$\int_0^\infty \psi(k^0, x_I^0, x_C^0, q^0, t) \, dt \geq \int_0^\infty \psi[k^1, x_I(k^1, q^0), x_C(k^1, q^0), q^0, t] \, dt. \tag{80}$$

For $0 \leq \xi \leq 1$ let us define

$$\alpha(\xi) = \int_0^\infty \psi(k^0, x_I^0, x_C^0, q^0, t) - \psi[k^\xi, x_I(k^\xi, q^0), x_C(k^\xi, q^0), q^0, t] \, dt \tag{81}$$

where

$$\begin{aligned} k^\xi(t) &= (1 - \xi)k^0(t) + \xi k^1(t), \\ \dot{k}^\xi(t) &= (1 - \xi)\dot{k}^0(t) + \xi \dot{k}^1(t). \end{aligned} \tag{82}$$

Then

$$\alpha'(\xi) = -\int_0^\infty \frac{\partial}{\partial \xi} \psi[k^\xi, x_I(k^\xi, q^0), x_C(k^\xi, q^0), q^0, t] \, dt \tag{83}$$

$$= -\int_0^\infty e^{-\delta t} \left[(k^1 - k^0) \frac{\partial}{\partial k} x(k^\xi, q^0) - q^0 \lambda (k^1 - k^0) - q^0(\dot{k}^1 - \dot{k}^0) \right] dt.$$

$$\alpha''(\xi) = -\int_0^\infty e^{-t}(k^1 - k^0)^2 \frac{\partial^2}{\partial k^2} x(k^\xi, q^0) \, dt.$$

By Table 7, we see that $(\partial^2/\partial k^2)x \leq 0$ for all (k, q). Therefore,

$$\alpha''(\xi) \geq 0 \qquad \text{for } 0 \leq \xi \leq 1. \tag{84}$$

Setting $\xi = 0$ in Equation 83 we obtain

$$\alpha'(0) = -\int_0^\infty e^{-\delta t} \left\{ \left[\frac{\partial}{\partial k} x(k^0, q^0) - \lambda q^0 \right] (k^1 - k^0) - q^0(\dot{k}^1 - \dot{k}^0) \right\} dt$$

$$= \int_0^\infty e^{-\delta t} [(\dot{q}^0 - \delta q^0)(k^1 - k^0) + q^0(\dot{k}^1 - \dot{k}^0)] \, dt$$

$$= e^{-\delta t} q^0(t)[k^1(t) - k^0(t)]|_0^\infty.$$

For $t = 0$, we have $q^0(0) = \tilde{q}(k_0) < \infty$, $k^1(0) = k^0(0) = k_0 > 0$. For $t = \infty$, we have $q^0(\infty) = q^*$, $k^0(\infty) = k^*$, $k^1(\infty) \leq \max(k_0, \tilde{k})$. Therefore,

$$\alpha'(0) = 0. \tag{85}$$

By Equations 84 and 85, we have

$$\alpha(1) \geq \alpha(0) = 0. \tag{86}$$

But Equation 86 is equivalent to Equation 80 and the lemma is proved.

In addition to the conditions of the lemma, every feasible trajectory must satisfy Equation 15. This fact gives us the following *theorem*.

The trajectory k^0, q^0, x_I^0, x_C^0 is optimal.

Proof: Substituting Equation 15 into Equation 78,

$$\psi[k(t), x_I(t), x_C(t), q(t), t] = e^{-\delta t} x_C(t) \tag{87}$$

for all feasible trajectories. Substituting Equation 87 into Equation 79,

$$\int_0^\infty e^{-\delta t} x_C^0(t) \, dt \geq \int_0^\infty e^{-\delta t} x_C^1(t) \, dt.$$

But k^1, x_I^1, x_C^1 may be any feasible trajectory. Therefore, k^0, x_I^0, x_C^0 is optimal, and the theorem is proved.

7. The Nature of the Optimal Path

Within the framework of this model, it is possible to determine the optimal growth path quantitatively, given quantitative assumptions on the forms of the functions $f_I(k_I)$, $f_C(k_C)$, and $\theta(z_I)$ and on the values of μ, n, δ, and k_0.

The qualitative nature of the optimal path will be strongly influenced by the configuration of patterns, but a few generalizations may be indicated. If the initial stock of capital k_0 is quite low, the optimal policy will be to specialize in the absorption of capital goods (that is, consume nothing, invest everything). Whether this should be achieved by autarky (specialization in the production of capital goods with no trade), international specialization (specialization in the production of the consumption good, all of which is traded for the capital good), or by partial international specialization (both goods produced, but all consumption goods traded for capital goods) is essentially a static question, to be determined at each instant by the relative marginal rates of transformation in production and in trade.

During an initial period of austerity, capital will be accumulated at the maximum possible rate until some critical capital-labor ratio is reached. Beyond this point, consumption will (in general) be gradually increased until we approach the stationary values k^*, q^*.

On the other hand, if the initial stock of capital is very high, the optimal policy will begin by emphasizing consumption, which will (in general) be gradually reduced as we approach the stationary values k^*, q^* from above.

8. Modification of Technical Assumptions

Now that we have completed the basic analysis, we can relax or modify some of the convenient assumptions made earlier.

If there are a finite number of reversals of factor intensities, we can break up the k-axis into segments within which no reversals occur. For each such segment, our analysis holds without modification. At any point of reversal, we have $k_I(\hat{\omega}) = k_C(\hat{\omega}) = \hat{k}$, $\hat{q} = p(\hat{\omega})$. Here we can no longer define $\breve{y}_I(\hat{k}, \hat{q})$, $\breve{y}_C(\hat{k}, \hat{q})$ by Equations 38. Instead we set

$$\breve{y}_I(\hat{k}, q) \equiv s(q)f_I(\hat{k}),$$
$$\breve{y}_C(\hat{k}, q) \equiv [1 - s(q)]f_C(\hat{k}), \tag{88}$$

where $s(q)$ is an upper-semicontinuous mapping defined by

$$s(q) = 1 \quad \text{if} \quad q > \hat{q},$$
$$s(q) = 0 \quad \text{if} \quad q < \hat{q}, \tag{89}$$
$$0 \le s(q) \le 1 \quad \text{if} \quad q = \hat{q}.$$

Although $\breve{y}_I$ and $\breve{y}_C$ are discontinuous at $\hat{k}$, $\hat{q}$, yet $y = \breve{y}_C(k, q) + q\breve{y}_I(k, q)$ is continuous, as is $\partial y/\partial k$.

Hence, $\partial x/\partial k$ and $\dot{q}$ are continuous. In general, the chances are good that the optimal trajectory will miss this point entirely, or if not, that it will not be the stationary point. If the optimal path does pass through this point, the continuity of $\dot{q}$ will prevent our tarrying there. Then, there is only a single point of time for which k is not uniquely determined. Thus, $k(t) = \int_0^t k \, dt + k_0$ is unaffected. If, however, we have

$$\dot{q}(\hat{k}, \hat{q}) = 0,$$
$$k(\hat{k}, \hat{q}_+) > 0 > k(\hat{k}, \hat{q}_-),$$

$$(90)$$

then $\hat{k}$, $\hat{q}$ is the stationary point k^*, q^* and $s^*(q^*)$ is uniquely determined by the condition $k(k^*, q^*) = 0$. In this exceptional case, the approach to k^*, q^* will not be gradual as previously described. Instead the optimal trajectory will reach the stationary point in a finite amount of time, and investment will then be suddenly shifted to the level that will maintain the capital-labor ratio k^*. If $\hat{k}$, $\hat{q}$ lies on the optimal trajectory but is not the stationary point, there will be a sudden shift in the levels of investment and consumption, after which the gradual approach to k^*, q^* is resumed.

The usual discussions of the Marshallian offer curve suggest that as the international price rises, the excess supply of the rest of the world for the investment good will rise. In our model, the international price is represented as

$$q_f = -\frac{\theta(z_I)}{z_I}.$$

But

$$\frac{dq_f}{dz_I} = \frac{\theta(z_I) - z_I\theta'(z_I)}{z_I^2} > 0$$

is a necessary but not a sufficient condition for $\theta''(z_I) < 0$. Therefore, it may be useful to consider the case where θ is not a strictly concave function. Then Equation 24 no longer has a unique solution for all values of q. However, the more basic condition of Equation 20, from which Equation 24 is derived, does determine the value of z_I and z_C within a limited range, while $x(k, q)$ and $\partial x/\partial k$ are determined uniquely and continuously. Except for prices $\hat{q}$ where $\breve{z}_I(\hat{q}_+) > \breve{z}_I(\hat{q}_-)$, $\breve{z}_C(\hat{q}_+) < \breve{z}_C(\hat{q}_-)$, the optimal trajectory does not differ from that already discussed. If $\hat{q} \neq q^*$, we shall have $\dot{q} \neq 0$ at that point. Then, the values of y_I and y_C will be uniquely determined except for one point of time, and the value of $k(t)$ is not affected by the choice of y_I, y_C at that point.

However, if $\hat{q} = q^*$, we are in trouble, since there may not exist a stationary solution. Here

$$\dot{q}(k^*, q^*) = 0,$$

$$\dot{k}(k^*, q_+^*) > 0 > \dot{k}(k^*, q_-^*). \tag{91}$$

In this case there is no optimal trajectory.

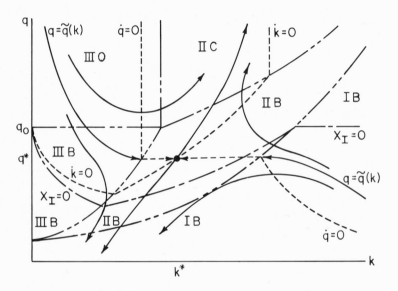

FIGURE 10. Optimal paths when gross disinvestment is permitted.

If we wish to modify the nonnegativity restrictions of Equation 14, this can be done with no trouble at all. The restriction $x_I \geq 0$ says that once an investment good has been installed domestically, it cannot be removed and exported. The removal of this restriction causes pattern A to disappear. In those regions of the k, q plane where pattern A held, we shall now have $x_I < 0$, $z_I < -y_I$. The functions $x_I(k, q)$, $x_C(k, q)$ will be defined in this region exactly as they are in pattern B. This modification will be irrelevant to any optimal trajectory beginning with $k_0 \leq k^*$. (See Figure 10.)

In recognition of the fact that the population cannot survive, let alone grow and work, unless some minimum amount of consumption is provided, we may wish to replace $x_C \geq 0$ by $x_C \geq w_{min}$ where w_{min} represents the minimum level of subsistence. This does not significantly alter the analysis. The region of the k, q plane where pattern C holds will be slightly enlarged and will no longer be characterized by complete specialization in the absorption of the investment good. Instead we shall have $x_C = w_{min}$ in pattern C. The optimal trajectory for a small k_0 will now imply an initial period during which consumption is held to a minimum, followed by a gradual rise as the stationary solution is approached. But if k_0 is so small that $x_C = w_{min}$ implies $\dot{k} < 0$, there is no feasible trajectory (optimal or otherwise). If w_{min} is a rigid minimum subsistence level, the economy is forced into a Malthusian trap that lies outside the assumptions of this model. (See Figure 11.)

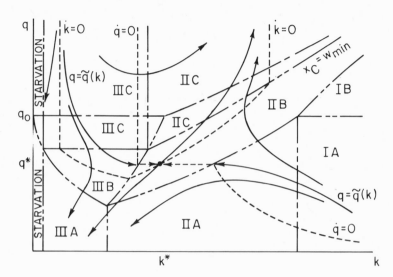

FIGURE 11. Optimal paths when consumption cannot fall below the subsistence level.

Exogenous technical progress of the Harrod-neutral type can easily be introduced into the model. The production function of the i-sector becomes:

$$F_i(K_i, e^{at}L_i), \qquad i = I, C.$$

We shall assume that the Marshallian offer curve is growing exponentially at the same rate $a + n$ as the effective labor force of the home country. The per capita quantities defined by Equation 9 are replaced by effective per capita quantities

$$k(t) = \frac{K(t)}{e^{at}L(t)}, \quad k_i(t) = \frac{K_i(t)}{e^{at}L_i(t)},$$

$$y(t) = \frac{Y(t)}{e^{at}L(t)}, \quad y_i(t) = \frac{Y_i(t)}{e^{at}L_i(t)},$$

$$x(t) = \frac{X(t)}{e^{at}L(t)}, \quad x_i(t) = \frac{X_i(t)}{e^{at}L_i(t)},$$

$$z_i(t) = \frac{Z_i(t)}{e^{at}L(t)}, \qquad i = I, C.$$

(9a)

The criterion functional becomes:

$$V[k(\cdot)] = \int_0^\infty e^{-\delta t} u[e^{at} x_C(t)] \, dt, \tag{17a}$$

or for a linear utility function

$$V_0[k(\cdot)] = \int_0^\infty e^{-(\delta - a)t} x_C(t) \, dt. \tag{18a}$$

In order that V_0 converge, it is necessary that

$$\delta > a.$$

The dynamic behavior of the shadow price of capital becomes

$$\dot{q} = (\delta - a + \lambda)q - \frac{\partial}{\partial k} x(k, q). \tag{22a}$$

Let us denote the stationary solution corresponding to the rate of technical progress a by $(k_a{}^*, q_a{}^*)$. Then, $(\delta - a + \lambda)q_0{}^* - (\partial/\partial k)x(k_0{}^*, q_0{}^*) = -aq_0{}^* < 0$. Since $(\partial/\partial k)\dot{q} \geq 0$, the curve $\dot{q} = 0|_{a>0}$ lies to the right of the curve $\dot{q} = 0|_{a=0}$. Thus $k_a{}^* > k_0{}^*$. That is, the stationary capital-effective labor ratio will be higher when there is technical progress than when there is not.

9. Concave Criterion Functional

Having solved our problem for the simple criterion function (Equation 18), let us examine how this analysis must be modified for the more general criterion

$$V[k(\cdot)] = \int_0^\infty e^{-\delta t} u[x_C(t)] \, dt. \tag{17}$$

The Pontryagin expression (Equation 19) now becomes

$$\Pi(k_I, k_C, z_I; k, p) = u(x_C) + p(x_I - \lambda k). \tag{92}$$

By Equation 20, x_C and x_I must be on the absorption frontier, which is traced out by $x_C(k, q)$, $x_I(k, q)$ as defined by Tables 2, 3, 4, and 5. Then Equation 20 implies

$$\frac{\partial \Pi}{\partial q} = u'(x_C) \frac{\partial x_C}{\partial q} + p \frac{\partial x_I}{\partial q} = 0. \tag{93}$$

This equation is satisfied when $q = p/u'[x_C(k, q)]$. The necessary conditions of optimality now become

$$qu'[x_C(k, q)] = p. \tag{94}$$

$$\dot{k} = x_I(k, q) - \lambda k. \tag{95}$$

$$\dot{p} = (\lambda + \delta)p - u'[x_C(k, q)] \frac{\partial}{\partial k} x_C(k, q) - p \frac{\partial}{\partial k} x_I(k, q)$$

(96)

$$= u'[x_C(k, q)] \left[(\lambda + \delta)q - \frac{\partial}{\partial k} x(k, q) \right].$$

$$k(0) = k_0, \quad \lim_{t \to \infty} e^{-\delta t} p(t) = 0.$$

(97)

Since the left-hand side of Equation 94 is a monotonically increasing function of q, we can invert it to obtain q as a function of p. As q increases to the upper boundary of pattern B, $x_C \to 0$, $u'(x_C) \to \infty$. Hence, pattern C is eliminated from consideration. In pattern A, we have $u'(x_C)$ as a function of k only, so that q and p are proportional.

Comparing Equations 95 and 96 to Equations 21 and 22, we see that $\dot{k}$ is unchanged as a function of k and q and that the sign of $\dot{q}$ under the linear criterion is the same as the sign of $\dot{p}$ under the concave criterion for any value of k and q. Thus, the loci $\dot{k} = 0$ and $\dot{p} = 0$ coincide with the earlier loci $\dot{k} = 0$ and $\dot{q} = 0$.

Before we can complete the phase diagram, we must determine the form of the loci representing a constant value of p. We have from Equation 94:

$$\left[u'(x_C) + qu''(x_C) \frac{\partial x_C}{\partial q} \right] dq + qu''(x_C) \frac{\partial x_C}{\partial k} dk = dp.$$

(98)

Holding $dp = 0$, we obtain

$$\left. \frac{\partial q}{\partial k} \right|_{p \text{ const}} = - \frac{qu''(x_C)(\partial x_C / \partial k)}{u'(x_C) + qu''(x_C)(\partial x_C / \partial q)} \sim \frac{\partial x_C}{\partial k}.$$

(99)

From Tables 3 and 5, we see that

$$\frac{\partial x_C}{\partial k} > 0 \qquad \text{in patterns IA, IIA, IIIA, IB.}$$

$$\frac{\partial x_C}{\partial k} = 0 \qquad \text{in pattern IIIB.}$$

$$\frac{\partial x_C}{\partial k} \sim k_C - k_I \qquad \text{in pattern IIB.}$$

(See Figure 12.)

As before, there is a unique stationary point—a saddle point. In fact, it is the same k^*, q^* as the stationary point we found under linear utility. We can show that there is a unique trajectory that converges to the stationary point. All other trajectories violate Equation 97, so that this trajectory is the only one satisfying all necessary conditions. The proof in section 6 can easily be modified to show that this trajectory is optimal. (See Figure 13.)

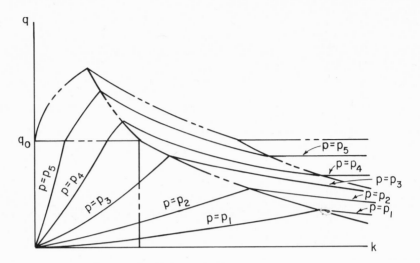

FIGURE 12. Loci of constant p when the utility function is concave.

The optimal path under concave utility converges to the same stationary state as the optimal path under linear utility. For every value of $k < k^*$, more is consumed under concave utility. In particular, there is no initial period of extreme austerity. Therefore, the approach to the stationary state is slower under concave utility.

The various modifications of technical assumptions discussed in the

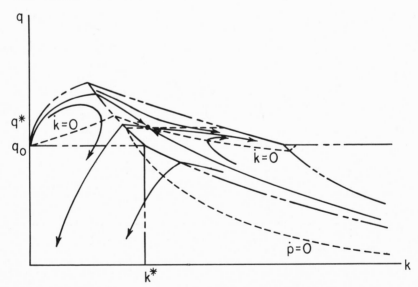

FIGURE 13. Optimal paths when the utility function is concave.

previous section can also be made under concave utility and do not in general present any difficulties. In the case of Harrod-neutral technical progress, however, it is convenient to confine our attention to the Cobb-Douglas utility function

$$u(x_C) = \frac{x_C^{1-b}}{1-b}, \qquad b > 0, b \neq 1,$$
$$u(x_C) = \log x_C, \qquad b = 1.$$
$$(100)$$

Then Expression 17a becomes

$$V[k(\cdot)] = \int_0^\infty e^{-\delta t} u[e^{at} x_C(t)] \, dt$$
$$= \int_0^\infty e^{-\delta t} e^{(1-b)at} u[x_C(t)] \, dt$$
$$(17b)$$

which converges when

$$\delta > (1 - b)a.$$

The dynamic behavior of the marginal utility of capital is now

$$\dot{p} = u'[x_C(k, q)]\left\{[\lambda + \delta - (1 - b)a]q - \frac{\partial}{\partial k} x(k, q)\right\}. \qquad (96a)$$

The effect of technical progress now depends on $-b$, the elasticity of marginal utility. When $0 < b < 1$, the effect of technical progress is to increase the stationary capital-effective labor ratio, but by less than it would be increased under a linear utility function ($b = 0$). When $b > 1$, the stationary capital-effective labor ratio is reduced. For a given, positive rate of technical progress, the effect of making marginal utility more elastic (increasing b) is to reduce the stationary capital-effective labor ratio.

References

1. Bardhan, P. K., "Optimum Accumulation and International Trade," *Review of Economic Studies*, Vol. 32 (1965), pp. 241–244.
2. Canitrot, A. M., "Patterns of Foreign Trade and Investment in a Growing Economy," dissertation, Stanford University, Stanford, Calif., 1965.
3. Diamond, P. A., "The Evaluation of Infinite Utility Streams," *Econometrica*, Vol. 33 (1965), pp. 170–177.
4. Goldman, S. M., "Economic Growth and International Trade: A Study in the Theory of Economic Development," dissertation, Stanford University, Stanford, Calif., 1966.
5. Goldman, S. M., H. E. Ryder, and H. Uzawa, "Optimum Patterns of Trade and Investment in a Two-Sector Model of International Trade," Technical Report No. 7, NSF: GS-420, Department of Economics, University of Chicago, Chicago, Ill., January 20, 1965.

6. Koopmans, T. C., "Stationary Ordinal Utility and Impatience," *Econometrica*, Vol. 28 (1960), pp. 287–309.
7. Koopmans, T. C., P. A. Diamond, and R. E. Williamson, "Stationary Utility and Time Perspective," *Econometrica*, Vol. 32 (1964), pp. 82–100.
8. Pontryagin, L. S., *et al.*, *The Mathematical Theory of Optimal Processes*, New York and London: Interscience Publishers, Inc., 1962.
9. Ryder, H. E., "Optimal Patterns of Foreign Trade and Investment in a Two-Sector Model of Capital Accumulation, II," Technical Report No. 8, NSF: GS-420, Department of Economics, University of Chicago, Chicago, Ill., January 30, 1965.
10. Srinivasan, T. N., "Optimal Savings in a Two-Sector Model of Growth," *Econometrica*, Vol. 32 (1964), pp. 358–373.
11. Strotz, R. H., "Myopia and Inconsistency in Dynamic Utility Maximization," *Review of Economic Studies*, Vol. 23 (1956), pp. 165–180.
12. Uzawa, H., "Optimal Growth in a Two-Sector Model of Capital Accumulation," *Review of Economic Studies*, Vol. 31 (1964), pp. 1–24.

VI

Optimum Foreign Borrowing[1]

PRANAB K. BARDHAN
Massachusetts Institute of Technology

The problem of optimum foreign borrowing or lending has usually been discussed in terms of a static model.[2] In this essay we analyze the problem of borrowing in the context of an intertemporal optimization model.[3] (Analogous reasoning is applicable if we choose to look at the problem from the point of view of a lending country.)

In order to pose the problem of borrowing in its simplest form, we assume that there is only one homogeneous commodity (consumable as well as accumulatable) in this world, so that there is no international trade.[4] Our country borrows from an international capital market that is imperfect, so that its extent of borrowing can influence the rate of interest at which it

---

[1] I am indebted to Sanjit Bose, Lionel McKenzie, and Harl Ryder for helpful discussion. Errors are, of course, mine.

[2] See, e.g., MacDougall [8], and Kemp [5], Chapter 14.

[3] In a recent paper [2] we considered the problem of optimum investment in an open economy in terms of a two-sector Ramsey model, but there we assumed away foreign investment and borrowing. In [1], Chapter 6, section IV, however, we discussed a Ramsey model of optimum foreign investment. Very recently we have come across a similar, and independent, analysis of the same problem in Hamada [4]. This essay may be regarded as a generalization of the results in [1] and [4].

[4] This is an enormous simplification. Any reader of [1], Chapter 7, Pearce and Rowan [9], and Kemp [6] knows how complicated the analysis becomes as soon as one introduces international trade and takes into account the effect of foreign investment on terms of trade.

117

borrows. With full employment, of the total amount of capital used in the home country K, a part is domestically owned K_d and the rest is foreign capital K_f. If we use lower-case letters to indicate per capita quantities,

$$k = k_d + k_f. \tag{1}$$

Per capita national income y in this model is given by

$$y = f(k) - r(k_f) \cdot k_f, \tag{2}$$

where $f(k)$ gives the functional relationship between output per capita and the amount of capital used per capita under conditions of constant returns to scale, and r, the rate of interest in the international capital market, is assumed to be an increasing function of the amount of foreign capital *per capita*[5] in the home country, so that $r'(k_f) > 0$.

The following is assumed about the production function:

$$f'(k) > 0, \quad f''(k) < 0,$$
$$f(0) = 0, \quad f'(0) = \infty, \tag{3}$$
$$f(\infty) = \infty, \quad f'(\infty) = 0.$$

It is assumed that there is an upper bound γ on the amount of k_f, with $r(\gamma) = \infty$, and that our home country at any moment of time either borrows from abroad or does not but never *lends* abroad (this is only a simplification), so that we may say

$$\gamma > k_f \geq 0. \tag{4}$$

By borrowing an extra unit of capital per capita we raise our *total* cost of borrowing by $\phi(k_f) \equiv r'(k_f)k_f + r > 0$. We assume, as in [1] and [4], that this marginal cost of per capita borrowing is an *increasing* function of the amount of per capita borrowing so that

$$\phi'(k_f) > 0. \tag{5}$$

The domestic accumulation equation is given by

$$k_d = s \cdot y - \mu \cdot k_d \quad \text{with } 1 > s \geq 0,[6] \tag{6}$$

where μ is the constant rate of growth of population, s is the savings ratio, and capital depreciation is ignored (depreciation at a fixed percentage rate could be easily taken care of).

---

[5] This, of course, implies some rate of growth in the availability of capital in the international capital market. If one wishes to take the case when r is a function of only the absolute amount of borrowing K_f, the subsequent analysis will remain essentially unchanged.

[6] Here $s = 1$ is ruled out by our later assumption of $\lim_{c \to 0} U'(c) = \infty$.

Per capita consumption c, as well as per capita domestic investment, is supposed to satisfy the usual nonnegativity constraints so that

$$c \geq 0 \quad \text{and} \quad k_d + \mu \cdot k_d \geq 0.$$

The social welfare function is given by[7]

$$V(c, k_f) = U(c) - D(k_f), \tag{7}$$

where $U(c)$ is the social utility of per capita consumption and $D(k_f)$ is the social *disutility* of having foreign capital in one's country.

The social objective is, in the fashion of Ramsey, to *minimize* over the infinite horizon the integral of the *shortfall* of the actual rate of social welfare from the *maximum sustainable level* of such welfare, that is, to minimize

$$\int_0^\infty [\hat{V} - V(c, k_f)] \, dt,$$

where $\hat{V}$ is the social welfare rate corresponding to the golden rule path.[8]

If, without loss of generality, we assume $\hat{V} = 0$, then our problem is to maximize

$$\int_0^\infty V(c, k_f) \, dt. \tag{8}$$

The following is assumed about $U(c)$ and $D(k_f)$:

$$U'(c) > 0, \qquad U''(c) < 0,$$

$$U'(0) = \infty,$$

$$D'(k_f) > 0, \qquad D''(k_f) > 0, \tag{9}$$

$$D'(0) = 0, \qquad D'(\gamma) < \infty.$$

---

[7] Our welfare function is slightly unconventional, but we think it is also slightly more realistic. You can call it extreme nationalism if you like, but it is a fact of life that many borrowing countries do derive some kind of disutility from their dependence on foreign capital: this is one of the reasons why self-sufficiency with respect to foreign investment is one of the major, ambitious goals of long-term planning in many poor countries. The problem is, of course, more serious in the case of equity capital, but even in the case of loan capital it is not nonexistent.

A separable form of the welfare function $V(c, k_f)$ is taken, first, because of convenience —a nonseparable $V(c, k_f)$ might easily lead to multiplicity of stationary solutions to our fundamental differential equations—and second, because it is difficult to give economic meaning to any assumed sign of the cross-partial derivatives of the function $V(c, k_f)$.

[8] This is to use the well-known Ramsey-Koopmans-Weizsäcker trick to make the limit of the welfare integral convergent. For detailed explanation, see Koopmans [7] and Phelps [10].

One of the implications of Conditions 9 is that while the utility function of consumption is concave, marginal disutility from the existence of foreign capital *increases* as the per capita amount of foreign capital increases ("extreme nationalism" once again!).

By applying Pontryagin's maximum principle [11] to the Hamiltonian representing the imputed value of national product, which is

$$H = U[(1 - s)y] - D(k_f) + \lambda(sy - \mu k_d),$$ (10)

with λ being the imputed price of a unit of domestic investment per head, we get the following conditions:

$$\dot{\lambda} = -\frac{\partial H}{\partial k_a} = -[U'(1 - s) + \lambda s]f'(k) + \mu\lambda,$$ (11)

$$\frac{\partial H}{\partial s} = -U'y + \lambda y \begin{cases} = 0, & \text{if } 1 > s > 0, \text{ in which case } \lambda = U'(c), \\ < 0, & \text{if } s = 0, \text{ in which case } \lambda < U'(y), \end{cases}$$ (12)

$$\frac{\partial H}{\partial k_f} = [(1 - s)U'(c + \lambda s)][f'(k) - \phi(k_f)] - D'(k_f) \begin{cases} = 0 & \text{if } k_f > 0, \\ < 0 & \text{if } k_f = 0. \end{cases}$$ (13)

We shall analyze the implications of these equations for three possible types of initial conditions: 1 $\mu > r(0) > 0$; (2) $r(0) > \mu > 0$; and (3) $\mu = r(0) > 0$, where $r(0)$ is the rate of interest in the international capital market when the home country is not a borrower (nor a lender).

1. The Case when $\mu > r(0) > 0$

Under this case let us first take the region of "nonspecialization" where $1 > s > 0$. It immediately follows from Equations 11 and 12 that

$$\dot{\lambda} = -\lambda[f'(k) - \mu],$$ (11a)

$$\lambda = U'(c).$$ (12a)

We shall now try to characterize the $\dot{\lambda} = 0$ curve. It is easy to prove that under our condition (1), this curve cannot belong to a region where $k_f = 0$. The proof is as follows: if $k_f = 0$, then from Equations 11a and 13 it must be true that

$$f'(k) - r(0) < 0,$$ (14)

since $\phi(0) = r(0)$; and, from Conditions 9, $U'(c) > 0$ and $D'(0) = 0$. But it follows from Equation 11a that along the $\dot{\lambda} = 0$ curve

$$f'(k) = \mu > r(0).$$ (15)

Thus if Expression 15 is valid, Expression 14 cannot be valid and k_f cannot be equal to zero. Since we have assumed away lending by the home country, the curve $\dot{\lambda} = 0$ must belong, under our conditions, to the region where $k_f > 0$. When $k_f > 0$, from Equations 13 and 12a,

$$\lambda[f'(k) - \phi(k_f)] - D'(k_f) = 0. \tag{13a}$$

From Equation 13a,

$$f'(k) - r(k_f) = \frac{D'(k_f)}{U'(c)} + r'(k_f)k_f > 0. \tag{16}$$

Equation 16 has an immediate policy conclusion: borrowing from abroad, if left to private borrowers, tends to be excessive. "Atomistic" private borrowers will fail to take account of the fact that an increase in the extent of (per capita) borrowing for the country as a whole raises the *total* cost of borrowing against it, and they are more likely to ignore the increase in disutility for the nation as a whole from extra borrowing: they would go on borrowing until the marginal product of capital at home is equal to the rate of interest (the average market cost of borrowing) in the international capital market, which is an inefficient solution for the borrowing country, as Equation 16 suggests. Private borrowers, left to themselves, thus tend to overborrow (unless they are few in numbers and, therefore, *individually* capable of influencing the world rate of interest and unless they are extremely socially conscious and nationalistic). There is here a clear case for an income tax on earnings from borrowed capital.[9] This is an atemporal efficiency condition of such borrowing models, just as the optimum-tariff argument is in usual trade models.

From Equation 16 it can easily be worked out, through differentiation of the implicit function, that

$$\left.\frac{dk_f}{dk_d}\right|_{\lambda \text{ const}} < 0, \tag{17a}$$

the absolute value of $\left.\dfrac{dk_f}{dk_d}\right|_{\lambda \text{ const}}$ is less than unity, $\qquad$ (17b)

and

$$\left.\frac{dk_f}{d\lambda}\right|_{k_d \text{ const}} > 0. \tag{17c}$$

In getting Inequalities 17a, 17b, and 17c we have used Conditions 5, 9, and 13a.

Now in Equation 11a,

$$\frac{\partial \dot{\lambda}}{\partial k_d} = \frac{-\lambda \cdot f''(k)\left(1 + \left.\dfrac{dk_f}{dk_d}\right|_{\lambda \text{ const}}\right)}{U''(c)[f''(k) - \phi'(k_f)] - D''(k_f)} > 0, \tag{18a}$$

---

[9] One can work out, from Equation 16, the formula for the optimum income tax rate with the help of the following equation: $f'(k) \cdot [1 - \tau] = r(k_f)$, where τ is the tax rate.

which follows from Conditions 5, 9, 12*a*, 17*a*, and 17*b*; and

$$\frac{\partial \dot{\lambda}}{\partial \lambda} = -\lambda \cdot f''(k) \cdot \frac{dk_f}{d\lambda}\bigg|_{k_d \text{ const}} > 0, \tag{18b}$$

which follows from Equations 9, 12*a*, and 17*c*. From Equations 11*a*, 18*a*, and 18*b*,

$$\frac{d\lambda}{dk_d}\bigg|_{\dot{\lambda}=0} < 0. \tag{18}$$

Inequality 18 implies that the $\dot{\lambda} = 0$ curve is downward sloping in the (k_d, λ) plane in the region where $1 > s > 0$ and $\mu > r(0) > 0$. Now from the equation for per capita income we know that

$$\dot{k}_d = f(k) - r(k_f) \cdot k_f - \mu \cdot k_d - c. \tag{19}$$

Let us try to find out the shape of the $\dot{k}_d = 0$ curve. From Equation 19,

$$\frac{\partial \dot{k}_d}{\partial \lambda} = -\frac{1}{U''(c)} + [f'(k) - \phi(k_f)] \cdot \frac{dk_f}{d\lambda}\bigg|_{k_d \text{ const}} > 0; \tag{20a}$$

where Conditions 9, 12*a*, 13*a*, and 17*c* are used,

$$\frac{\partial \dot{k}_d}{\partial k_d} = [f'(k) - \mu] + [f'(k) - \phi(k_f)] \cdot \frac{dk_f}{dk_d}\bigg|_{\lambda \text{ const}}. \tag{20b}$$

In view of Conditions 9, 13*a*, and 17*a*, it is difficult to be sure of the sign of $\partial \dot{k}_d / \partial k_d$. From Equation 11*a*, however, $f'(k) = \mu$ when $\dot{\lambda} = 0$, and hence at the intersection of the $\dot{k}_d = 0$ and $\dot{\lambda} = 0$ curves, $(\partial \dot{k}_d / \partial k_d) < 0$, which means, with Equations 19 and 20*a*, that at the point of stationary solution of the two differential Equations, 19 and 11*a*,

$$\frac{d\lambda}{dk_d}\bigg|_{\dot{k}_d=0}^{*} > 0, \qquad \text{where * denotes the stationary solution.}$$

Since for $k_d > k_d{}^*, f'(k) < \mu$, we have

$$\frac{d\lambda}{dk_d}\bigg|_{\dot{k}_d=0} > 0;$$

that is, $\dot{k}_d = 0$ is an upward sloping curve[10] in the (k_d, λ) plane for $k_d \geq k_d{}^*$. We are not sure of the sign of

$$\frac{d\lambda}{dk_d}\bigg|_{\dot{k}_d=0} \qquad \text{for the range } k_d < k_d{}^*.$$

---

[10] The $\dot{k}_d = 0$ curve is upward sloping for $k_d > k_d{}^*$ even when $k_f = 0$: this can be easily checked.

Figure 1 depicts the $\dot{\lambda} = 0$ and $\dot{k}_d = 0$ curves. Expanding the two differential Equations 11a and 19 around the point $(k_d{}^*, \lambda^*)$, it is easily shown that the characteristic roots of the resulting linear system are given by

$$\pm \sqrt{\left[\frac{\partial \dot{k}_d}{\partial k_d}\bigg|^*\right]^2 + \frac{\partial \dot{k}_d}{\partial \lambda}\bigg|^* \cdot \frac{\partial \dot{\lambda}}{\partial k_d}\bigg|^*}$$

which are real and opposite in sign. Hence $(k_d{}^*, \lambda^*)$ is a saddle-point solution. The stable branches of this saddle point are logical candidates for the optimum path, given $k_d(0) \neq k_d{}^*$.

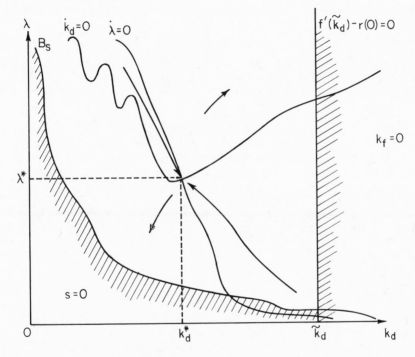

FIGURE 1. The case when $\mu > r(0) > 0$.

In spite of the undetermined shape of the $\dot{k}_d = 0$ curve in the range $k_d < k_d{}^*$, we can say that the intersection of the $\dot{k}_d = 0$ and $\dot{\lambda} = 0$ curves is *unique*, since for $k_d \geq k_d{}^*$, the $\dot{k}_d = 0$ curve is upward sloping and the $\dot{\lambda} = 0$ curve is downward sloping, as we have already noted.

In Figure 1, the B_s curve is the boundary that separates the region of "nonspecialization" (that is, $1 > s > 0$) from the region of specialization in consumption ($s = 0$), the latter being the region below the B_s curve in the positive quadrant.

It immediately follows from Equation 6 that the curve $\dot{k}_d = 0$ cannot belong to the region below the B_s curve. How about the shape of the curve $\dot{\lambda} = 0$ when it is in the latter region?

When $s = 0$, from Equation 11,

$$\dot{\lambda} = -U'(y) \cdot f'(k) + \mu \cdot \lambda. \qquad (11b)$$

From Equation 13, with $s = 0$ and $k_f > 0$,

$$U'(y)[f'(k) - \phi(k_f)] - D'(k_f) = 0. \qquad (13b)$$

Using Conditions 9, and with implicit differentiation, one can work out from Equation 13b the (negative) value of dk_f/dk_d. Using this in Equation 11b,

$$\frac{\partial \dot{\lambda}}{\partial k_d} > 0, \qquad \frac{\partial \dot{\lambda}}{\partial \lambda} > 0, \quad \text{and hence} \quad \frac{d\lambda}{dk_d}\bigg|_{\substack{\dot{\lambda}=0 \\ s=0}} < 0.$$

In other words, the $\dot{\lambda} = 0$ curve is downward sloping even in the region when $s = 0$. It is interesting to note, however, that unlike the case of $1 > s > 0$, with $s = 0$, our $\dot{\lambda} = 0$ curve may enter the region where $\dot{k}_f = 0$ even with our initial condition 1; that is, $\mu > r(0) > 0$. It is easy to check that even in that region the $\dot{\lambda} = 0$ curve will be downward sloping.

The B_s curve, characterizing the equation, $\lambda - U'(y) = 0$, can also easily be shown to be downward sloping at all times.

In conclusion to this section one can say that with the initial condition 1, that is, $\mu > r(0) > 0$, on the optimum growth path if $k_d(0) < k_d^*$, then k_d steadily increases and λ steadily decreases—and, hence, by virtue of Inequalities 17a and 17c, k_f the amount per capita of foreign capital, decreases—to asymptotically approach the golden rule path $(k_d^*, \lambda^*, k_f^*)$. The opposite holds good when $k_d(0) > k_d^*$.

2. The Case when $r(0) > \mu > 0$

It can be proved in the following way that under our initial condition 2, the curve $\dot{\lambda} = 0$ cannot be in the region where $k_f > 0$.

Let us first take the region of "nonspecialization" where $1 > s > 0$. When $k_f > 0$, we know from Equations 9 and 13a that

$$f'(k) - \phi(k_f) > 0. \qquad (21)$$

But with the present condition and Equations 11a and 12a, along the $\dot{\lambda} = 0$ curve

$$f'(k) = \mu < r(0). \qquad (22)$$

Since $\phi(k_f) > r(0)$, Equation 22 implies a contradiction with Inequality 21. This proves that with $1 > s > 0$, and the present initial condition, the curve $\dot{\lambda} = 0$ cannot be in the region where $k_f > 0$.

With $k_f = 0$ and $1 > s > 0$, along the $\dot{\lambda} = 0$ curve, $f'(k_d) = \mu$, and, therefore, the latter is vertically shaped as depicted in Figure 2. What about the shape of the $\dot{k}_d = 0$ curve?

In the region where $k_f = 0$, we know that

$$\dot{k}_d = f(k_d) - \mu k_d - c. \tag{23}$$

From Equation 23,

$$\frac{\partial \dot{k}_d}{\partial k_d} = f'(k_d) - \mu \tag{23a}$$

and

$$\frac{\partial \dot{k}_d}{\partial \lambda} = -\frac{dc}{d\lambda} = -\frac{1}{U''(c)} > 0, \tag{23b}$$

where Equations 9 and 12a have been used.

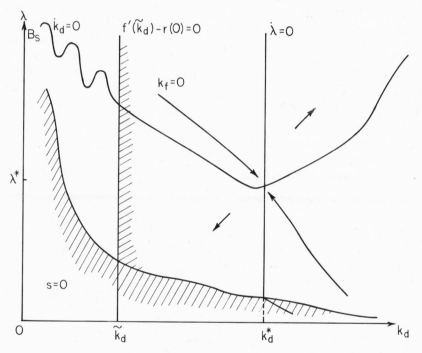

FIGURE 2. The case when $r(0) > \mu > 0$.

At the point of intersection of the curves $\dot{k}_d = 0$ and $\dot{\lambda} = 0$, we have $\partial \dot{k}_d / \partial k_d = 0$; the latter is positive or negative as $k_d \gtrless k_d{}^*$. Therefore, as depicted in Figure 2, for the $k_f = 0$ region the $\dot{k}_d = 0$ curve is downward or upward sloping as $k_d \gtrless k_d{}^*$.

It can be proved easily *à la* Cass [3], for example, that the unique intersection of the $\dot{k}_d = 0$ and $\dot{\lambda} = 0$ curves is a saddle point, and its stable branches are logical candidates for the optimum path, given $k_d(0) \neq k_d{}^*$.

As proved in Case 1, we are not sure of the shape of the $\dot{k}_d = 0$ curve in the region of $k_f > 0$ with $k_d < k_d{}^*$, as indicated in Figure 2. But this does not affect either the uniqueness or the saddle-point properties of the stationary solution of our differential equations.

As in Figure 1, a downward-sloping B_s curve serves as the boundary between the region where $1 > s > 0$ and that where $s = 0$. As before, the $\dot{k}_d = 0$ curve cannot belong to the region where $s = 0$. What about the shape of the $\dot{\lambda} = 0$ curve in the region where $s = 0$? With $s = 0$ and $k_f = 0$, it follows from Equation 11 that along the $\dot{\lambda} = 0$ curve,

$$\lambda = \frac{U'[f(k_d)] \cdot f'(k_d)}{\mu}. \tag{24}$$

From Equations 3, 9, and 24, we have $(d\lambda/dk_d) < 0$, and hence the $\dot{\lambda} = 0$ curve is downward sloping in the region where $s = 0$, as depicted in Figure 2. Under our initial condition 2 , in no case can the $\dot{\lambda} = 0$ curve belong to the region where $k_f > 0$.

One can thus verify from Figure 2 that under the present initial condition, that is, $r(0) > \mu > 0$, on the optimum growth path if $k_d(0) < k_d{}^*$, then k_d steadily increases and λ steadily decreases—and, hence, k_f *the amount per capita of foreign capital, decreases and ultimately becomes or is always zero—* to approach asymptotically the golden rule path $(k_d{}^*, \lambda^*)$.

3. The Case when $\mu = r(0) > 0$

In this case also the $\dot{\lambda} = 0$ curve cannot be in the region where $k_f > 0$.

Let us first take the region of "nonspecialization" where $1 > s > 0$. When $k_f > 0$, we know from Inequality 21 that $f'(k) - \phi(k_f) > 0$. But with this third condition and Equations 11a and 12a, along the $\dot{\lambda} = 0$ curve

$$f'(k) = \mu = r(0). \tag{25}$$

Since $\phi(k_f) > r(0)$, Equation 25 implies a contradiction with Inequality 21. This proves that with $1 > s > 0$ and the third initial condition, the $\dot{\lambda} = 0$ curve cannot be in the region where $k_f > 0$.

Arguments analogous to those in the preceding case are sufficient to explain why the $\dot{\lambda} = 0$ and $\dot{k}_d = 0$ curves are as in Figure 3. The unique intersection point is once again a saddle point, and k_f once again steadily decreases and ultimately approaches zero, as $k_d(0) < k_d{}^*$.

Taking all the three initial conditions together, the essential result of our model can be stated as follows: *On the optimum growth path, if the domestically owned capital stock is below the "balanced" capital stock, the amount per capita of foreign capital steadily decreases to a positive amount, becomes or is always equal to zero, depending on initial conditions.* The importance of the initial conditions is that by comparing the preborrowing rate of interest in

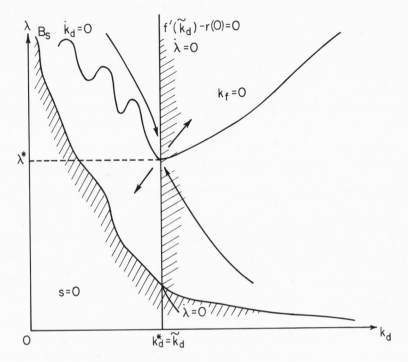

FIGURE 3. The case when $\mu = r(0) > 0$.

the world capital market with the golden rule rate of interest μ in the home country, they determine whether at the stationary solution the country is still a borrower or not.

References

1. Bardhan, P. K., "Economic Growth and the Pattern of International Trade and Investment: A Study in Pure Theory," Ph.D. dissertation, University of Cambridge, Cambridge, England, June 1965.
2. Bardhan, P. K., "Optimum Accumulation and International Trade," *Review of Economic Studies*, Vol. 32 (July 1965).
3. Cass, D., "Optimum Growth in an Aggregative Model of Capital Accumulation," *Review of Economic Studies*, Vol. 32 (July 1965).
4. Hamada, K., "Optimum Capital Accumulation of an Economy Facing an International Capital Market: The Case of an Imperfect World Capital Market," Technical Report No. 4, Department of Economics, University of Chicago, Chicago, Ill., November 1965.
5. Kemp, M. C., *The Pure Theory of International Trade*, Englewood Cliffs, N.J.: Prentice-Hall, Inc., 1964.
6. Kemp, M. C., "The Gain from International Trade and Investment: A Neo-Heckscher–Ohlin Approach," *American Economic Review*, Vol. 56 (September 1966).

7. Koopmans, T. C., "On the Concept of Optimal Economic Growth," in *Semaine d'Etude sur le Rôle de l'Analyse Econométrique dans la Formulation de Plans de Développement*, Vatican City: Pontifical Academy of Sciences, 1965, Vol. I, pp. 225–287.
8. MacDougall, C. D. A., "The Benefits and Costs of Private Investment from Abroad," *Economic Record*, Vol. 26 (March 1960).
9. Pearce, I. F., and D. C. Rowan, "A Framework for Research into Real Effects of International Capital Movements," to be published in *Essays in Honour of M. Fanno* (1966).
10. Phelps, E. S., "The Ramsey Problem and the Golden Rule of Accumulation," Cowles Foundation Discussion Paper No. 194, Yale University, New Haven, Conn., 1965.
11. Pontryagin, L. S., *et al.*, *The Mathematical Theory of Optimal Processes*, New York and London: Interscience Publishers, Inc., 1962.

VII

Optimum Allocation of Investments and Transportation in a Two-Region Economy

MRINAL DATTA-CHAUDHURI

Indian Statistical Institute, New Delhi

1. Introduction

Intertemporal investment planning essentially involves finding out the best allocation of investable resources among competing activities, with given constraints due to technology, behavioral relations, and initial resource availabilities. Competing activities can be alternative methods of producing a good, alternative collections of goods capable of providing the same satisfaction, the alternatives of producing a good and importing it, alternative locations for producing a good, and so on. In this essay, the question of optimality with respect to the last-choice element, that is, the locational choice, is examined under drastically simplified assumptions. Locational choice is interesting because of the crucial role of transportation activity, which, at some costs, can make goods produced at one place available at another.

In what follows, a simple aggregative planning model[1] is constructed for a country divided into two regions; for instance, the two wings of Pakistan separated by a thousand miles of Indian territory. Aggregative models are quite useless in analyzing the pattern of trade. It needs at least two goods to make a trading situation. The static theory of interregional trade, which is

[1] See two similar two-region, aggregative investment allocation models that do not use transport costs in Rahman [3] and Intrilligator [1]. The first uses the dynamic programming approach while the second uses optimal control theory to get optimal allocation.

based on the same principle as the pure theory of international trade—as Ohlin rightly pointed out in his celebrated book—is well developed, and the concepts are clear and well known by now. But in dynamic interregional analysis, a new kind of trading situation develops, that is, trade between present goods and future goods. The purpose of this aggregative model is to bring out the logic of the gains from this kind of trade in terms of the implied intertemporal pricing. It is fair to warn the reader at the beginning that the answers one can get from such simplistic models are usually simple and obvious, and the interest is essentially heuristic.

The optimality of an allocation model is judged in terms of a well-defined social objective. The difficulties of constructing a workable, as well as realistic, social welfare index are obvious to the initiated. The problem is much more vexed in the case of a multiregional economy; the marginal rate of substitution of one region's welfare for that of another is not easy to define in any situation involving real life. For the purposes of this article, the social objective is to reach a target level of national capital, however distributed geographically, in the minimum possible time. This seems to have an easy appeal in terms of national aspirations for an underdeveloped country.

The economy consists of two regions. At the beginning of the planning period each region is endowed with a given stock of capital and a given supply of labor. The labor force in each region is assumed to grow exponentially, not necessarily at the same rate. These are the only two factors of production necessary to produce the aggregate output, which can be either consumed or used for capital formation in either region. Both labor and capital (though not new investments) are assumed to be completely immobile interregionally. No depreciation of capital stocks is assumed explicitly, so regional output is to be interpreted as net replacements of depreciated capital. Replacement is independent of policy variables and is always carried out instantaneously. Each region is supposed to have an *ex ante* neoclassical production function: $Y_i = F_i(K_i, L_i) = L_i f_i(K_i/L_i)$ without technological change and with the usual diminishing returns assumptions. It is assumed that all wage incomes are consumed and a given fraction (maybe different for each region) of profit incomes is saved. Two different assumptions about the behavior of wages are made; these will be discussed later.

The simplest assumption about the nature of transport activity is made here; that is, a certain given fraction δ of the goods to be transported evaporates in the process of transportation. Another way of stating this assumption is that interregional transportation is carried on by foreigners who charge a fixed freight rate. Or, alternatively, the sending region provides transportation that is subject to the aggregate production function prevailing in that region, and the factors of production engaged in transportation are perfectly shiftable within production processes in the sending country. This is shown diagrammatically in Figure 1.

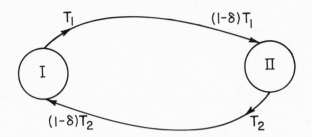

FIGURE 1. A diagrammatic representation of the possibilities of commodity movements between the regions.

Given the savings behavior of the two regions, the planning problem is to allocate the total savings of the nation among the two regions at each instant of time in such a way that the nation as a whole acquires a desired level of capital stock, irrespective of its geographical distribution, in the shortest possible time. Mathematically, the problem can be stated as:

$$\text{Minimize} \quad \int_{t_0}^{t_1} dt \tag{1}$$

subject to

$$Y_i(t) = L_i(t)f_i[k_i(t)] \quad \text{where } k_i(t) = K_i(t)/L_i(t), \tag{2}$$

$$L_i(t) = L_i(0)e^{n_i t}, \tag{3}$$

$$S_i(t) = s_i[Y_i(t) - w_i L_i(t)], \tag{4}$$

$$\dot{K}_i(t) = S_i(t) - T_i(t) + (1 - \delta)T_j(t) = [1 - u_i(t)]S_i(t) + (1 - \delta)u_j S_j(t), \tag{5}$$

$$T_i(t) = u_i(t)S_i(t), \tag{6}$$

$$0 \le u_i(t) \le 1, \tag{7}$$

$$K_i(t) = \overline{K_i(0)}, \quad i, j = 1, 2, \tag{8}$$

$$K_1(t_1) + K_2(t_1) = \overline{K}, \tag{9}$$

where Y_i, K_i, and L_i stand for net output, capital stock, and labor force, respectively, of region i. Similarly, k_i is the capital-labor ratio, $\dot{K}_i$ the net investment, S_i the savings, and T_i the transfer of investable resources from the ith region. Here u_i is the control variable that determines how much of the investable surplus of region i should be transported to the other region in the optimum plan. This is essentially a calculus of variation problem with phase variables K_i and control variables u_i. For an optimum program it is necessary that there exist nonzero continuous functions $\psi_1(t)$ and $\psi_2(t)$ such that for every point of time in the interval $t_0 \leq t \leq t_1$, the Hamiltonian expression

$$H = -1 + \psi_1[(1 - u_1)S_1 + (1 - \delta)u_2S_2 - \dot{K}_1]$$
$$+ \psi_2[(1 - u_2)S_2 + (1 - \delta)u_1S_1 - \dot{K}_2] \quad (10)$$

attains its maximum at the optimum values of the control variables u_1 and u_2. The functions ψ_1 and ψ_2 have the usual interpretation of the demand price of investments in the two regions.

Furthermore, the necessary Euler's equations,

$$\frac{\partial H}{\partial K_i} = \frac{d}{dt}\frac{\partial H}{\partial \dot{K}_i}, \quad i = 1, 2, \quad (11)$$

provide the following relationships:

$$\dot{\psi}_i = -\{\psi_1 - [\psi_1 - (1 - \delta)\psi_2]u_1\}\frac{\partial S_1}{\partial K_1} \quad (12)$$

and

$$\dot{\psi}_2 = -\{\psi_2 - [\psi_2 - (1 - \delta)\psi_1]u_2\}\frac{\partial S_2}{\partial K_2}. \quad (13)$$

The maximum of H implies maximization of the two following expressions subject to the two control variables:

$$\underset{u_1}{\text{Max}}\ [-\psi_1 + (1 - \delta)\psi_2]u_1S_1 \quad (14)$$

and

$$\underset{u_2}{\text{Max}}\ [-\psi_2 + (1 - \delta)\psi_2]u_2S_2. \quad (15)$$

This gives

$$u_1 = \begin{cases} 0 & \text{for } \psi_1 > (1 - \delta)\psi_2, \\ 1 & \text{for } \psi_1 < (1 - \delta)\psi_2, \end{cases} \quad (16)$$

and

$$u_2 = \begin{cases} 0 & \text{for } \psi_2 > (1 - \delta)\psi_1 \quad \text{or} \quad \psi_1 < \dfrac{1}{(1 - \delta)}\psi_2, \\ 1 & \text{for } \psi_2 < (1 - \delta)\psi_1 \quad \text{or} \quad \psi_1 > \dfrac{1}{(1 - \delta)}\psi_2. \end{cases} \quad (17)$$

The solution can be represented diagrammatically in the ψ_1–ψ_2 plane (Figure 2).

This means that if the price ratio is less than $1 - \delta$, all investment takes place in zone II. For a price ratio more than $1/(1 - \delta)$, all investment takes place in zone I. For $(1 - \delta) > \psi_1/\psi_2 > 1/(1 - \delta)$, the two regions are allowed to grow autarkically.

Once the forms of the production functions and wage behaviors are specified, the system of equations with the transversality condition

$$\psi_1(t_1) = \psi_2(t_1) \tag{18}$$

can be solved explicitly.

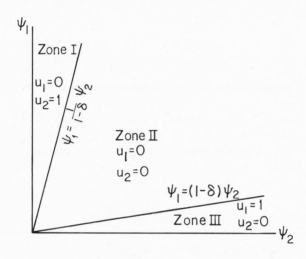

FIGURE 2. The three alternative patterns of efficient interregional commodity movements.

However, it is worth noting at this stage that the crucial factor in determining the movement of the demand price of investment (which determines the regional allocation in this model) is $\partial S_i/\partial K_i$. This is the familiar "reinvestment quotient" used as the "investment-criterion" in development literature. Here it is argued that if the long-run growth of an underdeveloped economy is to be maximized, the proper investment criterion is the allocation of investments to the technique that generates the maximum reinvestable surplus per unit of investments. The objective of reaching an "arbitrarily specified terminal capital stock" in the minimal time (as the problem is formulated here) is equivalent to maximizing the long-run growth of the total economy, since the terminal capital stock can be specified at as high a level as desired. Only this formulation clearly brings out the duality property of the allocation problem, that is, the price system implied in the planning process.

In the following two sections, two distinct cases involving different wage (and hence savings) behavior are analyzed. The first is the typical case of underdevelopment with excess labor, and the second of full-employment growth.

2. The Unlimited Supply of Labor

The economic facts of life behind growth models with unlimited supply of labor could be variously described. Essentially, the real wage in the system cannot go low enough to allow the full employment of the entire labor force with the existing stock of capital, even if it were technologically feasible. So, once the real wage is given (either as a minimum subsistence wage or a socially acceptable minimum) the optimum technique of production is known. In the present case of the smoothly substitutable neoclassical production function, equating the marginal product of labor with the wage rate uniquely determines the capital-labor ratio (and also the capital-output ratio); and in the absence of technological change, it remains fixed so long as labor does not become scarce.

In the present case it is assumed that labor remains in abundant supply throughout the relevant period. So capital-output and labor-output ratios and wage rates are fixed. Since no savings come from wage income, labor can be treated as a produced intermediate commodity with a fixed cost of production. The economic reality behind the model can be thought of as follows. People live self-sufficiently in a subsistence economy in either region. The task of planning involves only the building up of a modern sector in either region. In the process labor is brought to the modern sector from the subsistence sector. But once employed, labor has to be given wage goods from the production of the modern sector. No interactions between the two sectors are assumed to exist.

In this framework the planning problem can be solved mathematically from the following equations:

$$\dot{K}_1 = (1 - u_1)\alpha_1 K_1 + (1 - \delta)u_2\alpha_2 K_2, \tag{19}$$

$$\dot{K}_2 = (1 - \delta)u_1\alpha_1 K_1 + (1 - u_2)\alpha_2 K_2, \tag{20}$$

$$\dot{\psi}_1 = -\{\psi_1 - [\psi_1 - (1 - \delta)\psi_2]u_1\}\alpha_1, \tag{21}$$

$$\dot{\psi}_2 = -\{+\psi_2 - [\psi_2 - (1 - \delta)\psi_1]u_2\}\alpha_2, \tag{22}$$

$$K_1(t_0) = \overline{K_1(0)}, \tag{23}$$

$$K_2(t_0) = \overline{K_2(0)}, \tag{24}$$

$$K_1(t_1) + K_2(t_1) = \overline{K}, \tag{25}$$

$$\psi_1(t_1) = \psi_2(t_1), \tag{26}$$

$$u_1 = 0, \quad u_2 = 1 \quad \text{for } \psi_1 > \frac{1}{1 - \delta}\psi_2, \tag{27}$$

$$u_1 = 0, \quad u_2 = 0 \quad \text{for } \frac{1}{1 - \delta}\psi_2 > \psi_1 > (1 - \delta)\psi_2, \tag{28}$$

$$u_1 = 1, \quad u_2 = 0 \quad \text{for } \psi_1 < (1 - \delta)\psi_2, \tag{29}$$

where the effective production function $y_i = \min [A_i K_i, b_i L_i]$, w_i = wage rate in region i, and $\alpha_i = s_i A_i[1 - (w_i/b_i)]$.

The transversality condition (Equation 26) assures that the planning period should end in zone II (autarky), in the ψ_1–ψ_2 plane at some point on the 45° line. In zone II, the dynamic system is characterized by

$$\dot{K}_1 = S_1 = \alpha_1 K_1, \tag{30}$$

$$\dot{K}_2 = S_2 = \alpha_2 K_2, \tag{31}$$

$$\dot{\psi}_1 = -\psi_1 \alpha_1, \tag{32}$$

$$\dot{\psi}_2 = -\psi_2 \alpha_2. \tag{33}$$

Let

$$\psi_1(t_1) = \psi_2(t_1) = \bar{\psi}, \tag{34}$$

then from Equations 33 and 34,

$$\psi_1 = \bar{\psi} e^{-\alpha_1(t-t_1)}, \tag{35}$$

$$\psi_2 = \bar{\psi} e^{-\alpha_1(t-t_1)}. \tag{36}$$

If $\alpha_1 > \alpha_2$, $\psi_1(t)/\psi_2(t)$ is an increasing function of $t_1 - t$ and at time t^* before the terminal period t_1, the locus of optimum $[\psi_1(t), \psi_2(t)]$ crosses the $\psi_1 - (1 - \delta)\psi_2$ line, where $t_1 - t^*$ can be solved from

$$\frac{\psi_1(t^*)}{\psi_2(t^*)} = e^{(\alpha_1 - \alpha_2)(t_1 - t)} = \frac{1}{1 - \delta}$$

or

$$t_1 - t^* = \frac{1}{\alpha_2 - \alpha_1} \log_e (1 - \delta). \tag{37}$$

In zone I, the path is characterized by

$$\dot{K}_1 = S_1 + (1 - \delta)S_2 = \alpha_1 K_1 + (1 - \delta)\alpha_2 K_2, \tag{38}$$

$$\dot{K}_2 = 0, \tag{39}$$

$$\dot{\psi}_1 = -\alpha_1 \psi_1, \tag{40}$$

$$\dot{\psi}_2 = -(1 - \delta)\alpha_2 \psi_1. \tag{41}$$

The solutions of Equations 40 and 41 give

$$\psi_1(t) = \psi_1(t^*)e^{-\alpha_1(t-t^*)}, \tag{42}$$

$$\psi_2(t) = (1 - \delta)\psi_1(t^*)\left(1 - \frac{\alpha_2}{\alpha_1}\right) + (1 - \delta)\psi_1(t^*)\frac{\alpha_2}{\alpha_1} e^{-\alpha_1(t-t^*)}, \tag{43}$$

$$\frac{\psi_2(t)}{\psi_1(t)} = (1 - \delta)\left[\left(1 - \frac{\alpha_2}{\alpha_1}\right)e^{-\alpha_1(t^*-t)} + \frac{\alpha_2}{\alpha_1}\right]. \tag{44}$$

Given $0 < \delta < 1$ and $1 > \alpha_1 > \alpha_2 > 0$, the ratio $\psi_2(t)/\psi_1(t)$ increases with t. That means for $\alpha_1 > \alpha_2$, the locus of $[\psi_1(t), \psi_2(t)]$ throughout the range $t_0 - t^*$ remains in zone I.

Similarly, if $\alpha_2 > \alpha_1$, it can be shown that, except for a period $t_1 - t^*$ $[= 1/(\alpha_1 - \alpha_2) \log_e (1 - \delta)]$, at the end of the planning period when the two regions grow in autarky all the investment is channeled to region 2.

Diagrammatically, the optimum path can be traced in the ψ_1–ψ_2 plane as is shown in Figure 3.

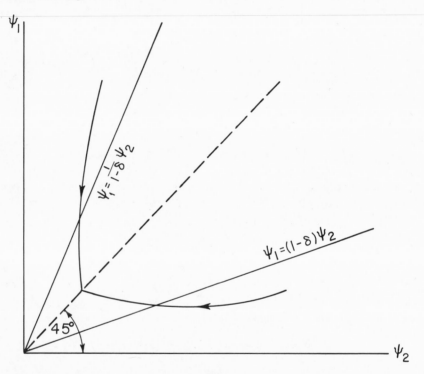

FIGURE 3. Typical trends in the relative shadow prices implied in efficient allocation programs.

The intuitive reason why the program always ends with a finite period of autarkic growth is that, given a positive transport cost for transferring investable resources, a certain period of time is always necessary before the productivity of the higher growing region can make up for the initial transport cost incurred in transferring investable resources.

Thus, the investment rule for allocating investments between two regions subject to a linear production function, fixed wage rates, stated savings assumptions, and the objective of the fastest program of capital accumulation for the nation as a whole can be stated as follows:

Invest all investable resources in the region with the higher "reinvestment quotient" until just before the attainment of the terminal objective when it no longer pays to incur the transport cost.

3. Full-Employment Growth

Once the growing economy hits full employment, the wage rate can move up. Competition among firms determines the wage rate as the marginal product of labor at full employment in the aggregate production function for the region. Under the same savings assumption, that is, that all wage income is consumed and a given fraction s_i of the profit income of the region is saved, the ith region's savings S_i become

$$S_i = s_i[L_i f_i(k_i) - w_i L_i]$$
$$= s_i L_i\{f_i(k_i) - [f_i(k_i) - k_i f_i'(k_i)]\} \tag{45}$$
$$= s_i K_i f_i'(k_i).$$

The reinvestment quotient, which is not constant any more, becomes

$$\frac{\partial S_i}{\partial K_i} = s_i[f_i'(k_i) + k_i f_i''(k_i)] = s_i f_i'(k_i)\left(1 + k_i \frac{f_i''}{f_i'}\right). \tag{46}$$

This again can be expressed in terms of the elasticity of substitution of the production function σ_i, because

$$\sigma_i = -\frac{f_i'}{k f_i''} + \frac{(f_i')^2}{f_i f_i''} = -\frac{f_i'}{k f_i''}\left(1 - \frac{k f_i'}{f_i}\right) = -\frac{f_i'}{k f_i''} \cdot v_i, \tag{47}$$

where v_i = relative share of wages. So, for instance,

$$\frac{\partial S_i}{\partial K_i} = s_i\left(1 - \frac{v_i}{\sigma_i}\right) \cdot f_i'$$
$$= s_i \alpha_i(k_i) f_i'(k_i). \tag{48}$$

Here again, given the specific forms of the production functions and initial and terminal conditions, the optimum growth path can be solved explicitly. However, without specifying the exact functional form, certain qualitative statements about the efficient path can be made. The demand price of investment ψ_i depends on $s_i \alpha_i f_i'$. Now suppose the initial conditions specifying capital stock and labor force in the two regions are such that the program starts in zone III (that is, all investments are made in region 2). Then with investments in region 2, capital intensity k_2 will increase and, given the usual first-order homogeneous production function, $f_2'(k_2)$ will diminish. At the same time, the naturally increasing labor force in region 1, with stationary capital stock, will push k_i down and $f_i'(k_i)$ up. So, the difference between the marginal productivities of capital will gradually diminish. See Figure 4.

Thus, in zone III, the ratio of the rates of changes of the two prices

$$\frac{\dot{\psi}_1}{\dot{\psi}_2} = (1 - \delta) \frac{s_1\alpha_1(k_1)f_1'(k_1)}{s_2\alpha_2(k_2)f_2'(k_2)} \tag{49}$$

is an increasing function of time, and the relative difference between the two prices narrows down.

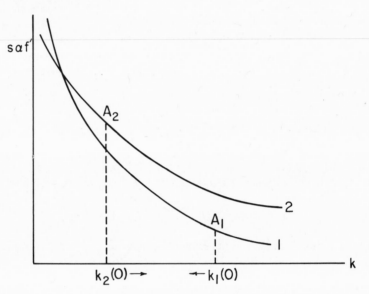

FIGURE 4. The direction of changes in the capital-labor ratios implied in certain initial conditions.

Similarly, starting with the opposite kind of initial conditions, that is, in zone I (all investments going to region 1), the locus of $[\psi_1(t), \psi_2(t)]$ moves toward zone II, the region of autarky. The optimum programs can be represented in the ψ_1–ψ_2 plane as shown in Figure 5.

Thus, in the linear case, the productivities of investments (and the reinvestment quotients) remain constant throughout the period, and only the transport cost disadvantage prevents all investments going to the higher growing region except for a short time only before meeting the terminal objectives. In the neoclassical full-employment case, however, changes in the capital intensities tend to diminish the initial differences in productivities (and in the reinvestment quotients), and the program moves toward autarky.

One interesting question can be asked in the context of this model where two neoclassical economies are interacting in trying to maximize their combined accumulation of capital. Is it ever optimal for the two regions to grow at their respective natural rates with the long-run equilibrium capital intensities?

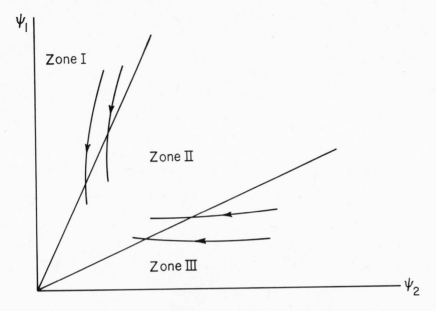

FIGURE 5. The phase diagram in the ψ_1–ψ_2 space.

The long-run equilibrium growth of a region in autarky under our savings assumption can be worked as follows:

$$\dot{K}_i = s_i K_i f_i'(k_i)$$

or

$$\frac{\dot{K}_i}{K_i} = \frac{\dot{k}_i}{k_i} + n_i = s_i f_i'(k_i); \tag{50}$$

for $\dot{k}_i/k_i = 0$, the solution of

$$n_i = s_i f_i'(k_i^*) \tag{51}$$

gives the equilibrium capital-labor ratio k_i^*. See Figure 6.

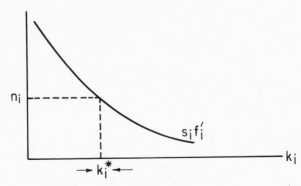

FIGURE 6. Equilibrium growth in autarky.

If the optimum path is for the two regions to grow at their natural rates in autarky, then the demand price of investment in the ith region ψ_i is given by

$$\frac{\dot{\psi_i}}{\psi_i} = -s_i\alpha_i(k_i{}^*)f_i{}'(k_i{}^*)$$

$$= -\alpha_i(k_i{}^*)n_i. \tag{52}$$

The sufficient condition for the locus of price $\psi_1-\psi_2$ to remain in zone II, once it is there, is the equality of the two rates of growth (which is negative, unless the elasticity of substitution σ_i is so small as to make $\alpha_i(k_i{}^*)$ negative).

Thus, *if* $n_1\alpha_1(k_1{}^*) = n_2\alpha_2(k_2{}^*)$, *then the optimum path eventually coincides with the natural growth paths of the two regions in autarky.*

References

1. Intrilligator, M., "Essay on Productivity and Savings," Ph.D. dissertation, Massachusetts Institute of Technology, Cambridge, Mass., 1963, Chapter 2.
2. Pontryagin, L. S., *et al., The Mathematical Theory of Optimal Processes,* New York and London: Interscience Publishers, Inc., 1962.
3. Rahman, A., "Regional Allocation of Investment," *Quarterly Journal of Economics,* Vol. 77, No. 1 (February 1963), pp. 26–39.

VIII

The Rate of Interest and the Value of Capital with Unlimited Supplies of Labor[1]

STEPHEN A. MARGLIN
Harvard University

1. Introduction

This essay investigates the choice of technique (labor-capital ratio) and the choice of the rate of saving as joint decisions linked by the following mechanism: (1) the supply of labor is always infinitely elastic at an exogenously determined wage rate; (2) all wage income is consumed; and (3) the marginal disutility of labor and its productivity unassisted by capital are nil.[2] The principal conclusions of this investigation are, first, that for the optimal technique and saving rate, the marginal productivity of labor in the capitalistic sector lies between the wage rate and zero. Second, and more important, neither the private nor the social rate of return (or marginal

---

[1] A seminar conducted jointly by Amartya Sen and myself at Delhi School of Economics in the spring of 1964 contributed substantially to the development of the ideas presented in this essay, and I am extremely grateful to Professor Sen and the members of the seminar. Subsequent exchanges of views with Sukhamoy Chakravarty have also been of considerable help in clarifying my ideas, and Robert Solow's comments on an earlier draft simplified the mathematics and sharpened the economics.

The essay was presented to the United Nations Interregional Symposium on Industrial Project Evaluation held in Prague, Czechoslovakia, during October 1965. The essay appears here with the kind permission of the United Nations Center for Industrial Development.

[2] These assumptions represent a theoretical simplification of the framework of growth going back at least to Karl Marx. For a modern discussion, see W. Arthur Lewis [10, 11, 12].

141

productivity) of capital is equal to the subjective rate of interest, defined by
the marginal premium on present over future consumption implicit in the
economy's social welfare function; optimally, the subjective rate of interest
is equal rather to the physical marginal productivity of capital. The difference
between the social and physical productivity of capital is the difference
between a *mutatis mutandis* and a *ceteris paribus* change. The social return
measures the extra output from an extra unit of output of capital if employment increases sufficiently to maintain the socially optimal labor-capital ratio,
which is, of course, the correct employment strategy under the assumptions
of this essay. The physical return to capital measures the extra output under
the assumption that employment does not change with the addition of a unit
of capital.

The implication of this second conclusion for investment planning will be
discussed later, but the extreme nature of our assumptions about the availability and behavior of labor compel at least cursory attention at the outset
to the relevance of these assumptions. Stated baldly they are far from realistic,
especially the assumption of perpetually unlimited supplies of labor at a fixed
wage. But the germ of truth that makes the assumption of unlimited supplies
of labor worth exploring is that in many underdeveloped economies unemployment and underemployment are large, and the wage rate of unskilled
labor is well in excess of its opportunity cost measured in terms either of
marginal disutility or of the alternative product forgone. And worse, in many
countries the creation of employment opportunities hardly keeps pace with
the growth of the labor force. In India, for example, the relative as well as
absolute amount of unemployment has apparently increased since indepen-
dence, despite fifteen years of planned economic development.[3] This is not a
state of affairs that will continue in perpetuity, one hopes, but certainly the
wage rate will exceed the opportunity cost of labor for some time to come;
and India is not unique in this respect.

The assumption that workers consume their entire wage income may seem
inappropriate in a model that attempts to simulate the choice of saving rate
as well as technique. With unlimited supplies of labor, surely the labor-
capital ratio should be increased until the marginal productivity of labor falls

---

[3] The following estimates are taken from V. R. K. Tilak [19], p. 27:

Year	At the beginning of	Number unemployed (*millions*)
1951	First Plan	Not available
1956	Second Plan	5.3
1961	Third Plan	$\begin{cases} 9.0 \text{ (original)} \\ 8.0 \text{ (revised)} \end{cases}$
1966	Fourth Plan	12.0 (anticipated)

The compound growth rate of unemployment is over 8 per cent, as compared with a
growth rate of population of the order of 2 per cent. Underemployment is, of course,
more difficult to estimate.

to zero; and the consumption of workers should be a separate issue. Even if workers cannot be induced to save voluntarily, it ought to be possible to force savings out of wages through a combination of taxation and a reduction of real wages by means of inflation.[4] However, governments are in general severely restricted in their ability to control the rate of consumption out of wage income. In decentralized, pluralistic societies, organized labor—along with other interested groups—can be expected to resist the taxation and inflation that would be required to force savings from wage income. And this resistance is likely to be effective, for the political advantages of increasing employment are relatively few. The unemployed, after all, are a minority of the labor force even in the most labor-surplus economies, so that even if man for man the unemployed were just as powerful politically as the employed, the sheer weight of numbers would make the interest of the employed in low taxes and price stability carry the day against the interest of the unemployed in expansion of the volume of investment and hence employment.[5]

Even in more highly planned and centralized economies, the latitude of the government to increase savings and investment by decreasing the consumption per employed worker is limited. Joseph Pajestka indicates that the attempts of the Polish government to do just this in the decade following the defeat of Nazi Germany "placed heavy burdens on certain social groups and brought in their wake the well-known social-political reactions and dispositions which resulted in checking further economic development."[6]

The Polish experience points up that it is consumption per *worker* rather than per *capita* that is at issue. More intensive use of existing capital goods makes it possible to increase total (and thus per capita) consumption and investment, at least to the point where the marginal productivity of labor falls to zero. But to increase the labor-capital ratio beyond the point where the marginal productivity of labor falls to the level of the wage necessitates either a fall in real consumption per *worker* or a fall in the rate of profit per unit of capital and hence in the rate of investment and growth. That consumption per worker rather than consumption per capita should be the politically sensitive magnitude is perhaps not so surprising after all. A society need not

---

[4] Such an assumption as this is implicit in Francis Bator's willingness to assume that the choice of a rate of saving can be made independently of the distribution of income. See [2] p. 98. Bator admits the logical possibility of a link between income distribution and savings (p. 103), but does not appear to take very seriously the problem such a link would pose.

[5] The irony of this conflict of interest is that the more successful a government in increasing the volume of savings and employment by taxation or inflation, the more difficulty it encounters. For the very people who are moved from the ranks of the unemployed to those of the employed, who might be expected to be the most vocal supporters of the taxation or inflation that created their jobs, now identify their interests with those who were already employed and, hence, lose from taxation and inflation.

[6] Pajestka [15], p. 323.

be Calvinistic for there to exist differences in expectations and aspirations between the employed and the unemployed. Individuals may become inured to chronic underemployment or unemployment, but similar individuals in possession of jobs may feel legitimately entitled to some minimum level of consumption in return for a day's work and may exercise all the political power at their command to resist taxation or inflation that might deprive them of their accustomed standard.

The preceding discussion is not intended to suggest a belief on my part in the absolute realism of the assumptions that underlie the model analyzed in this essay. The ingredients of theoretical models generally represent an extreme simplification of the actual environment of economic decisions, and the present case is no exception. Nevertheless, the model examined in subsequent sections of this essay captures sufficiently the distinctive features of a large number of countries in Asia and elsewhere to make it worth while to explore its implications for development policy.

2. Technique and Saving Divorced

To provide a basis of comparison, it may be a good idea first to set out the relevant results under the assumption that the government is able, by one means or another, to achieve any desired rate of savings regardless of the labor-capital ratio chosen. Thus the choice of technique can be divorced from the savings discussion. Given unlimited supplies of labor and our assumption that both the disutility of labor and labor productivity unassisted by capital are zero, we may suppose that the labor intensity is chosen to maximize the output-capital ratio regardless of the level of the wage rate. In other words, labor intensity is increased until the marginal productivity of labor in the capitalistic sector is driven to zero. So much for the choice of technique.

Following Ramsey [16], the optimal savings program is defined as one that minimizes the integral over the interval $[0, \infty)$ of the difference between "bliss" (the least upper bound on instantaneous utility) and the utility actually achieved. If we denote consumption at time t by $C(t)$, instantaneous utility by $U(C)$, and bliss by B, the objective function can be written

$$\text{Min} \int_0^\infty \{B - U[C(t)]\}\, dt. \tag{1}$$

Let ρ stand for the output-capital ratio,[7] K for capital, $\dot{K}$ for investment,[8] and Y for income. Then

---

[7] We shall assume throughout this essay that the production function is homogeneous of first degree, which means that ρ is a function of the labor-capital ratio alone.

[8] Dots will in general indicate time rates of change.

$$Y = \rho K, \tag{2}$$

$$Y = C + \dot{K}, \tag{3}$$

$$C = \rho K - \dot{K}. \tag{4}$$

Expression 1 becomes

$$\text{Min} \int_0^\infty \{B - U[\rho K(t) - \dot{K}(t)]\}\, dt. \tag{5}$$

If we apply the calculus of variations to Expression 5, the first-order Euler-Lagrange equation becomes[9]

$$-\rho U_C = \dot{U}_C \tag{6}$$

or

$$\rho = -\frac{\dot{U}_C}{U_C}. \tag{7}$$

In view of the zero marginal productivity of labor associated with the optimal technique, the output-capital ratio ρ becomes equal to both the social and the physical marginal productivity of capital. But both may differ from the private marginal productivity of capital, since a private computation of profit properly deducts any wage costs from the total return despite the assumed redundancy of labor. The right-hand side of Equation 7 is the percentage rate at which the marginal utility of consumption falls over time or the subjective rate of interest implied by society's utility function. Thus Equation 7 expresses the Fisherian balance of opportunity and impatience in the determination of the optimal program of capital accumulation, although in the present instance the balance is one of social rather than of private return with a social rather than a private subjective rate of interest.

Since the integral of Expression 5 is a function only of K and $\dot{K}$, we can integrate Equation 6 to obtain a solution in terms of $\dot{K}$:

$$\dot{K} = \frac{B - U}{U_C}. \tag{8}$$

Equation 8, the Ramsey-Keynes rule, says that the optimal rate of saving at any moment of time t is given by the ratio of the difference between bliss and utility at t to the marginal utility of consumption at t.[10]

To give concreteness to Equation 8 we shall adopt a specific form of the utility function, namely, the constant elasticity function,

$$U(C) = -aC^{-v}, \tag{9}$$

---

[9] Subscripts will in general indicate differentiation with respect to the variable indicated.
[10] Ramsey [16], p. 547.

where a and v are positive constants.[11] This function naturally suggests zero as the "bliss" level, that is, $B = 0$. The marginal utility of consumption is given by

$$U_C = vaC^{-(v+1)},\tag{10}$$

and Expression 8 becomes

$$\dot{K} = \frac{0 - (-aC^{-v})}{vaC^{-(v+1)}} = \frac{C}{v}.\tag{11}$$

Consumption plus savings are equal to total output; that is,

$$Y = C + \dot{K}.\tag{3}$$

So, Equation 11 is equivalent to

$$\frac{\dot{K}}{Y} = \frac{1}{1+v},\tag{12}$$

In other words, the optimal saving rate $\dot{K}/Y$ is constant over time and equal to the negative of the inverse elasticity of marginal utility with respect to consumption. Note that the optimal saving rate is independent of ρ.

For future reference we ought perhaps to specify society's subjective rate of interest (which henceforth we shall denote by r) implicit in the constant-elasticity utility function. Division of the negative of the time rate of change of marginal utility,

$$-\dot{U}_C = +(v + 1)vaC^{-(v+2)}\dot{C},$$

by the marginal utility of consumption (Equation 10) gives the subjective rate of interest,

$$r = -\frac{\dot{U}_C}{U_C} = (v + 1)\frac{\dot{C}}{C}.\tag{13}$$

It can be shown that $v + 1$ is the negative of the elasticity of marginal utility, and $\dot{C}/C$ is the rate of growth of consumption. The subjective rate of interest is equal to their product. For any program of capital accumulation that maintains a constant savings rate s over time, the rate of growth of consumption is simply the product $s\rho$. Expression 13 becomes

$$r = (1 + v)s\rho.\tag{14}$$

Since v is fixed by tastes (those, let us say, of the planning commission acting on behalf of "society"), implementation of the Fisherian balance $r = \rho$ consists of choosing s equal to $(1 + v)^{-1}$.

---

[11] Cf. J. Tinbergen [20 and 21] and S. Chakravarty [4]. This utility function has simplicity to recommend it but it also has the quality—compelling to some and distressing to others—of being the only utility function which implies that the subjective rate of interest depends only on the rate of growth of consumption and is independent of the level of consumption. A comprehensive discussion of the problems of defining a utility function in the context of infinite time can be found in Chakravarty [3].

3. Saving and Technique Functionally Related

Now we can proceed to the heart of the present inquiry, but not, unfortunately, without additional notation. Let w represent the exogenously fixed wage, and let l denote the labor-capital ratio. Each value of l is supposed to represent a different technique of production. The output-capital ratio ρ is a function of l alone by virtue of the assumption of a first-degree homogeneous production function,[12] and we shall assume $\rho(l)$ is a strictly concave function, that is, one reflecting strictly diminishing marginal returns of output to labor. Let α stand for the proportion of profits (surpluses) that are saved, which will be assumed to be a decision under the control of the planning commission. Assuming that all wages are consumed, we have s as the following function of l and α:

$$s(l, \alpha) = \frac{\alpha[\rho(l) - wl]}{\rho(l)}. \tag{15}$$

In order to avoid mathematical complications, we shall limit our attention here to capital accumulation programs in which l and α, and hence ρ and s, are fixed once and for all at time zero.

One extreme solution to the present problem is to proceed as before: to choose l so as to maximize immediate output, that is, to maximize ρ, but subject now to the constraint imposed by labor's insistence on consumption,

$$\rho - wl \geq 0. \tag{16}$$

Maximization of the productivity of capital represents a direct application to the labor-surplus economy of the social marginal productivity (SMP) criterion of Alfred Kahn [9] and Hollis Chenery [5]. But it should be observed that the context in which the SMP criterion was advanced was not one in which the rate of saving was linked to the choice of technique. Maximization of ρ subject to the constraint embodied in Expression 16 will—if the constraint is binding—lead to a zero rate of saving and, hence, a zero rate of growth of consumption. And precisely for this reason, the criterion of maximizing ρ is inapplicable under the present assumptions about the supply and behavior of labor. A decrease in the labor-capital ratio and the output-capital ratio in order to step up the savings ratio and the rate of growth of output and consumption seems clearly called for.

This suggests another extreme solution: to choose l and α to maximize the rate of growth of output and consumption. This solution, which—rightly or wrongly—has been associated with the names of Walter Galenson and Harvey Leibenstein,[13] has the attraction that maximal growth will eventually provide more consumption than any alternative program of capital accumulation.

---

[12] See footnote 7.
[13] See Galenson and Leibenstein [8].

Maximization of the growth rate $s\rho$ clearly involves setting α equal to the boundary value of unity, and choosing l to satisfy the first-order condition

$$\frac{\partial(s\rho)}{\partial l} = \frac{\partial[\alpha(\rho - wl)]}{\partial l} = \alpha(\rho_l - w) = 0$$

or, in other words, equality of the marginal productivity of labor and the wage:

$$\rho_l = w. \tag{17}$$

Maximization of the growth rate (which for $\alpha = 1$ is equal to the investable surplus per unit of capital) implies choosing l to equate the marginal productivity of labor with the wage.[14] This corresponds, by the way, to the choice of l to maximize the return on capital as a state capitalist or private entrepreneur would measure it: output less wage costs. This solution suffers from the defect of sacrificing the present to the future regardless of how poor, in consequence, the present may become relative to the future and of how distant the future may be for which the present is sacrificed.

Maurice Dobb [6], Otto Eckstein [7], and Amartya Sen [17, 18] have pointed out the extreme nature of these solutions, and each has sketched the outline of an alternative approach. My own approach, the choice of l, α, s, and ρ in terms of utility maximization, is more in the spirit of Eckstein than of Dobb or Sen. As before, we suppose that instantaneous utility and consumption are related by the function

$$U(C) = -aC^{-v}, \qquad a, v > 0. \tag{9}$$

Total utility $\mathcal{U}$ is given by

$$\mathcal{U} = \int_0^\infty U[C(t)] \, dt = \int_0^\infty -a[C(t)]^{-v} \, dt. \tag{18}$$

With bliss taken as zero, Ramsey's objective of minimizing the integral of the difference between B and U is equivalent to maximization of $\mathcal{U}$.

Since we are confining our attention to once-and-for-all choice of l, α, s, and ρ, we can substitute for the equations

$$Y(t) = \rho K(t) \tag{2}$$

$$Y(t) = C(t) + \dot{K}(t) \tag{3}$$

the equations

$$C(t) = (1 - s)\rho K(t) \tag{19}$$

$$\dot{K}(t) = s\rho K(t). \tag{20}$$

---

[14] The "marginal productivity of labor," unless qualified, means marginal productivity within the capitalistic sector; the marginal productivity of labor unassisted by capital is, by assumption, zero.

Integration of Expression 20 gives

$$K(t) = K(0)e^{s\rho t}, \tag{21}$$

where $K(0)$ is the given initial capital stock. This also gives

$$C(t) = (1 - s)\rho K(0)e^{s\rho t} \tag{22}$$

in place of Equation 19. If we substitute the right-hand side of Equation 22 for the left in Expression 19, we have

$$\mathcal{U} = \int_0^\infty -a[(1 - s)\rho K(0)e^{s\rho t}]^{-v} \, dt. \tag{23}$$

After integrating and substituting an equivalent expression for s from Equation 15, Equation 23 becomes

$$\mathcal{U} = \frac{-a[\rho - \alpha(\rho - wl)]^{-v}K(0)^{-v}}{v\alpha(\rho - wl)}. \tag{24}$$

Maximization of $\mathcal{U}$ is equivalent to minimization of $\log(-\mathcal{U})$ or to maximization of $-\log(-\mathcal{U})$, and this last is the easiest expression to work with. Now, $-\log(-\mathcal{U})$ is given by the equation

$$V = -\log(-\mathcal{U}) = \log a + v \log[\rho - \alpha(\rho - wl)] + v \log K(0)$$
$$+ \log v + \log \alpha + \log(\rho - wl). \tag{25}$$

Necessary conditions for maximization of Equation 25 are given by

$$\frac{\partial V}{\partial \alpha} \left\{ \begin{matrix} \geq \\ = \end{matrix} \right\} 0 \quad \text{as} \quad \left\{ \begin{matrix} \alpha = 1 \\ \alpha < 1 \end{matrix} \right\} \tag{26}$$

and

$$\frac{\partial V}{\partial l} = 0.^{15} \tag{27}$$

From Equation 25 we have

$$\frac{\partial V}{\partial \alpha} = \frac{v(\rho - wl)}{\rho - \alpha(\rho - wl)} + \frac{1}{\alpha}.$$

Thus Expression 26 becomes

$$\rho \left\{ \begin{matrix} \geq \\ = \end{matrix} \right\} (1 + v)\alpha(\rho - wl) \quad \text{as} \quad \left\{ \begin{matrix} \alpha = 1 \\ \alpha < 1 \end{matrix} \right\}. \tag{28}$$

---

[15] The boundary value $\alpha = 0$, which would correspond to $\partial V/\partial \alpha \leq 0$, and the SMP choice of l (with l such that $\rho = wl$), which would correspond to $\partial V/\partial l \geq 0$, can be eliminated simply by virtue of the fact that either of these choices would lead to the dominated utility value $\mathcal{U} = -\infty$. The possibility of $\partial V/\partial l < 0$, for the Galenson-Leibenstein choice of l (with l such that $\rho_l = w$), can be ruled out by appealing to continuity: since $\partial V/\partial l$ is positive for all values of l less than the Galenson-Leibenstein value, it cannot be negative at the Galenson-Leibenstein value.

Now combining Equations 14 and 15, we have

$$r = (1 + v)\alpha(\rho - wl), \tag{29}$$

so that Expression 28 becomes

$$\rho \begin{Bmatrix} \geq \\ = \end{Bmatrix} r \quad \text{as} \quad \begin{Bmatrix} \alpha = 1 \\ \alpha < 1 \end{Bmatrix}. \tag{30}$$

The derivative $\partial V/\partial l$ is given by

$$\frac{\partial V}{\partial l} = \frac{v[\rho_l - \alpha(\rho_l - w)]}{\rho - \alpha(\rho - wl)} + \frac{\rho_l - w}{\rho - wl}. \tag{31}$$

Thus, Equation 27 becomes

$$\rho - \rho_l l = (1 + v)\alpha(\rho - wl)\frac{\alpha(w - \rho_l) + \rho_l}{\alpha w} = r\frac{\alpha(w - \rho_l) + \rho_l}{\alpha w}. \tag{32}$$

Since the left-hand side of Equation 32 is smaller than ρ unless $\rho_l = 0$, and the right-hand side is greater than or equal to r, the equality in Expression 28 can hold only in the event $\rho_l = 0$, in which case both Equation 32 and Equation 30 reduce to the Euler-Lagrange equation (Equation 7) that characterizes the optimal growth path under the assumption that savings and technique are divorced. This should not be surprising, for if zero marginal productivity of labor is consistent with the optimal solution in the present problem, the constraint on savings imposed by the consumption of wage income is in fact not binding, and the present problem reduces to the previous one, in which technique and savings can be independently optimized.

If the solution of Equation 32 requires $\rho_l > 0$, the constraint arising from the consumption of wage income limits the choice of savings rate and the choice of technique, and strict inequality must hold in Expression 30. This is to say that α must equal unity; in other words, optimal growth requires reinvestment of all surpluses remaining after payment of the institutionally fixed wage bill wlK. In this case, the optimal technique is given by the value of l for which Equation 33 holds:

$$\rho - \rho_l l = r. \tag{33}$$

This is Equation 32 with α replaced by unity.

Equation 33 reflects a balance between "opportunity" and "impatience" when consumption of wage income is an effective constraint on choice of technique and savings rate. Marginal impatience is reflected in the value of the subjective rate of interest r. Opportunity is here represented by the physical marginal productivity of capital,

$$\left(\frac{\partial Y}{\partial K}\right)_{\text{employment = const}} = \rho - \rho_l l,$$

the extra output from an extra unit of capital with employment unchanged. The physical productivity should be distinguished from the marginal social productivity of capital,

$$\left(\frac{\delta Y}{\delta K}\right)_{l=\text{const}} = \rho,$$

which measures the extra output from an extra unit of capital when employment is increased to maintain a constant labor-capital ratio, which is the optimal employment strategy from the point of view of social utility maximization. The physical productivity of capital is equal to the return on capital measured by subtracting from the social productivity a labor cost computed by replacing the wage w with a lower shadow wage equal to the marginal productivity of labor ρ_l.[16] For the optimal technique and savings rate the following inequality holds:

$$\rho > \rho - \rho_l l = r > \rho - wl = s\rho. \tag{34}$$

Note that as v approaches zero, the $\mathscr{U}$-maximizing choice of l approaches the Galenson-Leibenstein growth-maximizing choice, and the physical productivity of capital and the subjective rate of interest approach the private rate of return to capital: $v \to 0$ implies $r \to (\rho - wl)$; hence from Equation 33 we have $\rho_l \to w$, which implies maximization of the rate of growth. A similar argument establishes that as $v \to \infty$, the optimal choice of l approaches the SMP choice of l to equate ρ with wl (unless a smaller value of l drives ρ_l to zero).

If we momentarily change the ground rules and assume that α is a parameter fixed exogenously rather than a choice variable, equality between the subjective rate of interest and the physical productivity of capital no longer characterizes the socially optimal choice of technique. In this case, which corresponds to a mixed economy in which the government controls employment but not savings (the value of α being determined, for example, by the behavior of private capitalists, just as the consumption of wage income is determined by the behavior of workers), Equation 32 alone characterizes the optimum, and the optimal physical productivity of capital exceeds the subjective rate of interest. The ratio of the physical productivity of capital to the subjective rate of interest,

$$\frac{\alpha w + (1 - \alpha)\rho_l}{\alpha w},$$

varies inversely with the propensity to save of capitalists.

---

[16] The shadow wage can be expressed in terms of w by substituting in Equation 33 an equivalent expression for l from Equation 15. This substitution gives
$$\rho_l = (\rho - r)w/(1 - s)\rho < w.$$

A numerical example might be useful in assessing the difference between optimization in terms of utility maximization and optimization in terms of the alternative criteria of choice to which reference has been made. Suppose production is governed by the Cobb-Douglas function (with L representing employment and with the other variables defined as before),

$$Y = L^{1/2}K^{1/2} = l^{1/2}K,$$

so that

$$\rho = l^{1/2}.$$

Further, let $v = 2$ and let $w = 2$. Then, Table 1 gives the values of the several variables associated with utility maximization and, for contrast, with maximization of immediate output ρ and with maximization of the rate of growth $s\rho$. It should be observed in Table 1 that the physical productivity of

Table 1. Parameter Values Resulting from Application of Alternative Criteria with $\rho = l^{1/2}, v = 2, w = 2$

	Criterion		
	Max ρ	Max $\mathcal{U}$	Max $s\rho$
α = proportion of profits saved	—*	1.0	1.0
l = labor-capital ratio	0.25	0.173	0.0625
ρ = output-capital ratio = social productivity of capital	0.5	0.416	0.25
s = rate of saving	0.0	0.166	0.5
$s\rho = \rho - wl$ = rate of growth = private rate of return on capital†	0.0	0.0695	0.125
ρ_l = marginal productivity of labor = shadow wage	1.0	1.2	2.0
$\rho - \rho_l l$ = physical productivity of capital	0.25	0.208	0.125
r = subjective rate of interest	0.0	0.208	0.375

* The value of α is irrelevant since $\rho - wl = 0$.
† Since either $\alpha = 1$ or $\rho - wl = 0$, it follows that $s\rho = \rho - wl$.

capital and the subjective rate of interest are equal only for the optimal growth path max $\mathcal{U}$. For growth rates less than optimal, of which the max ρ path is an extreme example, the physical productivity of capital exceeds the rate of interest; for growth rates greater than optimal, of which the max $s\rho$ path is the limiting case, the opposite is true.

Figure 1 illustrates some of the magnitudes of Table 1 graphically. The next three figures indicate the time profiles of output, consumption, and employment resulting from the three criteria. Initial capital stock $K(0)$ is assumed in all cases to be equal to 100.

4. The Value of Capital

In the economy of our model, output and consumption are governed by the simple relationships

$$Y(t) = \rho K(t) = \rho K(0)e^{s\rho t},$$

$$C(t) = (1 - s)\rho K(t) = (1 - s)\rho K(0)e^{s\rho t}.$$

But suppose we relax this assumption slightly to allow the planning commission to be presented with the possibility of an alternative use of one unit of capital at time t_0. The time pattern of consumption provided by the new opportunity, let us suppose, is given by the function $\Delta(t)$, $t_0 \leq t < \infty$. (This function is assumed to reflect reinvestment of surpluses over wage costs.)

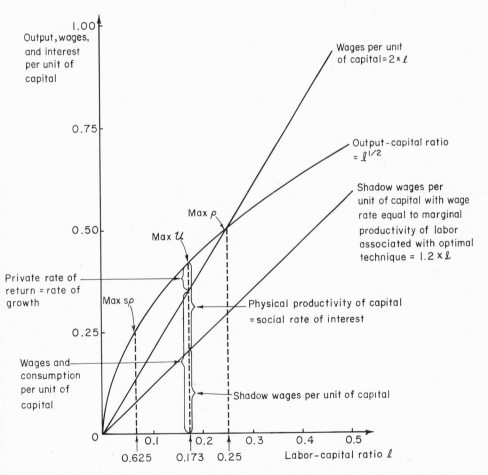

FIGURE 1. Output, wages, and interest as functions of the technique of production.

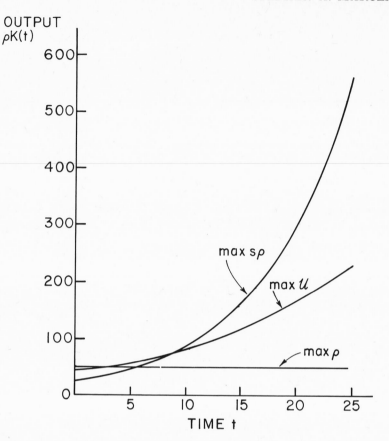

FIGURE 2. Time profile of output resulting from utility maximization and from alternative criteria.

The choice facing the planners is whether or not to divert one unit of investment to the new option when the opportunity arises.

How might planners make this decision? The first step is to compute the marginal utility afforded by the new opportunity. Denoting this marginal utility by $\mathscr{U}_\Delta$, we can write

$$\mathscr{U}_\Delta = \int_{t_0}^{\infty} U_C \, \Delta(t) \, dt = \int_{t_0}^{\infty} U_{C(0)} \, \Delta(t) e^{-rt} \, dt$$

$$= U_{C(0)} e^{-rt_0} \int_{t_0}^{\infty} \Delta(t) e^{-r(t-t_0)} \, dt,$$

where $U_{C(0)}$ equals the marginal utility of consumption at time $t = 0$, and (by virtue of the constancy of the elasticity of utility)

$$U_C = U_{C(0)} e^{-rt}.$$

The second step is to compare $\mathscr{U}_\Delta$ with the marginal utility of investment at time t in the optimal technique as determined by v, w, $\rho(l)$, and $s(l, \alpha)$. This marginal utility we denote $\mathscr{U}_{K(t_0)}$. We have

$$\mathscr{U}_{K(t_0)} = \int_{t_0}^{\infty} U_C \frac{\partial C(t)}{\partial K(t_0)} \, dt = U_{C(0)} e^{-rt_0} (1 - s)\rho \int_{t_0}^{\infty} e^{(s\rho - r)(t - t_0)} \, dt$$

$$= U_{C(0)} e^{-rt_0} \frac{(1 - s)\rho}{r - s\rho}.$$

For the $\mathscr{U}$-maximizing choices of s and l, substitution from Equations 15 and 33 gives the equality

$$\mathscr{U}_{K(t_0)} = U_{C(0)} e^{-rt} \frac{w}{w - \rho_l}. \tag{36}$$

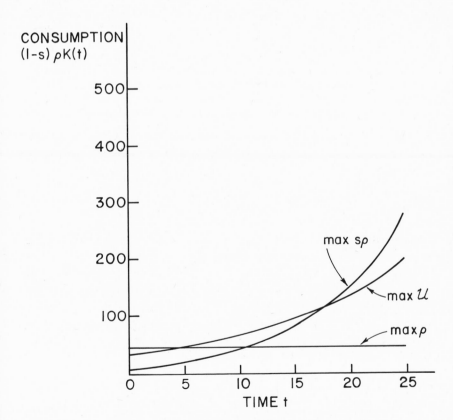

FIGURE 3. Time profile of consumption resulting from utility maximization and from alternative criteria.

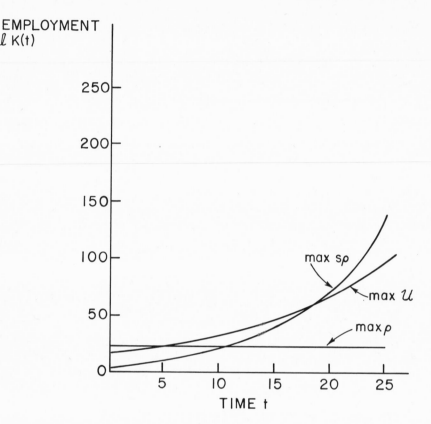

FIGURE 4. Time profile of employment resulting from utility maximization and from alternative criteria.

Now the new opportunity should be exploited only if $\mathcal{U}_\Delta > \mathcal{U}_{K(t_0)}$ or, in other words, only if

$$U_{C(0)}e^{-rt_0} \int_{t_0}^{\infty} \Delta(t)e^{-r(t-t_0)}\,dt > U_{C(0)}e^{-rt_0}\frac{w}{w-\rho_l}. \tag{37}$$

This criterion can be made a little more familiar by normalizing through the division of Expression 37 by $U_{C(t_0)} = U_{C(0)}e^{-rt_0}$, that is, by dividing both sides of Expression 37 by the marginal utility of consumption at time t_0. Then

$$\frac{\mathcal{U}_\Delta}{U_{C(t_0)}} = \int_{t_0}^{\infty} \Delta(t)e^{-r(t-t_0)}\,dt, \tag{38}$$

$$\frac{\mathcal{U}_{K(t_0)}}{U_{C(t_0)}} = \frac{w}{w-\rho_l}, \tag{39}$$

and Expression 37, the criterion of superiority of the new use of capital over the "optimal" technique, becomes

$$\int_{t_0}^{\infty} \Delta(t)e^{-r(t-t_0)}\, dt > \frac{w}{w - \rho_l}. \tag{40}$$

The integral $\int_{t_0}^{\infty} \Delta(t)e^{r(t-t_0)}\, dt$ is customarily called the present value at time t_0 of the consumption stream $\Delta(t)$ evaluated at the discount rate r. Similarly,

$$\frac{\mathcal{U}_{K(t_0)}}{U_{C(t_0)}} = \frac{w}{w - \rho_l} \tag{41}$$

is the marginal present value of investment in the "optimal" technique. Thus Expression 40 says that the present value of the new opportunity must exceed the marginal present value of investment in the "optimal" technique. This may be a bit surprising, for the physical trade-off rate between consumption and investment determined by the equation

$$Y(t) = C(t) + \dot{K}(t) \tag{3}$$

is unity, and we might therefore have expected that the new investment option would be attractive provided its present value $\int_{t_0}^{\infty} \Delta(t)e^{-r(t-t_0)}\, dt$ exceeded unity. But in the present model, limitations on the choice of s mean that the marginal rate of substitution, as reflected in the marginal present value of investment, is in excess of the technological transformation rate, and it is with the first rather than the second that the present value of alternative $\int_{t_0}^{\infty} \Delta(t)e^{-r(t-t_0)}\, dt$ must be compared.

The marginal present value of investment $w/(w - \rho_l)$ is thus the shadow price of investment. Since in the present model average and marginal values coincide, $w/(w - \rho_l)$ is also the shadow price of capital. This shadow price falls to unity only in the limiting case of $\rho_l = 0$ and $\rho = r$, when the production function $\rho(l)$, the elasticity of utility $-v$, and the wage rate w combine to make it possible to divorce the savings question from the technique question. At the other extreme, when v goes to zero and $\mathcal{U}$-maximization dictates the choice of l to provide a rate of growth of output and consumption that approaches the maximal feasible rate of growth, ρ_l goes to w and the shadow price of capital approaches infinity.

Measurement of the effectiveness of potential investments thus requires a more elaborate evaluation than would be necessary were it not for labor's effective insistence on consumption. Because the choice of the rate of saving cannot be divorced from the choice of technique, investment planning requires not only specification of a discount rate but also specification of a shadow price of capital. The present value of the consumption stream resulting from each investment opportunity (including whatever consumption is afforded by reinvestment) must be computed at the social rate of discount, and this present value must be compared with the capital cost computed with a shadow price equal to the economy's marginal present value of capital. Only in the event that $\rho = r$ for the optimal technique and the conflict between savings and growth, on the one hand, and immediate output, consumption, and employment, on the other, disappears does this evaluation procedure reduce to the more familiar procedure of comparing discounted present value with the nominal capital cost.[17]

5. Decentralization of Choice of Technique

It is evident that *laissez faire* cannot be relied upon to produce the optimal technique under the assumptions of the model. Decentralized entrepreneurs left to their own devices would maximize the private rate of return to capital $\rho - wl$ as would profit-maximizing state capitalists.

Decentralized "market socialists" of a Lange-Lerner type could be guided to the $\mathcal{U}$-maximizing choice of technique by an order from the planning commission to choose the technique of production to maximize the physical rate of return $\rho - \rho_l l$ computed with a shadow wage equal to the marginal productivity of labor associated with the optimal technique. This instruction would have to be supplemented by an order to reinvest all surpluses remaining after actual wage costs are paid.

---

[17] The analysis of this essay has been constrained by the assumption that the choice of technique and, hence, savings rate is a once-and-for-all decision. This limitation has been overcome in subsequent, as yet unpublished, work growing out of discussion in Karl Shell's spring 1965 seminar in optimal growth theory.

Formulating the problem as a variational one of choosing a labor-capital ratio $l(t)$ that maximizes total utility defined as the integral of a utility function $U(C)$ monotonically and smoothly approaching zero from below,

$$\mathcal{U} = \int_0^\infty U[C(t)]\, dt,$$

subject to the constraint

$$\dot{K}(t) = \alpha\{\rho[l(t)] - w\}K(t),$$

where

$$C(t) = \rho[l(t)]K(t) - \dot{K}(t) = \{(1 - \alpha)\rho[l(t)] + \alpha w l(t)\}K(t)$$

frees one from the restriction to constant technique and savings rates. The generalization turns out to add nothing for the constant elasticity utility function $U = -aC^{-v}$ analyzed here: in this case the optimal technique is constant over time even if the wider class of variable labor-capital ratios is admitted to consideration. But if a wider class of utility functions is considered, or if the (eventual) existence of an effective limit to the supply of labor is admitted, then constant $l(t)$ will in general not be optimal. The solution to the broader problem may involve changes in the shadow price of investment over time. In this case the optimality condition—Equation 33 when α is a choice variable, Equation 32 when α is a fixed parameter—becomes more complicated; the balance between "opportunity" and "impatience" must now include the capital gains or losses resulting from changes in the shadow price of investment.

Replacing w by ρ_l in choice of technique calculations amounts to an "as if" subsidy of $w - \rho_l$ per unit of labor. Choice of the optimal technique could be achieved through payment of an actual subsidy of $w - \rho_l$ to private entrepreneurs or state capitalists; but the taxes levied to pay the subsidy must not fall on the workers, for this would violate the rules of the game, which requires consumption of all wage income.[18]

The difficulty with decentralization of decision making on the basis of a shadow wage is a familiar one: the optimal technique must be known to the planning commission in order to determine the appropriate shadow wage. Hence, there might seem to be little advantage in decentralization. However, the optimal technique and shadow wage could be determined simultaneously by a decentralized *tâtonnement* procedure. If l is iteratively adjusted according to the formula

$$l^{n+l} - l^n = -\theta(\rho^n - \rho_l{}^n l^n - r^n) \qquad n = 1, 2, 3, \cdots, \tag{42}$$

where ρ^n, $\rho_l{}^n$, and r^n are values associated with $l = l^n$ and θ is a positive constant, then convergence of the sequence l^n to an arbitrarily small neighborhood of the optimal labor-capital ratio can be guaranteed by suitable choice of θ regardless of the initial choice of l.[19] Equation 42 says, in effect, that the labor-capital ratio should be decreased (in order to increase the rates of saving and growth) so long as the physical productivity of capital exceeds the social rate of discount, and vice versa. The social rate of discount would be recomputed from Equation 14 by the planning commission between iterations and transmitted to the decentralized managers, who, after computing the values of ρ and ρ_l, would calculate the new value of l from Equation 42 and transmit the associated values of ρ and s to the planning commission. This would in turn suggest a new value of r, which would form the basis for the next iteration.

6. Conclusions

The basic assumptions of the model explored in this essay are (1) the availability of unlimited supplies of labor in perpetuity at an exogenously

---

[18] The indirect control exercised through the subsidization of wages would have to be supplemented by direct control to ensure reinvestment of all profits remaining after payment of wages and taxes. But private capitalists would presumably tire very quickly of always having their cake and never eating it.

[19] This proposition presupposes that the optimal technique implies $\alpha = 1$. The more general case can be covered by suitably amending the algorithm embodied in Equation 42. The proof of the convergence of the sequence defined by Equation 42 to an arbitrary small neighborhood of the $\mathcal{U}$-maximizing value of l requires nothing more than modification of the proof of convergence of a continuous gradient process to allow for discrete changes in the values of variables. See Arrow, Hurwicz, and Uzawa [1], Chapter 10.

determined wage rate and (2) the consumption of all wage income. A third assumption is that labor neither involves disutility nor is productive without the assistance of capital. Without the second assumption, the choice of technique is a relatively simple affair: the goal is clearly to choose the labor-capital ratio l to maximize the output-capital ratio ρ. In this case the choice of a rate of saving s (which together with ρ determines the rate of growth of output, consumption, and employment) is a separate question. But insistence on the part of labor on consumption of its entire income makes it impossible to divorce the choice of technique from an upper bound on s; savings now can come only from profits. The greater the value of l and ρ (beyond the point where the marginal productivity of labor ρ_l falls to the level of the wage rate w), the lower is the upper limit on s. Others [6, 7, 17, and 18] have explored the conflict between immediate output and the rate of growth that the dependence of s on l poses, and it has been pointed out that, in general, the optimal technique can be expected to reflect a compromise between the maximal feasible immediate output and the maximal feasible rate of growth. The present analysis, couched in terms of maximization of an explicit utility function (chosen for convenience to reflect a constant elasticity with respect to consumption), confirms the wisdom of compromise, but our chief interest has been not in the compromise itself but rather in its implications with respect to wages and interest.

The principal conclusion was stated at the outset of this essay but certainly bears repeating. Neither the social rate of return (or social marginal productivity) of capital ρ nor the private rate of return $\rho - wl$ is equal to the subjective rate of interest r that reflects the marginal premium on present over future consumption that is implicit in the economy's utility function—even for the optimal technique and saving rate. The Fisherian balance of opportunity and impatience characterizing utility maximization is implemented instead by the following equality between the physical marginal productivity of capital and the subjective rate of interest:

$$\rho - \rho_l l = r. \tag{33}$$

The physical marginal productivity of capital on the left-hand side of Equation 33 is equivalent to the yield on capital measured by subtracting labor costs evaluated on the basis of a shadow wage (equal to the marginal productivity of labor associated with the optimal technique) from the output-capital ratio. Furthermore, the marginal productivity of labor optimally lies between zero and the actual wage, so that

$$\rho \geq \rho - \rho_l l = r > \rho - wl. \tag{34}$$

The private rate of return $\rho - wl$ is equal to the rate of growth of output, consumption, and employment $s\rho$ provided all surpluses remaining after payment of wages are reinvested,[20] so that Equation 34 can be interpreted as setting upper and lower bounds for the rate of interest as, respectively, the output-capital ratio and the rate of growth of the economy. The rate of interest will actually attain the upper bound only in the event the technology is such that it permits the best of both worlds simultaneously—the maximum output-capital ratio (which implies $\rho_l = 0$) and independent optimization with respect to the rate of saving.

The rate of interest appropriate for discounting the consumption stream generated by any new investment opportunities that may be afforded from time to time is r, for discounting at r is equivalent to weighting consumption at each moment of time by its marginal utility. But the decision whether or not to undertake any such investment cannot be made by comparing the present value of its consumption stream at r with its capital cost. The inability of the economy to optimize independently with respect to the rate of saving means that the marginal rate of substitution of consumption for investment, in other words, the marginal present value of investment at the social rate of discount, exceeds the physical rate of transformation of unity at "equilibrium." The present value afforded by any investment opportunity must therefore be compared with its capital cost evaluated at a shadow price equal to the marginal present value of investment in the economy. This marginal present value falls to unity only in the event that $\rho = r$ and the conflict between immediate output and employment, on the one hand, and savings and growth, on the other, disappears.[21]

Because of the difference between the private rate of return and the social rate of discount, *laissez faire* could not be expected to lead to an optimal choice of technology. A subsidy on labor costs to private entrepreneurs or state capitalists, or an "as if" subsidy to market socialists, would, however, make private and shadow returns coincide. In principle, the size of the subsidy $w - \rho_l$, with ρ_l as the marginal productivity of labor associated with the optimal technique, can be determined along with the optimal technique by a decentralized *tâtonnement* as well as by centralized planning.

The model on which the conclusions of this essay are based is an extremely simple one. It ignores the existence of a multiplicity of sectors, technologies,

---

[20] Reinvestment of all surpluses turns out to be a condition of optimality except in the limiting case $\rho = r$, in which event the conflict between immediate output and the rate of growth disappears.

[21] The point is a general one. When institutional constraints of any kind prevent optimization with respect to the rate of saving, the social, private, and physical productivities of capital will in general differ, and the price or "opportunity cost" of capital will differ from the purely physical marginal rate of transformation between consumption and investment goods. The question of interest rates and capital valuation for purposes of public investment is explored from a basis that reflects the conditions of mature mixed-enterprise economies rather than the destructive labor-surplus feature of underdeveloped economies in two articles by Marglin [13 and 14].

and outputs in the economy. It ignores foreign trade. It assumes unlimited supplies of labor not simply for the present but in perpetuity. It assumes absolute rigidity with respect to real wage rates and consumption by workers. Moreover, the choice of technique and the choice of savings rate are posited as once-and-for-all decisions. Finally, the utility function chosen—besides being extremely simple with respect to total consumption—does not take distribution of consumption into account at all, and distribution is surely an important aspect of the conflict of immediate output and employment against savings and growth. Nevertheless, the propositions I have sought to establish are qualitative rather than quantitative in nature, and for this purpose a simple model suffices as well as a complex one. The precise form of the conclusions will certainly be affected by added doses of realism, but not their nature.

References

1. Arrow, K. J., L. Hurwicz, and H. Uzawa, *Studies in Linear and Non-Linear Programming*, Stanford, Calif., Stanford University Press, 1958, Chapter 10.
2. Bator, F., "On Capital Productivity, Input Allocation, and Growth," *Quarterly Journal of Economics*, Vol. 71 (1957).
3. Chakravarty, S., "The Existence of an Optimal Savings Program," *Econometrica*, Vol. 30 (1962).
4. Chakravarty, S., "Optimal Savings With Finite Planning Horizon," *International Economic Review*, Vol. 3 (1962).
5. Chenery, H., "The Application of Investment Criteria," *Quarterly Journal of Economics*, Vol. 67 (1953).
6. Dobb, M., *An Essay on Economic Growth and Planning*, New York: Monthly Review Press, 1960, Chapters 3 and 4.
7. Eckstein, O., "Investment Criteria for Economic Development and the Theory of Intertemporal Welfare Economics," *Quarterly Journal of Economics*, Vol. 71 (1957).
8. Galenson, W., and H. Leibenstein, "Investment Criteria, Productivity and Economic Development," *Quarterly Journal of Economics*, Vol. 69 (1955).
9. Kahn, A. E., "Investment Criteria in Development Programs," *Quarterly Journal of Economics*, Vol. 65 (1951).
10. Lewis, W. A., "Economic Development With Unlimited Supplies of Labor," *Manchester School*, Vol. 22 (1954).
11. Lewis, W. A., *The Theory of Economic Growth*, London: Allen & Unwin Ltd., 1955.
12. Lewis, W. A., "Unlimited Labor: Further Notes," *Manchester School*, Vol. 26 (1958).
13. Marglin, S. A., "The Opportunity Costs of Public Investment," *Quarterly Journal of Economics*, Vol. 77 (1963).
14. Marglin, S. A., "The Social Rate of Discount and the Optimal Rate of Investment," *Quarterly Journal of Economics*, Vol. 77 (1963).

15. Pajestka, J., "Some Problems of Economic Development Planning," in O. Lange (ed.), *Problems of Political Economy of Socialism*, New Delhi: People's Publishing House, 1962.

16. Ramsey, F. P., "A Mathematical Theory of Saving," *Economic Journal*, Vol. 38 (1928).

17. Sen, A. K., "Some Notes on the Choice of Capital-Intensity in Development Planning," *Quarterly Journal of Economics*, Vol. 71 (1957).

18. Sen, A. K., *Choice of Techniques*, Oxford: Basil Blackwell & Mott, Ltd., 1960.

19. Tilak, V. R. K., "Unemployment Statistics in India," *Economic Weekly*, Vol. 27 (1965).

20. Tinbergen, J., "The Optimum Rate of Saving," *Economic Journal*, Vol. 66 (1956).

21. Tinbergen, J., "Optimum Savings and Utility Maximization Over Time," *Econometrica*, Vol. 28 (1960).

IX

A New Look at the Sandee Model[1]

NICHOLAS G. CARTER

International Bank for Reconstruction and Development

The application of optimal programming models to the problems of development economics is a relatively new and scarcely touched field. Moreover, it has a distinct tradition quite separate from that of optimal growth theory, arising in the work of Leontief in input-output models and Dantzig in linear programming. Possibly only in some of the more recent work of Eckaus [3] is the relationship with conventional growth theory explicitly brought forth. For the most part it remains a separate discipline.

In sharp distinction to optimal theory, published work in development programming is very scarce, the major examples being the work of Chenery [2], Manne [6], Sandee [7], Bruno [1], and Eckaus [4].[2] The reason for this scarcity probably lies in the close relationship this field must maintain with economic reality as distinct from economic theory. This means that the model builder is always acutely aware of the assumptions he must make in order to have a problem that is mathematically and computationally tractable. It also means that he is invariably occupied with the often frustrating task of data generation. Finally, because he is dealing with a real and detailed situation, he runs the risk of appearing to suggest policy, regardless of how clearly he points out the serious departures from reality caused by his

---

[1] I am indebted to Professor Shell for many helpful comments and criticisms, however I retain full responsibility for any mistakes contained herein.

[2] The last two works cited are not as yet published but are important and are available.

assumptions. It is with the first and third of these problems that this essay is concerned, the assumptions of programming models.

One of the most widely used of these assumptions is the specification of consumption as a fixed proportion bundle of goods;

$$c_i = l_i C, \quad l_i = \text{constant}, \quad i = 1, \cdots, n, \tag{1}$$

where C or $\sum c_i$ is the maximand. I shall explore the possibilities of changing this consumption form to one somewhat more realistic in the context of a small well-known, linear programming development model, the "Sandee" model.[3] The major change takes the form of allowing substitution to take place between goods in the consumption bundle. This is accomplished by the removal of constraints on consumption (which are present largely because of the lack of substitutability in the criterion function) and by the utilization of the techniques of nonlinear programming.

Since the work of Professor Sandee is well known, I shall do no more here than describe it briefly. Its purpose was to demonstrate and to teach the method of programming models rather than to produce a definitive development plan. It refers to the Indian economy in the decade 1960–1970 and works with variables that represent changes between those two dates. Its thirteen sectors explicitly describe the entire economy, and the whole decade is treated as one time period. This immediately suggests problems having to do with investment lags, thus an assumption is made that investment over the decade increases in a monotonic linear fashion. Furthermore, in order to make the model as compact as possible the B (investment) and S (inventory) matrices are converted into the corresponding flows and added to the A (technology) matrix. Since this is a difference model with capital restrained to grow in a linear fashion, there is no explicit problem of the postterminal period.[4] The maximand of the model is the sum of sectoral consumption over the decade.

The particular treatment of resource constraints creates certain problems. Labor is assumed to be free. Foreign trade is specified to be in balance (that is, $\sum E_i - \sum M_i = 0$), however the structure of the model is such that a unit of exports costs less than the imports required to produce it. Thus exports have to be supplied with specific maximum and minimum (import) levels. It is these levels that serve to bind the model. Finally, investment is restricted to be less than a certain fraction of consumption, a constraint that is always active. There is, however, no upper-level constraint on investment except in agriculture.

A discussion of the Sandee treatment of consumption will serve to introduce the central problem of this essay. Sandee's criterion function is typical of

---

[3] See Sandee [7].

[4] This problem is discussed extensively in the works of Eckaus; see, for example, [4], pp. 1–14 for a brief outline.

those found in development programming models and provides only a partial improvement over the standard treatment.

Current practice is to specify a model such as

$$X_i + M_i \geq \sum_j a_{ij} X_j + E_i + G_i + V_i + C_i \qquad i, j = 1, \cdots, n, \qquad (2)$$

where X_i represents output, M_i imports, E_i exports, G_i government consumption, V_i investment, $\sum a_{ij} X_j$ interindustry demand, and C_i consumption of the ith good. Usually E_i and G_i are specified exogenously, we have V_i as a function of X_k, $k = 1, \cdots, n$, by means of the B (investment) matrix, and $\sum M_i$ is constrained by $\sum E_i$. Then C_i goes into the maximand, and thus the dependent variable is X_i. The next question is how to incorporate C_i into the maximand. Linearity will only allow

$$\Phi = \sum w_i C_i \qquad i = 1, \cdots, n, \qquad (3)$$

and for lack of better knowledge in a single period w_i is usually specified to be equal to one. At this point a fundamental problem arises. In such a linear world as is described by Relations 2 and 3, substitution, limited only by absolute supply constraints, will take place with the cheaper (in terms of shadow prices) goods driving out the more expensive. Since the model always assumes constant real prices, the resulting patterns of expenditure are very distorted unless there happen coincidentally to be appropriate constraints on supply. There is nothing in the formulation of consumption that prevents unlimited substitution. In order to prevent this a specification such as Equation 1 is generally used. This however allows no substitution at all.

Economic theory about the consumer suggests that

$$U = U(C_i, \cdots, C_n) \qquad (4)$$

and particularly emphasizes that

$$\frac{\partial^2 U}{\partial C_i^2} < 0, \qquad (5)$$

that is, diminishing marginal utility. In the linear programming context we find

$$\frac{\partial^2 \Phi}{\partial C_i^2} = 0; \qquad (6)$$

in order to have the conditions of Equation 5 we must have a nonlinear maximand. Furthermore, consumer theory suggests that

$$\frac{\partial U / \partial C_i}{\partial U / \partial C_j} = \frac{p_i}{p_j}, \qquad (7)$$

and in the linear programming model this becomes

$$\frac{\partial \Phi / \partial C_i}{\partial \Phi / \partial C_j} = \frac{l_i}{l_j} = k, \tag{8}$$

which equals p_i/p_j only on a set of measure zero. Thus the problem would seem to lie directly in the constant marginal utility requirement of the linear model.

Objections to the consumption function described by Relations 1 and 3 are twofold. First, it cannot handle income effects, and second, it cannot deal with price effects. It commits the economy to expenditures on a constant proportion bundle of goods valued in base-year prices. The first problem has been treated partially in the linear context, the second has not been dealt with effectively in linear models and is the subject of this essay.

The problem of income effects, although treated partially, is still generally unsolved. Part of the trouble lies in the relatively inexact nature of the behavior of Engel's curve. Elasticities are useful but are probably not constant over time. Linear model builders usually assume that the time period involved is short enough so that elasticities can be considered constant. This being accepted, the approach is to state the arc definition:

$$\varepsilon_i = \frac{C_i - C_{i0}}{C_{i0}} \bigg/ \frac{C - C_0}{C}, \tag{9}$$

which solves out to

$$C_i = (1 - \varepsilon_i)C_{i0} + \varepsilon_i \frac{C_{i0}}{C_0} C, \tag{10}$$

which is equivalent to

$$C_i = \gamma_i + \beta_i C. \tag{11}$$

If C_0 and C_{i0} refer to some base period (usually the zeroth year of the model), then Equation 11 is a tangent to Engel's curve;

$$C_i = KC^{\varepsilon_i} \tag{12}$$

at that reference point. In the context of the Sandee model, which deals with differences, Equation 10 becomes

$$(C_i - C_{i0}) = l_i(C - C_0), \tag{13}$$

where

$$l_i = \frac{\varepsilon_i C_{i0}}{C_0}. \tag{14}$$

The base period is 1960, and elasticities of 0.8 for agriculture and 1.0 for transport are assumed. The remaining four consumption sectors (food, large and small manufacturing, and housing) are all given the elasticity (1.4) required to satisfy additivity in the base year. The l_i, however, do not satisfy this condition. One solution is to normalize them; Sandee prefers to leave them as they are and allow limited freedom (± 13 per cent) around these values. This has the added advantage of allowing some substitution. The freedom takes the form of upper and lower bounds for each consumption activity, that is,

$$C_i \leq l_i C + R, \quad C_i \geq l_i C - R. \tag{15}$$

This is referred to as a "compromise" between the strictly proportional consumption formulation and the unstable completely substitutable form, but it does little to remedy the basic problem of lack of ability to adjust to price relationships. Only occasionally will a consumption activity not be at one or the other of the bounds, typically exhibiting a flip-flop reaction to price changes. In the optimal solution, five of the six consumption activities are at bounds and the sixth is at an intermediate level only because of a production bound; thus there is not much benefit from such a formulation.

In approaching this problem, the general feeling has been that linearity is mandatory because of the binding nature of the computational constraint. Since the Sandee model was published the capacity of computing equipment has grown in size and speed, so that with a model so small one can begin to consider nonlinear possibilities. The first function that suggests itself is the log-linear form:

$$W = \sum \alpha_i \log C_i, \quad i = 1, \cdots, n, \tag{16}$$

which is equivalent to

$$\Phi = C_1{}^{\alpha_1}, C_2{}^{\alpha_2}, C_3{}^{\alpha_3}, \cdots, C_n{}^{\alpha_n}. \tag{17}$$

If we accept the income-effects approach of the Sandee model, Equation 16 could be adjusted to

$$W = \sum \alpha_i \log (C_i - C_{i0}), \quad i = 1, \cdots, n. \tag{18}$$

This function allows price substitution; moreover, the coefficients α_i are expenditure shares and thus present no data problem because

$$\alpha_i = \frac{l_i}{\sum l_i}. \tag{19}$$

Although the model still requires constant *expenditure* proportions, it can take account of shadow prices rather than having to assume constant base-year prices. Thus physical units of consumption can vary and prices can affect consumption directly, rather than indirectly via costs as in the Sandee model.

If we now maximize W in Equation 16 instead of Φ in Equation 3, subject to the constraints of the rest of the original model, we find the model reacting to relative prices but not exploding. Thus all the consumption constraints can be removed. The new maximand has the correct convexity and, moreover, is monotonic, thus it can be dealt with by the standard piecewise linear approximation method.[5] In this particular case the resulting tableau has five fewer constraints but a large number of additional activities.

What are the theoretical assumptions behind this form of utility function? First, it requires the usual belief in the "representative" consumer whose consumption function does not require fixed proportions. (In fact it is an assumption of fixed proportions that is often given as an "apology" for the use of a linear fixed-coefficient maximand.) This utility function does however require fixed *expenditure* proportions. In addition we are required to suppose that the consumer market is operating freely and the income distribution is essentially "correct."

The use of base-period values for C_{i0} presents some problems. If we accept the approach to income adjustment of the Sandee model we must have the C_{i0} somewhere near the actual levels, otherwise the tangencies will be strongly divergent from the Engel curves. On the other hand, the form of Equation 18 makes it impossible for consumption levels to fall below base-period values, which they well may in reality if prices are very much out of line. It is obvious that the larger the term $C_i - C_{i0}$, the more substitution will take place. In the particular experience of this essay it was found that C_{i0} levels significantly below the base period allowed considerably more substitution than could realistically be expected in the economy. Thus, the comparisons that follow are with reference to C_{i0} at base-period levels but with full realization of the problems involved.

I mention these objections to the form of the maximand in order to point out an awareness of the shortcomings in the specification of the functional form and to avoid the assumption that I am recommending this particular form as *the* answer in development programming. This essay is directed rather to the properties and possibilities of substitutable functions in linear programming models.

If Equation 17 is subjected to constrained (by the consumer's budget) maximization, we get the standard relationship:

$$\frac{\alpha_i}{p_i q_i} = \frac{\alpha_j}{p_j q_j}. \tag{20}$$

If p_i is the shadow price and q_i the quantity consumed, then this relationship will hold at the solution point of the reformulated Sandee model. It can also be used to indicate what the results will be in comparison to the original solution (referred to henceforth as model I). As the α_i are shares, the approximate relationship,

$$q_i = \alpha_i C \tag{21}$$

---

[5] This is a common programming technique. See, for example, Hadley [5], Chapter 4.

should hold; thus, if the solution to model I was in no way distorted, we would expect

$$p_i = p_j = p_k = \cdots = p_n. \tag{22}$$

Table 1 shows the shadow prices of model I.[6]

Table 1. Model I

Sector	Price	Sector	Price
Agriculture	.630	Food	.777
Large Manufacturing	1.890	Small Manufacturing	.720
Transport	1.600	Housing	3.144

Thus we should expect agriculture, food, and small manufacturing to be consumed more and housing considerably less. In addition we should expect that the value of the maximand would be higher; allowing substitution where there was none before will increase welfare.

The new formulation of the Sandee model as just outlined (hereafter referred to as model II) was run, and as can be seen in Table 2 the results were somewhat as expected.

Table 2. Model II

	Consumption Values in Rupees Crores	
Sector	Model I	Model II
Agriculture	3647	3802
Food	426	642
Transport	583	631
Large Manufacturing	316	316
Small Manufacturing	791	1825
Housing	561	300
Maximand	6331	7516

Most noticeable is the small rise in agriculture and the much larger gain in small industry. This is because agriculture is subject to certain capacity restraints, as Sandee quite correctly wished to emphasize this phase of Indian development. As already mentioned, the model has no explicit resource constraints and thus would increase without limit if not bounded in some other way. In the case of model II, substitution allows an avoidance of the export constraints that bind model I; instead it is bounded by an agricultural output (investment) constraint. As would be expected, this provides both a p and a q for that sector, thus all other consumption activities, being unbounded, can

---

[6] Sandee [7], p. 58.

come into balance with agriculture. Note that the gain in "welfare" due solely to the freedom of substitution is almost 20 per cent.

The only question now is the credibility of model II in terms of production capacity limits. In the particular sense of the Sandee model this is equivalent to maximum limits on sectoral investment. In all but a few cases the required growth in capacity is less than that required in model I. Heavy equipment requires a capacity twenty times that of the base period, but since that period had only a minute amount of such production capacity this rate of growth may not be unreasonable.[7] Other equipment and small industry require growth rates of 17 and 13 per cent per annum, respectively, and these are probably quite feasible figures.

The purpose of this essay has been to suggest a new departure in the treatment of consumption in development programming models and to present the results of one such experiment. It has been shown that a nonlinear function of the simple log type is relatively easy to handle, produces quite reasonable results, and, in allowing substitution, provides a substantial improvement over previous treatments of consumption. In the particular model it was shown that the shadow prices could give some indication of the relative shifts in consumption patterns but that these shifts were due solely to price effects—the problem of income effects remaining essentially the same as in previous formulations. In the Sandee model in particular, and in other models to a lesser extent, the removal of consumption constraints places a much greater burden on the production considerations.

There seems to be an immediate point of departure from the approach in this essay and that is to investigate this type of consumption function in an intertemporal as well as in an intersectoral sense. A suitable maximand might be

$$W = \sum_{t=1}^{\tau} \sum_{i=1}^{n} \alpha_{it} \log \left(C_{it} - C_{i0} \right) \tag{23}$$

where

$$\alpha_{it} = \alpha_{i1}[1/(1 + r)^{t-1}], \tag{24}$$

r being the intertemporal discount rate on consumption. Such experiments are now being conducted with the Eckaus model.

References

1. Bruno, M., "Experiments with a Multi-sectoral Programming Model," unpublished, Massachusetts Institute of Technology, 1965.
2. Chenery, H. B., "The Role of Industrialization in Underdeveloped Countries," Proceedings of the American Economic Association, May 1955.

---

[7] The rate in model I is fifteen times that of the base period.

3. Eckaus, R. S., and L. Lefeber, "Capital Formation: A Theoretical and Empirical Analysis," *Review of Economics and Statistics*, Vol. 44 (May 1962).
4. Eckaus, R. S., and K. S. Parikh, "Planning for Growth: Multisectoral, Intertemporal Models Applied to India," Center for International Studies, Massachusetts Institute of Technology, Cambridge, Mass., April 1966.
5. Hadley, G. F., *Nonlinear and Dynamic Programming*, Reading, Mass.: Addison-Wesley Publishing Co., 1964.
6. Manne, A. S., "Key Sectors in the Mexican Economy, 1960–1970," in A. S. Manne and H. M. Markowitz, *Studies in Process Analysis*, New York: John Wiley & Sons, Inc., 1963.
7. Sandee, J., "A Demonstration Planning Model for India," Calcutta, India, 1960.

X

Leisure and Consumption

ELIZABETH S. CHASE
Massachusetts Institute of Technology

Much of the current discussion of optimal economic growth is based on the assumption that the criterion for assessing various feasible growth paths depends upon the economy's ability to produce consumption goods, although, of course, the original paper on optimal saving by Ramsey [3] did include the disutility of labor as well as the utility of consumption. This essay deals with what is, essentially, the Ramsey model with slight elaborations, in which we find a modified form of the golden rule and discuss the difference between the dynamic and static determinations of the labor supply.

The main points of the present analysis are similar to those described by Cass [1], except that the labor force is not a fixed proportion of the total population, and the utility index to be maximized depends not only on per capita consumption c but also on leisure λ, or the fraction of the population that is not in the labor force. The population is assumed to grow at an exogenously given rate n. We note that

$$L = (1 - \lambda)P, \tag{1}$$

where L is the labor force and P the population, and that

$$\frac{\dot{P}}{P} = n. \tag{2}$$

The economy uses two homogeneous factors, capital K and labor L, to produce a single homogeneous output Y. If we make the usual assumptions

175

about linear homogeneity and the nature of marginal products, the production function can be described in per capita terms as

$$y = (1 - \lambda)f\left(\frac{k}{1 - \lambda}\right) = (1 - \lambda)f(\mathcal{K}), \tag{3}$$

where $\mathcal{K} = k/(1 - \lambda)$ is the stock of capital per worker.

$$f(\mathcal{K}) > 0, \quad f'(\mathcal{K}) > 0, \quad f''(\mathcal{K}) < 0, \quad \text{for } \mathcal{K} > 0, \tag{4}$$

and

$$f'(0) = \infty, \quad f'(\infty) = 0. \tag{5}$$

A fraction, $s(t)$, $0 \leq s \leq 1$, of output at time t is devoted to gross investment where it depreciates at a fixed rate μ, and the remainder is consumed instantaneously. The rate of change of capital stock per capita is therefore given by

$$\dot{k} = sy - \Delta k = s(1 - \lambda)f(\mathcal{K}) - \Delta k \quad \text{with } \Delta = \mu + n, \tag{6}$$

and the rate of consumption per capita by

$$c = (1 - s)y = (1 - s)(1 - \lambda)f(\mathcal{K}). \tag{7}$$

A positive Δ in conjunction with Equations 4 and 5 insures that there will be some maximum sustainable capital per capita $\bar{k}$.

The planning board has the task of choosing from among the feasible paths of capital accumulation the one that maximizes the sum of discounted social welfare over time, where social welfare is a function of both c and λ.

$$\text{Max} \int_0^\infty U(c, \lambda)e^{-\delta t}\, dt \quad \text{with } \delta \geq 0, c \geq 0, 0 \leq \lambda \leq 1, \tag{8}$$

subject to Equation 6. The function U displays positive marginal utilities for both c and λ,

$$U_1(c, \lambda) > 0, \quad U_2(c, \lambda) > 0 \quad \text{for } c, \lambda > 0, \tag{9}$$

as well as strictly decreasing marginal utilities for c and λ separately,

$$U_{11} < 0, \quad U_{22} < 0, \tag{10}$$

and for c and λ together,

$$U_{11}U_{22} - U_{12}^2 > 0. \tag{11}$$

The utility function also reflects the fact that the enjoyment of either consumption or leisure is enhanced by having more of the other,

$$U_{12} > 0, \tag{12}$$

and in line with the fact that the economy finds a complete absence of either consumption or leisure most odious, we have

$$U_1(0, \lambda) = \infty, \quad U_2(c, 0) = \infty, \tag{13}$$

which implies that no optimal path will have $s = 1$, $\lambda = 0$, or $\lambda = 1$.

We assume for the present that the planning board has control over both s and λ, and we introduce a shadow price q of gross investment, measured in utility units, so that the present value of national product is

$$\mathscr{H} = e^{-\delta t}[U(c, \lambda) + q\dot{k}]. \tag{14}$$

Using the maximum principle [2] on this, we obtain the following necessary conditions, and, because of Equations 4, 10, and 11, these are also sufficient:

$$q - U_1 \geq 0 \qquad \text{with strict equality for } s > 0, \tag{15}$$

$$U_2 - U_1 \cdot (f - f' \cdot \mathscr{K}) = 0, \tag{16}$$

$$\dot{q} = q(\Delta + \delta) - U_1 f', \tag{17}$$

and

$$\lim_{t \to \infty} q e^{-\delta t} = 0. \tag{18}$$

The boundary of the region wherein $s > 0$ is given by

$$(q - U_1)_{s=0} = 0, \tag{19}$$

$$U_2 - U_1 \cdot (f - f' \cdot \mathscr{K})_{s=0} = 0, \tag{20}$$

so that along the boundary

$$\frac{dq}{dk} < 0. \tag{21}$$

Along the stationary $\dot{k} = 0$, we have

$$c = y - \Delta k, \tag{22}$$

$$q - U_1(y - \Delta k, \lambda) = 0, \tag{23}$$

and

$$U_2(y - \Delta k, \lambda) - U_1(y - \Delta k, \lambda) \cdot (f - f' \mathscr{K}) = 0 \tag{24}$$

describing the curve in the (k, q)-plane along which $\dot{k} = 0$. By differentiation, we find that

$$\left. \frac{dq}{dk} \right|_{\dot{k}=0} \gtreqless 0 \qquad \text{as } k \gtreqless \check{k} \tag{25}$$

and

$$\lim_{k \to 0} q|_{\dot{k}=0} = \lim_{k \to \bar{k}} q|_{\dot{k}=0} = \infty, \tag{26}$$

which are the same as the results Cass obtained, except for the fact that $\check{k}$, at the minimum of the $\dot{k} = 0$ curve, is not the golden rule value of k.

Finally, when $\dot{q} = 0$,

$$\Delta + \delta - f' = 0 \qquad \text{for } s > 0,$$

$$(\Delta + \delta)q - U_1 f' = 0 \qquad \text{for } s = 0, \tag{27}$$

so that

$$\mathscr{K} = \mathscr{K}^* \qquad \text{for } s > 0,$$

$$q = \frac{U_1 f'}{\Delta + \delta} \qquad \text{for } s = 0, \tag{28}$$

and, differentiating, while bearing in mind that Equation 16 must hold,

$$\left.\frac{dq}{dk}\right|_{\dot{q}=0} > 0 \qquad \text{for } s > 0, \tag{29}$$

$$\left.\frac{dq}{dk}\right|_{\dot{q}=0} < 0 \qquad \text{for } s = 0. \tag{30}$$

It can be shown (see Figure 1) that the $\dot{q} = 0$ curve described by Equations 27 intersects both the boundary and the curve $\dot{k} = 0$ uniquely, and that the stationary point k^*, q^* is a saddle point, so that the heavy arrows in the diagram represent optimal paths.

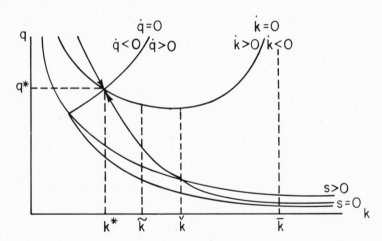

FIGURE 1. Optimal paths in (k, q)-space.

The minimum of the $\dot{k} = 0$ curve occurs at $\check{k}$, which is the steady-state value of k where dU/dc is least, since $q = U_1$. If, as in the analysis by Cass, we had U as a function of c alone, with the usual assumptions of monotonicity and diminishing marginal utility, then clearly $\check{k}$ would be the golden rule value of k, since c would be maximized there, and $f'(\check{k}) = \Delta$. But in the present situation, where U depends on λ as well as on c, the minimum of U_1

implies neither the maximum of c nor that $f'(\mathscr{K}) = \Delta$, so that $\check{k}$ is not the golden rule path. We do, however, have a generalized form of the golden rule when $\delta = 0$ and $f'[\check{k}/(1 - \lambda)] = \Delta$, although it does not refer to that balanced growth path which maximizes consumption per capita but rather to that for which $U(\tilde{c}, \check{\lambda})$ is a maximum. This may be seen by maximizing U subject to Equations 22, 23, and 24. Moreover, using the analysis by Cass ([1], pp. 238–239), we see that

$$k = \frac{U(\tilde{c}, \check{\lambda}) - U(c, \lambda)}{U_1(c, \lambda)}, \tag{31}$$

which is, of course, the Ramsey rule with golden rule utility $U(\tilde{c}, \check{\lambda})$ in place of bliss.

Suppose now that the planning board does not have control over the parameter λ, and the latter is chosen by the economy so as to maximize utility of consumption and leisure at every instant of time. For convenience we assume that the utility index for the economy is the same as that used as the optimizing criterion by the planning board. In other words, given k and s, the economy finds

$$\operatorname*{Max}_{\lambda} U(c, \lambda). \tag{32}$$

Note first that because of Equation 13, the economy will not have $\lambda = 0$ or $\lambda = 1$. Thus the necessary and sufficient condition for Expression 32 is

$$U_2 - U_1(1 - s)(f - f' \cdot \mathscr{K}) = 0, \tag{33}$$

or, if we assume that the wage rate is equal to the marginal product of labor,

$$\frac{U_2}{U_1} = (1 - s)w. \tag{34}$$

This is, of course, simply the equation behind the supply curve of labor, except that, since utility depends on consumption and not income, only that portion of the wage going into current consumption is considered. The equation for the determination of λ in a dynamic optimizing situation is Equation 16, which may be written

$$\frac{U_2}{U_1} = w. \tag{35}$$

The difference between Equations 34 and 35 may be loosely interpreted as the difference between a decision made on the basis of present consumption alone and one made on the basis of present plus future consumption as represented by the proportion of the wage that is saved. This suggests that it might be to the advantage of the planning board to introduce a propaganda campaign that would persuade the populace to think in terms of the future as well as concerning themselves with the present.

References

1. Cass, D., "Optimum Growth in an Aggregative Model of Capital Accumulation," *Review of Economic Studies*, Vol. 32, No. 3 (July 1965), pp. 233–240.
2. Pontryagin, L. S., *et al.*, *The Mathematical Theory of Optimal Processes*, New York and London: Interscience Publishers, Inc., 1962.
3. Ramsey, F. P., "A Mathematical Theory of Saving," *Economic Journal*, Vol. 38 (1928), pp. 543–559.

XI

Optimal Accumulation in Discrete Capital Models

MICHAEL BRUNO

Hebrew University, Jerusalem, and
Massachusetts Institute of Technology

1. Introduction[1]

This essay is concerned with optimal growth and valuation in multisectoral economies in which the technology is of the discrete, activity-analysis, type. The Ramsey formulation of our problem is in the tradition of Samuelson and Solow [21], Koopmans [12], Cass [5], Shell [22], and others. In all of these studies, however, only smooth neoclassical production functions have been used.

The importance of extending optimal growth theory to a discrete activity world does not stem only from a natural urge to try and see whether similar results obtain in this case. Full knowledge of the nature of such models is of considerable importance in throwing light on some basic issues in capital

---

[1] I owe my interest in the problems analyzed here to some very illuminating discussions with Paul A. Samuelson and Robert M. Solow. Thanks are also due to the patient participants of the M.I.T. 1966 Seminar in Optimal Economic Growth with whom I first discussed an earlier version of this study. Harl Ryder has been instrumental in making me choose finally the neater Pontryagin formulation over the more indirect Valentine approach (the two are ultimately equivalent) and also in helping me overcome my reluctance to use phase diagrams where they can be used.

For very helpful comments I am also indebted to Franklin M. Fisher and Karl Shell. This essay was written during a most enjoyable stay as Visiting Professor at M.I.T. and Research Associate at the Center for International Affairs, Harvard University. To both institutions goes a vote of thanks.

theory (the problem of technique reswitching, the behavior of consumption and the rate of interest, and the concept of aggregate capital). On the practical side, the type of model considered is believed to have a considerable degree of realism and usefulness, in particular for the field of development planning.

Pioneering work with discrete technologies was done by Dorfman, Samuelson, and Solow [8], Morishima [15], and, more recently, by Gale [10][2] and Chakravarty [6]. Gale's neat linear-algebra formulation could not, unfortunately, be applied to our problem. Chakravarty analyzed a one-technique Leontief model without a labor input and had to assume full utilization of factors rather than let it come out of the optimization process. It is the latter choice that turns out to give some of the more interesting aspects of a discrete technology. Also, a given labor supply is what is needed to make the model look more "human" than the ordinary von Neumann variety. However we owe our own initial approach to Chakravarty's use of the Valentine method.

Our main concern in this essay is to give a full characterization of the optimal path, the price behavior, and the nature of choice of alternative activities for some such models. Rather than go into generalities from the start, we shall confine most of our discussion to some well-specified two- and three-good models. We believe there is more insight to be gained from such a pragmatic approach.

Section 2 gives a very detailed analysis of optimal growth and price behavior in the simple fixed-proportions two-sector model. Some of the interesting price and production properties of this model are subsequently shown to be applicable also to more complex models. Section 3 next takes up the same model when there is choice of alternative activities for production of the consumption or the capital good. This is the discrete analogue to the two-sector Uzawa-type neoclassical model whose optimal growth properties have been analyzed by Cass [5] and Shell [22]. Section 4 is devoted to some generalizations to heterogeneous capital models. It briefly discusses the most general n-sector model, gives a more detailed treatment of the three-sector case, and finally analyzes one simple heterogeneous capital model with choice of alternative techniques. As we know, some of the simple neoclassical parables tend to break down when there is more than one capital good in the system, and it is from this angle that this discussion may derive most of its theoretical interest. We shall nonetheless confine ourselves in this essay to a technical analysis of optimal growth and leave further elaboration of some of the broader capital-theoretic issues to another occasion.[3]

---

[2] I owe this reference to E. Sheshinski.

[3] That paper is as yet unwritten. However, some underlying general duality properties of capital and growth models are discussed in [3].

2. The Two-Sector Single-Technique Model

Statement of the problem.   Consider an economy producing two goods, a consumption good C and a depreciable capital good I ($=$ gross investment) with an exponential depreciation rate μ. Each sector uses, as fixed proportion inputs, both capital and a primary factor of production, labor L, which is assumed to grow at an exogenously fixed rate n.[4]

The production technology is assumed to be given by a coefficient matrix

$$\begin{bmatrix} a_0 & a_{01} \\ a_1 & a_{11} \end{bmatrix}.$$

We also introduce the following notation:

$$c = \frac{C}{L} = \text{consumption per capita},$$

$$z = \frac{I}{L} = \text{gross investment per capita} = k + \lambda k, \qquad k = \frac{dk}{dt},$$

where

$$k = \frac{K}{L} = \text{capital-labor ratio},$$

and

$$\lambda = n + \mu = \text{gross natural rate of growth}.$$

We now wish to solve the following optimal growth problem:

$$\text{Maximize} \int_0^\infty ce^{-\delta t}\, dt, \qquad \text{where } \delta = \text{time rate of discount}, \qquad (1)$$

subject to the inequalities

$$a_0 c + a_{01} z \le 1 \qquad \text{(labor constraint)}, \qquad (2)$$

$$a_1 c + a_{11} z \le k \qquad \text{(capital constraint)}, \qquad (3)$$

$$-c \qquad\quad \le 0 \qquad \text{(consumption nonnegative)}, \qquad (4)$$

$$-z \le 0 \qquad \text{(gross investment nonnegative)}, \qquad (5)$$

where c, z, and k are all understood to be functions of time t, and we also keep in mind that

$$\dot{k} = -\lambda k + z. \qquad (6)$$

---

[4] In all that follows it should be clear that we could let n include the rate of growth of labor-augmenting *technical progress*, without thereby altering any of the results, providing we think of labor as measured in efficiency units. For simplicity, however, we stick to the no-technical-progress model.

The method of solution.   The literature on optimization techniques offers two alternative, but essentially equivalent, approaches to the solution of this problem. The "classical" approach is to treat the problem as a "Problem of Bolza" in the Calculus of Variations by applying the Euler-Lagrange equations to a Lagrangian expression involving the integrand and the differential side constraints.[5] The alternative method, leading to the same results but somewhat more directly, is to consider the problem as an "optimal control" problem and apply the Pontryagin [17] maximum principle. We shall follow the latter procedure here.[6]

We introduce the Hamiltonian form

$$H = e^{-\delta t}(c + \pi \dot{k}) = e^{-\delta t}[c + \pi(z - \lambda k)].$$

Here H can be interpreted as the net national product per capita where net investment is valued at the demand price for capital π.[7]

Applying Theorem 23 (page 298 in [17]) and the related analysis, we know that if a program $[c(t), z(t), k(t); 0 \leq t < \infty]$ is optimal, then there exists a continuous function $\pi(t)$ such that

$$\dot{k} = -\lambda k + z \tag{6}$$

with initially given $k(0) = k_0$,

$$\dot{\pi} = (\lambda + \delta)\pi - s, \qquad \text{perfect foresight equation}, \tag{7}$$

where, *at each moment of time*, GNP = $He^{\delta t} + \pi \lambda k = c + \pi z$ is maximized

---

[5] See Bliss [1], Chapter 7, for the theory and G. Leitmann [13], especially Chapter 4, for applications of this so-called Valentine method. See also Chakravarty [6]. Here the Lagrangian would conveniently be written as

$$\begin{aligned} F = e^{-\delta t}\{c &+ w[a_0 c + a_{01}(\dot{k} + \lambda k) + \varepsilon_0^2 - 1] \\ &+ s[a_1 c + a_{11}(\dot{k} + \lambda k) + \varepsilon^2 - k] \\ &+ p_0(\gamma_0^2 - c) + p[\gamma^2 - (\dot{k} + \lambda k)]\}, \end{aligned}$$

where ε_0^2, ε^2, γ_0^2, and γ^2 are nonnegative slacks (the squared form here is a matter of convenience) and w, s, p_0, and p are Lagrangian multipliers (for interpretation see p. 185).

The Euler-Lagrange equations are given by

$$\frac{\partial F}{\partial x} - \frac{d}{dt}\left(\frac{\partial F}{\partial \dot{x}}\right) = 0, \qquad \text{where } x \text{ stands for all variables}.$$

For all variables other than k, this boils down to $\partial F/\partial x = 0$ since no other explicit time derivative appears.

[6] In my original solution of the problem I used the former, "classical" method. I am indebted to Harl Ryder for pointing out to me that this could also be solved by direct application of Pontryagin [17], Chapter 6, which is the method adopted here. The equivalent "classical" analogue will be referred to in footnote 9.

[7] See also Cass [5] and Shell [22].

subject to the constraint Inequalities 2 through 5. The latter is a *linear programming problem*. Its dual is:

$$\text{Minimize } De^{\delta t} = w + sk$$

where D is discounted gross national income, subject to the price constraints:

$$wa_0 + sa_1 \geq 1, \tag{8}$$

$$wa_{01} + sa_{11} \geq \pi, \tag{9}$$

$$w \qquad \geq 0, \tag{10}$$

$$s \geq 0, \tag{11}$$

w has the interpretation of the real wage and s that of the gross rental price of capital.[8] All prices are measured in consumption units.

For continuity, $\pi(t)$ must satisfy the "jump condition" (Theorem 24, page 302 in [17]):

$$\lim_{\theta \to 0} [\pi(\tau + \theta) - \pi(\tau - \theta)] = 0 \tag{12}$$

for an optimal path crossing a phase k boundary at $t = \tau$. (Where these corner points arise will become clear from our subsequent discussion. Note that w and s need not be continuous.) In addition π must satisfy the transversality condition

$$\lim_{t \to \infty} e^{-\delta t}\pi(t) = 0. \tag{13}$$

All of these conditions together provide a set of necessary conditions for the existence of an optimal program.

It will be convenient to rewrite the constraints of Inequalities 2, 3, 8, and 9 in equality form. We then have the following:

The Production Equations:

$$a_0 c + a_{01} z + \varepsilon_0 = 1; \tag{2a}$$

$$a_1 c + a_{11} z + \varepsilon = k; \tag{3a}$$

The Price Equations:

$$wa_0 + sa_1 - p_0 = 1; \tag{8a}$$

$$wa_{01} + sa_{11} - p = \pi; \tag{9a}$$

---

[8] In Pontryagin's terminology k is the *state variable*, π is the *auxiliary variable*, c and z (with or without the production slacks) are the *control variables* and w and s are the *Lagrange multipliers*.

where ε_0, ε, p_0, p are nonnegative slack variables with the following economic interpretation:

ε_0 = rate of unemployment of labor,

ε = excess capacity (per unit of labor),

p_0 = difference between the supply price and demand price of consumption,

p = difference between the supply price and demand price of capital.

Also from basic linear-programming theory[9] we know that we must have

$$w\varepsilon_0 = s\varepsilon = p_0 c = pz = 0. \tag{14}$$

At any instant of time, π and k are given. The linear-programming system instantaneously maximizes national product or minimizes its dual. The pair of differential Equations 6 and 7 will determine a new pair of values π, k for the "next" instant of time, and so on. In practice, of course, both problems must be solved simultaneously. We solve the linear-programming problem for all possible ranges of π and k, solve the pair of differential equations for each such combination of values of the two variables, and use the "jump condition" (Equation 12), the transversality condition (Equation 13), and the initial condition k_0 to specify the optimal path completely. One loose end remains, and that is to be assured that the *necessary* conditions are also *sufficient*. Just as in the neoclassical model [5, 22], the diminishing marginal rate of substitution will assure us of that.

It will be clear from what follows how all of this generalizes to several goods and many techniques. However, we must first give a full solution of the two-sector one-technique model.

The full solution. The following is a compendium of useful formulas for the case $\varepsilon_0 = \varepsilon = p_0 = p = 0$. If we write

$$G = - \begin{vmatrix} a_0 & a_{01} \\ a_1 & a_{11} \end{vmatrix} = \begin{vmatrix} a_{01} & a_0 \\ a_{11} & a_1 \end{vmatrix}$$

---

[9] This may be a convenient place to state the analogous procedure along "classical" lines: Equations 8a, 9a, and 14 can be obtained from the Lagrangian formulation by taking $x = c$, z, ε_0, ε, γ_0, γ in the Euler-Lagrange equations (see footnote 5). Similarly, the perfect foresight Equation 7 is obtained by taking $x = k$. Corresponding to the "jump condition" (Equation 12), traditional theory has the so-called *Erdmann-Weierstrass corner condition* $(\partial F/\partial \dot{k})_+ = (\partial F/\partial \dot{k})_-$ (see Bliss [1] and Leitmann [13]), which, on substitution, turns out to give Equation 12. Finally, an exactly analogous transversality condition, Equation 13, must also hold. The equivalence of the two approaches is thus established.

and assume $G \neq 0$ ($G > 0$ means that the consumption good is more capital intensive than the investment good, and vice versa for $G < 0$),[10]

$$\rho = \frac{s}{\pi} = \text{gross rate of return } (= r + \mu),$$

$$h = \frac{z}{k} = \text{gross rate of growth of capital } \left(= \frac{\dot{K}}{K} + \mu \right).$$

We have (from Equations 2, 3, 8, and 9):

$$w = \frac{1 - a_{11}\rho}{a_0 + G\rho} \qquad \text{the } factor \ price \ frontier \text{ (FPF)}, \tag{15}$$

$$c = \frac{1 - a_{11}h}{a_0 + Gh} \qquad \begin{array}{l} \text{the identical } optical \ transformation \\ frontier \text{ (OTF);}[11] \end{array} \tag{16}$$

also

$$\pi = \frac{a_{01}}{a_0 + \rho G} = \frac{a_{11} + wG}{a_1} = \frac{1 - a_0 w}{a_1 \rho}, \tag{17}$$

$$w = \frac{a_1 \pi - a_{11}}{G}, \tag{18}$$

$$s = \rho \pi = \frac{a_{01} - a_0 \pi}{G} = \frac{1 - a_0 w}{a_1}, \tag{19}$$

$$c = \frac{a_{01}k - a_{11}}{G}, \quad z = \frac{a_1 - a_0 k}{G}, \quad h = \frac{1}{G}\left(\frac{a_1}{k} - a_0\right). \tag{20}$$

Figure 1 gives the factor price frontier (FPF) or the optical transformation frontier (OTF). Here AB is convex to 0 for $G > 0$, concave for $G < 0$.

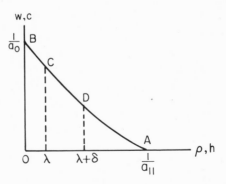

FIGURE 1. The factor-price (w, ρ) and the optimal-transformation (c, h) frontiers.

---

[10] The case $G = 0$ degenerates into a one-sector model, and will not be dealt with here.

[11] See [3] for a general statement and analysis of this duality property.

For $G > 0$, as ρ changes from $1/a_{11}$ (point A) to 0 (point B), so π rises from $a_{11}/a_1(A)$ to $a_{01}/a_0(B)$. Similarly, in a full-employment situation, k will lie between $a_{11}/a_{01}(A)$ and $a_1/a_0(B)$ as h changes from $1/a_{11}(A)$ to $0(B)$.

For $G < 0$ the same holds, only the signs are reversed: now $a_{11}/a_1 > a_{01}/a_0$ and $a_{11}/a_{01} > a_1/a_0$, and π falls as ρ falls and k falls as h falls.

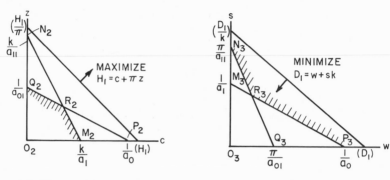

FIGURE 2. The single-technique model: FIGURE 3. The single-technique model:
the primal problem.   the dual problem.

Two points on FPF (OTF) are of special importance in what follows. We have D as the equilibrium point $\hat{\rho} = \lambda + \delta$ (write $\pi(\hat{\rho}) = \hat{\pi}$) for the price equations; and C as the equilibrium point $h^* = \lambda$ (steady state) for the production equations (write $k(h^*) = k^*$).

We assume: $0 \le \lambda \le \lambda + \delta \le \dfrac{1}{a_{11}}$.

Figures 2 and 3 describe the primal and dual linear programming problems, respectively, for the case $G > 0$: We get five different regions of solutions (points N, R, P, Q, M in the two diagrams, respectively) depending on the range of π and k.

As we shall see, only the first three regions are relevant for an optimal growth path (put differently, solutions for Q and M lie outside the FPF. In case Q, $w > 1/a_0$; in M, $\rho > 1/a_{11}$.) Table 1 gives a complete specification of the solutions in all five cases.

To get a full solution of the model we must substitute the values for ρ and h into the differential equations:

$$\frac{\dot{k}}{k} = -\lambda + h \qquad \text{or} \quad \dot{k} = -\lambda k + \dot{z};$$

$$\frac{\dot{\pi}}{\pi} = (\lambda + \delta) - \rho \qquad \text{or} \quad \dot{\pi} = (\lambda + \delta)\pi - s.$$

Also the solutions must satisfy initial (k_0) and terminal (transversality) conditions as well as the jump or corner condition $(\pi_+ = \pi_-)$ in transversing

Table 1. Solution of the Two-Sector One-Technique Model ($G > 0$)

Variable	N	R	Region P	Q	M
c	0	$\frac{a_{01}}{G}k - \frac{a_{11}}{G}$	$\frac{1}{a_0}$	0	$\frac{k}{a_1}$
z	$\frac{k}{a_{11}}$	$\frac{a_1}{G} - \frac{a_0}{G}k$	0	$\frac{1}{a_{01}}$	0
ε_0	$1 - \frac{a_{01}}{a_{11}}k$	0	0	0	$1 - \frac{a_0}{a_1}k$
ε	0	0	$k - \frac{a_1}{a_0}$	$k - \frac{a_{11}}{a_{01}}$	0
p_0	$\frac{a_1}{a_{11}}\pi - 1$	0	0	$\frac{a_0}{a_{01}}\pi - 1$	0
p	0	0	$\frac{a_{01}}{a_0} - \pi$	0	$\pi - \frac{a_1}{a_{11}}$
w	0	$\frac{a_1\pi - a_{11}}{G}$	$\frac{1}{a_0}$	$\frac{\pi}{a_{01}}$	0
s	$\frac{\pi}{a_{11}}$	$\frac{a_{01} - a_0\pi}{G}$	0	0	$\frac{1}{a_1}$
$\rho\left(=\frac{s}{\pi}\right)$	$\frac{1}{a_{11}}$	$\frac{a_{01}}{\pi G} - \frac{a_0}{G}$	0	0	$\frac{1}{a_1\pi}$
$h\left(=\frac{z}{k}\right)$	$\frac{1}{a_{11}}$	$\frac{a_1}{kG} - \frac{a_0}{G}$	0	$\frac{1}{ka_{01}}$	1
Definition of Region	$0 < k \leq \frac{a_{11}}{a_{01}}$	$\frac{a_{11}}{a_{01}} \leq k \leq \frac{a_1}{a_0}$	$\frac{a_1}{a_0} \leq k < \infty$	$\frac{a_{11}}{a_{01}} \leq k < \infty$	$0 < k \leq \frac{a_1}{a_0}$
	$\frac{a_{11}}{a_1} \leq \pi < \infty$	$\frac{a_{11}}{a_1} \leq \pi \leq \frac{a_{01}}{a_0}$	$0 < \pi \leq \frac{a_{01}}{a_0}$	$\frac{a_{01}}{a_0} \leq \pi < \infty$	$0 < \pi \leq \frac{a_{11}}{a_1}$
Charac-terization of Region	Insufficient Capital	Full Employment	Insufficient Labor	"Inefficient" Regions $w > \frac{1}{a_0}$	$\rho > \frac{1}{a_{11}}$

from one region to another. The phase diagram, Figure 4, helps to explain what is going on.

The optimal path. Suppose we start with insufficient capital to ensure full employment, that is, $k_0 < a_{11}/a_{01}$ (and $\pi \geq a_{11}/a_1$) in region N. We have $c = 0$, $z = k/a_{11}$, $\varepsilon_0 > 0$.

$$\frac{\dot{k}}{k} = \frac{1}{a_{11}} - \lambda; \quad \frac{\dot{\pi}}{\pi} = \lambda + \delta - \frac{1}{a_{11}} = -\left[\frac{1}{a_{11}} - (\lambda + \delta)\right], \quad (21)$$

with solutions for $t \leq t_1$:

$$k = k_0 \exp\left(\frac{1}{a_{11}} - \lambda\right)t; \quad \pi = A_1 \exp\left\{-\left[\frac{1}{a_{11}} - (\lambda + \delta)\right]t\right\}. \quad (22)$$

(A_1 to be determined later.)

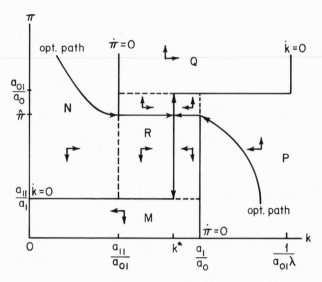

FIGURE 4. Phase diagram for the single-technique model ($G > 0$).

At time $t = t_1$ we have a corner ("jump") point determined by

$$k_0 \exp\left[\left(\frac{1}{a_{11}} - \lambda\right)t_1\right] = \frac{a_{11}}{a_{01}}$$

and we pass into region R (full employment with $\varepsilon_0 = 0$) where

$$\frac{\dot{k}}{k} = \frac{a_1}{kG} - \frac{a_0}{G} - \lambda, \qquad \dot{k} = 0 \rightarrow k = k^*,$$

$$\frac{\dot{\pi}}{\pi} = -\frac{a_{01}}{\pi G} + \frac{a_0}{G} + \lambda + \delta, \qquad \dot{\pi} = 0 \rightarrow \pi = \hat{\pi}. \quad (23)$$

This gives the solutions:

$$k = \left(\frac{a_{11}}{a_{01}} - k^*\right) \exp\left[-\left(\lambda + \frac{a_0}{G}\right)(t - t_1)\right] + k^*,$$

$$\pi = A_2 \exp\left[\left(\frac{a_0}{G} + \lambda + \delta\right)t\right] + \hat{\pi} \qquad \text{for } t_2 \leq t < \infty. \quad (24)$$

(A_2 to be determined later.)

Since $a_0/G + \lambda + \delta > 0$ for $G > 0$, the transversality condition [(13) $\pi e^{-\delta t} \to 0$ as $t \to \infty$] requires that $A_2 = 0$. It follows that

$$\pi = \hat{\pi} \quad \text{for } t_1 \leq t < \infty. \tag{24a}$$

Now we can determine A_1 backwards from the jump condition at $t = t_1$:

$$\hat{\pi} = A_1 \exp\left\{-\left[\frac{1}{a_{11}} - (\lambda + \delta)\right]t_1\right\};$$

and thus for $t \leq t_1$ we must have

$$\pi = \hat{\pi} \exp\left[\left(\frac{1}{a_{11}} - \lambda - \delta\right)(t_1 - t)\right]. \tag{22a}$$

where t_1 is determined from $t_1 = 1/[(1/a_{11}) - \lambda]$ anti ln $a_{11}/k_0 a_{01}$. It is obvious that if we start from $k_0 > a_1/a_0$ (region P) we decumulate capital (produce the consumption good only) until region R is reached (when $k = a_1/a_0$) and then proceed to the saddle point $\Lambda(k^*, \hat{\pi})$ (see Figure 4). It is similarly clear how the system behaves starting from anywhere inside R,

if $k_0 < k^* \quad k \uparrow k^*$⎫ In either case we write k_0 instead of
if $k_0 > k^* \quad k \downarrow k^*$⎭ a_{11}/a_{01} and $t_1 = 0$ in Equation 24.

Here the Leontief (full-employment) trajectory[12] is the optimal path once the system *can* achieve full employment.[13]

By using the solution for k we can similarly work out the solution for c. In the case $k_0 < a_{11}/a_{01}$,

$$\text{for } t \leq t_1 \quad c = 0,$$

$$\text{for } t \geq t_1 \quad c = \frac{a_{01}k}{G} - \frac{a_{11}}{G},$$

and therefore

$$c = c^*\left\{1 - \exp\left[-\left(\lambda + \frac{a_0}{G}\right)(t - t_1)\right]\right\}, \tag{25}$$

where $c^* = (a_{01}k^* - a_{11})/G = (1 - a_{11}\lambda)/(a_0 + \lambda G)$. See point C on Figure 1: the movement of c will be along OTF from A to C.

Note that c is *monotonically increasing* (monotonically *decreasing* in the case of $k_0 > k^*$).

A modified golden rule. Evaluating the Integral 1 (by means of Equation 25) we find after some manipulation:

$$\int_0^\infty ce^{-\delta t}\, dt = e^{-\delta t_1}\frac{1 - a_{11}\lambda}{\delta[(\delta + \lambda)G + a_0]} = e^{-\delta t_1}\frac{\hat{\omega}}{\delta} + \pi_0 k_0. \tag{26}$$

---

[12] For use of this term see [8], p. 298.
[13] In contrast see the case $G < 0$ on page 192.

When $k_0 \geq a_{11}/a_{01}$ we have $t_1 = 0$ and obtain

$$\hat{w} = \delta\left(\int_0^\infty ce^{-\delta t}\, dt - \pi_0 k_0\right),$$

$$= \frac{\int_0^\infty ce^{-\delta t}\, dt}{\int_0^\infty e^{-\delta t}\, dt} - \delta\pi_0 k_0.$$

The economic interpretation of this result is that *the weighted average of consumption* over the planning horizon, *net of the imputed income stream* derived from the initial full-employment endowment of wealth, *equals the long-run real wage* $\hat{w}$. An analogous result holds for the case $t_1 > 0$.

This can be viewed as a modification of the simple golden rule ($\delta = 0$, $c^* = w$) for the case in which $\delta \neq 0$.

The value of capital.   Writing $V = \pi k$ (wealth per capita), for $t \leq t_1$, we have

$$\frac{\dot{V}}{V} = \frac{\dot{k}}{k} + \frac{\dot{\pi}}{\pi} = \delta$$

from Equation 21. Thus:

$$V_t = V_0 e^{\delta t}, \qquad \text{where } V_0 = \pi_0 k_0; \tag{27}$$

that is, *the discounted present value of capital is constant.*[14] For $t \geq t_1$ we have

$$\frac{\dot{V}}{V} = \frac{\dot{k}}{k} = -\left(\frac{a_0}{G} + \lambda\right) + \frac{a_{11}}{kG} = h - \lambda, \tag{28}$$

which is not constant, starting from $[(1/a_{11}) - \lambda]$ at $t = t_1$ and gradually falling to zero as $t \to \infty$.

We can also work out explicitly the shape of the optimal path in the $\pi - k$ plane for the region N. For $t \leq t_1$ this is

$$\pi = V_0 k_0^\alpha k^{-(1-\alpha)} \qquad \text{where } \alpha = \frac{\delta}{(1/a_{11}) - \lambda}. \tag{29}$$

The smaller the δ, the closer this is to a rectangular hyperbola.

The case $G < 0$.   The case where the capital goods industry is more capital intensive than the consumer goods industry can be worked out in

---

[14] See also Dorfman, Samuelson, and Solow [8], p. 322, for a similar finding. Note that this is no longer true for $t > t_1$.

analogous fashion. In fact, we can read the full solution from Table 1 with only one change. The definition of region R should now read:

$$\frac{a_1}{a_0} \le k \le \frac{a_{11}}{a_{01}}, \quad \frac{a_{01}}{a_0} \le \pi \le \frac{a_{11}}{a_1},$$

and we should keep in mind the reverse movement of k and π as h and ρ change.

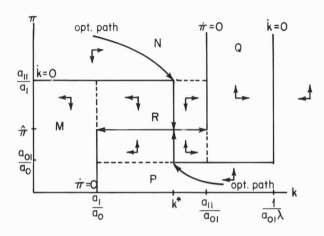

FIGURE 5. Phase diagram for the case $G < 0$.

Figure 5 shows what becomes of the phase diagram. Note that now, in contrast to the $G > 0$ case, *the system reaches full employment only at the point $k = k^*$*. The optimal policy for $k_0 \le k^* \le a_{11}/a_{01}$ is to accumulate only and produce no consumption until $k = k^*$ is reached, when the system enters into region R (from N). At that point ($t = t_2$, determined by $k^* = k_0 \exp{[(1/a - \lambda)t_2]}$) we settle at k^* and c^*. The motion of π is accordingly different:

$$\text{For } t \le t_2, \quad \pi = A_1 \exp\left[\left(\lambda + \delta - \frac{1}{a_{11}}\right)t\right],$$

$$\text{for } t = t_2, \quad \pi = \frac{a_{11}}{a_1},$$

$$\text{for } t \ge t_2, \quad \pi = A_2 \exp\left[\left(\lambda + \delta + \frac{a_0}{G}\right)t\right] + \hat{\pi}. \tag{30}$$

Now

$$\lambda + \delta + \frac{a_0}{G} = \frac{1}{\hat{\pi}}\frac{a_{01}}{G} < 0.$$

Thus we do *not* require $A_2 = 0$ (that is, the transversality condition is satisfied for all A_2); and instead obtain:

$$A_1 = \frac{a_{11}}{a_1} \exp\left[-\left(\lambda + \delta - \frac{1}{a_{11}}\right)t_2\right],$$

$$A_2 = \left(\frac{a_{11}}{a_1} - \hat{\pi}\right) \exp\left[-\left(\lambda + \delta + \frac{a_0}{G}\right)t_2\right].$$

The movement of the rate of return:

$$\text{In region } N, \qquad \rho = \frac{1}{a_{11}};$$

$$\text{in region } R, \qquad \rho = \frac{1}{\pi}\frac{a_{01}}{G} - \frac{a_0}{G},$$

which falls *gradually* from $1/a_{11}$ to $\lambda + \delta$ as π decreases from a_{11}/a_1 to $\hat{\pi}$; that is, we move *along* the FPF smoothly from A to D. But note that this movement of the rate of interest has no marginal-productivity-of-capital interpretation in any real sense (since $k = k^*$ throughout this movement). It is a pure *Wicksell effect* (see Joan Robinson [18], p. 391).

The Value of Capital:

$$\text{For } 0 \le t \le t_1 \qquad \frac{\dot{V}}{V} = \delta > 0,$$

$$\text{for } t_1 \le t < \infty \qquad \frac{\dot{V}}{V} = \lambda + \delta - \rho < 0; \tag{31}$$

that is, V is falling and at a decreasing rate since $\rho \downarrow (\lambda + \delta)$.

Concluding remarks. The cases $G > 0$ and $G < 0$ are best contrasted in terms of Figure 6 where we have drawn side by side the behavior of the dual (price) solution in terms of the factor price frontier (FPF) and that of the primal (quantity) solution in terms of the identical optimal transformation frontier (OTF). Figure 6 is drawn for the capital-scarce starting point ($k_0 \le a_{11}/a_{01}, a_1/a_0$). The capital-abundant case is exactly symmetrical.

In the case $G > 0$, we find (ρ, w) jump discretely when full employment is reached (at time t_1) from the point A_1 ($1/a_{11}$, 0) to D_1 ($\lambda + \delta$, $\hat{w}$), whereas (h, c) follow a smooth quasi-turnpike along the Leontief trajectory from the moment full employment is reached. The steady state at C_1 (λ, c^*) is only reached at $t = \infty$.[15]

---

[15] But the system spends only a finite amount of time along a portion of the arc $A_1 C_1$ arbitrarily close to C_1.

As against that, in the case $G < 0$, the system follows a von Neumann trajectory at the maximal rate of growth $1/a_{11}$, producing no consumption until $k = k^*$ is reached (at $t = t_2$), when the rate of growth falls discretely to the steady rate λ and consumption jumps from zero to c^* and stays there.

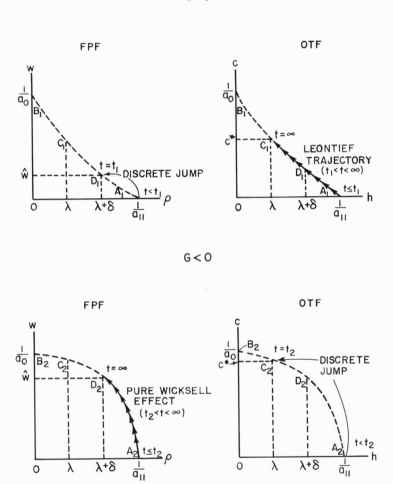

FIGURE 6. The dual price and production behavior of the single-technique model.

Only at that point is full employment reached, and only then do prices gradually start to adjust to the long-run equilibrium at $D_2(\lambda + \delta, \hat{w})$.

This contrasting behavior of the dual systems in the two cases is closely linked with the nature of instability attached to the saddle point in the two cases. As we know from other studies,[16] and as is readily shown here, the case of $G < 0$ is one in which the steady state $k = k^*$ is unstable for the production side of the system, whereas in the case $G > 0$ it is stable. Had the system started along the Leontief trajectory in the case $G < 0$ (at any point other than C_2) it would never reach the steady state. The price system, on the other hand, exhibits an *exactly polar property*, being stable for the case $G < 0$, and unstable for $G > 0$.[17]

As we shall see, some of these results generalize to the case in which there is more than one capital good. First we must deal with the case of alternative production activities.

3. Choice of Alternative Techniques: Homogeneous Capital

We now modify our model, still confining ourselves to one capital good but allowing for alternative production activities. The following models will be analyzed:

Model H_1. One activity to produce c
Two activities to produce z
order of capital intensity: $c - z_1 - z_2$

Model H_2. One activity for z
Two activities for c
order of intensity: $c_1 - c_2 - z$

Model H_3. One activity for c
Two activities for z
order of intensity: $z_1 - c - z_2$

It is easy to generalize from these three basic models to any number of activities for c and z (still only one homogeneous capital good!). The interest in this class of models lies in providing the discrete analogue to the two-sector neoclassical model [22].

Model H_1.

$$\text{Maximize} \quad \int_0^\infty ce^{-\delta t}\, dt$$

---

[16] See, for example, Shell [22] for the two-sector neoclassical case.
[17] For the dual instability properties of the Leontief system see Solow [23], Jorgenson [11], and Morishima [15]. See also section 4.

subject to

$$a_0c + a_{01}z_1 + b_{01}z_2 + \varepsilon_0 = 1, \tag{32}$$

$$a_1c + a_{11}z_1 + b_{11}z_2 + \varepsilon = k, \tag{33}$$

$$c, z_1, z_2, \varepsilon_0, \varepsilon, \geq 0 \quad \text{and } k_0 \text{ is given.}$$

The problem again boils down to finding the solution to the following linear programming problem:

$$\text{Maximize} \quad H_1 = c + \pi(z_1 + z_2)$$

subject to Equations 32 and 33, and the *dual* is

$$\text{Minimize} \quad D_1 = w + sk$$

subject to

$$1 = a_0w + a_1s - p_0, \tag{34}$$

$$\pi = a_{01}w + a_{11}s - p_1, \tag{35}$$

$$\pi = b_{01}w + b_{11}s - p_2, \tag{36}$$

with

$$z_1p_1 = z_2p_2 = cp_0 = w\varepsilon_0 = s\varepsilon = 0; \tag{37}$$

and the *dynamic equations* now are

$$\dot{k} = -\lambda k + z_1 + z_2, \tag{38}$$

$$\dot{\pi} = (\lambda + \delta)\pi - s \tag{39}$$

as before.

In the present case it is easier to give a geometric picture for the dual problem (the primal problem involves three dimensions). This is given in

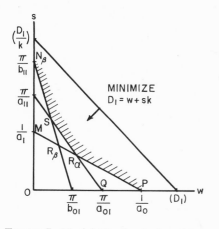

FIGURE 7. Model H_1: the dual problem.

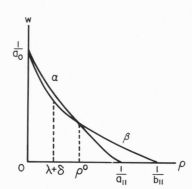

FIGURE 8. Model H_1: the factor price frontier.

Figure 7 and the factor price frontier in Figure 8. Without loss of generality we assume $1/b_{11} > 1/a_{11}$. We also assume $1/a_{01} > 1/b_{01}$, so that one technique will not completely dominate the other.

Next we assume $0 < (\lambda + \delta) < \rho^0$, so as to be able to get technique switching.[18] Write

$$G_\alpha = \begin{vmatrix} a_{01} & a_0 \\ a_{11} & a_1 \end{vmatrix} > 0$$

$$G_z = \begin{vmatrix} a_{01} & b_{01} \\ a_{11} & b_{11} \end{vmatrix} < 0$$

$$G_\beta = \begin{vmatrix} b_{01} & a_0 \\ b_{11} & a_1 \end{vmatrix} > 0.$$

We now have seven regions of solutions corresponding to the seven marked points on Figure 7 (listed in Table 2). All of these, with the exception of the point S, can be read off Table 1 with only minor alterations.

Characterization of the optimal path. We now have four relevant regions for the optimal path. Figure 9 gives the phase diagram for this case. Suppose k_0 is "small," that is, $k_0 < b_{11}/b_{01}$. We start accumulating capital by the β technique, the rate of return is $1/b_{11}$, and $w = 0(\varepsilon_0 > 0)$, until full employment is reached with $k = b_{11}/b_{01}$. At this point it pays to go on *accumulating only* ($c = 0$) *and with both activities*. We are at the switching point $\rho = \rho_0$ until a sufficient quantity of capital is accumulated to reach $k = a_{11}/a_{01}$. At this instant, region R_α is entered, which is the same as R in Figure 4. Then ρ jumps to $(\lambda + \delta)$ and stays there.

Note that what determines the choice of this path is the fact that at $\hat{\rho} = \lambda + \delta$, technique α gives a higher real wage ($\hat{w}_\alpha$) than technique β ($\hat{w}_\beta$). Technique α will therefore be chosen (cf. Samuelson's *nonsubstitution theorem* [14] and [19]) from the moment k reaches the minimum (a_{11}/a_{01}) required for full-employment production of z_1 and c with that technique.

The optimal path therefore consists of the sequence $[\varepsilon_0, z_2]; [z_2, z_1]; [z_1, c]$. Going "backwards," if $k_0 > a_1/a_0$, it is $[\varepsilon, c]; [z_1, c]$. Note that *c is monotonic* and so is ρ, but again the latter changes in *discrete jumps*:

$$\rho = \frac{1}{a_{11}}; \quad \rho^0; \quad \lambda + \delta. \quad \text{Or} \quad 0; \quad \lambda + \delta$$

while

$$w = 0; \quad w_\pi{}^0; \quad \hat{w}. \quad \text{Or} \quad \frac{1}{a_0}; \quad \hat{w}.^{19}$$

---

[18] For a definition and analysis of technique switching see [4] and [16].

[19] Here $w_\pi{}^0$ is *not* on the FPF (!) since π at $\rho = \rho^0$ is not the competitive long-run π at that point (note that π falls systematically during the S regime). We have $\dot{\pi}/\pi = (\lambda + \delta) - \rho^0 < 0$. During S, we find $w_\pi{}^0$ falls with π.

Table 2. Solutions for Model H_1

Definition of Point	Range of k	Range of π	Source of Data	Policy	
N_β	$0 \le k \le \dfrac{b_{11}}{b_{01}}$	$\dfrac{b_{11}}{a_1} \le \pi < \infty$	Col. N, Table 1 with (b_{01}, b_{11}) instead of (a_{01}, a_{11})	z_2	ε_0
S	$\dfrac{b_{11}}{b_{01}} \le k \le \dfrac{a_{11}}{a_{01}}$	$\dfrac{a_{11}}{a_1} \le \pi < \infty$	See below*	$z_1 z_2$	
R_α	$\dfrac{a_{11}}{a_{01}} \le k \le \dfrac{a_1}{a_0}$	$\dfrac{a_{11}}{a_1} \le \pi \le \dfrac{a_{01}}{a_0}$	Col. R, Table 1	z_1	c
P	$\dfrac{a_1}{a_0} \le k < \infty$	$0 < \pi \le \dfrac{a_{01}}{a_0}$	Col. P, Table 1	c	ε
Q	$\dfrac{a_{11}}{a_{01}} \le k < \infty$	$\dfrac{a_{01}}{a_0} \le \pi < \infty$	Col. Q, Table 1	z_1	ε
M	$0 \le k \le \dfrac{a_1}{a_0}$	$0 < \pi \le \dfrac{b_{11}}{a_1}$	Col. M, Table 1	c	ε_0
R_β	$\dfrac{b_{11}}{b_{01}} \le k \le \dfrac{a_1}{a_0}$	$\dfrac{b_{11}}{a_1} \le \pi \le \dfrac{a_{11}}{a_1}$	Col. R, Table 1 with (b_{01}, b_{11}) instead of (a_{01}, a_{11})	z_2	c

* In the S-region we have:

$$c = 0, \quad z_1 = \frac{b_{11} - k b_{01}}{G_z}, \quad z_2 = \frac{a_{01} k - a_{11}}{G_z}, \quad \varepsilon_0 = \varepsilon = 0,$$

$$p_0 = \pi\left(\frac{G_\alpha - G_\beta}{G_z} - 1\right), \quad p_1 = p_2 = 0, \quad w = \frac{\pi(b_{11} - a_{11})}{G_z},$$

$$s = \frac{\pi(a_{01} - b_{01})}{G_z}, \quad \rho = \frac{a_{01} - b_{01}}{G_z} = \rho^0, \quad \text{switching point,}$$

$$h = \frac{b_{11} - a_{11}}{k G_z} + \frac{a_{01} - b_{01}}{G_z}.$$

Had we assumed $\lambda + \delta > \rho^0$, the switching point would not have been crossed and technique β would have been preferred right through (maximization in R_β with $k = k_\beta{}^*$).

The way we can specify the path of k and π exactly should be clear from our previous discussion (using the same continuity considerations) and will not be repeated here.

Simulating the neoclassical model. It should now be clear how this model is generalized to the case of more than one alternative activity for production of the homogeneous capital good. We can arrange these techniques by order of capital intensity. In Figure 9 the curve $k = 0$ will now consist of numerous steps (with number equal to the number of distinct activities for z) and there will be a corresponding number of switching points $\rho_i{}^0$. If we make this array

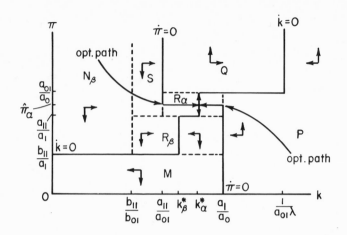

FIGURE 9. Model H_1: the phase diagram.

a very dense one, we shall gradually approach a smooth curve (and the switching points $\rho_i{}^0$ will get close to each other). Finally we shall be back in a neoclassical world (compare our phase diagram with that given in Shell's two-sector model [22]).[20] Here is another constructive illustration of the neoclassical parable [20].

Model H_2. The productive system is now given by

$$a_0 c_1 + b_0 c_2 + a_{01} z + \varepsilon_0 = 1, \tag{40}$$

$$a_1 c_1 + b_1 c_2 + a_{11} z + \varepsilon = k, \tag{41}$$

and prices by

$$w a_0 + s a_1 - p_{01} = 1, \tag{42}$$

$$w b_0 + s b_1 - p_{02} = 1, \tag{43}$$

$$w a_{01} + s a_{11} - p = \pi. \tag{44}$$

Now assume $1/a_0 > 1/b_0$ (an arbitrary choice) and $1/b_1 > 1/a_1$, to get a heterogeneous FPF with a switching point. Write $G_a = G_\alpha = G > 0$, as before, and

$$G_b = \begin{vmatrix} a_{01} & b_0 \\ a_{11} & b_1 \end{vmatrix} > 0,$$

and define

$$G_c = \begin{vmatrix} a_0 & b_0 \\ a_1 & b_1 \end{vmatrix} < 0.$$

---

[20] To complete the analogy we would still have to consider alternative activities for production of the consumption good. See further on.

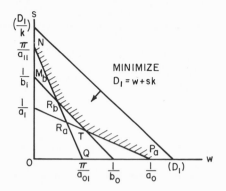

FIGURE 10. Model H_2: the dual problem.

FIGURE 11. Model H_2: the factor price frontier.

Figure 10 describes the dual problem and Figure 11 the factor price frontier. Again we have seven regions, which can be summarized as in Table 3.

The phase diagram is given in Figure 12. In the present case $\lambda + \delta < \rho^0$ ($\hat{\pi}_a > \pi^0$) and the optimal sequence for $k_0 < a_{11}/a_{01}$ is $N(z\varepsilon_0)$; $R_a(zc_1)$, and for $k_0 > a_1/a_0$ it is $P_a(c_1\varepsilon)$; $R_a(zc_1)$. Again c *is monotonic*. Note that we do *not* pass through the switching point (T regime) in this case but ignore technique b altogether.

If $\lambda + \delta > \rho_0$ ($\hat{\pi}_b < \pi^0$), the optimal sequence becomes $N(z\varepsilon_0)$; $R_b(zc_2)$, if $k_0 < a_{11}/a_{01}$. The switching regime T is passed through only when starting from a capital-abundant point ($k_0 \geq a_1/a_0$). The optimal sequence in that case becomes $P_a(c_1\varepsilon)$; $T(c_1c_2)$; $R_b(zc_2)$.

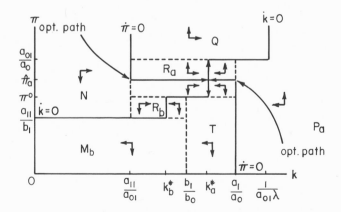

FIGURE 12. Model H_2: the phase diagram.

Model H_3. This is identical with the H_1 model except that the order of capital intensities is changed: we assume z_2 to be more capital intensive than c (that is, now $G_\alpha < 0$) and c, as before, more capital intensive than z_1. (See Figure 13: note the complete analogy in notation with Figure 7.)

Table 3. Solutions for Model H_2

Definition of Point	Range of k	Range of π	Source of Data	Policy	
N	$0 < k \le \dfrac{a_{11}}{a_{01}}$	$\dfrac{a_{11}}{b_1} \le \pi < \infty$	Col. N, Table 1	z	ε_0
R_a	$\dfrac{a_{11}}{a_{01}} \le k \le \dfrac{a_1}{a_0}$	$\pi^0 \le \pi \le \dfrac{a_{01}}{a_0}$	Col. R, Table 1	z	c_1
R_b	$\dfrac{a_{11}}{a_{01}} \le k \le \dfrac{b_1}{b_0}$	$\dfrac{a_{11}}{b_1} \le \pi \le \pi^0$	Col. R, Table 1 with (b_0, b_1) instead of (a_0, a_1)	z	c_2
P_a	$\dfrac{a_1}{a_0} \le k < \infty$	$0 \le \pi \le \dfrac{a_{01}}{a_0}$	Col. P, Table 1	c_1	ε
Q	$\dfrac{a_{01}}{a_{11}} \le k < \infty$	$\dfrac{a_{01}}{a_0} \le \pi < \infty$	Col. Q, Table 1	z	ε
M_b	$0 < k \le \dfrac{b_1}{b_0}$	$0 \le \pi \le \dfrac{a_{11}}{b_1}$	Col. M, Table 1	c_2	ε_0
T	$\dfrac{b_1}{b_0} \le k \le \dfrac{a_1}{a_0}$	$0 \le \pi \le \pi^0$	See below*	$c_1 c_2$	

* In a T regime we have:

$$c_1 = \frac{b_1 - b_0 k}{G_c}, \quad c_2 = \frac{a_0 k - a_1}{G_c}, \quad z = \varepsilon_0 = \varepsilon = 0, \quad p_{01} = p_{02} = 0,$$

$$w = \frac{b_1 - a_1}{G_c}, \quad s = \frac{a_0 - b_0}{G_c}, \quad \rho = \frac{a_0 - b_0}{G_a - G_b} \, (= \rho^0), \quad h = 0.$$

The FPF is given in Figure 14 (note that the α portion is now concave to 0) and the phase diagram in Figure 15. The optimal sequence for $k_0 < b_{11}/b_{01}$ is given by

$$N_\beta(z_2 \varepsilon_0); \quad S(z_1 z_2); \quad R_\alpha(z_1 c) \quad \text{for } k_0 > k_a{}^* \quad P(c\varepsilon); \quad R_\alpha(z_1 c).$$

In all cases c is monotonic (we have assumed $\lambda + \delta < \rho^0$). The behavior of ρ and w in this case is somewhat "perverse":

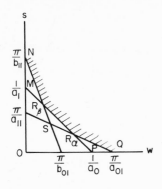

FIGURE 13. Model H_3: the dual problem.

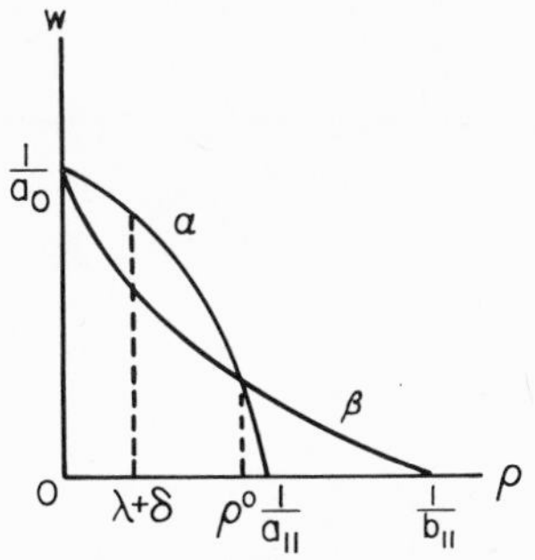

FIGURE 14. Model H_3: the factor price frontier.

In region N_β: $\qquad \rho = \dfrac{1}{b_{11}}, \qquad w = 0.$

In region S: $\qquad \rho = \dfrac{a_{01} - b_{01}}{G_z} = \rho^0, \qquad w = \dfrac{\pi(b_{11} - a_{11})}{G_z}.$

In region R_α: $\qquad \rho = \pi \dfrac{a_{01}}{G_\alpha} - \dfrac{a_0}{G_\alpha}, \qquad w = \dfrac{a_1\pi - a_{11}}{G_\alpha}.$

At the border line between N_β and S (suppose this is at $t = t_1$), we find ρ drops from $1/b_{11}$ to ρ^0, and w rises (both jump discretely).

In the S zone, we find ρ remains constant at ρ^0 and w falls gradually (since

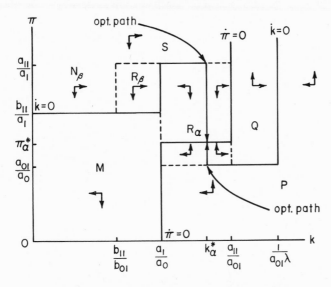

FIGURE 15. Model H_3: the phase diagram.

π falls) to $(a_{11}/a_1)[(b_{11} - a_{11})/G_z]$. At the second "jump," between S and R_α (suppose at $t = t_2$), there is another discontinuity in both ρ and w. Here ρ jumps back up to $1/a_{11}$ and then falls smoothly to $(\lambda + \delta)$ as $t \to \infty$ (again a *Wicksell effect* see p. 194) whereas w drops to zero and then rises smoothly to $\hat{w}_\alpha$. In this model (H_3) w and ρ are *not monotonic* with respect to time as long as $t \le t_2$.[21]

4. Models With Heterogeneous Capital Goods

The stage is now set for consideration of models in which there is more than one capital good. Some of what was found in the context of the various one-capital models considered previously can be carried over to a hetero-geneous capital world. At the same time, as is now well known, some of the most interesting capital-theoretic problems arise only in the case in which there is more than one capital good in the system.[22]

We begin by a statement of the problem in the general n-sector case and then proceed, in the spirit of our previous discussion, to give explicit con-sideration to two specific models. The method of solution will be exactly the same as before.

The general model.   Consider now an economy producing $n + 1$ goods, a consumption good (simple or composite) C, and n depreciable capital goods I_i with exponential depreciation rates μ_i $(i = 1, 2, \cdots, n)$. As before we assume labor to be growing at an exogenously fixed rate n. We keep the same notation except that we now add a subscript to the variables involving the capital goods $(z, k, \lambda, \varepsilon, s, \pi, \rho, p)$. In the most general model each of the $n + 1$ goods can be thought of as being producible by m_i alternative activities $(i = 0, 1, \cdots, n)$.

The Ramsey problem now becomes

$$\text{Maximize} \quad \int_0^\infty ce^{-\delta t}\, dt \tag{1}$$

subject to the $n + 1$ constraints:

$$\sum_{j=1}^{m_0} a_r^j c_j + \sum_{i=1}^{n} \sum_{j=1}^{m_i} a_{ri}^j z_i^{\,j} + \varepsilon_r = k_r \qquad r = 0, 1, \cdots, n \tag{45}$$

where $k_0 = 1$, $\sum_{j=1}^{m_i} z_i^{\,j} = z_i$,[23] $\sum_{j=1}^{m_0} c_j = c$ and a_{ri}^j is the input coefficient of

---

[21] However, since $c = 0$ for $t \le t_2$, and $c = c_\alpha^*$ for $t > t_2$, then c, as a function of ρ, will formally be monotonic.

[22] In particular, the reswitching phenomenon to be referred to again later on (see also [4]).

[23] This notation should not be confused with the notation used in the previous section where z_1, z_2 related to two activities for the *same* capital good.

the rth factor in the jth activity for the production of the ith good (a_r^j is the same for the consumption good). Again all variables (c_j, z_i^j, k_r) are understood to be nonnegative.

The *dual system* now is

$$wa_0^j + \sum_{r=1}^{n} s_r a_r^j - p_{0j} = 1 \qquad j = 1, 2, \cdots, m_0,$$

$$wa_{0i}^j + \sum_{r=1}^{n} s_r a_{ji}^r - p_{ij} = \pi_i \qquad i = 1, 2, \cdots, n \tag{46}$$

$$j = 1, 2, \cdots, m_i$$

(there are $\sum_{i=0}^{n} m_i$ constraints in this system).

The Hamiltonian to be maximized, subject to the Constraints 45, is

$$e^{\delta t} H = c + \sum_{i=1}^{n} \pi_i(z_i - \lambda_i k_i),$$

or the dual to be minimized, subject to the Constraints 46, is

$$e^{\delta t} D = w + \sum_{r=1}^{n} s_r k_r.$$

Also we must have, from the duality conditions,

$$z_i^j p_{ij} = c^j p_{0j} = w \varepsilon_0 = s_r \varepsilon_r = 0 \qquad \text{for all } i, j, r. \tag{47}$$

We now have a pair of dynamic equations for *each* capital good:

$$\dot{k}_i = -\lambda_i k_i + z_i \qquad \text{or} \quad \frac{\dot{k}_i}{k_i} = -\lambda_i + h_i, \tag{48}$$

and

$$\dot{\pi}_i = (\lambda_i + \delta)\pi_i - s_i \quad \text{or} \quad \frac{\dot{\pi}_i}{\pi_i} = (\lambda_i + \delta) - \rho_i, \tag{49}$$

where

$$\lambda_i = n + \mu_i, \quad z_i = \sum_{j=1}^{m_i} z_i^j, \quad h_i = \frac{z_i}{k_i}, \quad \rho_i = \frac{s_i}{\pi_i} \qquad i = 1, 2, \cdots, n.$$

To complete the specification of the optimal path of $k_i(t)$, $\pi_i(t)$, and the rest of the system, we are also given n initial stocks $k_i(0)$ and, exactly as in the one capital good models, for *each* capital good the transversality condition of Expression 13 and the jump condition at corner points of Expression 12 must hold.

Once we leave the single capital good world we can no longer apply simple two-dimensional phase diagrams and straightforward methods of solution of single differential equations. Instead Equations 48 and 49 are *systems* of differential equations, the nature of whose solutions will depend on the characteristic roots of these equations, which, as we know, will contribute geometrically growing, geometrically decaying, and oscillatory components to the solution.[24] Since we allow for choice of alternative techniques there is little that one can say about the complete characterization of the optimal path with all its phases unless one makes more specific assumptions about the nature of this spectrum of techniques. Certain general statements can nonetheless be made:

1. A singular solution $\hat{\pi}_i$ to Equation 49 ($\dot{\pi}_i = 0$) implies that $\lambda_i + \delta = \rho_i$ or $r_i = n + \delta$ for all i. Thus if the system has an equilibrium point,[25] stable or unstable, it must be one in which all the own rates of interest equal the *sum* of the biological rate n and the rate of discount δ (which is the system's "money" rate of interest). This much we already know from our simpler models, and it is equally well known for neoclassical models.[26] In the present context this has a very clear implication. Whatever techniques the system will choose to employ along the optimal path, it will always end up choosing that technique on the factor price frontier which *maximizes the real wage at the rate of interest* $(n + \delta)$. This we would also expect from application of Samuelson's *nonsubstitution theorem* [9]. Substituting the relevant technique matrix into the equation of motion for production (Equation 48), we obtain the singular point $k_i = k_i^*$, which gives the balanced growth solution ($h_i = \lambda_i$).

2. Looking at the dual sets of differential Equations 48 and 49 and at the dual systems of constraints, Expressions 45 and 46, it is easy to show that to each characteristic root γ_i of the first system there must correspond a dual characteristic root $-\gamma_i + \delta$ in the price system. This has some simple implications for the dual stability-instability property of the two systems, which has already been noted in the two-sector model.[27] This is best illustrated by means of the two capital good case ($n = 2$) which will now briefly be discussed.

The three-sector single-technique model. The *production system* for the case $n = 2$ will be[28]

$$a_0 c + a_{01} z_1 + a_{02} z_2 + \varepsilon_0 = 1,$$

$$a_1 c + a_{11} z_1 + a_{12} z_2 + \varepsilon_1 = k_1, \qquad (50)$$

$$a_2 c + a_{21} z_1 + a_{22} z_2 + \varepsilon_2 = k_2.$$

[24] See Solow [23], Jorgenson [11], and Morishima [15].

[25] We require, essentially, that the coefficient matrix satisfy some variant of the Hawkins-Simon condition (see Solow [23]).

[26] See Cass [5] and Shell [22].

[27] A similar result was stated by Solow [23] and proved, for a *closed* Leontief model, by Jorgenson [11]. Ours is basically an *open* model.

[28] We are here assuming that there is only one technique or that we are considering the final phase of the optimal program in which only the considered technique is viable.

To this the *dual price system* corresponds:

$$wa_0 + s_1a_1 + s_2a_2 - p_0 = 1,$$
$$wa_{01} + s_1a_{11} + s_2a_{21} - p_1 = \pi_1, \tag{51}$$
$$wa_{02} + s_1a_{12} + s_2a_{22} - p_2 = \pi_2.$$

Figure 16 gives the generalized factor price frontier (in terms of w, ρ_1, ρ_2) or the identical optimal transformation frontier (in terms of full-employment values of c, h_1, h_2).[29]

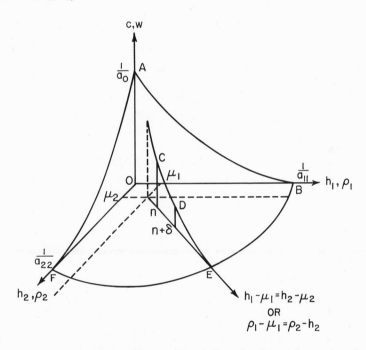

FIGURE 16. The three-sector factor price and optimal transformation frontiers.

The FPF (OTF) is given by the surface $ABEF$. The curve AE on that surface is the ordinary two-dimensional OTF for the case in which both capital goods grow in fixed proportions and is also the FPF for the case in which the relative prices of the two capital goods remain constant. In either of the two cases, we note, the system can be looked upon as a one (composite) capital good model. The point C is the balanced growth point and D corresponds to price equilibrium (compare with Figure 1 in the one capital good model).

If we denote the minor of a_{ij} in the coefficient matrix by M_{ij} and the

---

[29] For the basic duality theorem underlying this identity see [3].

determinant of the coefficient matrix by M_0, one can show (see [3]) that the equation of the FPF is given by [30]

$$-w\rho_1\rho_2 M_0 + w\rho_1 M_{33} + w\rho_2 M_{22} + \rho_1\rho_2 M_{11}$$
$$- wa_0 - \rho_1 a_{11} - \rho_2 a_{22} + 1 = 0. \quad (52)$$

Likewise one can see from Equations 50 that the system can produce nonnegative quantities of the three goods at full employment of all factors if and only if the capital stocks k_i $(i = 1, 2)$ satisfy three nonnegativity constraints. For example, the condition $c \geq 0$ implies

$$\frac{M_{11} - k_1 M_{21} + k_2 M_{31}}{M_0} \geq 0. \quad (53)$$

Similarly $w \geq 0$ implies the following dual constraint on π_i $(i = 1, 2)$:

$$\frac{M_{11} - \pi_1 M_{12} + \pi_2 M_{13}}{M_0} \geq 0. \quad (54)$$

(The equality sign in Equations 53 or 54 implies being right on the curve *BEF* in Figure 16.)

It is easy to see how Equations 52 through 54 generalize when $n > 2$. It is also a straightforward check to see that for the case $n = 1$ these equations boil down to the analogous expressions already derived in section 2.

The configuration of the dual problem is given in Figure 17. This is drawn for the case

$$\frac{a_{11}}{a_1} < \pi_1 < \frac{a_{01}}{a_0}, \qquad \text{assuming } M_{33} < 0;$$

$$\frac{a_{12}}{a_2} < \pi_2 < \frac{a_{02}}{a_2}, \qquad \text{assuming } M_{22} < 0.$$

The three commodity boundaries define three planes in a three-dimensional diagram with a vertex at X. Minimization of the dual $w + s_1 k_1 + s_2 k_2$ will take place at X if Equation 53 is satisfied. Let us see under what conditions a full-employment path will approach equilibrium at point C (production) and D (prices) on Figure 16.

The equations for $k_1 k_2$ now are

$$k_1 = -\lambda_1 k_1 + z_1 = -\frac{M_{12}}{M_0} + k_1\left(\frac{M_{22}}{M_0} - \lambda_1\right) - k_2\frac{M_{32}}{M_0};$$

$$k_2 = -\lambda_2 k_2 + z_2 = \frac{M_{13}}{M_0} - k_1\frac{M_{23}}{M_0} + k_2\left(\frac{M_{33}}{M_0} - \lambda_2\right); \quad (55)$$

---

[30] OTF is given by the same expression when substituting (c, h_1, h_2), respectively, for (w, ρ_1, ρ_2). The way Figure 16 is drawn it is assumed that $M_{33} < 0$, $M_{22} < 0$. The principal minors M_{33}, M_{22} fulfill the same role in respect to convexity or concavity of the curves *AB*, *AF*, as the determinant $(-G)$ did in the two-sector case.

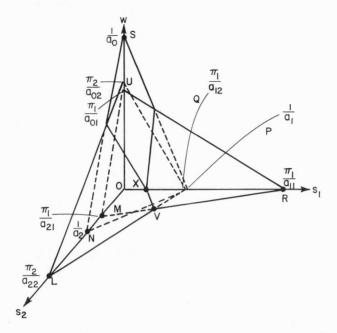

FIGURE 17. The three-sector dual problem.

and for π_1, π_2 we have

$$\dot{\pi}_1 = \pi_1(\lambda_1 + \delta) - s_1 = \frac{M_{21}}{M_0} - \pi_1\left[\frac{M_{22}}{M_0} - (\lambda_1 + \delta)\right] + \pi_2\frac{M_{23}}{M_0};$$

$$\dot{\pi}_2 = \pi_2(\lambda_2 + \delta) - s_2 = -\frac{M_{31}}{M_0} + \pi_1\frac{M_{32}}{M_0} - \pi_2\left[\frac{M_{33}}{M_0} - (\lambda_2 + \delta)\right].$$

(56)

Let us denote the singular points for Equations 55 by k_1^*, k_2^* and for Equations 56 by $\hat{\pi}_1$, $\hat{\pi}_2$. Following known procedures for solution of systems of differential equations (see, for example, W. Kaplan, *Ordinary Differential Equations*, p. 417), we can write

$$\alpha_1 = \frac{M_{22}}{M_0} - \lambda_1; \qquad \beta_1 = -\frac{M_{32}}{M_0};$$

$$\alpha_2 = -\frac{M_{23}}{M_0}; \qquad \beta_2 = \frac{M_{33}}{M_0} - \lambda_2.$$

Consider the characteristic roots γ_1, γ_2 given by

$$\begin{vmatrix} \alpha_1 - \gamma & \beta_1 \\ \alpha_2 & \beta_2 - \gamma \end{vmatrix} = 0;$$

write $\gamma^2 - p\gamma + q = 0$, with

$$p = \gamma_1 + \gamma_2 = \alpha_1 + \beta_2 = \left(\frac{M_{22}}{M_0} - \lambda_1\right) + \left(\frac{M_{33}}{M_0} - \lambda_2\right)$$

$$= \sum \left(\frac{\partial z_i}{\partial k_i} - \lambda_i\right);$$

$$q = \gamma_1\gamma_2 = \alpha_1\beta_2 - \alpha_2\beta_1 = \frac{a_0}{M_0} - \lambda_2\frac{M_{22}}{M_0} - \lambda_1\frac{M_{33}}{M_0} + \lambda_1\lambda_2;$$

and the discriminant

$$\Delta = \left[\left(\frac{M_{22}}{M_0} - \lambda_1\right) - \left(\frac{M_{33}}{M_0} - \lambda_2\right)\right]^2 + \frac{M_{23}M_{32}}{M_0{}^2}.$$

Summarizing the major cases for the first set of Equations 55, we have, for the singular point $k_i{}^*$:

1. *Stable node:* if $\Delta > 0$ (for example, this will always be the case if $M_{23}M_{32} = M_{22}M_{33} - a_0M_0 > 0$) *and* $q > 0$, $p < 0$. There will thus be two negative roots (for example, if $M_{22} < 0$, $M_{33} < 0$, and $\partial z_i/\partial k_i < \lambda_i$).

2. *Unstable node:* if $\Delta > 0$, $q > 0$, and $p > 0$, there will be two positive roots (that is, if $\sum [(\partial z_i/\partial k_i) - \lambda_i] > 0$).

3. *Saddle point:* if $q < 0$, there will be one positive and one negative root so there will be only one optimal path on OTF (for example, this will be the case if $\partial z_i/\partial k_i < \lambda_i$ for at least one of the goods and $M_0 < 0$).

4. *Focus:* if $\Delta < 0$ but $p < 0$, there is a spiral approach to *stable* equilibrium at $k_i{}^*$. If $\Delta < 0$ but $p > 0$, there is an *unstable* focus.

The key relationships in determining the nature of the equilibrium solution seem to be $\partial z_i/\partial k_i \gtrless \lambda_i$.[31]

If we perform the same analysis for Equations 56 and write the characteristic equation as $\gamma^2 - p'\gamma + q' = 0$, we find

$$p' = 2\delta - p = -\sum \left[\frac{\partial s_i}{\partial \pi_i} - (\lambda_i + \delta)\right],$$

$$q' = 2 + \delta^2 - \delta p,$$

$$\Delta' = \Delta.$$

We have the following results:

1. Whenever $k_i{}^*$ gives a *stable node*, $\hat{\pi}_i$ gives an *unstable node*, and if $\hat{\pi}_i$ gives a stable node, $k_i{}^*$ must be an unstable node. The converse is not necessarily true; that is, if one of the solution sets is an unstable node, then

---

[31] The condition $G \gtrless 0$ for the one capital good model is similar: from Equation 20, we have $\partial z/\partial k = -(a_0/G)$ and $\partial z/\partial k = h - (a_1/kG)$, when $G > 0$, $\partial z/\partial k < 0$, when $G < 0$, $\partial z/\partial k > h$.

its dual set may give a saddle point or may also be an unstable node (the latter can happen only if $0 < p < 2\delta$).

2. A similar result holds in the case of a *focus* ($\Delta = \Delta' < 0$): a *stable focus* for one solution set necessarily implies an *unstable focus* for its dual. Again the converse does not necessarily hold. We shall get an unstable focus in both cases if $0 < p < 2\delta$.

Put in a different form, what this result says is that the price and quantity solutions exhibit a polar characteristic. We can never have both sets of solutions stable. When one is stable (whether a node or a focus), the other is not. At the same time, the possibility of a completely unstable solution for both sets is confined to the case $0 < p < 2\delta$, which in a more economically meaningful way can be stated as

$$\sum \left[\frac{\partial z_i}{\partial k_i} - \lambda_i \right] > 0; \quad \sum \left[\frac{\partial s_i}{\partial \pi_i} - (\lambda_i + \delta) \right] < 0;$$

where

$$\frac{\partial z_i}{\partial k_i} = \frac{\partial s_i}{\partial \pi_i} = \frac{M_{22}}{M_0}, \quad \frac{M_{33}}{M_0} \quad \text{for } i = 1, 2.^{32}$$

These conclusions for the three-sector model thus generalize a similar conclusion already found for the two-sector case (see section 2).

Without going into a very detailed analysis of the optimal path itself, we can use our one capital good discussion to draw some analogous conclusions for the present heterogeneous capital case. Suppose the nature of the coefficient matrix is such that the balanced growth solution is stable. We would expect, as in the previous case, that once k_i satisfies the output-nonnegativity conditions it will pay the system to follow the Leontief trajectory (that is, move along the OTF). At the same time, since the price solution must be *unstable*, the transversality condition will see to it that the prices settle at their long-run equilibrium level (point D on Figure 16, $\pi_i = \hat{\pi}_i$) *from the moment the system enters the full-employment phase.* In a heterogeneous capital model this has a particularly interesting implication. What it means is that in this case relative prices of the capital goods remain constant, and for all practical purposes we are back to a one (composite) capital good world!

Similarly if the price solution is stable, the quantity solution will be unstable, and, just as in the one capital good model, we expect the optimal path of the quantities to be more like in a von Neumann model. Full employment, positive consumption, and balanced growth will be reached at the same

---

[32] Our analysis of the nature of stability of the quantity and price solution thus seems to verify and also to supplement that of Solow [23] and Jorgenson [11]. The case of complete instability mentioned here can arise only if $\delta \neq 0$. In their analysis such a case is ruled out by the assumption (which Solow [23] states as not very convincing) that the rate of interest cannot be higher than the rate of balanced growth. In our model the rate of interest will *always* end up being higher than the rate of balanced growth.

time (point C on Figure 16) while prices (π_i, w, and ρ_i) go on moving along the FPF (Wicksell effect) as $t \to \infty$. Again, once production settles at the balanced growth stage, we are back to a one (composite) capital good model, even though relative prices may go on changing through time (since relative quantities now remain constant).

To complete the analysis we would have to look at the pattern of dynamic behavior when the system is not in full employment and then use the "jump" conditions and the initial conditions to give a complete characterization of the optimal path. To prevent undue repetition we leave the model at that.

Choice of alternative techniques: the canonical model. Consider now a heterogeneous capital model with alternative production activities of a highly simplified nature. We assume that there are two (or more) techniques for production of the consumption good (c_1, c_2) each using and producing only its own specific capital good (z_1, z_2).[33] This model, first used by Samuelson [20], derives its main interest in the present context from the fact that it is the simplest capital model for which the phenomenon of technique reswitching has been exhibited (see [4]). In general in this model no ordering of techniques is possible as between low and high interest rates for different *steady states*. As we move from one steady state with a high interest rate to one with a lower interest rate, we may return to the use of a technique α that had not been in use at an intermediate interest rate (in favor of a different technique β). In other words, as the rate of interest falls, the sequence of techniques becomes $\alpha - \beta - \alpha$.

The question that arises in the present context is whether such "perverse" sequencing of techniques can also take place in a Ramsey model along an optimal path *to* a steady state. The answer, interestingly enough, turns out to be no, at least for this simple case.[34]

With two techniques we have the following linear programming problem:

$$\text{Maximize} \quad c_1 + c_2 + \pi_1 z_1 + \pi_2 z_2$$

subject to

$$a_0 c_1 + b_0 c_2 + a_{01} z_1 + b_{01} z_2 + \varepsilon_0 = 1, \tag{57}$$

$$a_1 c_1 \quad\quad + a_{11} z_1 \quad\quad\quad + \varepsilon_1 = k_1, \tag{58}$$

$$b_1 c_2 \quad\quad\quad + b_{11} z_2 + \varepsilon_2 = k_2. \tag{59}$$

---

[33] Again we sacrifice consistency of notation for sake of simplicity, and c_1 and c_2 are assumed to be the *same* consumption good whereas z_1 and z_2 are *different* capital goods.

[34] On the basis of this and the previous discussion, we have good reason to believe that this result is of a much more general nature, but this must remain a subject for another paper.

The dual linear programming problem is

$$\text{Minimize} \quad w + s_1 k_1 + s_2 k_2,$$

subject to

$$wa_0 + s_1 a_1 \qquad\qquad - p_{01} = 1, \tag{60}$$

$$wb_0 \qquad\quad + s_2 b_1 - p_{02} = 1, \tag{61}$$

$$wa_{01} + s_1 a_{11} \qquad\qquad - p_1 = \pi_1, \tag{62}$$

$$wb_{01} \qquad\quad + s_2 b_{11} - p_2 = \pi_2. \tag{63}$$

For simplicity let us assume that for both techniques the consumption good is more capital intensive than the respective capital good, so that $(a_0 a_{11} - a_1 a_{01})$ and $(b_0 b_{11} - b_1 b_{01})$ are negative. Also assume $1/a_{11} > 1/b_{11}$;

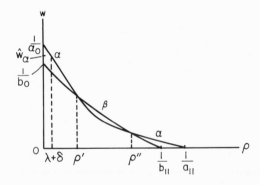

FIGURE 18. Canonical heterogeneous capital model: the factor price frontier.

$1/a_0 > 1/b_0$, to allow for the possibility of two switching points,[35] and suppose that at $\hat{\rho} = \lambda + \delta$, we have $\hat{w}_\alpha > \hat{w}_\beta$ (see Figure 18).[36]

It is impossible to give a complete picture of the model in a two-dimensional diagram, but we can use two auxiliary diagrams in the planes $c_1 - z_1$ and $c_2 - z_2$ simultaneously (Figure 19). We use the following notation:

$$g_1 = 1 - b_0 c_2 - b_{01} z_2, \qquad 0 \le g_1 \le 1,$$

$$g_2 = 1 - a_0 c_1 - a_{01} z_1, \qquad 0 \le g_2 \le 1,$$

and

$$g_1 + g_2 = 1 + \varepsilon_0.$$

The solutions are obtained by juggling the lines $P_1 Q_1$ and $P_2 Q_2$ subject to the constraint $g_1 + g_2 = 1 (+ \varepsilon_0)$ and using the simplex criterion on

---

[35] See [4].

[36] Figure 18 superimposes the factor price curves for the two techniques in one diagram, under the simplifying assumption $\mu_1 = \mu_2$. There is no need to make this assumption in what follows.

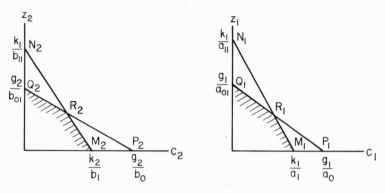

FIGURE 19. Canonical heterogeneous capital model: production constraints.

$c_1 + c_2 + \pi_1 z_1 + \pi_2 z_2$. We obtain the following four main regions in terms of k_1 and k_2 with a further breakdown into subregions (depending on whether $\hat{w}_\alpha \gtrless 1/b_0$). These are listed in Table 4.

The enumeration of phases in Table 4 helps to give the full characterization of the optimal path. The following conclusions emerge:

1. The choice of technique is determined by the real wage $\hat{w}$ at the long-run rate $\lambda + \delta$. By an arbitrary assumption $\hat{w}_\alpha > \hat{w}_\beta$. Since technique α does not require β-capital in its production, the system will never invest in k_2 (that is, $z_2 = 0$), *no matter how high the initial endowment of k_2.*

Table 4. Solutions for the Canonical Model

Region	Range of k_i		Points in Figure 19	Optimal Policy*				
I	$\dfrac{a_{01}}{a_{11}} k_1 + \dfrac{b_{01}}{b_{11}} k_2 \leq 1$		N_1, M_2	z_1		c_2	ε_0	
II	$\begin{cases} \dfrac{a_{01}}{a_{11}} k_1 + \dfrac{b_{01}}{b_{11}} k_2 \geq 1 \\ \dfrac{a_{01}}{a_{11}} k_1 + \dfrac{b_0}{b_1} k_2 \leq 1 \end{cases}$		N_1, M_2	z_1		c_2	ε_0	
IIIa		$\hat{w}_\alpha < \dfrac{1}{b_0}$	R_1, M_2	z_1	c_1	c_2		
IIIb	$\dfrac{a_{01}}{a_{11}} k_1 + \dfrac{b_0}{b_1} k_2 > 1$	$\hat{w}_\alpha = \dfrac{1}{b_0}$	$R_1 \equiv N_1, P_2$	z_1		c_2		ε_2
IIIc		$\hat{w}_\alpha > \dfrac{1}{b_0}$	$R_1, P_2 \equiv 0$	z_1	c_1			ε_2
IV	$k_1 \geq \dfrac{a_1}{a_0}$		$P_1, P_2 \equiv 0$		c_1		ε_1	ε_2

* In all cases in which c_2 appears it is assumed that $k_2 > 0$.

2. The last point is particularly well brought out by what happens in region II. The only difference between I and II is that in II full employment could, in principle, be achieved (by producing z_1 and z_2), and yet the system is foresighted enough to use up the existing k_2 endowment for the production of c_2 and wait to go into full employment only when region III is reached, having accumulated sufficient amounts of k_1.

3. The particular production schedule chosen in region III depends on whether it pays to go on operating β-capital to produce consumption c_2 at marginal (variable) cost $\hat{w}_\alpha b_0$. Since $z_2 = 0$, then k_2 will eventually decay to zero and the system will go on producing only z_1 and c_1 in the full-employment amounts, just as in a two-sector single-technique model (see Section 2).

4. *Consumption need not be monotonic* in this model. If k_2 dies out before k_1 catches up, we can have a temporary fall in $c = c_2$ before $c = c_1 + c_2$ starts rising again.

5. There *is no technique reswitching* along the optimal path (that is, no sequences of the type $\alpha - \beta - \alpha$). The own rates of interest ρ_i jump discretely, avoiding intermediate switching points.[37]

It should be clear from our discussion how this analysis is trivially generalized to the case of more than two alternative techniques (and thus more than two capital goods).

5. Some Concluding Remarks

No attempt will be made to summarize this essay. The various models considered here all belong to the same family, and their behavior does follow some common rules (especially with respect to duality, stability, and the choice of alternative techniques). At the same time it is the product diversification on which we should like to lay stress. Each of the models considered was analyzed not so much for the sake of contributing to some general statements about "n-sector models with m_i alternative activities for the ith good" but rather to help illuminate some particular question, and these cannot be summarized conveniently. Instead, let us point out some of the things that were left out and need further elaboration.

---

[37] In a sense there is only one steady-state interest rate in our system (namely $n + \delta$) and therefore only one technique that is eventually viable. The only way reswitching can still be brought about in this model is by allowing for a change of n and/or δ as between generations, but is this a realistic assumption to make?

If we nonetheless believe in transitions from one steady state to another (i.e., suppose $n + \delta$ changes abruptly to a new level), the present analysis can be used to trace out efficient transition to a new steady state. Given the k_1^*, k_2^* levels of the first steady state, we take these as the initial endowments of the new Ramsey problem. The new level of $n + \delta$ will determine which of the techniques maximizes the long-run real wage, and now the optimal path from one steady state to another can be worked out, as before.

It should be clear that, on the production side, all the results can be extended to include the case in which Leontief-type intermediate goods are produced along with durable capital goods.[38] The one consumption good should be understood to include the case in which there is a fixed basket of consumer goods or the case in which relative prices of different consumer goods remain constant. All this is trivial. There is one important extension to be worked out, however. Rather than let the model maximize consumption, it should be modified to maximize a nonlinear welfare function in which consumption (or a consumption vector) appears as an argument. Clearly this makes the explicit solution of the model much messier. But there may be some gain in realism. For one thing, it need no longer be the case that the quantity and price equations can be solved independently, even within any one phase.

Next we should mention the question of the planning horizon. We have confined ourselves to infinite horizon models. Obviously the same method can be used to solve for the case of a finite planning horizon. In fact the only change that has to be introduced is in the transversality conditions.[39] The latter modification may not be important for the pure theory aspects of our discussion but becomes quite relevant when we think of the application of this type of model in actual development planning. It is, in fact, in bridging a gap between existing optimal growth theory and the type of empirical input-output models increasingly used in development planning that there lies, we believe, the main possible use of this type of model.[40]

Finally, we believe this type of capital model to be particularly suited for the realistic introduction of technical progress in an optimal growth context. This will here take the form of the appearance of new activities in the spectrum of techniques as time goes on. And we should end by paying our lip service to uncertainty.

When we have introduced these "minor" modifications, will any characteristics that we have found remain valid? Clearly there is a lot that remains to be done. In this field of research the steady state has not yet been reached. Let us at least hope that we have contributed a small discrete step on the optimal path.

---

[38] One can always think of our coefficient matrix as being derived from a larger system in which intermediate inputs also appear by application of Leontief inverse matrices.

[39] If we specify a terminal stock k_T for the period $t = T$, the transversality condition for that capital good becomes $e^{-\delta t}\pi(T) [k(T) - k_T] = 0$, which implies either $k(T) = k_T$ or $\pi(T) = 0$.

[40] Another deficiency of our model, in a planning context, is its confinement to a closed economy. This, however, can be overcome when we think of foreign exchange being, in one respect, just like another capital good. Also one should think in terms of discrete, rather than continuous time. For recent empirical examples of this type of optimizing planning model see Stoleru [24], Eckaus and Parikh [9], Chenery and MacEwan [7], and Bruno [2].

References

1. Bliss, G. A., *Lectures on the Calculus of Variations*, Chicago, Ill.: University of Chicago Press, Seventh Impression, 1963.
2. Bruno, M., "A Programming Model for Israel," in I. Adelman and E. Thorbecke (eds.), *The Theory and Design of Economic Development*, Baltimore, Md.: The Johns Hopkins Press, 1966.
3. Bruno, M., "Fundamental Duality Relations in the Pure Theory of Capital and Growth," Department of Economics, Massachusetts Institute of Technology, Cambridge, Mass., July 1966.
4. Bruno, M., E. Burmeister, and E. Sheshinski, "The Nature and Significance of the Reswitching of Techniques," *Quarterly Journal of Economics*, Vol. 80 (November 1966).
5. Cass, D., "Optimum Growth in an Aggregative Model of Capital Accumulation," *Review of Economic Studies*, Vol. 32 (July 1965).
6. Chakravarty, S., "Optimal Programme of Capital Accumulation in a Multi-Sector Economy," *Econometrica*, Vol. 33 (July 1965).
7. Chenery, H. B., and A. MacEwan, "Optimal Programs of Aid and Development," in I. Adelman and E. Thorbecke (eds.), *The Theory and Design of Economic Development*, Baltimore, Md.: The Johns Hopkins Press, 1966.
8. Dorfman, R., P. A. Samuelson, and R. M. Solow, *Linear Programming and Economic Analysis*, New York: McGraw-Hill Book Company, 1958.
9. Eckaus, R. S., and K. S. Parikh, "Planning for Growth: Multi-Sectoral Inter-Temporal Models Applied to India," Center for International Studies, Massachusetts Institute of Technology, Cambridge, Mass., April 1966.
10. Gale, D., "Optimal Programs for a Multi-Sector Economy with an Infinite Time Horizon," Technical Report No. 1, Department of Mathematics, Brown University, Providence, R.I., 1965.
11. Jorgenson, D. W., "A Dual Stability Theorem," *Econometrica*, Vol. 28 (October 1960).
12. Koopmans, T. C., "On the Concept of Optimal Economic Growth," Cowles Foundation Discussion Paper No. 163, Yale University, New Haven, Conn., December 1963.
13. Leitmann, G., *et al.*, *Optimization Techniques*, New York: Academic Press, 1962.
14. Levhari, D., "A Non-Substitution Theorem and the Switching of Techniques," *Quarterly Journal of Economics*, Vol. 79 (February 1965).
15. Morishima, M., *Equilibrium, Stability and Growth*, London: Oxford University Press, 1964.
16. Pasinetti, L. L., "Changes in the Rate of Profit and Switches of Techniques," *Quarterly Journal of Economics*, Vol. 80 (November 1966).
17. Pontryagin, L. S., *et al.*, *The Mathematical Theory of Optimal Processes*, New York and London: Interscience Publishers, Inc., 1962.
18. Robinson, J., *The Accumulation of Capital*, London: Macmillan and Company, 1956.
19. Samuelson, P. A., "A New Theorem on Nonsubstitution," in H. Hegeland (ed.), *Money, Growth and Methodology* (essays in honor of Johan Åkerman), Lund, Sweden, 1961; reproduced in J. Stiglitz (ed.), *The Collected Scientific Papers of Paul A. Samuelson*, Cambridge, Mass.: The M.I.T. Press, 1966, Vol. I, pp. 520–536. Hereafter referred to as *Samuelson Papers*.

20. Samuelson, P. A., "Parable and Realism in Capital Theory: The Surrogate Production Function," *Review of Economic Studies*, Vol. 29 (June 1962); reproduced in *Samuelson Papers*, Vol. I, pp. 325–338.
21. Samuelson, P. A., and R. M. Solow, "A Complete Capital Model Involving Heterogeneous Capital Goods," *Quarterly Journal of Economics*, Vol. 70 (November 1956); reproduced in *Samuelson Papers*, Vol. I, pp. 261–286.
22. Shell, K., "Optimal Programs of Capital Accumulation for an Economy in which there is no Exogenous Technical Change," Essay I in this volume.
23. Solow, R. M., "Competitive Valuation in a Dynamic Input-Output System," *Econometrica*, Vol. 27 (January 1959).
24. Stoleru, L. G., "An Optimal Policy for Economic Growth," *Econometrica*, Vol. 33 (April 1965).

XII

Indeterminacy of Development in a Heterogeneous-Capital Model with Constant Saving Propensity[1]

PAUL A. SAMUELSON

Massachusetts Institute of Technology

1. Introduction

Much attention has been paid to growth models in which saving is a constant fraction of income. Thus, Solow [12] showed that the one-sector well-behaved neoclassical version of the full-employment Harrod-Domar model would asymptotically approach a stable golden-age equilibrium.

A two-sector model, in which labor and a homogeneous capital good can make a consumption good (simple or composite) or new capital goods, has been analyzed by Uzawa, Solow, Inada, Drandakis, Findlay, Burmeister, and many others. For this "canonical model," there need not be convergence to a golden-age equilibrium of exponential growth; there can be locally unstable equilibria and limit cycles; there can even be causal indeterminacy in the sense that, for a given amount of capital and labor and prescribed propensities to save out of wage and profit incomes, there may exist a variety of different possible short-term outcomes. However, a number of alternative sufficiency conditions are known that rule out causal indeterminacy and locally unstable equilibria. (See Burmeister [1] for a review and extension of this literature, most of which appeared in the *Review of Economic Studies* since 1963.)

Recently Frank Hahn [4, 5] has investigated the considerable complications

[1] My thanks go to the Carnegie Corporation for granting me a reflective 1965–1966 year and to Felicity Skidmore for research assistance.

219

that arise for the determinacy of a model involving constant propensities to save when the assumption of a homogeneous capital good is replaced by the assumption of two or more heterogeneous capital goods. Need the system approach a golden-age equilibrium as in the simple Solow model? Is a unique short-run growth path defined and followed by the system? Hahn presents strong reasons to doubt that an affirmative answer can be given to these questions. I propose here to reinforce those doubts, elucidate the nature of the problem, and suggest some heuristic ways that the difficulties might be partially circumvented.

2. Solow Model with Homogeneous Capital

Denoting labor, homogeneous capital, consumption, and output by (L, K, C, Y), Solow's simple system is defined by

$$\dot{K} + C = Y = F(K, L) = LF(K/L, 1) = Lf(K/L) = Lf(k), \qquad f'' < 0. \quad (1)$$

The behavior equation $\dot{K}/Y = s$, a constant, leads when labor grows exponentially at rate n to the differential-equation system.

$$\frac{\dot{k}}{k} = s\frac{f(k)}{k} - n \qquad (2)$$

with stable fixed point k^{∞} by virtue of the fact that $f(k)/k$ is a declining function of k. Had saving been a constant function of profit income only, Equation 2 would be replaced by

$$\frac{\dot{k}}{k} = s_k f'(k) - n, \qquad (3)$$

which is also stable because $f'' < 0$.

The two-sector canonical model is more complicated. Now Equation 1 becomes the production-possibility frontier

$$\dot{K} = T(K, L; C) = T(K/L, 1; C/L)L = T(k, 1; c)L, \qquad (4)$$

where T is a concave function as well as being homogeneous of degree one.[2] Using small letters for per capita magnitudes, Equation 4 becomes

$$\dot{k} = T(k, 1; c) - nk \qquad (5)$$

---

[2] Because the two sectors do not involve joint production, along with the singularity of the 3-by-3 Hessian matrix $[T_{ij}]$, where subscripts depict partial differentiation with respect to the numbered arguments $(T, L; C)$, it is known (Samuelson [10]) that the 2-by-2 principal minor must vanish:

$$\begin{vmatrix} T_{11} & T_{12} \\ T_{21} & T_{22} \end{vmatrix} \equiv 0.$$

with the right-hand side being concave in its (k, c) arguments by virtue of diminishing returns in each sector.

For simplicity, I stick with the Harrod-Solow case of constant saving s out of *all* income. This can be written in a variety of ways:

$$\dot{K} = s[KT_1 + LT_2]$$

$$\dot{K} = \frac{s}{1 - s} \qquad \text{(value of consumption in machine } \textit{numéraire} \text{ units)} \qquad (6)$$

$$= \frac{s}{1 - s} C(-T_3).$$

Equating the last right-hand expression with the right-hand expression of Equation 4 and writing $s/(1 - s) = \beta$, we end up with the system

$$T(k, 1; c) + \beta c T_3(k, 1; c) = 0,$$
$$\dot{k} = T(k, 1; c) - nk. \qquad (7)$$

The first part of Equation 7 can be solved for $c = c(k)$, because its Jacobian

$$T_3(1 + \beta) + \beta c T_{33}$$

is necessarily one-signed, being negative. Hence, with an equal savings rate from profit and wages, no causal indeterminacy is possible in the two-sector model, inasmuch as substitution of $c(k)$ into the last part of Equation 7 yields

$$\dot{k} = T[k, 1; c(k)] - nk, \qquad (8)$$

a determinate system. A golden-age equilibrium k^∞ must satisfy

$$0 = T[k^\infty, 1; c(k^\infty)] - nk^\infty. \qquad (9)$$

This will be unique if $T[k, 1; c(k)]/k$ is an ever declining function of k. Sufficient conditions for this are that the consumption-good industry be relatively capital intensive. This entails that T_{31} and $c'(k)$ be positive in sign; since $T(k, 1; c)/k$ diminishes with k when c is held constant, it will diminish still more when c grows with k. Hence, the golden-age equilibrium is unique and globally stable when the consumption industry is relatively capital intensive.

It is well known that in the case of opposite factor intensities, that is, when the consumption-good industry is relatively labor intensive (and particularly when both industries have very low elasticities of substitution σ_i), there may exist two or even an infinity of equilibria, none being globally stable and some being locally unstable.

If one considers the failure to approach a golden age somehow annoying, a radically different approach can be taken. Instead of assuming constant saving propensity $\dot{K}/Y$, one can take a programmer's approach in the spirit of Ramsey. Thus, a planned society might determine its investment $\dot{K}(t)$ and capital development $K(t)$ in order to maximize some per capita social-utility integral of the form

$$\operatorname*{Max}_{K(t)} \int_0^T e^{-\rho t} U\!\left(\frac{C}{L}\right) dt. \tag{10}$$

Subjecting the system to production restraints of the Solow-Ramsey type shown in Equation 2 or of the canonical type shown in Equation 5 is known to lead, for $T = \infty$, *asymptotically* to a golden-age equilibrium, with $\dot{K}$ *ultimately* ending up as a constant fraction of Y (depending on n and ρ). Thus, when $\rho = 0$, the system approaches the Swan-Phelps golden rule golden age of maximum permanent per capita consumption, with the interest rate asymptotically at $r = n$ and the proportion of income saved constant at the same fractional value as the factor share of capital.

It must be emphasized that Ramsey planners do contrive convergence to golden ages that might be unstable under *laissez faire* with constant saving propensities. How do they do this? Consider the bombing of some capital, which perturbs K and k from their golden-age paths. If the rule $\dot{K}/Y = s$ leads to instability, it should be clear that the planners—in *aiming* to maximize their integral—make sure that they depart from such a rule until they are again back on their turnpike target. A teleological purpose is definitely involved. Just as eternal vigilance is the price of liberty, eternal vigilance is the price of maintaining an optimal growth path. Each exogenous shock requires the planner to reaim his decision variables.

The role of teleology is reinforced when we recognize the *catenary* nature of the Euler differential equations.[3] These extremals surround the golden-age equilibrium point in a saddle point, not in a convergently spiraling focus or damped node. Only for one knife-edge direction of aim will the motion be convergent to equilibrium: for all other initial directions, the system ultimately fans out from the golden-age turnpikes. Indeed it is this catenary property of the motions around the turnpike that is essential for the truth of the fundamental turnpike theorem (which says you must spend most of the time indefinitely near to golden-age balanced growth even if your distant target is away from the golden-age configuration).

An analogy to the problem of stability and planning is provided by a bicycle. A bicycle is highly unstable: unless set just right (and reset just right if perturbed), it will fall cumulatively away from equilibrium. But a bicycle manned by a trained rider is stable. The biological link provides its governor.

---

[3] A catenary has the form $a \exp(\lambda t) + b \exp(-\lambda t)$, or more generally has exponentials with opposite-signed exponents, and is therefore generally unstable forward as well as backward and at best approaches "asymptotically" to the equilibrium and ultimately diverges from it. "Asymptotically" is used here in the sense of "asymptotic" rather than convergent series. The equilibrium of an upright bicycle has the catenary property. (See Samuelson [9] for catenary turnpike discussion.)

The governor, or his muscles, knows how to reaim it every instant to retain stability.

An interesting question is whether a competitive market of futures prices can provide the teleological foresight and reaimings that ideal planning is able to provide. I come back to this complex question later.

3. Heterogeneous Capital Goods

Now let us begin to grapple with models involving heterogeneous capital goods. Dynamic programming techniques, involving discrete time periods, can handle the blue-prints technology studied by Joan Robinson. However, the analogy with standard methods in the calculus of variations and with Solow's work will be closer if we make the neoclassical assumptions used earlier by Solow and Samuelson [6, 8] in generalizing the Ramsey model. Let $(K_1, \cdots, K_m)$ be a vector of different capital goods which can be used with labor to produce consumption goods $(C_1, \cdots, C_s)$ and their own net capital formations. All this can be summarized in the concave, homogeneous-of-first-degree social transformation function:

$$C_1 = F(L; K_1, \cdots, K_m; \dot{K}_1, \dot{K}_2, \cdots, \dot{K}_m; C_2, \cdots, C_s). \tag{11}$$

Just as Equations 1 and 4 could be transformed into per capita functions Equations 2 and 5, so can Equation 11 be transformed into per capita

$$c_1 = F(1; k_1, \cdots, k_m; \dot{k}_1 + nk_1, \cdots, \dot{k}_m + nk_m; c_2, \cdots, c_s), \tag{12}$$

a function concave in its arguments.

As shown in Samuelson [10], it is easy for a programmer to generalize the Ramsey problem and plan, subject to Equation 12, to maximize a per capita integral of the form

$$\max_{\left[\substack{k_j(t) \\ c_i(t)}\right]} \int_0^T e^{-\rho t} U(c_1, \cdots, c_s) \, dt, \tag{13}$$

ending up as $T \to \infty$ with an asymptotic state of golden-age equilibrium, with value of net investment a constant fraction of value of income.

But the last remarks reverse the order of our previous exposition. Suppose we ask, with Hahn, what happens when we generalize the Solow constant-saving model to heterogeneous capitals?

Recalling the definition of income as the sum of all factor payments, we write it in terms of the C_1 *numéraire* as

$$\begin{aligned}
Y &= L \frac{\partial F}{\partial L} + K_1 \frac{\partial F}{\partial K_1} + \cdots + K_m \frac{\partial F}{\partial K_m} \\
&= LF_0(1, k_1, \cdots, k_m; \dot{k}_1 + nk_1, \cdots; c_2, \cdots, c_s) \\
&\quad + \sum_{j=1}^m K_j F_j(1, k_1, \cdots, \dot{k}_1 + nk_1, \cdots; c_2, \cdots, c_s),
\end{aligned} \tag{14}$$

where L is treated as the zeroth argument and F_j denotes partial derivatives.

The total value of net capital formation or investment in terms of the same C_1 *numéraire* is

$$I = -\left[\dot{K}_1 \frac{\partial F}{\partial \dot{K}_1} + \cdots + \dot{K}_m \frac{\partial F}{\partial \dot{K}_m}\right]$$

$$= -L\left[\sum_{j=1}^{m} (\dot{k}_j + nk_j)F_{n+j}(1, k_1, \cdots; k_1 + nk_1, \cdots; c_2, \cdots)\right]. \quad (15)$$

The behavior equation $I/Y = s$ becomes, from Equations 14 and 15 in per capita terms,

$$-\sum_{j=1}^{m} (\dot{k}_j + nk_j)F_{n+j}(1, k_1, \cdots; \cdots; \cdots, c_s)$$

$$= s\left[F_0(1, k_1, \cdots; \cdots; \cdots, c_s) + \sum_{j=1}^{m} k_j F_j(1, k_1, \cdots; \cdots; \cdots, c_s)\right]. \quad (16)$$

Obviously Equations 12 and 16 are but two equations and are insufficient to determine the paths of the $m + s$ unknowns $[k_j(t); c_i(t)]$. We can easily make good the equations needed to determine the $[c_i(t)]$ by invoking consumers' sovereignty and current preference-maximizing demand functions, which allocate the funds not going to investment among the available (c_i) goods while taking account of their scarcity or market prices. Or, even simpler, we might assume fixed proportions for a composite market basket of consumption goods: with $c_i/c_1 = a_i$, we could express Equations 11 and 12 in terms of a single consumption good c_1. Or, if indifference curves are always homothetic and entail unitary income elasticities for all consumption goods, we can rigorously define a single composite consumption good (made up of changing proportions of the c_i components, depending upon relative prices). Hence, for expositional simplicity, we may often deal here with a single consumption good c_1, setting $s = 1$ and omitting the last variables to the right of the semicolon $(c_2, \cdots,)$.

With multiple capital goods $m > 1$, Equation 16 still leaves us short $m - 1$ conditions for a determinately developing system. We shall see that this is inevitable: for until we add further assumptions, such as where the system is to terminate (at some future date), how can it know precisely where to aim now?

4. Intertemporal Efficiency Conditions

But first I must digress to derive the efficiency conditions that it is known a well-running system must satisfy. (See Dorfman, Samuelson, Solow [2] and Samuelson [7].) These are also $m - 1$ in number; but, involving as they do the new variables $\ddot{K}_j$, we are left short $m - 1$ terminal conditions.

The problem of intertemporal efficiency conditions can be stated simply, omitting all mention of price or dual variables. For prescribed consumption requirements $c_i(t)$, between $t = 0$ and $t = T$, and *all but one* terminal capitals prescribed at T $(k_2^T, \cdots)$, and for *all* initial capitals initially prescribed $(k_1^0, k_2^0, \cdots)$, the planners (or the "Invisible Hand" under ideal laissez-faire futures-market pricing) are to select $k_j(t)$ in order to maximize the terminal stock of the one remaining capital k_1^T. Why? If this is not done, everybody can be made better off. Mathematically,

$$\underset{k_j(t)}{\text{Max}} \; k_1^T = \int_0^T \dot{k}_1 \, dt \tag{17}$$

subject to given $(k_1^0, k_2^0, \cdots)$, $(k_2^T, \cdots)$, $[c_i(t)]$, and

$$c_1 = F(1; k_1, k_2, \cdots; \dot{k}_1 + nk_1, \dot{k}_2 + nk_2, \cdots; c_2(t), \cdots)$$

$$= G(k_1, k_2, \cdots, k_m; \dot{k}_1, \dot{k}_2, \cdots, \dot{k}_m; t)$$

$$= G(k, \dot{k}; t), \qquad \text{for short.}$$

Replacing $\dot{k}_1$ by the Lagrangian integrand

$$\dot{k}_1 + \lambda(t)[G(k_1, k_2, \cdots; \dot{k}_1, \dot{k}_2, \cdots) - c_1],$$

we derive in the usual fashion the Euler efficiency conditions

$$\frac{d}{dt}(\lambda G_{m+j}) - \lambda G_j = 0, \qquad j = 1, \cdots, m. \tag{18}$$

We can eliminate λ from Equation 18 by substitution to get $m - 1$ efficiency conditions

$$\frac{(d/dt)G_{m+1} - G_1}{G_{m+1}} = \cdots = \frac{(d/dt)G_{m+m} - G_m}{G_{m+m}}. \tag{19}$$

A typical one of these, written out after performing the indicated time differentiation, is of the form

$$\sum_{j=1}^m A_{ij}(k, \dot{k}, t)\ddot{k}_j + B_i(k, \dot{k}, t) = \sum_{j=1}^m A_{1j}(k, \dot{k}, t) + B_1(k, \dot{k}, t), \tag{20}$$

$$i = 2, \cdots, m,$$

subject of course, from Equation 17, to

$$\dot{c}_1(t) = \frac{d}{dt} G(k, \dot{k}, t) = \sum_{j=1}^m H_j(k, \dot{k}, t)\ddot{k}_j + H_0(k, \dot{k}, t).$$

Hence, our efficiency conditions (Equation 19) introduce as many new unknowns $(\ddot{k}_j)$ as themselves. This digression on efficiency therefore shows that escape from the impasse of indeterminacy is not to be found from this direction. Yet the subject was worth elucidating for its own sake. And, what is important in linking up this discussion with that of Hahn, these efficiency conditions enable us to have the full content of his perfect-foresight price-fulfillment conditions without having to introduce any price or dual variables into the discussion.

In leaving the subject of intertemporal efficiency conditions, I stress the fact that these are quite divorced from the Ramsey problem of optimal saving. If the Ramsey integral (Integral 13) is maximized, the efficiency conditions (Equation 19) will automatically be satisfied; but not vice versa. No matter how arbitrarily consumption and total investment are determined, an ideal market system (with a complete set of futures markets) or an optimally planned program will ensure that efficiency conditions are satisfied.

5. Reduction to a von Neumann Model

The system satisfying Equations 12, 16, and 19 is seen to be indeterminate, lacking $m - 1$ terminal conditions. Nevertheless, there does exist, in general at least, one balanced-growth or golden-age equilibrium path defined by

$$k_j(t) \equiv k_j^*, \quad K_j(t) = k_j^* L(t) = k_j^* e^{nt},$$

$$c_1^* = F(1, k_1^*, \cdots; 0 + nk_1^*, \cdots; \cdots),$$

$$- \sum_{j=1}^{m} nk_j^* F_{n+j}(1, k_1^*, 111) = s\left[F_0(1, k_1^*, \cdots) + \sum_{j=1}^{m} k_j^* F_j(1, k_1^*, \cdots)\right],$$
$$\tag{21}$$

$$r^* - n = -\frac{G_j}{G_{m+j}} = -\frac{F_j}{F_{m+j}} - n, \quad j = 1, \cdots, m.$$

I suspect that one might show that this stationary point $(k, \dot{k}, \ddot{k}) = (k^*, 0, 0)$ has, for fixed (c_i^*), a catenary saddle-point property. (That is, utilizing the local linear approximation to the differential equations, we determine that the characteristic roots come in opposite-signed pairs.) Rather than investigate this problem here, I shall consider an artifice that will turn our problem into a von Neumann model whose properties have already been worked out. For simplicity of exposition I work with the case of a single consumption good $c_1 = c_s$. My argument will be heuristic rather than rigorous (but at least for certain special cases, like the Cobb-Douglas technology of Hahn, I suspect it can be made rigorous).

If a constant fraction of income is being saved and a constant fraction is being consumed, we might think of the amount consumed as being a necessary input—just the way fodder for horses, or petrol for machines, is a necessary input. The surplus producible by the system, *after* subtracting off this necessary consumption, is all plowed back for growth in the familiar von Neumann manner. The effect then of a positive propensity to consume, $1 - s$, is to leave us with a von Neumann system capable of less rapid growth than our original system with $1 - s$ zero and all c zero. (This trick of creating a new pseudo-Neumann system by treating induced consumption as necessitous was used, following up an insight of Bator, in Samuelson [8], to demonstrate why $r = n$ in the golden rule state of maximum per capita consumption.)

If this heuristic trick can be made to work, successfully duplicating the constant saving case, it is just as if we have a new F function, call it f, exactly like Equation 11 but now with *all* c_s zero. This analogue to Equation 11 can be written as

$$0 = f(L, K_1, \cdots, K_m; \dot{K}_1, \cdots, \dot{K}_m; 0, \cdots), \tag{22}$$

where f is concave and homogeneous of the first degree. In per capita terms, the analogue to Equation 12 becomes

$$0 = f(1, k_1, \cdots, k_m; \dot{k}_1 + nk_1, \cdots, \dot{k}_m + nk_m; 0, \cdots)$$
$$= g(k, \dot{k}), \qquad \text{for short,} \tag{23}$$

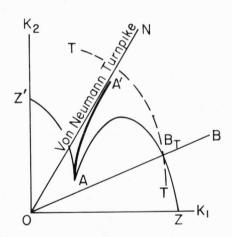

FIGURE 1. Treating the fractional amount consumed as necessitous input, we consider our system as a pseudo-Neumann model, capable of maximal balanced growth along the indicated golden-age turnpike. From any initial point, like A (which could have been on the turnpike), there streams out an infinite number of efficient paths, only one of which, namely AA', approaches the golden age (by virtue of the catenary property). For a wide class of systems, this convergent path is the only one that can be *permanently* efficient, since all others eventually hit an axis (as at Z or Z') and then, presumably, reveal themselves to be inefficient. If we supply the system with terminal-goal conditions (so-called transversality conditions), such as that at time T we be as far out as possible on the ray OB from the origin, then the path AB_T will be the determinate outcome. If $T \to \infty$, and we insist on *permanent* efficiency, the convergent heavy path will be the determinate outcome.

where $g(k, \dot{k})$ is concave in its arguments, and where we may expect (save possibly for singular cases) that $0 = g(k^*, 0)$ has a unique solution for a golden-age state or von Neumann turnpike.

Now it is fairly well known from catenary turnpike theory (cf. Samuelson [7]) that von Neumann turnpikes do have the catenary property. Still reasoning heuristically, I depict in Figure 1 the behavior to be expected of such a two-variable system that begins at any point A in the K_1, K_2 space (where $m = 2$). The diagram tells its own story: only one path from A approaches the golden-age turnpike, and (by a theorem of Furuya and Inada [3]) this is the only path through A that does not eventually hit an axis and (presumably) reveal itself subsequently to be inefficient.[4]

If one insists on permanent efficiency, a way out of the impasse of indeterminacy does seem provided—namely, by the heavy path from A which uniquely converges to the golden-age turnpike.

Alternatively, if society knows where it wants to end up at some future time T (or, what leads to the same thing, if society knows the pecuniary valuations of the K_j that will hold at terminal time T), there can be determined a unique original direction of aim—that is, a unique quantitative mix of current capital formations to reach that goal.

6. Reaiming Behavior of Speculators

My analysis, culminating in Figure 1, has confirmed Hahn's finding that merely to postulate over-all saving propensities leaves a heterogeneous system indeterminate in its development. When there was only one homogeneous good K, with $m = 1$ and $m - 1 = 0$, no similar problem of allocation of saving funds among alternative capital formations would arise.

Now how do actual economic systems resolve these indeterminacies? For a planned society of the Soviet type, the authorities presumably aim (and reaim) the system at each time period so as to achieve whatever goal they want to attain. (Of course, all this is highly idealized. Many so-called planned systems do not in fact know what they are doing at any instant of time, much less know where they are going or just why they want to end up there.)

But what about a modern mixed economy run largely by consumer sovereignty (including freedom to advertise and affect consumer demand) and by profit-seeking competitive investors? Even if we waive Chamberlinian problems of monopolistic competition, where does such a system get its guidance?

Well, for one thing we can imagine ideal futures markets. Just as there exists a price quotation today for wheat delivered in Chicago next May, we

---

[4] This exposition lacks rigor. How can I be sure it does not take an infinite time to reach Z or Z'? If Z is reached in finite time, could the motion somehow be *efficiently* extended along the axis itself?

can imagine prices quoted today for each future $[K_j(t)]$ or $[C_i(t)]$. We can imagine this, but it takes a strong imagination to indulge in such an unrealistic exercise. Very few activities are able to rely on a viable organized futures market; and even for wheat and other staples, such markets are only able to overcome the hurdle of indivisible costs for a year or two ahead (when the contingency risks are sufficiently foreseeable to motivate hedgers to pay for the transference of risks to speculators, while having to pay brokerage commissions and other costs of market maintenance).

Let us, though, indulge our imaginations and conceive of futures markets. What determines the profile of futures prices that will be self-fulfilling? Each path through A in Figure 1 calls for, and is evoked by, a different profile of futures prices (or dual variables to the primal variables of my equations). As Hahn suggests, we are left with the problem of indeterminacy of the future-price profile. Mathematically, if we knew $m - 1$ terminal price ratios $(P_{K_j}/P_{K_1})^T$, we could pick out a determinate path from the $(m - 1)$-parameter family of curves through A. Why should a laissez-faire system select that particular point in the $m - 1$ space corresponding to convergence to the golden age?

Heuristically, I feel that the fact underlying the Furuya-Inada theorem about permanent inefficiency may provide something of an answer. In the long, long future, any path but the convergent one is going to frustrate somebody's expectations and, crudely, is going to lead to bankruptcy for someone and to reaiming for the system. "Whom the Gods would destroy, they first make mad." And, I may add, "There will generally be a sharp-shooting speculator around, both to pick up the pieces after the debacle and—by foreseeing the debacle—to make money by doing some of the things that keep it from happening."

The image in my mind is that of a bicycle. The rider of the bicycle is the bulk of the market, a somewhat mystical concept to be sure—like its analogue, the well-informed speculator who gets his way in the end because his way is the correctly discerned way of the future; and those who think differently are bankrupted by their bets against (him and) the future. (It is easier to identify the well-informed speculator *ex post* than *ex ante*, and the image can easily dissolve into an empty tautology.) For a time, the less than omniscient market may chase down a false path emanating from A; but when the system is led too far from the balanced-growth configuration, some entrepreneurs begin to foresee the shoals ahead at Z, and they act to push the system back toward the turnpike. Even if there is something valid in this heuristic reasoning, one must admit that the system need not—and, generally, will not—move from its present position to the golden age in the most efficient way: it will hare after false goals, get detoured, and begin to be corrected only after it has erred. But, pragmatically, this may be the best one can hope for in an uncertain world, where changes in technology and tastes are going on continuously, making it impossible to certify *ex ante* just what is the golden-age turnpike that the system should aim for even if it possessed a greater approximation to omniscience than it actually does.

The reader may draw into Figure 1 my poetic image of a pragmatic path that streams out of *A* in the "wrong" direction but that gets repointed back toward the turnpike discontinuously by entrepreneurs sensing an opportunity for profit or for avoidance of future loss. Perhaps this would lead to a quasi-random walk that stays with considerable probability in some cone neighborhood around the golden-age path of balanced growth.

I leave this heuristic discussion with a reminder that it lacks both analytical rigor and empirical documentation.[5] And I must give warning that, in at least one economic model, there exists an *infinity* of self-fulfilling motions that are *permanently* explosive. I refer to the tulip-mania phenomenon (discussed in Samuelson [6]). If people think tulips will appreciate at 10 per cent per month, they can be motivated to act so that this will happen. Happen for how long? As far as theory can tell, forever. Even though every tulip mania and stock-market bubble have come to an end in history, economists have no good theory to explain why they last as long as they do and not twice or half as long.

One feels that the real world of tools, plant, and inventory contrasts with the purely financial dream world of indefinite group self-fulfillment. But can this feeling be given documentation and plausible explication?

References

1. Burmeister, E., "Stability and Causality in Two-Sector Models of Economic Growth," Ph.D. dissertation, Massachusetts Institute of Technology, Cambridge, Mass., 1965.
2. Dorfman, R., P. A. Samuelson, and R. M. Solow, *Linear Programming and Economic Analysis*, New York: McGraw-Hill Book Company, 1958, Chapters 11 and 12.
3. Furuya, H., and K. Inada, "Balanced Growth and Intertemporal Efficiency in Capital Accumulation," *International Economic Review*, Vol. 3 (1962), pp. 94–107.

---

[5] Empirically, the lifetime statistical studies of speculative prices by Holbrook Working suggest, for a market like wheat or onions, that the outcome is to have prices fluctuate quasi-randomly around trends that do serve to allocate goods over time so as to minimize positions of scarcity and glut and to lead to that optimal carry-over and storage that minimize fortuitous variance of price movements. Keynes was a good personal speculator; but when he described commodity markets as if they were merely gambling casinos—in which the winners guess not who really is the prettiest girl, but whom the majority will think (the majority will think . . .) is the prettiest girl—Keynes was apparently not being an accurate empirical scientist. [Since this paper was written, K. Shell and J. Stiglitz have advanced the subject, proving that *permanent* efficiency and *correct* price anticipation do rule out all indeterminacy.]

4. Hahn, F., "On the Stability of Growth Equilibrium," memorandum, Institute of Economics, University of Oslo, 1966.

5. Hahn, F., "Equilibrium Dynamics with Heterogeneous Capital Goods," *Quarterly Journal of Economics*, Vol. 80 (1966), pp. 633–646.

6. Samuelson, P. A., "Intertemporal Price Equilibrium: A Prologue to the Theory of Speculation," *Weltwirtschaftliches Archiv*, Band 79, Heft 2 (Hamburg: Hoffmann & Campe Verlag, 1957), pp. 181–219; reproduced in J. Stiglitz (ed.), *The Collected Scientific Papers of Paul A. Samuelson*, Cambridge, Mass.: The M.I.T. Press, 1966, Vol. II, pp. 946–984. Hereafter referred to as *Samuelson Papers*.

7. Samuelson, P. A., "Efficient Paths of Capital Accumulation in Terms of the Calculus of Variations," in K. J. Arrow, S. Karlin, and P. Suppes (eds.), *Mathematical Methods in the Social Sciences, 1959*, Stanford, Calif.: Stanford University Press, 1960, pp. 78–88; reproduced in *Samuelson Papers*, Vol. I, pp. 287–298.

8. Samuelson, P. A., "Comment," *Review of Economic Studies*, Vol. 29, No. 3 (1962), pp. 251–254.

9. Samuelson, P. A., "A Catenary Turnpike Theorem Involving Consumption and the Golden Rule," *American Economic Review*, Vol. 55 (1965), pp. 486–496.

10. Samuelson, P. A., "The Fundamental Singularity Theorem for Non-Joint Production," *International Economic Review*, Vol. 7 (1966), pp. 34–41.

11. Samuelson, P. A., and R. M. Solow, "A Complete Capital Model Involving Heterogeneous Capital Goods," *Quarterly Journal of Economics*, Vol. 70 (1956), pp. 537–562; reproduced in *Samuelson Papers*, Vol. I, pp. 261–286.

12. Solow, R. M., "A Contribution to the Theory of Economic Growth," *Quarterly Journal of Economics*, Vol. 70 (1956), pp. 65–94.

XIII

Individual Saving, Aggregate Capital Accumulation, and Efficient Growth[1]

DAVID CASS AND MENAHEM E. YAARI

Cowles Foundation for Research in Economics, Yale University

1. Introduction

In the present essay we shall try to explore the growth-theoretic implications of what is essentially the Modigliani-Brumberg [7] life-cycle theory of saving. More specifically, we shall attempt to study growth and capital accumulation in a model where production is neoclassical but aggregate saving is due entirely to the desire of individuals to achieve an optimal lifetime consumption pattern.

Upon casual examination, the Modigliani-Brumberg life-cycle hypothesis may seem especially well suited for incorporation in a neoclassical growth theory. For this hypothesis implies that after the economy has "settled down" aggregate saving will depend on such parameters as the rate of population growth and the rate of technological improvement. However, attempts so far to construct a dynamic theory on this basis suggest that the task is not as simple as it appears at first sight. The particular studies to which we have reference here are Samuelson's 1958 article on an exact consumption-loan model of interest [10] and Diamond's 1965 article on a neoclassical model of national debt [3]. This essay may very well be thought of as a continuation of the investigation begun by these authors.[2]

[1] Research support from the National Science Foundation is gratefully acknowledged. We are indebted to various members of the Cowles Foundation, in particular, Richard Attiyeh, Tjalling Koopmans, and Herbert Scarf, for helpful discussions and criticism.

[2] Elsewhere [2], we have presented an extensive analysis of Samuelson's model.

233

On the production side of the economy we shall assume a single, competitive sector that hires labor and capital, produces a homogeneous output under neoclassical conditions, and sells this output (indifferently) on the capital and consumption goods markets. Our view of aggregate production and distribution is thus essentially that of Solow [11].

On the consumption side we assume that each individual is born with a labor endowment only and that he plans his lifetime consumption pattern given the relevant wage rates, interest rates, and output prices. Since, in general, a particular individual's desired level of consumption at a moment of time will not coincide with his earnings at that moment, he will be engaged in saving or dissaving. Net aggregate saving, and therefore aggregate capital accumulation, is thus simply the sum of all individuals' saving or dissaving. This is, essentially, the Modigliani-Brumberg view.

Given the analogue of perfect information in static equilibrium analysis, perfect foresight, the interaction of the production and consumption sectors determines a competitive equilibrium growth path. Our major concern will be the properties, for instance, efficiency and Pareto optimality, of this path.[3]

2. The Model

The population at time t is composed of all individuals born at times v for $t - 1 \le v \le t$; that is, all individuals live a lifetime of length one "year." The group of individuals born at time v will be referred to as "generation v." Generation v consists of $e^{nv} \, dv$ individuals, where n is thus the constant rate of population growth. We assume that n is nonnegative. It is further assumed that generation v is born into the labor force and continues therein until death.[4] Hence, the total labor force at time t, denoted $L(t)$, is given by

$$L(t) = \int_{t-1}^{t} e^{nv} \, dv = \frac{1 - e^{-n}}{n} e^{nt}. \tag{1}$$

Total output at time t, denoted $Y(t)$, is produced with the cooperation of this labor force and the capital stock at time t, denoted $K(t)$, in many competitive firms whose aggregate activity can be described by a neoclassical production function. More precisely, letting lower-case letters stand for per capita quantities, it is assumed that[5]

$$y(t) = f[k(t)],$$

---

[3] After this essay was completed, we became aware of Meade's investigation of the bequest motive in a similar model [6].

[4] The implications of modifying this assumption will be explored in section 6.

[5] There is no technical progress in this economy. However, as is usual in neoclassical growth theory, labor augmenting or Harrod-neutral technical progress at a constant rate could easily be assumed. The only difference that this assumption would make is that it would require a reinterpretation of all intensive variables and some parameters of the model.

where f is a real function that is twice continuously differentiable, strictly concave, and that satisfies the derivative conditions $f'(0) > n > f'(\infty)$. It is also assumed that f is strictly increasing for $0 \le k \le \hat{k}$, where $0 < \hat{k} \le \infty$ is the point of capital saturation. The distribution of total output is determined in competitive factor markets, where the competitive real wage and real interest rates are given by the marginal productivities of labor and capital

$$w(t) = f[k(t)] - k(t)f'[k(t)]$$

and

$$r(t) = f'[k(t)],$$

respectively.

In order to complete the picture, we must describe the behavior of an individual from generation v.[6] For such a description we have at our disposal the classical analysis of consumer behavior over time, as introduced, basically, by Irving Fisher [4]. The difficulty is that we do not have much else at our disposal, and using the Fisher analysis involves one assumption that, in the present context, is very drastic indeed. We are referring here to the *perfect foresight* assumption. To plan his consumption today, the Fisher consumer must know with certainty what he will earn in wages during the balance of his lifetime and what returns can be earned in the future from the ownership of assets. In the model under discussion, however, the effects of consumer decisions on wage and interest rates play a central role, so that the perfect foresight assumption amounts to the assertion that consumers take into account wage and interest rates that accurately reflect their own present and future actions. Clearly, what lies in the background of such an assumption is the notion of a general equilibrium model for which the commodities are dated output, labor, and capital, prices (with output as *numéraire*) are the wage and interest rates at every moment of time, and the equilibrium conditions are summarized in Equation 8 from the sequel.

The existence of such an equilibrium is by no means obvious; in particular, the restrictions on trades, which are imposed by the time structure of the model and are not found in the standard static general equilibrium theory, may preclude existence. Only if this equilibrium exists is the perfect foresight assumption legitimate. Demonstrating the existence of equilibrium for initial conditions that give rise to a *stationary* path is a fairly easy matter, as will be seen in the following section. For arbitrary initial conditions, we shall present an existence argument only in the case of a specific example that is discussed in section 4. It is possible to generalize the methods of section 4 and thereby

---

[6] For the time being we assume that all individuals of generation v behave identically. This assumption will be relaxed slightly in section 6.

prove the existence of equilibrium in the general case; however, this requires a rather lengthy argument, and we have decided to omit it.

Notice, in passing, that the alternatives to assuming perfect foresight are either to adopt an arbitrary rule of expectation (and a concomitant arbitrary rule by which to reconcile *ex ante* with *ex post*) or to incorporate into the model a full-fledged theory of decisionmaking under uncertainty; the former alternative leads to rather unconvincing results, while the latter lies beyond our present investigative ability.

Given the perfect foresight assumption, one can write down the allocation problem confronting an individual of generation v. Let $C(t, v)$ be the rate of consumption and let $A(t, v)$ be the asset holdings (in capital goods) of an individual of generation v at time t where $v \leq t \leq v + 1$. We assume that the individual's preferences depend only on his consumption of output[7] and, furthermore, that they can be represented by a utility function of the form

$$\int_v^{v+1} U[C(t, v)]e^{-\delta(t-v)} \, dt,$$

where U is a nondecreasing, concave, and twice-differentiable real function, and δ is the individual's constant and nonnegative subjective rate of time preference. The allocation problem may now be stated as follows:

$$\text{Maximize} \quad \int_v^{v+1} U[C(t, v)]e^{-\delta(t-v)} \, dt$$

subject to

$$C(t, v) = w(t) + r(t)A(t, v) - \frac{\partial A(t, v)}{\partial t},$$

$$A(v, v) = A(v + 1, v) = 0,$$

and

$$C(t, v) \geq 0.$$

The first of the constraint equations is simply the individual's budget identity. The second equation states that an individual is born with no assets, that is, that bequests are absent in this economy and that an individual dies with no assets. (Actually, the wealth constraint should be written $A(v + 1, v) \geq 0$, but the monotonicity of the function U entails that it hold with equality.) Finally, the last of the constraints merely formalizes the fact that a negative rate of consumption of output is meaningless.

---

[7] Leisure as a second consumption good can easily be incorporated into the model. In fact, we originally carried out a good deal of the subsequent analysis under this assumption. However, as it is cumbersome and yields little if any added insight into the central results, we now just mention it as a feasible extension.

By solving the budget equation for $A(t, v)$, which yields

$$A(t, v) = \exp\left[\int_v^t r(x)\, dx\right]$$
$$\times \left\{\int_v^t [w(s) - C(s, v)] \exp\left[-\int_v^s r(x)\, dx\right] ds + A(v, v)\right\},$$

(2)

it is possible to rewrite the allocation problem as

$$\text{Maximize} \quad \int_v^{v+1} U[C(t, v)]e^{-\delta(t-v)}\, dv$$

subject to

$$\int_v^{v+1} [w(s) - C(s, v)] \exp\left[-\int_v^s r(x)\, dx\right] ds = 0$$

and

$$C(t, v) \geq 0.$$

The solution to this maximization problem is well known from the theory of consumer behavior over time.[8] For each moment t at which the non-negativity constraint is not binding, the optimal consumption plan satisfies the following differential equation:

$$\frac{\partial C(t, v)/\partial t}{C(t, v)}\, \eta[C(t, v)] = r(t) - \delta,$$

where $\eta(x) = -xU''(x)/U'(x)$ is the elasticity of marginal utility.

At this point we make the simplifying assumption that η is identically equal to one, which reduces the function U to the logarithm.[9] Such an assumption is essentially equivalent to postulating a Friedman consumption function, with permanent income elasticities all equal to unity. The optimal consumption plan is now given by the differential equation

$$\frac{\partial C(t, v)/\partial t}{C(t, v)} = r(t) - \delta,$$

which has the closed solution

$$C(t, v) = C(v, v) \exp\left\{\int_v^t [r(x) - \delta]\, dx\right\}$$

(3)

---

[8] See, for example, Yaari [13].

[9] Here η equal to any constant could just as well be assumed. Note that this assumption ensures that the nonnegativity constraint is never binding (except in the trivial case where the economy produces no output).

for all t satisfying $v \leq t \leq v + 1$. The initial rate of consumption is determined from the wealth constraint after substitution from Equation 3:

$$C(v, v) = \frac{\int_v^{v+1} w(s) \exp\left[-\int_v^s r(x)\, dx\right] ds}{(1 - e^{-\delta})/\delta}. \tag{4}$$

Finally, the asset holdings corresponding to the optimal consumption plan are derived from Equation 2 after substitution from Equations 3 and 4:

$$
\begin{aligned}
A(t, v) = {}& \int_v^t w(s) \exp\left[-\int_t^s r(x)\, dx\right] ds \\
& - \frac{1 - e^{-\delta(t-v)}}{1 - e^{-\delta}} \int_v^{v+1} w(s) \exp\left[-\int_t^s r(x)\, dx\right] ds
\end{aligned} \tag{5}
$$

for all t satisfying $v \leq t \leq v + 1$.

Let $c(t)$ be the rate of aggregate consumption per capita and $a(t)$ be aggregate asset holdings per capita at time t. From Equations 1, 3, 4, and 5 these two quantities are given explicitly by

$$
\begin{aligned}
c(t) = {}& \frac{n}{1 - e^{-n}} \frac{\delta}{1 - e^{-\delta}} \\
& \times \int_{t-1}^t \left\{ \int_v^{v+1} w(s) \exp\left[-\int_t^s r(x)\, dx\right] ds \right\} e^{-(n+\delta)(t-v)}\, dv
\end{aligned} \tag{6}
$$

and

$$
\begin{aligned}
a(t) = {}& \frac{n}{1 - e^{-n}} \int_{t-1}^t \left\{ \int_v^t w(s) \exp\left[-\int_t^s r(x)\, dx\right] ds - \frac{1 - e^{-\delta(t-v)}}{1 - e^{-\delta}} \right. \\
& \left. \times \int_v^{v+1} w(s) \exp\left[-\int_t^s r(x)\, dx\right] ds \right\} e^{-n(t-v)}\, dv.
\end{aligned} \tag{7}
$$

If we now identify the asset holdings of individuals with the capital stock,[10] we get the basic equilibrium condition for the economy

$$a(t) = k(t). \tag{8}$$

By differentiating Equation 8 and simplifying the result, or, more directly, by equating the rate of net saving per capita to the rate of gross investment per capita, we also have the equilibrium growth equation for the economy

$$
\begin{aligned}
\dot{k}(t) &= f[k(t)] - nk(t) - c(t) \\
&= [r(t) - n]k(t) + [w(t) - c(t)].
\end{aligned} \tag{9}
$$

---

[10] Negative asset holdings (debt) for some consumers could be expressly accounted for by assuming competitive financial intermediaries which hold as assets capital goods and consumer-issued bonds and as liabilities intermediary-issued bonds. Equation 8 then represents a netting of the consumer and financial intermediary sectors. We shall have more to say about intermediaries of this sort in sections 6 and 8.

For some purposes the representation in Equation 9 will be more useful than the representation in Equation 8; note, however, that Equation 8 implies Equation 9, but not conversely.

3. Competitive Growth Equilibrium: Balanced Growth Paths

We initiate the analysis of the equilibrium condition of Equation 8 by restricting attention to balanced growth paths, that is, to growth paths on which the capital-labor ratio remains constant over time. The question to be answered is thus: Are there constant capital-labor ratios which satisfy Equation 8?

To begin with, observe that if k = constant, then $r = f'(k)$ = constant and $w = f(k) - f'(k)k$ = constant. (In fact, because of these constancies, balanced growth in our economy is easily shown to be equivalent to stationary consumer behavior, that is, to the statement that $C(t, v)$ and $A(t, v)$ depend only on the difference $t - v$ for all t satisfying $v \le t \le v + 1$.) Hence, utilizing Equation 9 with appropriate simplification, it follows that a necessary condition for balanced growth equilibrium is

$$0 = [f(k) - nk] - w\left[\frac{n}{1 - e^{-n}}\frac{\delta}{1 - e^{-\delta}}\frac{1 - e^{-r}}{r}\frac{1 - e^{-(n+\delta-r)}}{n + \delta - r}\right]. \quad (10)$$

For convenience, let us rewrite Equation 10 as an equation in the rate of interest r (which is legitimate by virtue of the strict concavity of the function f),

$$\psi(r) = \phi(r), \quad (11)$$

where we define the function ψ as

$$\psi(r) = \frac{f(k) - nk}{f(k) - f'(k)k} \quad \text{with } r = f'(k)$$

and the function ϕ as

$$\phi(r) = \frac{n}{1 - e^{-n}}\frac{\delta}{1 - e^{-\delta}}\frac{1 - e^{-r}}{r}\frac{1 - e^{-(n+\delta-r)}}{n + \delta - r}.$$

Properties of the functions ψ and ϕ, relevant now and later on, are for ψ,

$$\psi(r) \lessgtr 1 \qquad \text{as } r \lessgtr n \quad (12a)$$

and

$$\psi'(r) = \frac{1}{f''(k)}\frac{f'(k) - n}{f(k) - f'(k)k} + \psi(r)\frac{k}{f(k) - f'(k)k}, \quad (12b)$$

while for ϕ,

$$\phi\left(\frac{n+\delta}{2}+x\right) = \phi\left(\frac{n+\delta}{2}-x\right) \qquad \text{for all } x, \qquad (12c)$$

$$\phi(\delta) = \phi(n) = 1, \qquad (12d)$$

$$\phi'(r) = [g(r) - g(n+\delta-r)]\phi(r) \lesseqgtr 0 \qquad \text{as } r \lesseqgtr \frac{n+\delta}{2}. \qquad (12e)$$

and

$$\phi''(r) = \{[g'(r) + g'(n+\delta-r)] + [g(r) - g(n+\delta-r)]^2\}\phi(r) > 0, \qquad (12f)$$

where it is useful to introduce the function g, defined by

$$g(x) = \frac{(1+x)e^{-x} - 1}{x(1 - e^{-x})} \qquad \text{for all } x,$$

and shown in Figure 1.

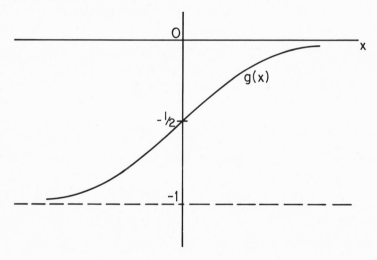

FIGURE 1. Properties of the function $g(x) = \dfrac{(1+x)e^{-x} - 1}{x(1 - e^{-x})}$.

From the properties just listed it becomes clear that Equation 11 yields at least one candidate $r = n$, and in general more than one candidate $r = n$, $r = \bar{r}_1, \cdots, r = \bar{r}_m$ for balanced growth equilibrium. As an illustration, in Figure 2, ψ, ϕ and the two solutions to Equation 11 are depicted under the assumptions $0 < \delta < n$ and $f(k) = Ak^\alpha$, $0 < \alpha/(1-\alpha) < n[g(n) - g(\delta)]$. Now, by examining Equation 8 we can show that $r = n$ represents a balanced growth equilibrium if and only if $\psi'(n) = \phi'(n)$ (that is, if and only if the functions ψ and ϕ are actually tangent to each other at $r = n$) whereas $r = \bar{r}_j \neq n, j = 1, \cdots, m$, always represents a balanced growth equilibrium.

Let k^* be the golden rule capital-labor ratio, that is, let $f'(k^*) = n$. Then the first part of the assertion follows simply by writing out the expression for assets per capita from Equation 7 when $r = n$,

$$a^* = [f(k^*) - f'(k^*)k^*]\left[\frac{1}{n}\left(\frac{n}{1-e^{-n}} - 1\right) - \frac{1}{\delta}\left(\frac{\delta}{1-e^{-\delta}} - 1\right)\right]$$

$$= [f(k^*) - f'(k^*)k^*]\phi'(n),$$

(13)

and noting that therefore $k^* = a^*$ if and only if

$$\frac{k^*}{f(k^*) - f'(k^*)k^*} = \phi'(n),$$

or, from Equations 12a and 12b, $\psi'(n) = \phi'(n)$. On the other hand, let k be any other capital-labor ratio. Then the second part of the assertion follows

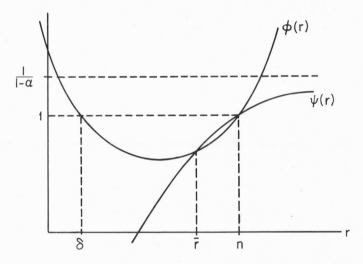

FIGURE 2. Illustration of possible balanced growth equilibria.

by differentiating the expression for assets per capita from Equation 7 when $r \neq n$,

$$0 = (r - n)a + [f(k) - f'(k)k][1 - \phi(r)]$$

or

$$a = \frac{[f(k) - f'(k)k][1 - \phi(r)]}{n - r},$$

(14)

and noting that therefore $k = a$ if and only if

$$\frac{f(k) - nk}{f(k) - f'(k)k} = \phi(r)$$

or

$$\psi(r) = \phi(r).$$

It should be mentioned that if $\phi'(n) < \psi'(n)$, then a balanced growth equilibrium may not exist. For example, consider the production technology described by

$$f(k) = k(A + Bk), \qquad A > 0, \quad B < 0,$$

so that

$$\psi(r) = \frac{A - 2n + r}{A - r} \qquad \text{for } r \leq A.$$

If $n < A < \delta$, then $\phi'(n) < 0 < \psi'(n)$, while $r = n$ is the only solution to Equation 11. (Note that if $\phi'(n) > \psi'(n)$, then there must be at least one solution to Equation 11 in the interval $(0, n)$; that is, for the opposite case the situation depicted in Figure 2 is typical.) In the following discussion, however, we simply assume the existence of a balanced growth equilibrium, which is equivalent to imposing appropriate additional conditions on the production function. For example, the conditions

$$\lim_{k \to 0} r = \infty \tag{15}$$

and

$$\psi''(r) \leq 0 \qquad \text{for } r \geq \hat{r}, \quad 0 \leq \hat{r} < \infty, \tag{16}$$

entail that if $\phi'(n) < \psi'(n)$, then there must be at least one solution to Equation 11 in the interval (n, ∞), and thus these conditions would be sufficient (if not especially transparent).

What conclusions can be drawn from the foregoing? First, that there may be no, one, or several balanced growth equilibria. And second, that any feasible, positive rate of interest[11] may represent a balanced growth equilibrium, depending, in particular, on the specific production technology, rate of population growth, and rate of time preference prevailing in the economy. Citing a result conjectured by Phelps [8], proved by Koopmans, and then elaborated by Phelps [9]—that if $r(t) \leq n - \varepsilon$ for some $\varepsilon > 0$ and all $t \geq \hat{t}$, then the growth path represented by $r(t)$ is inefficient[12]—we can therefore deduce a further important result: the balanced growth equilibrium in our stylized competitive economy need not be an efficient growth path.

---

[11] As we have not forestalled the possibility of capital saturation, for a sufficiently "perverse" rate of time preference Equation 11 might have a nonpositive solution. This exceptional case is at present excluded by assumption ($\delta \geq 0$) but will receive further attention in section 6.

[12] In this context, inefficiency means simply that, given the same initial capital-labor ratio, there is another feasible growth path that provides at least as much total consumption all of the time, and in fact provides more total consumption some of the time.

Additional results on inefficiency in the neoclassical growth model, which will be utilized later on in the essay, are contained in the appendix.

4. Competitive Growth Equilibrium: An Example

In this section we shall present a complete characterization of the competitive growth equilibria for a specific production function. The example is both interesting in its own right and suggestive of the general case, which we discuss briefly in the following section.

Suppose that the production technology in our economy is described by

$$f(k) = k(A + B \log k), \qquad B < 0, \tag{17}$$

which is the general representation of the class of production functions for which

$$w = -Bk, \tag{18a}$$

that is, the wage rate is proportional to the capital-labor ratio. Notice also that the production function of Equation 17 exhibits capital saturation at $\tilde{k} = e^{-(1 + A/B)}$. Some further properties we shall use are

$$r = A + B + B \log k \tag{18b}$$

and

$$\psi(r) = 1 + \frac{n}{B} - \frac{r}{B}. \tag{18c}$$

The significance of the production function of Equation 17 is that it permits a substantial simplification of the equilibrium condition of Equation 8. More specifically, if we substitute from Equation 18a into the right-hand side of Equation 8, invert the order of integration in the right-hand side of Equation 8, and then multiply both sides of the equation by the factor

$$\exp\left[-\int_0^t r(x)\,dx\right],$$

we get the following standard linear integral equation for Equation 8:

$$x(t) = \int_{-\infty}^{\infty} G(t - s)x(s)\,ds, \tag{19}$$

where

$$x(t) = k(t) \exp\left[-\int_0^t r(x)\,dx\right] \tag{20}$$

and

$$G(t - s) = B\frac{n}{1 - e^{-n}} \int_{t-1}^{s} \left(1 - \frac{1 - e^{-\delta(t-v)}}{1 - e^{-\delta}}\right) e^{-n(t-v)}\,dv,$$

$$t - 1 \leq s \leq t, \tag{21}$$

$$= -B\frac{n}{1 - e^{-n}} \int_{s-1}^{t} \left(\frac{1 - e^{-\delta(t-v)}}{1 - e^{-\delta}}\right) e^{-n(t-v)}\,dv,$$

$$t \leq s \leq t + 1,$$

$$= 0 \quad \text{otherwise}.$$

In order to characterize the competitive growth equilibria for an economy having such a production function, we need only characterize the real, positive solutions of Equation 19. But the solutions to this integral equation are well known; they are essentially exponentials in which the exponents are the roots of the equation

$$\int_{-1}^{1} G(s)e^{us} \, ds = 1. \tag{22}$$

More precisely, all solutions of Equation 19 are of the general form,

$$x(t) = \sum_{i=1}^{n} \sum_{j=1}^{m_i} a_{ij} t^{j-1} e^{-u_i t}, \tag{23}$$

where $u_1, u_2, \cdots, u_n$ are the n distinct roots of Equation 22 and m_i is the multiplicity of the root u_i. The a_{ij} are arbitrary constants. Thus, we need only characterize the roots of Equation 22.[13]

Rather than attempt this task directly, it is much easier to utilize the fact that, for the production function of Equation 17, the equilibrium growth equation may be rewritten in terms of the present value of capital per head as

$$\frac{\dot{x}(t)}{B} + \left(1 + \frac{n}{B}\right)x(t) = \int_{-\infty}^{\infty} H(t - s)x(s) \, ds, \tag{24}$$

where

$$H(t - s) = \frac{n}{1 - e^{-n}} \frac{\delta}{1 - e^{-\delta}} \int_{t-1}^{s} e^{-(n+\delta)(t-v)} \, dv, \qquad t - 1 \le s \le t,$$

$$= \frac{n}{1 - e^{-n}} \frac{\delta}{1 - e^{-\delta}} \int_{s-1}^{t} e^{-(n+\delta)(t-v)} \, dv, \qquad t \le s \le t + 1, \tag{25}$$

$$= 0 \qquad \text{otherwise.}$$

What this means is that any root of Equation 22 must also be a root of the equation obtained by substituting

$$x(t) = e^{-ut}$$

into Equation 24, that is, of the equation

$$1 + \frac{n}{B} - \frac{u}{B} = \int_{-1}^{1} H(s)e^{us} \, ds. \tag{26}$$

Consider first the real roots that Equations 22 and 26 have in common.

---

[13] See, for example, Titchmarsh [12], pp. 305–307.

If u is real, for instance $u = r$, then it is easily verified that Equations 22 and 26 are in fact the balanced growth counterparts of Equations 8 and 9, respectively. In particular, Equation 26 reduces to Equation 11 with ψ given by Equation 18c. But then from the analysis of the preceding section we know immediately that $\bar{r}$, the rate of interest corresponding to balanced growth equilibrium, is the unique real root that Equations 22 and 26 have in common, as is illustrated in Figure 3 under the assumptions $0 < \delta < n$ and $\psi'(n) = -1/B > g(n) - g(\delta) = \phi'(n)$.

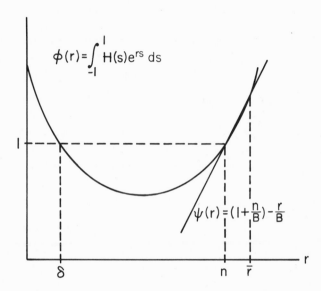

FIGURE 3. Balanced growth equilibrium for the example $f(k) = k(A + B \log k)$.

Consider now the complex roots that Equations 22 and 26 have in common. If u is complex, for instance $u = \alpha + i\beta$, then by equating real and imaginary parts Equation 26 may be rewritten as the pair of equations

$$1 + \frac{n}{B} - \frac{\alpha}{B} = \int_{-1}^{1} H(s)e^{\alpha s} \cos \beta s \, ds \qquad (28)$$

and

$$-\frac{\beta}{B} = \int_{-1}^{1} H(s)e^{\alpha s} \sin \beta s \, ds. \qquad (29)$$

It follows directly from Equation 28 that if $\beta \neq 0$, then $\alpha \neq \bar{r}$ (as H is a positive function while the cosine is an even function less than or equal to one). Thus, without any further analysis we may conclude that if a solution to Equation 23 is to be real and positive, then it can only be of the form

$$x(t) = Ce^{-\bar{r}t}, \qquad C > 0. \tag{30}$$

Converting from present to current values of capital per head, the foregoing can be summarized in the following proposition:

For an economy with the production function of Equation 17, every competitive growth equilibrium is represented by the asymptotically balanced growth path

$$k(t) = [r(t) - \bar{r}]k(t), \quad k(0) > 0, \qquad \lim_{t \to \infty} k(t) = \bar{k}, \tag{31}$$

along which total consumption is a constant proportion of labor's competitive income

$$c(t) = \left(1 + \frac{n - \bar{r}}{B}\right)w(t). \tag{32}$$

Equation 32 is easily checked by substituting from Equations 17, 18a, and 18b into Equation 31 in order to obtain Equation 9.

We mention for emphasis that the equilibria for this example are not necessarily efficient, because (again appealing to the Phelps-Koopmans result)

$$\lim_{t \to \infty} r(t) = \bar{r} < n \qquad \text{whenever} \quad -\frac{1}{B} < g(n) - g(\delta),$$

the rate of interest will eventually lie below its natural value for certain parameter configurations. This leads naturally to certain sorts of questions: Under what conditions is the competitive growth equilibrium efficient? Given that it is efficient, is it therefore Pareto optimal? For this example, the following proposition and attached footnote contain a complete answer:[14]

If $-1/B > g(n) - g(\delta)$, or $\bar{r} > n$, then the competitive growth equilibrium represented by the growth path of Equation 31 maximizes

$$\int_{-1}^{\infty} \left[\int_{\max(o,v)}^{v+1} \log C(t, v)e^{-\delta(t-v)} \, dt \, e^{-\bar{r}v}\right] e^{nv} \, dv$$

$$= \int_{0}^{\infty} \left[\int_{t-1}^{t} \log C(t, v)e^{(\rho-\delta)(t-v)} \, dv\right] e^{-\rho t} \, dt, \qquad \text{with } \rho = \bar{r} - n, \tag{33}$$

---

[14] It may puzzle the reader to find that Pareto optimality is defined only for welfare enjoyed after time zero, because up to now we have been implicitly assuming that the competitive growth equilibrium exists forever. The answer to this seeming contradiction is that we are also implicitly assuming that the behavior of the economy before time zero is past history, that is, that observation of the economy only begins at time zero. Perhaps a better (though certainly more difficult) assumption to accord with the latter would be that, given an arbitrary distribution of the capital stock among generations existing at time zero, just then does perfect foresight become a pervasive phenomenon.

the social welfare function which gives the total welfare of an individual of generation v (measured from time zero) the weight $e^{-\bar{r}v}$.[15] This proposition is based on the facts, whose proof we do not spell out here, first, that the individual consumption rate

$$C(t, v) = \frac{1 - e^{-h}}{n} \frac{n + \delta - \bar{r}}{1 - e^{-(n+\delta-\bar{r})}} c(t)e^{(\bar{r}-\delta)(t-v)} \tag{34}$$

is the solution to the variational problem

$$\text{Maximize} \int_{t-1}^{t} \log C(t, v)e^{(\rho-\delta)(t-v)} \, dv \tag{35}$$

subject to

$$\frac{n}{1 - e^{-n}} \int_{t-1}^{t} C(t, v)e^{-n(t-v)} \, dv = c(t)$$

and

$$C(t, v) \geq 0$$

of selecting the "best" intergenerational distribution of consumption at each point along an arbitrary feasible growth path, and second, that the growth path of Equation 31 is the solution to the variational problem

$$\text{Maximize} \int_{0}^{\infty} \log c(t)e^{-\rho t} \, dt \tag{36}$$

subject to

$$\dot{k}(t) = [A - n + B \log k(t)]k(t) - c(t), \quad \text{given } k(0) > 0$$

and

$$c(t) \geq 0$$

of selecting the "best" feasible growth path.[16] From inspection of the social welfare function of Equation 33 it is easily seen that, by solving the first problem, substituting the value of its solution into the social welfare function, and then solving the second problem, the asserted conclusion is obtained.

One further point is worth remarking in connection with the relationship between the efficiency and Pareto optimality of the growth path of Equation 31. Namely, by virtue of the property of Equation 18a, the weight given to

---

[15] Furthermore, if $-(1/B) = g(n) - g(\delta)$, or $\bar{r} = n$, then the growth path of Equation 31 maximizes the social welfare function that gives the amount by which each individual's total welfare deviates from his hypothetical golden rule welfare (measured from time zero) the weight $e^{-\bar{r}v}$.

[16] The distribution problem is, given constant wage and interest rates, precisely that analyzed in section 2, while the growth problem is, given specific production and utility functions, precisely that analyzed in Cass [1] and Koopmans [5]. We should also note that Koopmans' analysis provides a justification for the claim made in the preceding footnote.

the welfare of an individual of generation v in the social welfare function of Equation 33 is proportional to the present value of his labor endowment in the competitive growth equilibrium itself

$$e^{-\bar{r}v} = \left[w(0) \frac{1 - e^{-\bar{r}}}{\bar{r}} \right]^{-1} \int_v^{v+1} w(s) \exp \left[-\int_0^s r(x)\, dx \right] ds. \qquad (37)$$

This feature, which will be the basis for generalization in the following section, is peculiar to the specific utility function assumed, as is well known from the standard static general equilibrium theory.

5. Competitive Growth Equilibrium: The General Case

Unlike the example just discussed, for a general neoclassical production function it is not possible to derive an explicit expression representing the competitive growth equilibria. However, taking our cue from that example, it is possible to construct a conventional fixed-point argument for the existence of a competitive growth equilibrium that starts close to and goes asymptotically to a balanced growth path. We omit this argument, partly because it is somewhat tedious but mostly because it is somewhat beside the point.

By the last we mean simply that much more pertinent to our understanding of the nature of competitive growth equilibrium would be, for example, the demonstration of the asymptotic balance of *all* competitive growth equilibria. And while, primarily on the basis of the example of the preceding section, we conjecture this property, we have as yet been unable to demonstrate it.

What we shall do in this section is to present a general theorem on the relationship between the efficiency and Pareto optimality of the equilibrium for our model. This theorem is closely related, though not perfectly analogous to the proposition outlined in the last part of the preceding section. It is intended to answer, at least in part, the same questions posed there.

For this purpose we require two things, first, a more sophisticated criterion for recognizing inefficiency than the Phelps-Koopmans result, and second, a weaker definition of Pareto optimality than the usual notion (which was employed earlier).

With regard to the first requirement, in the appendix the following necessary and sufficient condition for inefficiency in the neoclassical growth model is provided: a feasible growth path $k^0(t)$ for $t \geq 0$ is inefficient if and only if there exists another feasible growth path $k^1(t)$ for $t \geq 0$ such that [17]

---

[17] The notion of feasible growth from a given initial capital-labor ratio is precisely defined in the appendix to this essay.

$$0 < \liminf_{T \to \infty} \int_0^T [c^1(t) - c^0(t)] \exp\left\{-\int_0^t [r^0(x) - n]dx\right\} dt. \quad (38)$$

This condition simply says that a growth path is inefficient when there are feasible deviations in aggregate consumption whose present value, calculated at the rates of interest generated by the growth path, is unambiguously positive.

With regard to the second requirement, an increase in an individual's welfare from society's viewpoint is defined thus: the individual consumption $\tilde{C}(t, v)$ for max $(0, v) \le t \le v + 1$ provides more welfare than the individual consumption $\bar{C}(t, v)$ for max $(0, v) \le t \le v + 1$ if and only if

$$0 \le \int_{\max(0,v)}^s [\log \tilde{C}(t, v) - \log \bar{C}(t, v)]e^{-\delta(t-v)} dt$$

$$\text{for max } (0, v) \le s \le v + 1, \quad (39)$$

with strict inequality for $s = v + 1$. That is, an increase in an individual's welfare must occur throughout his lifetime to be recognized as such from society's viewpoint.[18]

We proceed to show that *if a competitive growth equilibrium is not Pareto optimal in the latter sense, then it is inefficient.*

We shall let variables with a bar represent quantities along the particular competitive growth equilibrium under consideration and variables with a tilde represent quantities along a *dominating* growth path, that is, another feasible growth path that, after time zero, provides at least as much and sometimes more individual welfare than the competitive growth equilibrium. Without loss of generality we can assume that along the dominating growth path all individuals of generation v are treated identically. Also let

$$\bar{P}(0, v) = \int_v^{v+1} \bar{w}(s) \exp\left[-\int_0^s \bar{r}(x) \, dx\right] ds$$

$$= \bar{P}(t, v) \exp\left[-\int_0^t \bar{r}(x) \, dx\right] > 0 \quad (40)$$

represent the present value of the labor endowment of an individual of generation v along the competitive growth equilibrium. From Equations 39

---

[18] The appeal of our weaker definition of Pareto optimality in the present dynamic context arises from the following observation. Namely, if uncertainty about a particular individual's (or perhaps generation's) presence in the future is introduced explicitly (or even implicitly) into the model, then it more accurately reflects the fundamental idea that reallocation is obviously called for only when in fact somebody's welfare will be increased but nobody's welfare will be decreased. However, it is arguable and is adopted basically because it permits a definite conclusion.

and 40 it follows directly that

$$0 < \lim_{T \to \infty} \int_{-1}^{T} \left\{ \int_{\max(0,v)}^{\min(T,v+1)} [\log \tilde{C}(t, v) - \log \overline{C}(t, v)]e^{-\delta(t-v)} \, dt \overline{P}(0, v) \right\} e^{nv} \, dv$$

$$= \lim_{T \to \infty} \int_{0}^{T} \left\{ \int_{t-1}^{t} [\log \tilde{C}(t, v) - \log \overline{C}(t, v)]\overline{P}(t, v)e^{-(n+\delta)(t-v)} \, dv \right\} \quad (41)$$

$$\times \exp\left\{ -\int_{0}^{t} [\bar{r}(x) - n] \, dx \right\} dt,$$

some positive number is assigned to the dominating growth path by the social welfare function that gives the amount by which each individual's welfare deviates from his competitive equilibrium welfare (measured from time zero) the weight $\overline{P}(0, v)$.

Now consider the intergenerational distribution of consumption along the dominating growth path. From Equation 41 it should be clear that if, say, $\hat{C}(t, v)$ represents the solution to the variational problem

$$\text{Maximize} \quad \int_{t-1}^{t} \log C(t, v)\overline{P}(t, v)e^{-(n+\delta)(t-v)} \, dv \quad (42)$$

subject to

$$\frac{n}{1 - e^{-n}} \int_{t-1}^{t} C(t, v)e^{-n(t-v)} \, dv = \tilde{c}(t)$$

and

$$C(t, v) \geq 0$$

of picking the "best" intergenerational distribution of consumption at each point along the dominating growth path, then

$$0 < \lim_{T \to \infty} \int_{0}^{T} \left\{ \int_{t-1}^{t} [\log \hat{C}(t, v) - \log \overline{C}(t, v)]\overline{P}(t, v)e^{-(n+\delta)(t-v)} \, dv \right\}$$

$$\times \exp\left\{ -\int_{0}^{t} [\bar{r}(x) - n] \, dx \right\} dt. \quad (43)$$

But each problem of this type is essentially the consumer lifetime allocation problem discussed in section 2 (now with a variable subjective discount rate). Again employing the result quoted there, we can easily derive its closed solution

$$\hat{C}(t, v) = \frac{\overline{C}(t, v)}{\tilde{c}(t)} \tilde{c}(t). \quad (44)$$

Finally, substituting from Equation 44 into Equation 43 and manipulating the resulting expression we find that

$$0 < \lim_{T \to \infty} \int_0^T \left\{ \int_{t-1}^t \left[\log \frac{\overline{C}(t, v)}{\tilde{c}(t)} \tilde{c}(t) - \log \frac{\overline{C}(t, v)}{\bar{c}(t)} \bar{c}(t) \right] \overline{P}(t, v) e^{-(n + \delta)(t - v)} \, dv \right\}$$

$$\times \exp \left\{ -\int_0^t [\bar{r}(x) - n] \, dx \right\} dt$$

$$= \lim_{T \to \infty} \int_0^T \left\{ \int_{t-1}^t \overline{P}(t, v) e^{-(n + \delta)(t - v)} \, dv \right\} \{ \log \tilde{c}(t) - \log \bar{c}(t) \}$$

$$\times \exp \left\{ -\int_0^t [\bar{r}(x) - n] \, dx \right\} dt \tag{45}$$

$$= \frac{1 - e^{-n}}{n} \frac{1 - e^{-\delta}}{\delta} \lim_{T \to \infty} \int_0^T \bar{c}(t)[\log \tilde{c}(t) - \log \bar{c}(t)]$$

$$\times \exp \left\{ -\int_0^t [\bar{r}(x) - n] \, dx \right\} dt$$

$$\le \frac{1 - e^{-n}}{n} \frac{1 - e^{-\delta}}{\delta} \lim_{T \to \infty} \int_0^T [\tilde{c}(t) - \bar{c}(t)] \exp \left\{ -\int_0^t [\bar{r}(x) - n] \, dx \right\}.$$

By virtue of the condition of Equation 38, this completes the proof of our assertion.

6. An Interpretation

In this section, for convenience of exposition, we concentrate on balanced growth. Hereafter (for the most part) we also adopt the simplifying assumption that the production technology satisfies the conditions of Equations 15 and 16 with $\hat{r} = 0$, which guarantees a unique balanced growth equilibrium. The central question we are addressing is: Why may competitive capital accumulation go astray?

The answer to this question is, in fact, straightforward. At efficient rates of interest consumers may want to hold more real assets than are available in the existing capital stock. (Or, to put the matter another way, at the rate of interest that equilibrates desired real assets and the actual capital stock, the private rate of return may differ from the social rate of return—which is surely minus infinity on an inefficient balanced growth path.) More precisely, given the conditions of Equations 15 and 16 with $\hat{r} = 0$, from Equations 13 and 14 we know that

$$a \gtreqless k \qquad \text{as } r \gtreqless \bar{r}$$

and

$$\bar{r} \gtreqless n \qquad \text{as } \psi'(n) \gtreqless \phi'(n),$$

which, taken together, entail the relationship

$$a > k \qquad \text{for } r \ge n \quad \text{whenever } \psi'(n) < \phi'(n). \tag{46}$$

An extreme example points up this difficulty especially well. Suppose, in a more classical tradition, that population is stationary ($n = 0$) and that capital saturation is possible ($f'(\tilde{k}) = 0$ for some $0 < \tilde{k} < \infty$). Also suppose that consumers exhibit "perverse" time preference ($\delta < 0$). Finally, suppose that production technology entails that $\psi'(0) < \phi'(0)$. Then, there is a unique stationary solution to Equation 8 at some $\bar{r} < 0$ (depicted in Figure 1 by shifting the vertical axis to the point n on the horizontal axis) that obviously represents a grossly inefficient situation; merely by utilizing less than the whole capital stock, total output could be increased. However, for this example, because consumers can carry inventories without cost or hold capital as assets, the rate of interest would never fall below zero, and Equation 8 is an incomplete statement of the equilibrium condition, which instead should be

$$a(t) = k(t) + z(t), \tag{8'}$$

with

$$k(t) \le \tilde{k}$$

and

$$z(t) \ge 0, \quad \text{equality for } k(t) < \tilde{k},$$

where $z(t)$ stands for inventories of consumption goods per head at time t. Therefore, it is easily seen that the true stationary state for this stylized, classical competitive economy must occur at the rate of interest $r = n = 0$, which, on the production side, is clearly efficient. On the other hand, on the consumption side, this stationary state is just as clearly inefficient: from the relationship of Equation 46 it follows that $z > 0$ when $r = 0$, or that, in the stationary state, consumers desire to carry an inventory of consumption goods over and above their holdings of capital, an inventory that will in actuality never be consumed. We recall for emphasis that from each consumer's viewpoint, carrying such a dead weight is quite sensible; he is doing the best he can *given* the wage rate $w = f(\tilde{k})$ and interest rate $r = 0$ prevailing.

Given our interpretation, the question naturally arises: Have we overlooked something, some aspect of consumer behavior or perhaps some institution, that will in fact *ensure* the "right" relationship between real asset preferences and opportunities? Let us consider these possibilities in turn.

One point, purposely left in the background until now, is that a sufficiently high rate of time preference would guarantee (at least) efficient balanced growth equilibrium under all conceivable neoclassical production technologies. That is, if $\delta \ge n$, then

$$\phi'(n) = g(n) - g(\delta) \le 0, \tag{47}$$

which rules out the possibility of a solution to Equation 11 for $r < n$. Intuitively this is a rather plausible result. If a consumer strongly prefers consumption today to consumption tomorrow, then, even at relatively high rates of interest, his total savings will be small algebraically at every instant during his lifetime (cf. Equation 5). However, the requisite balancing of parameters cannot be depended on in theory and, indeed, loses a degree of support if we admit some variation among consumers' rates of time preference.[19]

Suppose now that each generation has a proportion of individuals $\lambda_j > 0$ with rate of time preference $\delta_j \geq 0$, $j = 1, \cdots, m$ and $\sum_{j=1}^{m} \lambda_j = 1$. Then we have

$$\phi(r) = \sum_{j=1}^{m} \lambda_j \phi_{\delta_j}(r),$$

where

$$\phi_{\delta_j}(r) = \frac{n}{1 - e^{-n}} \frac{\delta_j}{1 - e^{-\delta_j}} \frac{1 - e^{-r}}{r} \frac{1 - e^{-(n + \delta_j - r)}}{n + \delta_j - r},$$

and the stylized competitive economy will exhibit efficient balanced growth equilibrium for every neoclassical production technology if and only if

$$\phi'(n) = \sum_{j=1}^{m} \lambda_j \phi'_{\delta_j}(n) = g(n) - \sum_{j=1}^{m} \lambda_j g(\delta_j) \leq 0. \tag{48}$$

If we now associate the rate of time preference δ introduced in section 2, with the average rate of time preference here $\sum_{j=1}^{m} \lambda_j \delta_j$, then by the strict concavity of $g(x)$ for $x > 0$, it follows that

$$-g(\delta) < -\sum_{j=1}^{m} \lambda_j g(\delta_j),$$

which means that the inequality in Equation 48 might not be satisfied even if that in Equation 47 were satisfied. While not placing too much weight on this example, it illustrates that diversity in consumer behavior cannot be expected, a priori, to reduce the likelihood that consumers may want to hold more real assets than are available in the capital stock at efficient rates of interest.

Another aspect of consumer behavior whose effects we have investigated is biological or sociological restrictions on the length of and efficiency during the work life.[20] As a gross approximation to these restrictions, suppose that the individuals of each generation enter the labor force at age m_1 (because they are maturing and undergoing education from age 0 to age m_1) and leave

---

[19] Some support is regained in the concluding section, where we analyze an economy in which uncertainty about the end of the world contributes to positive time preference.

[20] Both Diamond [3] and Samuelson [10] adopt one such restriction, forced retirement, as an integral part of their models. Unlike them, we prefer to treat these restrictions as less fundamental, partly because their particular formulation seems somewhat more arbitrary than that of the other elements in the basic model but mostly because we feel that their introduction at the outset tends to obscure the basic issue presently being discussed.

it at age m_2 (because they are no longer able to work) where $0 \le m_1 \le m_2 \le 1$. In the spirit of the two preceding paragraphs, it is easily shown that under these additional assumptions the function ϕ remains strictly convex, while $\phi'(n) \le 0$ if and only if

$$-g(\delta) \le -(m_2 - m_1)g[n(m_2 - m_1)] + m_1. \qquad (49)$$

The right-hand side of this inequality is depicted in Figure 4 under the further assumption that the growing-up and retirement periods are of equal length, $m_1 = \varepsilon$ and $m_2 = 1 - \varepsilon$ for $0 \le \varepsilon < 1/2$. Again, though one can certainly derive conditions from such restrictions that would ensure the efficiency of competitive behavior (for instance, $\varepsilon \ge \varepsilon^*(n, \delta)$ in Figure 4), a presumption that they would be satisfied is not justified.

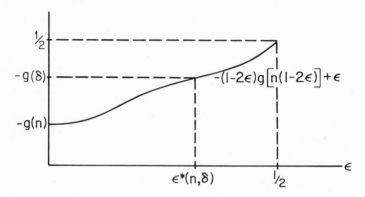

FIGURE 4. Illustration of the sufficient condition for efficient balanced growth equilibrium when the growing-up and retirement periods are equal.

It is clear to us, after analyzing these and other aspects of consumer behavior, that further complications along similar lines do not basically alter the general conclusion stated at the beginning of this section. What, then, about an overlooked institution, one that might be expected to exist in an *inefficient economy*[21] and whose existence might be expected to forestall the possibility of inefficiency?

That any such institution would have as its essential function the provision of assets to be held by consumers in lieu of capital goods should be apparent after a moment's reflection on the relationship of Equation 46. The logical candidate is thus an intermediary sector, holding as assets capital goods

---

[21] Hereafter this term signifies an economy in which (1) the production technology satisfies the conditions of Equations 15 and 16 with $\hat{r} = 0$ (balanced growth equilibrium is unique) and (2) the production technology, rate of population growth, and rate of time preference together entail $\psi'(n) < \phi'(n)$ (the balanced growth equilibrium is inefficient).

while issuing as liabilities various types of financial instruments. We deduce immediately,[22] however, that in an inefficient economy private ownership of the intermediary sector and an efficient balanced growth equilibrium are mutually exclusive. This conclusion follows from the fact that the only efficient balanced growth path consistent with a competitive consumer sector is the golden rule path (that is, the rate of interest $r = n$ is the only efficient solution to Equation 11 for an inefficient economy). Hence, assuming for simplicity that consumers hold only financial assets, if an intermediary sector were to provide the real assets consumers desire on this balanced growth path $L(t)a^*$, then it would have negative and, indeed, continually decreasing net worth $L(t)(k^* - a^*) < 0$.

But, public ownership of the intermediary sector—for instance in the form of a social saving system or, like in Diamond's model [3], a fiscal authority, or, as suggested by Samuelson [10], a monetary authority—is certainly possible. And, in contrast to the conclusion of the preceding paragraph, given proper policies a public intermediary sector could ensure an efficient balanced growth equilibrium precisely because it need not back its liabilities with specific assets—but rather with the general fiscal and monetary authority vested in government—and can therefore supply assets to the consumer sector somewhat independently of the existing capital stock.

In part to exemplify the last statement, we take up Samuelson's suggestion and present a rigorous treatment of the effects stemming from the existence of a monetary system.

7. A Monetary Authority

Suppose that we introduce into our economy a monetary authority that has nominal liabilities equal to the nominal money supply $M(t) > 0$ and that pays a nominal rate of interest $-\infty < \rho(t) < \infty$.[23] Then the basic model of section 2 must be modified accordingly. First, there is an additional growth equation for the money supply per capita $m(t)$,

$$\frac{\dot{m}(t)}{m(t)} = \rho(t) - n. \tag{50}$$

---

[22] And also somewhat reluctantly. Notice, especially, that this conclusion is independent of the type or behavior of private intermediaries postulated. In an earlier stage of this research we thought that a sector of private intermediaries with existence in their own right (that is, owning capital goods purchased from internal funds) would set matters right. Though this conjecture proved wrong, such a private intermediary sector does generate effects of some interest, and therefore will be detailed in section 8.

[23] This is the simplest monetary policy to analyze in the framework of our model. However, essentially the same results would carry over for any monetary policy that is perfectly foreseen by all individuals, as it is the mere *existence* of a monetary system that is critical here.

Second, the money price level $p(t)$, that is, the price of output in terms of money, must be accounted for. Third, individual holdings of real assets may now be composed of both real money balances $M(t, v)/p(t)$, and capital goods $K(t, v)$,

$$A(t, v) = \frac{M(t, v)}{p(t)} + K(t, v). \tag{51}$$

Fourth, the equilibrium condition of Equation 8 becomes one requiring equality of real assets per capita to the sum of the real money supply per capita and the capital stock per head

$$a(t) = \frac{m(t)}{p(t)} + k(t). \tag{8''}$$

And finally, observing that individuals will hold capital goods if and only if the rate of interest is at least as large as the real rate of return on money, while they will hold real money balances—say, money will *matter*—if and only if the real rate of return on money is at least as large as the rate of interest, we deduce a second equilibrium condition requiring equality of these two rates:

$$r(t) = \rho(t) - \frac{\dot{p}(t)}{p(t)}. \tag{52}$$

Clearly Equation 9 is still a necessary condition for equilibrium. It should also be obvious that the interpretation accompanying the model just outlined only makes sense [24] when

$$0 < \frac{m(t)}{p(t)} = a(t) - k(t) < \infty. \tag{53}$$

This enables a simple characterization of balanced growth equilibrium in which $0 < m/p < \infty$ or money matters. Recall from the analysis in section 3 that $r = n$ is the only solution to Equation 11 for which possibly $a - k \neq 0$, while $a^* - k^* > 0$ if and only if $\psi'(n) < \phi'(n)$. We can conclude immediately that (1) for the inefficient economy with money there is a *unique* balanced growth equilibrium at the golden rule while (2) for the efficient economy with money (that is, an economy with money in which $\psi'(n) \geq \phi'(n)$) there is *no* balanced growth equilibrium.

The latter results are somewhat misleading, as, in addition to the possibility that there is no equilibrium in which money matters, there is also the possibility that there are equilibria in which money matters in the short run but not in the long run. This observation is borne out by further analysis based on the example of section 4: For the production function of Equation 17 with

_____

[24] But see section 8 for an alternative interpretation that only makes sense when, in effect, $-\infty < m(t)/p(t) < 0$.

$-1/B \neq g(n) - g(\delta)$, the equilibrium condition of Equation 8″ can be reduced to

$$x(t) = \int_{-\infty}^{\infty} I(t - s)x(s) \, ds, \tag{54}$$

where now

$$x(t) = k(t) \exp\left\{ -\int_{0}^{t} [r(x) - n] \, dx \right\} + \frac{m(0)/p(0)}{1 - \int_{-1}^{1} I(s) \, ds} \tag{55}$$

and

$$I(t - s) = G(t - s)e^{n(t-s)}. \tag{56}$$

Detailed analysis of Equation 54, omitted here because it is basically similar to the earlier analysis of Equation 19, reveals that the nature of its real, positive solutions depends on whether the economy is efficient or inefficient. On the one hand, if $-1/B > g(n) - g(\delta)$ (the efficient economy), then in fact there are no solutions with $m(0)/p(0) > 0$. On the other hand, if $-1/B < g(n) - g(\delta)$ (the inefficient economy), then all solutions with $m(0)/p(0) > 0$, after converting from present values of capital to current values of capital per head and introducing explicitly the real value of the money supply per capita, are of the form

$$\dot{k}(t) = [r(t) - \bar{r}]k(t) + \left\{ (n - \bar{r}) \middle/ \left[1 - \int_{-1}^{1} I(s) \, ds \right] \right\} \frac{m(t)}{p(t)}, \qquad k(0) > 0, \tag{57}$$

and

$$\left[\frac{m^{\cdot}(t)}{p(t)} \right] = [r(t) - n]\left[\frac{m(t)}{p(t)} \right], \qquad \frac{m(0)}{p(0)} > 0. \tag{58}$$

The permissible solutions to this pair of differential equations are depicted in the phase diagram in Figure 5, which shows up clearly that equilibria abound in which money does not matter in the long run (for example, the paths marked I and II are such equilibria).

Even though money may not matter, perhaps the most interesting property of the economy with money is that *if money does matter in the long run, then the equilibrium is efficient*. More formally, if

$$\limsup_{t \to \infty} \frac{m(t)}{p(t)} > 0, \tag{59}$$

then the equilibrium is efficient and, therefore, by virtue of the theorem proved in section 5 (which, it is easy to see, also pertains here), Pareto optimal. We emphasize, in particular, that this property is essentially independent of the monetary policy pursued—in the present discussion it is the nominal rate of interest promised, but in general it could be any scheme

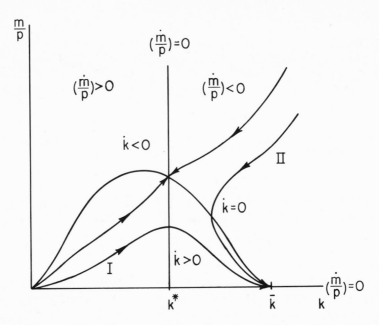

FIGURE 5. Equilibrium with money for the example $f(k) = k(A + B \log k)$.

that systematically puts the monetary authority in debt to the public—provided that it is perfectly foreseen by all individuals.

To verify this property, we demonstrate in the appendix the following sufficient condition for efficiency in the neoclassical growth model: the feasible growth path $k(t)$ for $t \geq 0$ is efficient if there exists a finite number M such that

$$\liminf_{t \to \infty} \exp\left\{-\int_0^t [r(x) - n]\, dx\right\} < M. \tag{60}$$

As from Equations 50 and 52

$$\frac{m(t)}{p(t)} = \frac{m(0)}{p(0)} \exp\left\{\int_0^t [r(x) - n]\, dx\right\}, \tag{61}$$

this condition is simply the asserted property.

To summarize the effects stemming from the existence of a monetary system: On the one hand, there may be no equilibrium in which individuals will desire to hold money balances. On the other hand, even when there is such an equilibrium, money may or may not matter in the long run. However, if money does matter in the long run, then the economy is assuredly efficient and Pareto optimal.

8. A Mixed Neoclassical-Marxian Model

One of the characteristics of neoclassical economics (in the broad sense of the term) is the notion that consumers are the sole source of independent decision making in the decentralized economy. Firms and financial institutions act as agents of their shareholders, who are consumers. At another extreme we find the Marxian view, which holds that in a private economy all the relevant decision making is concentrated in the hands of capitalists whose sole objective is accumulation, and consumption enters the picture only to the extent that the labor force must be kept at a subsistence level.

In the foregoing discussion we have seen that a purely consumer-oriented economy may be inefficient. Consumer decisions were not sufficient to guarantee an efficiently operating system. Indeed, sometimes in order to achieve efficiency we had to introduce into the model an institution that could not be thought of as a privately owned (that is, consumer-owned) firm whose actions represent the interest of its owners. In this section, we shall take a brief look at the role that a similar institution might play in the efficient economy. Our model will turn out to be a blend of the neoclassical (consumer-oriented) and the Marxian (accumulation-oriented) points of view.

Let us assume that individuals cannot hold capital goods as an instrument of saving but must, rather, save by holding corporate bonds. These bonds are issued by a multitude of competitive firms which, in turn, hold capital goods as assets. We now depart from the neoclassical tradition by assuming that the ownership of these firms is not located in the consumer sector. In other words, firms behave according to certain independent objectives that are not reducible to consumer decisions. In particular, we shall assume that firms act so as to *maximize* the rate of increase in net worth at every moment of time. This is indeed a Marxian postulate. Firms must of course repay their debt to consumers (at competitive interest rates), but with this repayment their commitment to the consumer sector ends.

Let $B(t)$ be the total number of corporate bonds[25] outstanding at time t, and let $S(t)$ be the aggregate net worth of firms at time t. Then, the consolidated balance sheet equation for all firms is

$$K(t) = B(t) + S(t),$$

which is equivalent to

$$k(t) = b(t) + s(t), \tag{62}$$

where $b(t) = B(t)/L(t)$ and $s(t) = S(t)/L(t)$. At time t firms hire labor and issue bonds so as to maximize the rate of increase of net worth. To find this

---

[25] By a "bond" we mean a debt instrument that is traded by whoever issues it for one unit of output and that is recontracted at every instant at the current rate of interest.

rate of increase, we must write down the profit-and-loss statement for the firms at time t under the assumption that profits are never distributed:

$$\dot{S}(t) = L(t)f[k(t)] - L(t)w(t) - r(t)B(t),$$

which, we note for later reference, reduces immediately to

$$\dot{s}(t) = f[k(t)] - ns(t) - w(t) - r(t)b(t).$$

It is the quantity $\dot{S}(t)$ that the firms are assumed to maximize, given the wage and interest rates. This maximization leads, once again, to the conditions

$$f[k(t)] - k(t)f'[k(t)] = w(t)$$

and

$$f'[k(t)] = r(t).$$

The first of these equations may be regarded as a demand-for-labor equation and the second as a supply-of-bonds equation. These two equations may now be used in our equation for $\dot{s}(t)$ to obtain the following result:

$$\frac{\dot{s}(t)}{s(t)} = r(t) - n. \tag{63}$$

The dynamic behavior of this system is described by Equations 62 and 63, together with the equilibrium condition for the bond market, namely,

$$a(t) = b(t). \tag{64}$$

Again, Equations 62, 63, and 64 entail the equilibrium growth equation

$$\dot{k}(t) = f[k(t)] - nk(t) - c(t). \tag{9}$$

Let us now consider balanced growth equilibrium. Along a balanced growth path k is constant by definition and a is constant by virtue of the stationarity of consumer decisions. Thus, from Equation 64, we find b must also be constant and, since $s = k - b$, we conclude that along a balanced growth path s must be constant. It now follows from Equation 63 that $r = n$; that is, the only possible balanced growth path in our new model is the golden rule path.

Let k^*, a^*, b^*, and s^* denote the values of k, a, b, and s, respectively, along the golden rule path. We have already seen (Equation 13) that

$$a^* = [f(k^*) - nk^*]\phi'(n),$$

and since $a^* = b^*$ and $s^* = k^* - b^*$, we get

$$s^* = k^* - [f(k^*) - nk^*]\phi'(n).$$

Thus, using Equation 12b, we obtain

$$s^* \geq 0 \qquad \text{if and only if } \psi'(n) \geq \phi'(n).$$

In other words, the statement $s^* \geq 0$ is equivalent to the statement that the economy is efficient. By the same token, $s^* < 0$ means that the economy is inefficient, so that in the inefficient case our firms reduce to the negative net worth intermediaries that were discussed in sections 6 and 7.[26] Indeed, by identifying the quantity $s(t)$ with the quantity $-m(t)/p(t)$ of section 7, we see immediately that our present model and the model of section 7 are really the same, except that now we are concentrating on the efficient case whereas in section 7 we concentrated on the inefficient case.

We turn now to a brief comment about the actual equilibrium path along which the economy will travel, a path that will not, in general, be the balanced growth path. We shall restrict our attention to the efficient case, that is, to the case $s^* \geq 0$. The first point to notice is that if $s(0) = 0$, then it follows from Equation 63 that $s(t) = 0$ for all $t \geq 0$. In other words, if our firms start out with zero net worth, there is no way for them to get to a state of positive net worth (since payments to laborers and creditors always exhaust the firms' receipts). Thus, when $s(0) = 0$, we find ourselves back in the original model of section 2. However, if $s(0) > 0$, then it follows from Equation 60 that $s(t) > 0$ for all $t \geq 0$. In other words, if our firms start out with positive net worth, then they will continue to have positive net worth. Even so, it may happen that the firms' net worth will become relatively insignificant in the long run, that is, that $\lim_{t \to \infty} s(t) = 0$. By the concluding argument of the preceding section, if this is not the case, then equilibrium will be efficient and (again taking account of only consumers' welfare) Pareto optimal.

9. The End of the World

Many of the properties of the economic system that we have been discussing in this study depend upon the assumption that civilization will survive forever. This fact is duly emphasized, indeed sometimes overemphasized, by both Diamond and Samuelson.[27] Before bringing our discussion to a close,

---

[26] Of course, in the inefficient case our firms can no longer be viewed as maximizing the rate of growth of net worth because by shutting down they can guarantee themselves a net worth of zero.

[27] A viewpoint pursued more thoroughly in [2]. There it is argued that a more pertinent difference between the present dynamic general equilibrium model and the standard static general equilibrium model is that in the former we are explicitly confronted with the fact that a central role of markets is to *intermediate indirect trade* between individuals when direct trade is not feasible and/or desirable (for example, by means of the use of money).

let us, therefore, indicate briefly how the grim prospect of the end of the world might be incorporated in the foregoing discussion. We confess that this remark will be made somewhat tongue in cheek.

The end of the world only matters in the foregoing discussion if it enters into the expectations of decision makers. Now, it seems to us somewhat extreme to assume that all decision makers expect with certainty that the world will come to an end at some definite time, say T. It is more plausible that if the end of the world enters decision makers' expectations at all, it enters in a probabilistic fashion. In other words, the date T on which the world will end is not a fixed number but a random variable with a subjective probability distribution. To make things simple, suppose that each individual's subjective density function for this random variable (measured from his birth date) is the same and given by the exponential density with parameter λ. The subjective probability for each individual of the event that his world will end when he is τ years old is thus given by

$$\pi(\tau) = \lambda e^{-\lambda \tau}, \qquad 0 \le \tau < 1,$$
$$= e^{-\lambda}, \qquad \tau = 1. \tag{65}$$

From Equation 65 it follows that each consumer believes he will be alive at age τ with probability

$$1 - \Pi(\tau) = e^{-\lambda \tau}, \qquad 0 \le \tau < 1,$$
$$= 0, \qquad \tau = 1. \tag{66}$$

Finally, suppose that individuals behave according to the expected utility hypothesis, which simply means that the lifetime allocation problem of section 2 now becomes, from Equation 66,

Maximize $\displaystyle\int_{v}^{v+1} [1 - \Pi(t - v)] \log C(t, v)\, e^{-\delta(t-v)} dt$

$$= \int_{v}^{v+1} \log C(t,v) e^{-\delta'(t-v)}\, dt$$

subject to

$$\int_{v}^{v+1} [w(t) - C(t, v)] \exp\left[-\int_{v}^{t} r(x)\, dx \right] dt = 0$$

and

$$C(t, v) \ge 0,$$

where $\delta' = \delta + \lambda$, that is, the consumer's rate of time preference is the sum of his "pure" rate of time preference and the reciprocal of his expectation of the world's end (measured from his birth date). It is now obvious that the stylized competitive economy in which people have probabilistic expectations with regard to the world's end behaves just like the stylized competitive economy that is infinite with certainty, except that in the former consumers have a higher rate of time preference. Indeed, this may serve as one rationalization for the existence of a positive rate of time preference.

APPENDIX

Our purpose here is to develop the two conditions for recognizing (in)efficiency in the neoclassical growth model that were utilized in the text. As a preliminary we require two definitions.

DEFINITION 1. *Given a positive initial capital-labor ratio k^0, the growth path $k(t)$ for $t \geq 0$ is* feasible *if and only if*

$$k(t) \geq 0 \tag{A.1}$$

and

$$\dot{k}(t) = f[k(t)] - nk(t) - c(t) \quad \text{with } k(0) = k^0 \tag{A.2}$$

for some nonnegative, piecewise continuous rate of consumption per capita $c(t)$ for $t \geq 0$.

An immediate implication of this definition is that any feasible growth path $k(t)$ for $t \geq 0$ satisfies the condition

$$k(t) \leq \max (k^0, \hat{k}) = \bar{k}, \tag{A.3}$$

where the maximum sustainable long-run capital-labor ratio $\hat{k}$ is given by the unique solution to the equation

$$f(\hat{k}) - n\hat{k} = 0. \tag{A.4}$$

DEFINITION 2. *The feasible growth path $k^0(t)$ for $t \geq 0$ is* inefficient *if and only if there exists another feasible growth path $k^2(t)$ for $t \geq 0$ such that*

$$c^2(t) \geq c^0(t) \quad \text{with strict inequality for some } t \geq 0. \tag{A.5}$$

Likewise, the feasible growth path $k^0(t)$ for $t \geq 0$ is efficient *if and only if there does not exist such a feasible growth path $k^2(t)$ for $t \geq 0$.*

An immediate implication of the first definition for the second is that the strict inequality in Equation A.5 must hold over an open interval.

Armed with these definitions we proceed to restate and demonstrate the conditions in the order of their appearance in the text.

THEOREM 1. *A feasible growth path $k^0(t)$ for $t \geq 0$ is inefficient if and only if there exists another feasible growth path $k^1(t)$ for $t \geq 0$ such that*

$$\liminf_{t \to \infty} \int_0^t [c^1(s) - c^0(s)] \exp\left\{-\int_0^s [r^0(x) - n]\, dx\right\} ds > 0. \qquad (A.6)$$

Proof (necessity): This is obvious from Definition 2 and the remark following it.

Proof (sufficiency): Assume that there is a feasible growth path $k^1(t)$ for $t \geq 0$ satisfying this condition. Then there must be some finite time T such that

$$\int_0^t [c^1(s) - c^0(s)] \exp\left[-\int_0^s [r^0(x) - n]\, dx\right] ds > 0 \qquad (A.7)$$

$$\text{for all } t \geq T.$$

Substituting from Equation A.2 into Equation A.7 we derive

$$\int_0^t \left(\{f[k^1(s)] - nk^1(s) - k^1(s)\} - \{f[k^0(s)] - nk^0(s) - k^0(s)\} \right)$$

$$\times \exp\left\{-\int_0^s [r^0(x) - n]\, dx\right\} ds$$

$$= -\int_0^t \{f[k^0(s)] - f[k^1(s)] - f'[k^0(s)][k^0(s) - k^1(s)]\}$$

$$\times \exp\left\{-\int_0^s [r^0(x) - n]\, dx\right\} ds \qquad (A.8)$$

$$+ [k^0(t) - k^1(t)] \exp\left\{-\int_0^t [r^0(x) - n]\, dx\right\} > 0$$

$$\text{for all } t \geq T.$$

Rearranging the latter inequality in Equation A.8 we find

$$k^0(t) - k^1(t) > \int_0^t \{f[k^0(s)] - f[k^1(s)] - f'[k^0(s)][k^0(s) - k^1(s)]\}$$

$$\qquad (A.9)$$

$$\times \exp\left\{-\int_t^s [r^0(x) - n]\, dx\right\} ds > 0 \qquad \text{for all } t \geq T,$$

where the second inequality holds because both $k^0(t)$ and $k^1(t)$ are continuous, while f is strictly concave. We shall utilize Equation A.9 to construct a growth path that is feasible and satisfies the condition of Equation A.5.

First, let

$$\varepsilon(t) = \int_0^t \{f[k^0(s)] - f[k^1(s)] - f'[k^0(s)][k^0(s) - k^1(s)]\}$$

$$\times \exp\left\{-\int_t^s [r^0(x) - n] \, dx\right\} ds \qquad \text{for all } t \geq T, \tag{A.10}$$

which by virtue of Equation A.9 satisfies the inequalities

$$0 < \varepsilon(t) < k^0(t) - k^1(t) < k^0(t). \tag{A.11}$$

Second, let

$$\dot{z}(t) = f[z(t)] - nz(t) - [c^0(t) + c] \qquad \text{with } z(T) = k(T) \atop \text{for } T \leq t \leq T' \tag{A.12}$$

where c is an arbitrary positive number and T' is the first point $t > T$ for which $z(t) = k^0(t) - \varepsilon(t)$, or, if there is no such point, ∞. Finally, let

$$\begin{aligned} k^2(t) &= k^0(t), & 0 &\leq t \leq T, \\ &= z(t), & T &\leq t \leq T', \\ &= k^0(t) - \varepsilon(t), & T' &\leq t. \end{aligned} \tag{A.13}$$

It is easily seen from Equations A.10 through A.12 that the growth path of Equation A.13 is feasible and satisfies the condition of Equation A.5 provided

$$c^2(t) \geq c^0(t) \qquad \text{for } t \geq T'. \tag{A.14}$$

To verify this inequality we simply write out $c^2(t)$ for $t \geq T'$:

$$\begin{aligned} c^2(t) &= f[k^2(t)] - nk^2(t) - \dot{k}^2(t), \\ &= \{f[k^0(t)] - nk^0(t) - \dot{k}^0(t)\} \\ &\quad + \{f[k^2(t)] - f[k^1(t)] - f'[k^0(t)][k^2(t) - k^1(t)]\}, \\ &> c^0(t) + \{f[k^2(t)] - f[k^1(t)] - f'[k^2(t)][k^2(t) - k^1(t)]\}, \\ &> c^0(t). \end{aligned} \tag{A.15}$$

THEOREM 2. *The feasible growth path $k^0(t)$ for $t \geq 0$ is efficient if there exists a finite number M such that*

$$\liminf_{t \to \infty} \exp\left\{-\int_0^t [r^0(x) - n] \, dx\right\} < M.$$

Proof: We shall show that for any feasible growth path $k^1(t)$ for $t \geq 0$

$$\liminf_{t \to \infty} \int_0^t [c^1(s) - c^0(s)] \exp \left\{ -\int_0^s [r^0(x) - n]\, dx \right\} ds \leq 0, \quad \text{(A.16)}$$

which by Theorem 1 implies that the growth path $k^0(t)$ for $t \geq 0$ is efficient. To begin with, we know from the derivation of Equation A.8 that

$$\int_0^t [c^1(s) - c^0(s)] \exp \left\{ -\int_0^s [r^0(x) - n]\, dx \right\} ds$$

$$= -\int_0^t \{f[k^0(s)] - f[k^1(s)] - f'[k^0(s)][k^0(s) - k^1(s)]\} \quad \text{(A.17)}$$

$$\times \exp \left\{ -\int_0^s [r^0(x) - n]\, dx \right\} ds + [k^0(t) - k^1(t)]$$

$$\times \exp \left\{ -\int_0^t [r^0(x) - n]\, dx \right\} \qquad \text{for all } t \geq 0.$$

In order to evaluate the limit inferior of this expression, consider the sequence of points

$$t_0 = \min \left(t : t \geq 0, \exp \left\{ -\int_0^t [r^0(x) - n]\, dx \right\} \leq M \right)$$

$$t_1 = \min \left(t : t \geq t_0 + 1, \exp \left\{ -\int_0^t [r^0(x) - n]\, dx \right\} \leq M \right) \quad \text{(A.18)}$$

$$\vdots$$

$$t_i = \min \left(t : t \geq t_{i-1} + 1, \exp \left\{ -\int_0^t [r^0(x) - n]\, dx \right\} \leq M \right)$$

$$\vdots$$

whose existence is guaranteed by hypothesis. For each point t_i and some positive number $1 \geq \delta > 0$, define the closed interval

$$T_i = [t_i, t_i + \delta], \quad \text{(A.19)}$$

and for each interval T_i define the lower bound

$$\varepsilon_i = \min_{t \in T_i} \left([k^0(t) - k^1(t)] \exp \left\{ -\int_0^t [r^0(x) - n]\, dx \right\} \right). \quad \text{(A.20)}$$

Now because the function f is concave, the first term in Equation A.17 must be nonpositive. Thus, on the one hand, if $\limsup_{i \to \infty} \varepsilon_i \leq 0$, then the limit inferior of Equation A.17 is clearly nonpositive. On the other hand, suppose that $\limsup_{i \to \infty} \varepsilon_i > 0$, so that there exists a subsequence $\{t_{i_j}\}$ and some positive number $\varepsilon > 0$ such that

$$0 < \varepsilon \leq [k^0(t) - k^1(t)] \exp \left\{ -\int_0^t [r^0(x) - n]\, dx \right\} \qquad \text{for } t \in T_{i_j}. \quad \text{(A.21)}$$

Without any loss of generality we can assume that the subsequence $\{t_{i_j}\}$ is in fact the original sequence $\{t_i\}$. On the basis of Equation A.21 we shall construct an upper bound to Equation A.17 for $t = t_i$ that is strictly negative for i sufficiently large.

We know (by hypothesis and the definition in Equation A.19) that

$$\exp\left\{-\int_0^t [r^0(x) - n]\,dx\right\} < Me^{n\delta} \qquad \text{for } t \in T_i \qquad \text{(A.22)}$$

and (by the feasibility condition of Equation A.1 and remark in Equation A.3) that

$$[k^0(t) - k^1(t)] < \bar{k} \qquad \text{for all } t \geq 0. \qquad \text{(A.23)}$$

By combining Equations A.21 through A.23 we can deduce further that

$$\exp\left\{-\int_0^t [r^0(x) - n]\,dx\right\} > \frac{\varepsilon}{\bar{k}} \qquad \text{for } t \in T_i \qquad \text{(A.24)}$$

and

$$[k^0(t) - k^1(t)] > \frac{\varepsilon}{Me^{n\delta}} \qquad \text{for } t \in T_i. \qquad \text{(A.25)}$$

Hence, substituting from Equations A.22 through A.25 into Equation A.17, we can derive the following inequalities:

$$\int_0^{t_i} [c^1(s) - c^0(s)] \exp\left\{-\int_0^s [r^0(x) - n]\,dx\right\} ds$$

$$< -\sum_{j=1}^i \int_{T_{j-1}} \{f[k^0(s)] - f[k^1(s)] - f'[k^0(s)][k^0(s) - k^1(s)]\}$$

$$\times \exp\left\{-\int_0^s [r^0(x) - n]\,dx\right\} ds + \bar{k}Me^{n\delta}$$

$$< -\frac{\varepsilon}{\bar{k}}\sum_{j=1}^i \int_{T_{j-1}} \left\{f[k^0(s)] - f\left[k^0(s) - \frac{\varepsilon}{Me^{n\delta}}\right]\right. \qquad \text{(A.26)}$$

$$\left. - f'[k^0(s)]\frac{\varepsilon}{Me^{n\delta}}\right\} ds + \bar{k}Me^{n\delta}$$

$$\leq -\left\{\frac{\varepsilon\delta}{\bar{k}}\left[f(\tilde{k}) - f\left(\tilde{k} - \frac{\varepsilon}{Me^{n\delta}}\right) - f'(\tilde{k})\frac{\varepsilon}{Me^{n\delta}}\right]\right\}i + \bar{k}Me^{n\delta},$$

where $\tilde{k}$ is the solution to the minimization problem

$$\underset{\frac{\varepsilon}{Me^{n\delta}} \leq k \leq \bar{k}}{\text{Minimize}}\left[f(k) - f\left(k - \frac{\varepsilon}{Me^{n\delta}}\right) - f'(k)\frac{\varepsilon}{Me^{n\delta}}\right].$$

But because the function f is *strictly* concave, the value of the solution to this last problem is positive and the *limit* of the last expression in Equation A.26 is minus infinity.

References

1. Cass, D., "Optimum Growth in an Aggregative Model of Capital Accumulation," *Review of Economic Studies*, Vol. 32 (1965), pp. 233–240.
2. Cass, D., and M. E. Yaari, "A Re-Examination of the Pure Consumption Loans Model," *Journal of Political Economy*, Vol. 74 (1966), pp. 353–367.
3. Diamond, P. A., "National Debt in a Neoclassical Growth Model," *American Economic Review*, Vol. 55 (1965), pp. 1126–1150.
4. Fisher, I., *The Theory of Interest*, New York: The Macmillan Company, 1930.
5. Koopmans, T. C., "On the Concept of Optimal Economic Growth," in *Semaine d'Etude sur le Rôle de l'Analyse Econométrique dans la Formulation de Plans de Développement*, Vatican City: Pontifical Academy of Sciences, 1965.
6. Meade, J. E., "Life-Cycle Savings, Inheritance and Economic Growth," *Review of Economic Studies*, Vol. 33 (1966), pp. 61–78.
7. Modigliani, F., and R. Brumberg, "Utility Analysis and the Consumption Function: An Interpretation of Cross-Section Data," in K. K. Kurihara (ed.), *Post-Keynesian Economics*, London: Allen & Unwin Ltd., 1955.
8. Phelps, E. S., "The End of the Golden Age in Solovia: Comment," *American Economic Review*, Vol. 52 (1962), pp. 1097–1099.
9. Phelps, E. S., "Second Essay on the Golden Rule of Accumulation," *American Economic Review*, Vol. 55 (1965), pp. 793–814.
10. Samuelson, P. A., "An Exact Consumption-Loan Model of Interest with or without the Social Contrivance of Money," *Journal of Political Economy*, Vol. 66 (1958), pp. 467–482; reproduced in J. Stiglitz (ed.), *The Collected Scientific Papers of Paul A. Samuelson*, Cambridge, Mass.: The M.I.T. Press, 1966, Vol. I, pp. 219–234.
11. Solow, R. M., "A Contribution to the Theory of Economic Growth," *Quarterly Journal of Economics*, Vol. 32 (1956), pp. 65–94.
12. Titchmarsh, E. C., *Introduction to the Theory of Fourier Integrals*, London: Oxford University Press, 1937.
13. Yaari, M. E., "On the Consumer's Lifetime Allocation Process," *International Economic Review*, Vol. 5 (1964), pp. 304–317.

XIV

A Turnpike Refutation of the Golden Rule in a Welfare-Maximizing Many-Year Plan

PAUL A. SAMUELSON
Massachusetts Institute of Technology

1. Introduction

In 1958 I showed [8] that, in a model of exponential population growth without capital, the golden rule consumption configuration among different age groups that will maximize the representative man's *ex ante* and *ex post* lifetime utility is that which would be realized if every man faced a competitive interest rate equal to the biological rate of population growth.

In 1965 Peter Diamond [2] added productive (neoclassical) capital to this model and showed that, along with the consumption golden rule, maximization of the representative man's utility requires that the Swan-Phelps (production) golden rule be satisfied, in which the marginal productivity of capital is also equal to the rate of population growth [5, 10].

In 1966, A. Asimakopulos [1] pointed out that Diamond had not mentioned the A. P. Lerner [4] objection to the Samuelson maximum-representative-man biological optimum. Lerner proposed the alternative Benthamite criterion of maximizing a social welfare function that consisted of the sum of the utilities of all individuals in every age period, and concluded that its optimum would be achieved for a capital-less model by an interest rate of zero. Asimakopulos went on to show that this same paradoxical discrepancy was called for even with real capital in the model: for the optimal Lerner-Asimakopulos consumption allocation, a zero rate of interest, $r = 0$, would be called for even if the system were, in terms of production, in a Swan-Phelps golden

269

age—with marginal productivity of capital equal to population growth, $f'(k) = r = n > 0$.[1]

2. Paradox Upon Paradox

It is indeed paradoxical that the policy which maximizes social utility in every period should, when applied to a permanently growing exponential, result in a configuration such that every man who ever lives is worse off. This paradox, like most paradoxes,[2] arises from the infinity assumption involved in the concept of a *permanently* growing exponential. Lerner presumably would bypass the pitfalls of divergent geometric series by insisting that the assumption of a permanently growing exponential is an absurd and monstrous one, involving a Ponzi-game or chain-letter swindle. (If golden-age assumptions are successfully ruled out by Lerner as monstrous, he will in one swoop kill off a sizable fraction of the modern growth-theory literature.)

Presumably Asimakopulos would let the production golden rule, $r = n$, stand in order to maximize the total of consumption to be allocated among all living generations, but would achieve by redistributional intervention of the state the $r = 0$ lifetime allocation of the maximized total. Within the tyranny of a golden-age exponential that had been agreed upon this might be deemed optimal. But many will argue that a limited universe cannot tolerate such a permanently growing state.

Suppose we are to be for a very long time in such an exponential state— say a billion or a trillion years. Is not the indicated optimum of a Bentham-Lerner social welfare function achieved by straddling both stools, equating $f'(k) = r = n$ in terms of production and allocating lifetime consumption as if $r = 0$, thereby getting the best of both worlds? The answer, surprisingly I think, is no.

3. An Odd Result

CATENARY TURNPIKE THEOREM. Even if society starts out with the capital-labor ratio of the Swan-Phelps golden rule age k^* such that $f'(k^*) = n$, and after a long period of time T is to end up in that same k^* configuration, the

---

[1] In this regard, Asimakopulos is almost out-Lernering Lerner, since the latter had said: "The Samuelson plan *would* be optimal if one could really get $2 for $1 [i.e., $1 + f'(k) > 1$] by postponing consumption and reaping the rewards of a positive marginal efficiency of investment." (A. P. Lerner, [4], p. 525.)

[2] Canceling out, so to speak, the above paradox that seems to tell in favor of the Samuelson-Diamond state rather than the Lerner-Asimakopulos one, is the following. Up to *any* instant of time, the L-A state has produced more social utility than the S-D state. And departing from an ever held S-D state in favor of an L-A state leads to an increase in social utility in *every* subsequent period.

path that optimizes Bentham-Lerner social welfare must have k arch above k^*, approaching the Schumpeter zero-interest level k^{**} at which $f'(k^{**}) = 0$, remaining long in the neighborhood of this saturation level, and penultimately reverting back to the S-P golden rule state. Most of the time, so to speak, society must be indefinitely near a zero rate of interest, which means most of the time definitely away from the golden rule state.

Paradoxically, this turnpike theorem requires the system to be most of the (very long) time definitely in the region where Phelps and Koopmans [6] forbid it to be permanently!

To demonstrate this odd result I employ the analysis of my 1965 catenary turnpike discussion [9]. Before generalizing it to discrete time and to lifetime optimization, I shall briefly review its contents.

4. Review of Catenary Turnpike Analysis

Frank Ramsey [7] taught us how to maximize undiscounted utility in a population with stationary population, by having capital grow from its initial limited level to the "bliss" or "turnpike" level k^{**} at which the interest rate is zero,

$$f'(k^{**}) = 0. \tag{1}$$

If population grows exponentially at rate n and society acts to maximize utility per capita, the turnpike becomes the golden rule state at which the interest rate equals population growth, or

$$f'(k^*) = n. \tag{2}$$

Now let society aim to maximize a discounted integral of per capita utility, of the form

$$\int_0^\infty e^{-\rho t} U(c) \, dt.$$

Then the turnpike shifts once again to the level where

$$f'(k^*) - n = \rho. \tag{3}$$

Usually the time-preference rate is considered to favor present over future, with $\rho > 0$ and the infinite integral finite. However, the catenary turnpike theorem deals with long, finite times and applies for $\rho \lesseqgtr 0$. Figure 1 illustrates the alternative cases where $\rho > 0$ and $\rho < 0$ in the special situation where beginning and ending capital is at the golden rule level.

To prepare us for the Bentham-Lerner optimum, suppose in Figure 1 we set $\rho = -n$ and drop the interpretation of it as reflecting subjective time preference by anyone. Instead let $\int e^{nt} U(c) \, dt = \int L(t) U(c) \, dt$ be the total of social utility accruing to the absolute number of all individuals over time.

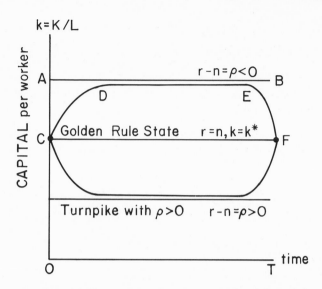

FIGURE 1. Starting and ending the system at the golden rule level of capital, the optimal path arches toward a lower turnpike with positive time preference and toward a higher turnpike with negative time preference.

This means that e^{nt} or $L(t)$ are weighting factors which make it desirable to have more consumption *at a later date* when there are more people and, hence, when less diminishing marginal utility will have been reached for each total of consumption. And now we understand why it pays to go from C to F via the roundabout path through D and E: the path of greater capital deepening makes more consumption *possible in toto* and gives more of it at a later date when there are more people and hence more social need.[3]

The necessary Euler-Lagrange condition for an optimizing extremal to

$$\underset{k(t)}{\text{Max}} \int_0^T e^{nt} U[f(k) - nk - \dot{k}]\, dt \qquad \text{for } k(0) = k_0, k(T) = k_T \qquad (4)$$

---

[3] If we let $T \to \infty$, the optimizing path will approach the upper horizontal asymptote. This limiting path is easily seen to be worse, in terms of individual *and* social utility, than the golden rule path through CF, and is dominated in terms of consumption by the latter, being in this sense Phelps-Koopmans "inefficient." The reason is clear: the limiting path never harvests the late-stage surplus of consumption: it is a case of no jam today and no jam tomorrow, because jam is being put in the bank forever. Needless to say, the integral $\int_0^\infty e^{nt} U(c)\, dt$ is divergent and infinite even when $U(c^*)$ by convention is set equal to zero. Along the Lerner optimizing extremal, $C_T(t)$,

$$\int_0^T e^{nt} U[C_T(t)]\, dt > 0;$$

and

$$\lim T \to \infty, \quad \int_0^T e^{nt} U[C_T(t)]\, dt \to \infty \neq \int_0^\infty e^{nt} U[\lim_{T \to \infty} C_T(t)]\, dt = -\infty.$$

is

$$0 \equiv E_t[\ddot{k}, \dot{k}, k] \equiv \frac{d}{dt} \frac{\partial}{\partial \dot{k}} \{e^{nt} U[f(k) - nk - \dot{k}]\}$$

$$- \frac{\partial}{\partial k} \{e^{nt} U[f(k) - nk - \dot{k}]\}, \tag{5}$$

with the sole stationary turnpike solution, like that of Schumpeter or Ramsey in Equation 1,

$$E_t(0, 0, k^{**}) \equiv 0, \quad \text{where } f'(k^{**}) - n = -n \quad \text{or} \quad f'(k^{**}) = 0. \tag{6}$$

In Figure 1, with the proviso that $\rho = -n$, the higher AB turnpike can be identified as the Ramsey-Schumpeter bliss level, where $r = 0$.

5. Discrete Analogue to Calculus of Variations

I shall sketch rapidly the parallelism between the continuous-time differential equation model of a maximized integral and the discrete-time difference equation of a maximized sum. First, I write down a self-explanatory glossary of correspondences for the traditional one-sector neoclassical growth model.[4]

$$
\begin{aligned}
C_t + \dot{K}_t &= G(K_t, L_t) - \delta K_t & C_t + (K_{t+1} - K_t) &= G(K_t, L_t) - \delta K_t \\
&= F(K_t, L_t) & &= F(K_t, L_t) \\
&= L_t F\left(\frac{K_t}{L_t}, 1\right) & &= L_t F\left(\frac{K_t}{L_t}, 1\right) \\
&= L_t f(k_t), f'' < 0 & &= L_t f(k_t), f'' < 0
\end{aligned}
$$

$$\frac{K_t}{L_t} = k_t, \quad \frac{C_t}{L_t} = c_t \tag{7}$$

$$
\begin{aligned}
\frac{\dot{L}}{L} &\equiv n, \quad \frac{\dot{k}_t}{k_t} = \frac{\dot{K}_t}{K_t} - n & \frac{L_{t+1} - L_t}{L_t} &\equiv n \\
\frac{C_t}{L_t} + \frac{\dot{K}_t}{K_t} \frac{K_t}{L_t} &= f(k_t) & \frac{C_t}{L_t} + \frac{K_{t+1}}{K_t} \frac{L_{t+1}}{L_t} - \frac{K_t}{L_t} &= f(k_t) \\
c_t &= f(k_t) - nk_t - \dot{k}_t & c_t &= f(k_t) + k_t - (1 + n)k_{t+1}
\end{aligned}
$$

$$
\operatorname*{Max}_{c_t} \int_0^T e^{-\rho t} U(c_t) \, dt \qquad\qquad \operatorname*{Max}_{c_t} \sum_0^T \lambda^{-t} U(c_t)
$$

---

[4] Note that the same symbol n is used in both cases but with a small difference of meaning, and likewise for the symbol F and G.

Now consider the discrete analogue of maximizing an integral of the form $\int L(x, dx/dt, t)\, dt$, which is the sum

$$\text{Max} \sum_{x_t}^{T} L(x_{t+1}, x_t, t) \quad \text{subject to } (x_0, x_{T+1}) \text{ prescribed.} \quad (8)$$

Ordinary partial differentiation gives the standard calculus conditions for an extremum

$$0 \equiv E(x_{t+1}, x_t, x_{t-1}, t) \equiv L_2(x_{t+1}, x_t, t) + L_1(x_t, x_{t-1}, t - 1), \quad (9)$$

where subscripts L_i indicate partial derivatives with respect to the indicated argument. If the conditions of Equation 9 are all satisfied, and the L functions are concave, Equation 9 represents sufficient as well as necessary conditions for the maximum.[5]

The generalized Ramsey problem now becomes in discrete form

$$\text{Max} \sum_{c_t}^{T} \lambda^{-t} U(c_t) = \max_{k_t} \sum_{0}^{T} \lambda^{-t} U[f(k_t) + k_t - (1 + n)k_{t+1}], \quad (10)$$

$$(k_0, k_{T+1}) \text{ prescribed.}$$

This entails the extremal condition

$$0 \equiv \lambda^t E(k_{t+1}, k_t, k_{t-1}, t) \equiv U'(c_t)[1 + f'(k_t)] - (1 + n)\lambda U'(c_{t-1}). \quad (11)$$

A stationary turnpike exists for Equation 11 when

$$\lambda^t E(k, k, k, t) = e(k^*, k^*, k^*) = 0,$$

or

$$1 + f'(k^*) = (1 + n)\lambda. \quad (12)$$

This corresponds to the general Equation 3 of the continuous-time model.

For the Ramsey special case, where $n = 0$, $\lambda = 1$, we have the bliss level corresponding to Equation 1,

$$1 + f'(k^{**}) = 1, \quad \text{or} \quad f' = r = 0. \quad (13)$$

For the golden rule state of Phelps-Swan with $\lambda = 1$, corresponding to Equation 2 we have

$$1 + f'(k^*) = 1 + n, \quad f' = r = n. \quad (14)$$

---

[5] If x_{t+1} is replaced by x_{t+h} and we properly let $h \to 0$, we can rearrange the terms of Equation 9 to get the standard Euler differential equation for an extremal in the calculus of variations. Actually it was by such a limit process that Euler first derived his equation.

For the Bentham-Lerner welfare turnpike, where $\lambda^{-1} = 1 + n$, we have corresponding to Equation 6 the Schumpeter-Ramsey bliss level (but with a growing population),

$$1 + f'(k^{**}) = \frac{1 + n}{1 + n} = 1, \quad f'(k^{**}) = r = 0. \tag{15}$$

Note that the extremals of Equation 11 become for this special Lerner case, where $\lambda^{-1} = 1 + n$ and we maximize the absolute total of all persons' utilities,

$$\operatorname*{Max}_{c_t} \frac{1}{L_0} \sum_0^T L_t U(c_t) = \max_{c_t} \sum_0^T (1 + n)^t U(c_t), \tag{16}$$

the customary Fisher [3] relation between marginal utilities and the interest rate,

$$\frac{U'(c_{t-1})}{U'(c_t)} = 1 + f'(k_t) = 1 + r_t. \tag{17}$$

The continuous analogue to Equation 17, derivable from the extremal condition of Equation 5, is

$$\frac{-(d/dt)U'(c_t)}{U'(c_t)} = \frac{-d \log U'(c_t)}{dt} = r_t. \tag{18}$$

In completing this brief sketch of the discrete case, I mention (but do not give the proofs) that all the catenary turnpike theorems (and local stability analysis) of the continuous-time case hold without essential modifications in the discrete-time case. Specifically, as in Samuelson [9], we have:

GENERALIZED CATENARY TURNPIKE THEOREM. If a system is given specified initial and terminal per capita capitals, and maximizes over a long period of time a discounted sum of per capita utilities, it will arch toward the turnpike defined in Equation 11 and spend most of its time in a near neighborhood of that turnpike, before finally moving to the prescribed terminal capital stock.

6. Welfare Optimum of Life-Cycle Consumption

With the analysis of the discrete case in hand, the intralife allocation of consumption can be treated definitely. As in the Samuelson-Diamond model, the persons L_t born (as economic units) at time t consume in the first, working stage of their lives per capita consumption of c_t^1 units, their total consumption in time t being $L_t c_t^1 = C_t^1$. At time t the number of people in the second, retirement stage of life is L_{t-1}, the number born one period earlier; their per capita consumption at time t is denoted by c_t^2, and their total consumption is $L_{t-1}c_t^2 = C_t^2$. The total of all consumption at time t is $C_t^1 + C_t^2 = C_t = L_t c_t$, where the c's without superscripts are precisely the consumptions dealt with in this essay until now.

The utility of any man born at time t is given by $u(c_t^1, c_{t+1}^2)$. Utility *ex ante*, as seen at the beginning of life, might differ from that *ex post*, as evaluated upon retrospective reflection. The difference might be Böhm-Bawerkian subjective-time preference, as for example

$$u = v(c_t^1) + .9v(c_{t+1}^2), \qquad ex\ ante,$$

$$u = v(c_t^1) + v(c_{t+1}^2), \qquad ex\ post.$$

My 1958 model was content to work with *ex ante* utility. However, if *ex ante* and *ex post* utility differ for the individual, a problem is created for the Bentham-Lerner social welfare function. Which shall an ethical observer respect and add up for his social total? To bypass this complication and also the complication if u is a joint function of consumptions in the different stages of life, I shall stick to the hypothesis that individual utility—both *ex ante* and *ex post*—is the sum of identical, independent—and hence time-symmetric—utility functions for each life stage. Always,

$$u(c_t^1, c_{t+1}^2) = v(c_t^1) + v(c_{t+1}^2), \qquad v' \geq 0, \quad v'' < 0. \tag{19}$$

Now, if labor grows exponentially with $L_t = (1 + n)L_{t-1}$, in each golden age when capital does likewise, with $K_t/L_t = k_t$ frozen to constancy, the Samuelson-Diamond maximum utility enjoyed by each and every man is given by

$$\underset{c^i}{\text{Max}}\ u(c^1, c^2)$$

subject to

$$C_t^1 + C_t^2 = C_t = \gamma L_t, \qquad \text{where } \gamma \text{ depends on } k \text{ as in Equations 7,}$$

$$L_t c_t^1 + L_{t-1} c_t^2 = \gamma L_t, \tag{20}$$

$$c^1 + \frac{c^2}{1 + n} = \gamma,$$

which entails

$$\frac{\partial u(c^1, c^2)/\partial c^1}{\partial u(c^1, c^2)/\partial c^2} = 1 + n = 1 + r. \tag{21}$$

This is the consumption golden rule of the biological interest rate, where, for consumption purposes, $r = n$.

But now let us turn to the Bentham-Lerner social sum of individual utilities, defined at time t as the sum of utilities enjoyed by all (identical) people alive in all stages of life:

$$W_t = L_t v(c_t^1) + L_{t-1} v(c_t^2). \tag{22}$$

For each available total of consumption,

$$C_t = C_t^1 + C_t^2 = L_t c_t^1 + L_{t-1} c_t^2, \qquad (23)$$

Bentham-Lerner require

$$\underset{c_t{}^i}{\text{Max}} \, [L_t v(c_t^1) + L_{t-1} v(c_t^2)], \qquad (24)$$

and, hence, equal[6] marginal utilities everywhere of the transferable consumption goods

$$v'(c_t^1) = v'(c_t^2). \qquad (25)$$

Once this good rule is followed, the maximized social welfare becomes a function of the available c_t total, and of course the amounts of population. Specifically, Expressions 22, 23, and 24 lead to

$$\underset{c_t{}^1, \, c_t{}^2}{\text{Max}} \, W_t = L_t w\left(\frac{C_t}{L_t}, \frac{L_t}{L_{t-1}}\right),$$

$$= L_t w(c_t, 1 + n), \qquad (26)$$

$$= L_t w(c_t), \quad \text{if } n \text{ is frozen, with } w' \geq 0, w'' < 0.$$

But note this remarkable fact: the social welfare function $w(c_t)$ has *all* the properties of the $U(c_t)$ individual per capita functions used earlier in the Ramsey-type maximized integrals $\int e^{-\rho t} U(c_t) \, dt$ or sums $\sum \lambda^{-t} U(c_t)$. All of the apparatus of the catenary turnpike can be put at the disposal of Lerner, and his calculated optima can be compared with those of Samuelson, Diamond, Phelps, and others. I shall do so, assuming that the ethical hedonist has no telescopic time preference, knowing that the experienced reader will be able to introduce in a straightforward way such e^{-Pt} and Λ^{-t} functions of social time preference.

We set up the definitive Lerner problem

$$\underset{c_t}{\text{Max}} \frac{1}{L_0} \sum_0^T L_t w(c_t) = \underset{k_t}{\text{max}} \sum_0^T (1 + n)^t w[f(k_t) + k_t - (1 + n)k_{t+1}] \quad (27)$$

for fixed (k_0, k_{T+1}), ending up with the extremum conditions of the type of Equation 11:

$$0 = E(k_{t+1}, k_t, k_{t-1}, t)$$

$$= (1 + n)^t \{w'(c_t)[1 + f'(k_t)] - (1 + n)^{-1} w'(c_{t-1})(1 + n)\}, \qquad (28)$$

---

[6] If older people systematically, *ex ante* and *ex post*, individually, and as seen by the ethical observer, had a greater or lesser utility—as, for instance, $v_2(c_t^2) = .8 v_1(c_t^1)$ now that wine and song have lost 20 per cent of their charm—the analysis would be changed only trivially, since $v_2' = v_1'$ is still implied but with $c_t^1 \neq c_t^2$.

with a unique stationary turnpike defined by the Schumpeter-Ramsey bliss level

$$1 + f'(k^{**}) = 1 + r = 1 + 0. \tag{29}$$

Our knowledge of demonstrated results about catenary turnpike theorems tells us that those who plan for a long period of time T will want to move close to the zero-interest-rate turnpike and stay near it most of the time.

Figure 2 shows, on semilogarithmic paper where golden-age motions appear as straight lines of slope n, optimal paths of total capital (not per capita capital as in Figure 1) as heavy curves. Note that the light AB Swan-Phelps golden

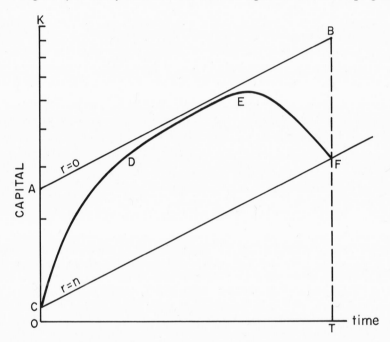

FIGURE 2. To go from C in the Phelps golden rule configuration to F in that same state, social utility is maximized by departing from the golden rule golden-age path CF: instead, if T is large, one should arch (as in AD) toward the zero-interest-rate bliss turnpike, staying near it for most of the time (as in DE), and finally arching down (along EF) back to F. Thus, any golden-age path that differs from the AB golden-age path—like CF, the golden rule path—can definitely be bettered. This is in no conflict with the truth that social (and individual) utility along "efficient" AB is *less* than it would be along "inefficient" CF; it is this last odd fact that explains why *permanent* movement along the "finite-time-efficient" AB path is "Phelps-Koopmans inefficient" in comparison with *permanent* movement along the "finite-time inefficient" CF path. (The reader will realize that the best path from A to F, which he can draw between AB and $ADEF$, involves more utility than either.)

rule golden age is *not* optimal under the hedonist criterion, and this remains true no matter how long T is—a day, a year, a century, or a trillion millennia.[7]

An alternative direct solution to the welfare maximization of Equations 25 through 27 can be given as follows:

$$\underset{c_t^1, c_t^2}{\text{Max}} \frac{1}{L_0} \sum_0^T [L_t v(c_t^1) + L_{t-1} v(c_t^2)]$$

$$= \underset{k_t, c_t^2}{\text{max}} (1 + n)^t \sum_0^T \left\{ v\left[f(k_t) + k_t - (1 + n)k_{t+1} - \frac{c_t^2}{1 + n} \right] + \frac{v(c_t^2)}{1 + n} \right\},$$

$$\tag{30}$$

with extremal conditions

$$v'(c_t^1) = v'(c_t^2), \tag{30a}$$

$$\frac{v'(c_{t-1}^1)}{v'(c_t^1)} = 1 + f'(k_t) = 1 + r_t. \tag{30b}$$

Laissez faire will *not* lead to satisfaction of these conditions, even under perfect competition. From these two sets of equations, we can derive a third set that will be satisfied under perfect competition, namely,

$$\frac{v'(c_{t-1}^1)}{v'(c_t^2)} = 1 + f'(k_t) = 1 + r_t. \tag{30c}$$

Together Equations 30c and 30a would produce the optimum; but perfect competition by consumers who maximize only over their own lifetimes provides only Equation 30c and not Equation 30a. The latter presupposes direct intervention by the state to redistribute consumptions by lump-sum taxation.

7. Conclusion

Even if one rejects the Samuelson-Diamond representative-man criterion in favor of the Bentham-Lerner criterion, one must be grateful to Diamond for his positive analysis of the incidence of internal and external public debt. However, the normative interpretation of debt incidence must be modified under the new criterion.

Thus, Diamond shows that larger internal debt impinging on a situation in which the competitive market produces a golden age with interest less than the rate of population growth, will raise the interest rate. By his criterion, this is a good thing in that it moves r toward the golden rule identity with n.

---

[7] This shows how limited and precise must be the claims for the Phelps-Koopmans notion of (permanent!) dynamic inefficiency, as footnote 3 on divergent limits had warned.

But a Lernerite would have to disagree. Anything that raises the interest rate for a very long period (but not forever) stands to lessen the total of social utility.

Indeed since Lerner himself disbelieves in the relevance of exponentials that grow over infinite time, he would ask Diamond to elaborate his analysis of debt incidence. Instead of asking, "What new golden age will result from this new element of per capita debt?" we ask, "If new debt is created now and maintained afterward at such and such a time profile, what will be the resulting change in total and intrageneration consumption, and in the cumulative total of social utility?" I shall not enter into this matter here.

References

1. Asimakopulos, A., unpublished, Massachusetts Institute of Technology, 1966.
2. Diamond, P., "National Debt in a Neoclassical Growth Model," *American Economic Review*, Vol. 55 (1965), pp. 1126–1150.
3. Fisher, I., *The Theory of Interest*, New York: The Macmillan Company, 1930.
4. Lerner, A. P., "Consumption-Loan Interest and Money" (Reply), *Journal of Political Economy*, Vol. 67 (1959), pp. 512–518; P. A. Samuelson, "Reply," *Ibid.*, pp. 518–522; A. P. Lerner, "Rejoinder," *Ibid.*, pp. 523–525.
5. Phelps, E. S., "The Golden Rule of Accumulation: A Fable for Growthmen," *American Economic Review*, Vol. 51 (1961), pp. 638–643.
6. Phelps, E. S., "Second Essay on the Golden Rule of Accumulation," *American Economic Review*, Vol. 55 (1965), pp. 793–814.
7. Ramsey, F. P., "A Mathematical Theory of Saving," *Economic Journal*, Vol. 38 (1928), pp. 543–559.
8. Samuelson, P. A., "An Exact Consumption-Loan Model of Interest with or without the Social Contrivance of Money," *Journal of Political Economy*, Vol. 66 (1958), pp. 467–482; reproduced in J. Stiglitz (ed.), *The Collected Scientific Papers of Paul A. Samuelson*, Cambridge, Mass.: The M.I.T. Press, 1966, Vol. I, pp. 219–234.
9. Samuelson, P. A., "A Catenary Turnpike Theorem Involving Consumption and the Golden Rule," *American Economic Review*, Vol. 55 (1965), pp. 486–496.
10. Swan, T. W., "Of Golden Ages and Production Functions," 1960 Gamagori *IEA* paper published in K. Berrill (ed.), *Economic Development with Special Reference to East Asia*, New York: International Economic Association, 1964, pp. 3–16.

XV

Stability, Marginal Products, Putty, and Clay[1]

GEORGE A. AKERLOF

University of California at Berkeley

This essay is a proof of the stability of the putty-clay model without technical change. As such, it could be an addendum to several papers: Johansen [2], Solow [4], Phelps [3], Inada [1].

But there is something more important at stake here than a stability exercise. For we have a model founded on the principle that in the short run labor is paid its short-run marginal product; the natural question arises whether in the long run labor will be paid its long-run marginal product. (The role of stability is that both the long-run wage and the long-run marginal product are well-defined concepts.) The answer to the question is a conditional "yes": in the long run labor is paid its long-run marginal product if producers respond to a given wage by building the profit-maximizing machine for that wage rate. Thus, perhaps surprisingly, the chain between short-run marginal products and long-run marginal products depends upon the construction of the proper machines. This appears to be a more tenuous link than in the usual putty-putty models, where the choice of technique is not made irrevocably at the time of construction of the capital good, where the capital-labor ratio can be costlessly changed at the whim of the entrepreneur, and where, consequently, long-run marginal product and short-run marginal product are one and the same.

---

[1] This essay was inspired by Eytan Sheshinski. The author, who is responsible for all errors, would also like to thank Robert M. Solow for valuable comments. The writing of this essay was supported by the National Science Foundation.

At the risk of repetition, but for the sake of specificity and clarity, we briefly spell out the model. Labor is growing at a constant rate λ. There are two production functions: an *ex ante* production function and an *ex post* production function. The *ex ante* production function F is neoclassical:

$$Q = F(K, L); \qquad \frac{\partial F}{\partial K} > 0, \quad \frac{\partial F}{\partial L} > 0; \qquad \frac{\partial^2 F}{\partial K^2} < 0, \quad \frac{\partial^2 F}{\partial L^2} < 0;$$

and F is homogeneous of degree one. Here Q is output, K is capital, and L is labor. Once machines have been produced, it is no longer possible to substitute capital for labor. An old machine has fixed labor requirements for the production of output.

New capital is produced by savings. Savings are assumed to be a constant share of output. The wage rate is the average product of labor on the least efficient machine used; labor is allocated first to the most efficient machines then to successively less efficient machines until it is exhausted. There is a qualification to this process, however. Labor will not accept a wage less than $\bar{w} > 0$. Therefore machines that produce less than $\bar{w}$ with one unit of labor will never be used; and labor will be unemployed if there is not a large enough number of sufficiently productive machines.

Entrepreneurs have stationary expectations; accordingly, they choose the current capital-labor ratio (for newly produced capital) such that $(\partial F/\partial L)$ $(K, L) = w(t)$, where $w(t)$ is the wage rate at time t. (F was already introduced.)

Machines are retired only because their use would be inefficient; and old machines never die or fade away; they live forever. We add one further assumption that is not necessarily indigenous to putty-clay models. This assumption could be stated (imprecisely) as follows: call $k_{\bar{w}}$ the minimum capital intensity used when the wage is $\bar{w}$ (or $f(k_{\bar{w}}) = \bar{w}$). Suppose that at time 0 there is a machine of capital intensity $\hat{k}$, then, according to our assumption, "there is a machine" of all intensities between $k_{\bar{w}}$ and $\hat{k}$. Furthermore, there is some $\varepsilon > 0$ such that "there are more than ε machines" of each intensity between $k_{\bar{w}}$ and $\hat{k}$. This last statement is not quite precise because we are dealing with a whole continuum of machines, therefore the statement "there is a machine" needs some further exposition. We repeat our assumption in more precise form: let $g_0(k)$ be the distribution function of machines of type k. If $dg_0(k) > 0$, or if k is an atom, then either x is an atom or $dg_0(x) > \varepsilon_k > 0$ for all $x\varepsilon(k_{\bar{w}}, k)$.

At this point let us introduce the cast of leading actors in our drama: $k(t)$ is the capital-labor ratio of capital built at time t; $k_{\min}(t)$ is the capital-labor ratio of the minimum capital intensity at time t; $S(t)$ is the economy's total savings at time t; s is the constant proportion of income that is saved; λ is the rate of growth of labor; $f(\cdot) = F(\cdot, 1)$, where F has been introduced already; it is assumed that if F, s, and λ were the corresponding data for a Solow-1956 model, there would be a unique nonzero stable equilibrium k^*.

Then k^* is the positive root of the equation $sf(k) = \lambda k$. For feasibility we require that the minimum wage $\bar{w}$ meet the requirement $\bar{w} < f(k^*) - k^*f'(k^*)$; that is, the marginal product of labor with the maximum sustainable capital-labor ratio is greater than the minimal wage. We also mention $g_t(k)$, which is the "distribution function" of machines of intensity k at time t; and $k_{\bar{w}}$, which has the property $f(k_{\bar{w}}) = \bar{w}$. By "distribution function" we mean that $g_t(k)$ is the number of machines of capital intensity greater than or equal to k at time t, where the unit of machines is the number of workers employed.

We list these symbols for easy future reference:

$k(t)$ = capital-labor ratio built at time t,
$S(t)$ = total savings at time t,
$f(k)$ = average product of labor with capital-labor ratio k,
λ = rate of growth of labor $L(t)$,
$\dot{L}(t)$ = change in labor supply at time t,
k^* = maximum sustainable capital-labor ratio: $sf(k^*) = \lambda k^* > 0$,
s = constant rate of savings,
$w(t)$ = the wage at time t,
$\bar{w}$ = minimum wage,
$g_t(k)$ = distribution function of machines of type k,
$k_{\bar{w}}$ = capital intensity with the property $f(k_{\bar{w}}) = \bar{w}$.

Our object is to prove the following theorem: under the conditions already outlined $\lim_{t \to \infty} k(t) = k^*$. Rather than plunge immediately into a morass of algebraic detail, we present first an outline of our strategy of proof.

The basic relation of our system is the inequation between new jobs, new labor, and capital intensity. If new jobs exceed new laborers, the wage will not fall—because old equipment will be retired; however, if new jobs fall short of new laborers, old equipment will be returned to service (if possible) and wages will not rise. (PROPOSITION I)

Suppose that the economy is producing capital-labor ratios below k^*. These low capital-labor ratios foster enough savings to support their own maintenance for an exponentially growing labor force; or, to be more technical and more precise, suppose that all the machines were of the same capital intensity $x < k^*$, and the whole labor force is working on such capital. Then the number of new jobs created, by using the economy's savings to produce new capital goods of this intensity x, would exceed the new laborers. The result is that if the initial capital intensity produced at time 0 is less than k^*, eventually $k(t)$ must rise. The reader is reminded that $k(t)$ is the capital intensity produced at time t. (PROPOSITION II)

Analogously, if $k(0) > k^*$, eventually $k(t)$ must fall. (PROPOSITION III)

Propositions IV and V are based on the same logic as Propositions II and III. The results are surprisingly strong. Suppose that at time t the number of jobs created just match the new entrants to the labor force. Then $k(t)$ the capital intensity of capital newly produced will fall (not rise) or rise (not fall), within a small neighborhood of t, depending upon whether $k(t) \gtrless k^*$. The reason for this behavior is the "savings" created by the extra output from the new machines themselves.

Summarizing Propositions II through V, either $k(t)$ will cross k^* an infinite number of times, or $k(t)$ will be monotonic after some time t.

Proposition VI duly limits the number of times that $k(t)$ can cross k^*. Here $k(t)$ can only cross k^* once in an upward direction: the reason is that savings generated by producing capital of intensity greater than k^* is enough to supply new workers with jobs on capital of intensity k^*, even though no higher capital-intensity can be permanently maintained.

Propositions VII and VIII show that $k(t)$ does not approach an asymptote $\hat{k} \neq k^*$. This is natural, since for such a case, savings get closer and closer to the savings of a Solow-1956 economy. And in this Solow-1956 analogue the capital-labor ratio approaches k^*.

Again summarizing our results to date: we have found $k(t)$ is monotonic beyond a certain point; it does not approach an asymptote not equal to k^*; it does not approach ∞; it must approach k^*.

With this battle plan in mind, we begin our proof. Before any further presentation it is necessary to deal with a technicality. Here $k(t)$ need not be differentiable, although we shall prove that it must be continuous. At time t, $k(t)$ may have the property that within some neighborhood of t, $k(t + \Delta t) - k(t) \geq 0$, for $\Delta t > 0$. We shall denote this property $\Delta k(t) \geq 0$. It is important to note that $\Delta k(t)$ is not a number but a property of the function k at time t. However, $\Delta k(t) \leq 0$, $\Delta k(t) > 0$, $\Delta k(t) < 0$ have natural and analogous interpretations.

For our purposes $\Delta k(t)$ replaces the time derivative of $k(t)$ at time t. For the reader who does not worry about technicalities, the sign of $\Delta k(t)$ could be interpreted as the sign of $\dot{k}(t)$, if that animal should exist.

We begin our proof with the following basic proposition:

PROPOSITION I.

$$\frac{S(t)}{k(t)} - \dot{L}(t) > 0 \to \Delta k(t) \geq 0, \tag{1}$$

$$\frac{S(t)}{k(t)} - \dot{L}(t) < 0 \to \Delta k(t) \leq 0, \tag{2}$$

$$\Delta k(t) > 0 \to \frac{S(t)}{k(t)} - \dot{L}(t) > 0, \tag{3}$$

$$\Delta k(t) < 0 \to \frac{S(t)}{k(t)} - \dot{L}(t) < 0. \tag{4}$$

The reader is referred to Appendix A for a rigorous proof of this proposition.

Below we present the economics of the situation. (Note: numbers in "proof" refer to Relations 1 through 4 in Proposition I.)

"*Proof.*"   (1) $S(t)/k(t)$ is the number of new jobs. Suppose $S(t)/k(t) - \dot{L}(t) > 0$, then the number of new jobs exceeds the number of new laborers. Therefore old capital equipment must be retired, and the wage will not fall; correspondingly, $k(t)$ will not fall. Expression 2 is analogous.

(3) If $\Delta k(t) > 0$, then old equipment is being retired. Therefore $S(t)/k(t) - \dot{L}(t) > 0$. Expression 4 is analogous.

This first proposition enables us to prove our theorem with minimal effort; we need worry about only three interrelationships: $S(t)$, $k(t)$, and $\dot{L}(t)$. Through the judicious use of inequalities it is unnecessary to maintain a complex catalogue of all the machines on hand.

PROPOSITION II.   If $k(T) < k^*$ for some time T, eventually $S(t)/k(t) - \dot{L}(t) \geq 0$ for some time $t \geq T$.

Proof: Suppose the contrary. Suppose $S(t)/k(t) - \dot{L}(t) < 0$ for all $t \geq T$. In this case

$$\dot{S}(t) \geq \frac{sf[k(t)]}{k(t)} S(t) \tag{5}$$

since the right-hand side of Expression 5 is the savings from new labor placed on new machines; in addition, output may increase by the use of some machines that were not previously in service.
But

$$\frac{sf[k(t)]}{k(t)} \geq \min\left\{\frac{sf[k(T)]}{k(T)}, \frac{sf(\bar{k})}{\bar{k}}\right\} > \lambda + \varepsilon, \quad \text{for some } \varepsilon > 0; \tag{6}$$

where $\bar{k}$ is the capital intensity produced when $w(t) = \bar{w}$. (Here $\bar{k}$ has the property $f(\bar{k}) - \bar{k}f'(\bar{k}) = \bar{w}$.)

Relation 6 is true because $k(t) \leq k(T)$ for all $t \geq T$ by Proposition I and the assumption that $S(t)/k(t) - \dot{L}(t) < 0$.

Combining Expressions 5 and 6, $\dot{S}(t) > (\lambda + \varepsilon)S(t)$ or $S(t) > S(T)e^{(\lambda + \varepsilon)t}$. Eventually

$$\frac{S(t)}{k(t)} - \lambda L_0 e^{\lambda t} \geq \frac{S(t)}{k(T)} - \lambda L_0 e^{\lambda t} > 0.$$

Hence $\Delta k(t) \geq 0$ for some $t \geq T$.

PROPOSITION III.   Analogously, if $k(T) > k^*$ for some time $t \geq T$, then

$$\frac{S(t)}{k(t)} - \dot{L}(t) \leq 0.$$

Proof: Suppose the contrary. Then

$$\frac{S(t)}{k(t)} - \dot{L}(T) > 0 \quad \text{and} \quad \Delta k(t) \geq 0 \qquad \text{for all } t \geq T.$$

Then

$$\dot{S}(t) \leq sf[k(t)]\frac{S(t)}{k(t)} \leq \frac{sf[k(T)]S(t)}{k(T)} \leq (\lambda - \varepsilon)S(t) \qquad \text{for some } \varepsilon > 0,$$

$$S(t) \leq S(T)e^{(\lambda - \varepsilon)t}.$$

Eventually

$$\frac{S(t)}{k(t)} - \dot{L}(t) \leq \frac{S(t)}{k(T)} - \lambda L_0 e^{\lambda t} < 0.$$

Therefore, there is some $t \geq T$ such that $S(t)/k(t) - \dot{L}(t) \geq 0$.

PROPOSITION IV.   If $S(t)/\dot{L}(t) - k(t) = 0$ and $k(t) < k^*$, then

$$\Delta k(t) \geq 0.$$

Proof: We show that $k(t + \Delta t) - k(t) \geq 0$ for sufficiently small $\Delta t > 0$. We do so by estimating $\Delta[S(t)/\dot{L}(t) - k(t)]$ and showing that this is greater than 0. Here Δ means the same thing as when applied to $k(t)$.

Assume $k(t + \Delta t) < k(t)$. We shall show that this is not true. We estimate

$$\left[\frac{S(t + \Delta t)}{\dot{L}(t + \Delta t)} - \frac{S(t)}{\dot{L}(t)}\right] - [k(t + \Delta t) - k(t)]. \tag{8}$$

If $k(t + \Delta t) < k(t)$, then $k_{\min}(t + \Delta t) < k_{\min}(t)$. Also, $S(t + \Delta t) \geq S(t) + \dot{L}(t)\Delta t sf[k(t)] + o(\Delta t^2)$. Here it is greater than or equal to, because in this case old machines have been brought back into service. Also

$$\dot{L}(t + \Delta t) = \Delta t \lambda \dot{L}(t) + \dot{L}(t) + o(\Delta t^2).$$

Hence

$$\frac{\dot{L}(t)S(t + \Delta t) - S(t)\dot{L}(t + \Delta t)}{\dot{L}(t)\dot{L}(t + \Delta t)} \geq \frac{[sf(k)\dot{L}(t)^2 - \lambda S(t)\dot{L}(t)]\Delta t + o(\Delta t^2)}{\dot{L}(t)\dot{L}(t + \Delta t)}$$

$$= \frac{[sf(k) - \lambda k][\dot{L}(t)]^2 \Delta t + o(\Delta t^2)}{\dot{L}(t)\dot{L}(t + \Delta t)} > 0$$

for Δt sufficiently small.

But $k(t + \Delta t) < k(t)$, hence

$$\left[\frac{S(t + \Delta t)}{\dot{L}(t + \Delta t)} - \frac{S(t)}{\dot{L}(t)}\right] - [k(t + \Delta t) - k(t)] > 0,$$

hence

$$\frac{S(t + \Delta t)}{\dot{L}(t + \Delta t)} - k(t + \Delta t) > 0.$$

Therefore, by Proposition 1,

$$k(t + \Delta t) \geq k(t). \quad \text{Contradiction.}$$

Hence

$$k(t + \Delta t) \geq k(t).$$

PROPOSITION V.   Similarly, for $k(t) > k^*$, if $S(t)/k(t) - \dot{L}(t) = 0$, then

$$\Delta k(t) \leq 0.$$

The proof is exactly analogous to the proof of Proposition IV.

The implications of Propositions IV and V are that $k(t)$ is monotonic on one side of k^*, once $S(t)/k(t) - \dot{L}(t) \geq 0$. For if $S(t)/\dot{L}(t) - k(t) = 0$, then $\Delta k(t) \geq 0$ and $\Delta[S(t)/\dot{L}(t) - k(t)] > 0$, where Δ has the same meaning applied to the expression $[S(t)/\dot{L}(t) - k(t)]$ that it did applied to $k(t)$. Therefore $S(t)/\dot{L}(t) - k(t)$ cannot cross 0. And therefore $k(t)$ cannot decrease for $k < k^*$ or increase for $k > k^*$.

PROPOSITION VI.   Suppose $k(T) = k^*$ at some time $T \geq 0$. Suppose $\Delta k(T) > 0$, then

$$k(t) \geq k^* \qquad \text{for all } t \geq T.$$

Proof: Let $\hat{T}$ be the time of first return to k^* after T. We show that $\Delta k(\hat{T}) \geq 0$.

$$\frac{S(\hat{T})}{k^*} = \frac{S(T)}{k^*} + \int_T^{\hat{T}} \frac{sf[k(t)]}{k^*} [\dot{L}(t) + R(t)] \, dt \qquad (9)$$

where $R(t)$ is the (algebraic) number of workers retired from old machines to work on (newer) more capital-intensive machines at time t.

$$\int_T^{\hat{T}} R(t) \, dt = 0,$$

since the net number of workers retired must be zero; all machines in use at time T are in use at time $\hat{T}$, since the wage is exactly the same at T as at $\hat{T}$. From Equation 9 and the fact that $k(t) \geq k^*$ for all t, we find $T \leq t \leq \hat{T}$,

$$\frac{S(\hat{T})}{k^*} \geq \frac{S(T)}{k^*} + \int_T^{\hat{T}} \lambda[\dot{L}(t) + R(t)] \, dt,$$

$$> \dot{L}(T) + \lambda[L(\hat{T}) - \dot{L}(T)] + \lambda \int_T^{\hat{T}} R(t) \, dt,$$

$$= \dot{L}(T) + \dot{L}(\hat{T}) - \dot{L}(T) = \dot{L}(\hat{T}).$$

Actually $\Delta k(\hat{T}) > 0$, since $\hat{T}$ was the moment of first return; if $\Delta k(T) > 0$, then $\Delta k(\hat{T}) > 0$ also.

PROPOSITION VII.   Either k crosses k^* or approaches an asymptote, by Propositions II, III, and IV.

We shall show that $k(t)$ does not approach an asymptote $\hat{k} < k^*$. Suppose the contrary, that $k \to \hat{k} < k^*$:

$$S(T) \sim \int_{-\infty}^{T} sf(\hat{k})\dot{L}(t)\, dt \qquad \left(A \sim B \text{ means } \frac{A}{B} \to 1\right),$$

$$\frac{S(T)}{\hat{k}} \sim \int_{-\infty}^{T} \frac{sf(\hat{k})}{\hat{k}} \dot{L}(t)\, dt > (\lambda + \varepsilon)L(T) \qquad \text{some } \varepsilon > 0.$$

Therefore,

$$\frac{S(T)}{\hat{k}} > (\lambda + \varepsilon)L(T) \qquad \text{for all } T \geq T_0 \text{ for some time } T_0.$$

But this implies that eventually all workers are working on capital of capital intensity greater than or equal to $\hat{k}$. Furthermore, there is a surplus of new jobs over new workers. But then $w(T) \geq f(\hat{k}) - \varepsilon$ eventually for any $\varepsilon > 0$. But for ε sufficiently small, $k(T) > \hat{k}$. Therefore, k does not approach $\hat{k}$.

PROPOSITION VIII. Suppose $k \to \hat{k} > k^*$.

$$\frac{S(T)}{\hat{k}} \sim \int_{-\infty}^{T} \frac{sf(\hat{k})}{\hat{k}} \dot{L}(T) < (\lambda - \varepsilon)L(T) \qquad \text{for some } \varepsilon > 0.$$

This implies that there will eventually be unemployment and therefore k does not approach $\hat{k}$.

Propositions V through VIII imply that $\lim_{t \to \infty} k = k^*$.

1. k does not approach an asymptote $k \neq k^*$.
2. k does not approach ∞.
3. k cannot cross k^* more than two times by Proposition VI.
4. Yet after being on one side of k^* for more than a time T, we find k is monotonic, by Propositions II, III, IV, and V.

Therefore k has no choice: it must approach k^*. Q.E.D.

It is clear from the nature of our proof and our logic that a stronger and more general theorem is in fact true. Given an *ex ante* production function $Q/L = f(k)$ and an *ex post* production function $Q/L = g(k; \bar{k})$, where $\bar{k}$ is the capital-labor ratio originally chosen for optimal production, where k is the *ex post* capital-labor ratio, and furthermore where f is the envelope of the g's, then if labor is paid its short-run marginal product and $\bar{k}(t)$ is chosen such that $f[\bar{k}(t)] - \bar{k}f'[\bar{k}(t)] = w(t)$, this model will also have a stable capital intensity k^*. The specific assumption of fixed Leontief coefficients was by no means necessary for the completion of our appointed task. The reader can quickly verify that Propositions I through VIII will hold with this more general "envelope" model.

Before these results are passed on either as a bequest or as a burden to future generations, some criticism is well deserved. It is a remarkable fact that in the long run almost all workers will be working on capital stock with capital of intensity within some ε-neighborhood of k^*, while an ancient machine whose average product is almost $f(k^*) - k^*f'(k^*)$ determines the wage rate of labor. If all machines die after a fixed period of time, havoc breaks loose in our previously well-ordered model. As Ken-Ichi Inada has shown, it is not possible to have a steady state in such a system. But, at least, we can say something about the difference between Inada's model and the Sheshinski-Kemp contradiction. In the Inada system, if machines of intensity k^* were the only machines produced, there would soon be no machine of average product $f(k^*) - k^*f'(k^*)$. But it is necessary to have at least some machines of this type to maintain a wage w^*, which in turn will induce producers to make machines of intensity k^*.

We are faced with one of those rare situations in economic theory where the difference between ε and 0 qualitatively changes the results. Another example of such a predicament is the decomposability of a von Neumann matrix; according to a famous but fallacious argument, a decomposable matrix is "almost" indecomposable, for tiny ε's could be fed into the appropriate slots to replace 0's.

The reason for the irregularity, in the case at hand, is that the model we have chosen has certain singular assumptions. If we had isoquants that were not quite fixed-coefficient, and if labor were paid its short-run marginal product on the existing capital, it is no longer obvious that the death of old machines would be disastrous for the stability of $k(t)$.

As promised in the beginning, the stability of our system has something to say about marginal products. In the long run we know that the wage will be approximately w^* and all the capital will be of intensity close to k^*. Thus the long-run marginal product of labor is well defined. Since $w^* = f(k^*) - k^*f'(k^*)$, we know that the long-run wage is equal to the long-run marginal product.

Suppose, however, that producers had a different response to a given wage: suppose $k(t) = \phi[w(t)]$, where $\phi'(w) > 0$. Then, if k^* is a feasible solution (that is, if there is a $w^* > w_{\min}$ such that $\phi(w^*) = k^*$), it will be a stable solution independent of ϕ. But, in general, $\phi^{-1}(w^*) \neq f(k^*) - k^*f'(k^*)$. This makes precise what we said in the beginning—producers must build "the proper machines" in order that the long-run wage be equal to the long-run marginal product.

APPENDIX A

We wish to prove Proposition I. By a basic relation of our system

$$L(t) = \int_{k_{\min}(t)}^{\infty} dg_t(x) \tag{A.1}$$

or

$$k_{\min}(t) = k_{\bar{w}} \quad \text{and} \quad L(t) \geq \int_{k_{\min}(t)}^{\infty} g_t(x)\, dx$$

where $dg_t(x)$ is the measure associated with the distribution function of machines of intensity greater than or equal to x, and where $k_{\min}(t)$ is the index of the least productive machine used at time t (or the lim inf of these numbers).

It is immediately clear that the continuity, differentiability, and direction of $k_{\min}(t)$ are equivalent to the continuity, differentiability, and direction of $k(t)$; for the wage is the average product of capital of type $k_{\min}(t)$, or $w(t) = f[k_{\min}(t)]$, where f is continuous, differentiable, and monotonic, and $k(t)$ is a continuous, differentiable, monotonic function of the wage.

To show that $k_{\min}(t)$ is continuous, we calculate its change in value in a neighborhood of time t; we show that this value is small if the neighborhood itself is small.

But certain problems present themselves. Namely, to show the continuity of $k_{\min}(t)$ it is necessary to show that $dg_t(k_{\min})$ is positive for $k_{\min}(t + \Delta t)$ within a Δt-neighborhood of time t. A backward glance at Equation A.1 will show why this last statement is true.

So our argument must be more complex than originally planned. We must simultaneously show that $dg_t(k_{\min}) > 0$ and $k(t)$ is continuous. To do this we proceed by induction. We divide time into short intervals of length $\overline{\Delta t}$. Later in our argument we place upper limits on $\overline{\Delta t}$. We show that $k(t)$ is continuous during the period $n\overline{\Delta t} \leq t \leq (n + 1)\overline{\Delta t}$ if $k(t)$ was continuous up to that time.

LEMMA 1. *$k(t)$ is continuous in the period $0 \leq t \leq \overline{\Delta t}$.*

Our induction property can be shown to hold in the period $0 \leq t \leq \overline{\Delta t}$, (1) by our initial conditions—remember the assumption about $dg_0(x)$—and (2) by the logic which shows that if $k(t)$ is continuous in period $n\overline{\Delta t} \leq t \leq (n + 1)\overline{\Delta t}$ if $k(t)$ was continuous up to time $n\overline{\Delta t}$. We do not try the reader's patience with such an exercise, though he may later wish to check to see that the claim made here is in fact correct.

LEMMA 2. *$k(t)$ is continuous in the interval $n\overline{\Delta t} \leq t \leq (n + 1)\overline{\Delta t}$, and $k(t)$ is continuous for $0 \leq t \leq n\overline{\Delta t}$.*

Proof: We show that $dg_t(x) > 0$ for $k_{\bar{w}} < x < \max[k_{\min}(t + \Delta t), k_{\min}(t)]$. Suppose that this is not true. Then $k(\tau) < \max[k_{\min}(t + \overline{\Delta t}), k_{\min}(t)]$ for $\tau \leq n\overline{\Delta t}$. The reason is that up to time $n\overline{\Delta t}$, $k(t)$ has been continuous.

$$g_t(k) = g_0(k) + \int_{t|k(t) \geq k} \frac{S(t)}{k(t)}\, dt;$$

that is, the distribution of jobs on machine of type k is the original distribution plus the jobs created at times when the capital intensity of machines built was greater than k. Since $k(t)$ was continuous up to $n\overline{\Delta t}$, and $S(t)$ was greater than $S(0)$, if $k_{\min}(t) = k(\tau)$ for some time τ before $n\overline{\Delta t}$ or if $g_0(k_{\min}) > 0$, then $g_t(x) > 0$ for $k_{\bar{w}} \le x \le k_{\min}(t)$. Therefore, $g_{n\overline{\Delta t}}(x) = 0$ for all $x \ge \max [k_{\min}(t), k_{\min}(t + \Delta t)]$ if $dg_t\{\max [k_{\min}(t), k_{\min}(t + \Delta t)]\} = 0$.

This indicates that a massive amount of capital building has taken place since $n\overline{\Delta t}$. For all workers now have jobs on machines of capital intensity greater than or equal to $\max [k_{\min}(t), k_{\min}(t + \Delta t)]$. Thus

$$\int_{\substack{n\overline{\Delta t} \\ k(t) \text{ in use}}}^{t+t\Delta} \frac{S(t)}{k(t)} \, dt = L(t + \Delta t). \tag{A.2}$$

We make three comments on Expression A.2: (1) We shall hereafter consider $k_{\min}(t + \Delta t)$ to be $\max [k_{\min}(t), k_{\min}(t + \Delta t)]$. This will simplify the notation. (2) The integral in Expression A.2 is subscripted by the phrase "$k(t)$ in use," since some capital built since time $n\overline{\Delta t}$ may not be in use. (3) Expression A.2 is an equality since $g_0(k_{\bar{w}}) > 0$.

But Expression A.2 places an impossible strain on the system to produce capital in a short period. $S(n\overline{\Delta t}) \le sf[k_{\min}(t + \Delta t)]L(n\overline{\Delta t})$ since all machines at time $n\overline{\Delta t}$ have capital intensity less than $k_{\min}(t + \Delta t)$. And $k(t)$ in use $\ge k(\tau)$ for $0 < \tau < n\overline{\Delta t}$. Therefore, for $\overline{\Delta t}$ sufficiently small Expression A.2 cannot hold; and therefore, $g_0[\max (k_{\min}(t), k_{\min}(t + \Delta t))] > 0$ or $k(\tau) = \max [k_{\min}(t + \Delta t), k_{\min}(t)]$ for some time $0 \le \tau \le n\overline{\Delta t}$.

It is important to note that $\overline{\Delta t}$ was chosen sufficiently small, independent of $k_{\min}(t)$ or t itself. A closer look at Expression A.2 will indicate why. For a proof of this proposition, see Appendix B.

We know that $dg_t(x) > 0$ for $k_{\bar{w}} \le x \le \max [k_{\min}(t), k_{\min}(t + \Delta t)]$.

We now show that $k_{\min}(t)$ is continuous. There are four cases to consider. We show that $[k_{\min}(t) - k_{\min}(t + \Delta t)]$ is small in each of these cases.

Case 1.

$$L(t) = \int_{k_{\min}(t)}^{\infty} dg_t(k), \tag{A.3}$$

$$L(t + \Delta t) = \int_{k_{\min}(t + \Delta t)}^{\infty} dg_{t + \Delta t}(k); \tag{A.4}$$

Case 2.

$$L(t) = \int_{k_{\min}(t)}^{\infty} dg_t(k), \tag{A.5}$$

$$L(t + \Delta t) = \int_{k_{\bar{w}}}^{\infty} dg_{t + \Delta t}(k); \tag{A.6}$$

Case 3.

$$L(t) < \int_{k_{\tilde{w}}}^{\infty} dg_t(k), \tag{A.7}$$

$$L(t + \Delta t) = \int_{k_{\min}(t + \Delta t)}^{\infty} dg_{t + \Delta t}(k); \tag{A.8}$$

Case 4.

$$L(t) < \int_{k_{\tilde{w}}}^{\infty} dg_t(k), \tag{A.9}$$

$$L(t + \Delta t) < \int_{k_{\tilde{w}}}^{\infty} dg_{t + \Delta t}(k). \tag{A.10}$$

Case 4 is easy. $k_{\min}(t) = k_{\min}(t + \Delta t) = k_{\tilde{w}}$.

We proceed with *Case* 1: Subtracting Expression A.3 from Expression A.4,

$$\begin{aligned}
L(t + \Delta t) - L(t) &= \int_{k_{\min}(t + \Delta t)}^{\infty} dg_{t + \Delta t}(k) - \int_{k_{\min}(t)}^{\infty} dg_t(k) \\
&= \int_{k(t) \text{ in use}}^{t + \Delta t} \frac{sQ(t)}{k(t)} \, dt + \int_{k_{\min}(t + \Delta t)}^{k_{\min}(t)} dg_t(k) \\
&= \int_{t}^{t + \Delta t} \frac{sQ(t)}{k(t)} \, dt = \int_{k_{\min}(t + \Delta t)}^{k_{\min}(t)} dg_t(k).
\end{aligned}$$

Since $dg_t(k) > 0$ in the relevant range, it is clear that for Δt sufficiently small, $k_{\min}(t + \Delta t) - k_{\min}(t)$ must be sufficiently small.

Case 2. If $k_{\min}(t) \neq k_{\tilde{w}}$, it is possible to choose a neighborhood of t such that Expression A.6 does not hold since $dg_t(k)$ varies slowly as does $L(t)$. Therefore $k_{\min}(t) = k_{\tilde{w}}$; $k_{\min}(t + \Delta t) = k_{\tilde{w}}$; and $k_{\min}(t + \Delta t) - k_{\min}(t) = 0$ in a sufficiently small neighborhood.

Case 3. Likewise, if $k_{\min}(t) = k_{\tilde{w}}$ and Expression A.7 is satisfied, it is possible to choose a neighborhood such that

$$L(t + \Delta t) < \int_{k_{\tilde{w}}}^{\infty} g_{t + \Delta t}(k) \, dk.$$

Summarizing these cases, $k(t)$ is continuous for $n \overline{\Delta t} \leq t \leq (n + 1) \overline{\Delta t}$, given that $k(t)$ was continuous for $0 \leq t \leq n \overline{\Delta t}$.

We can now show the truth of Proposition I, using the following formula:

$$L(t + \Delta t) - L(t) = \int_{t}^{t + \Delta t} \frac{sQ(t)}{k(t)} \, dt + \int_{k_{\min}(t)}^{k_{\min}(t + \Delta t)} dg_t(k). \tag{A.11}$$

Expression A.11 should make Proposition I obvious.

APPENDIX B

To show that $\overline{\Delta t}$ can be fixed independently of $k_{max} = \max\limits_{t \le n\overline{\Delta t}} k(t)$ is the second part of this appendix.

The question at hand is what is the minimum time $\overline{\Delta t}$ beyond time t_0 so that workers can all be working on machines newly built since t_0 and with intensity greater than or equal to k_{max}.

First, it is clear that this is an optimization problem: to create more than $L(t_0)$ jobs on machines of intensity greater than k_{max} in the minimum time.

Second, it is also clear that this time is reduced (or not increased) if we assume that the stock of capital at time t_0 contains an infinite supply of capital of intensity k_{max}. It is also logically clear that workers will work only with this intensity. Then

$$\dot{S}(t) = \frac{S(t)}{k(t)} \{sf[k(t)] - sf(k_{max})\},$$

because $S(t)/k(t)$ represents the new jobs created at time t, and $f[k(t)]$ represents the output per worker on new jobs at time t—but these workers must be transferred from machines with average output $f(k_{max})$.

We wish to minimize the time Δt such that

$$\int_{t_0}^{t_0 + \Delta t} \frac{S(t)}{k(t)} \, dt \ge L(t_0)$$

subject to

$$S(t_0) = L(t_0) sf(k_{max})$$

$$\dot{S}(t) = \frac{S(t)}{k(t)} \{sf[k(t)] - sf(k_{max})\}$$

$$k(t) \ge k_{max}.$$

A third transformation of our problem makes it still simpler.

$$\dot{S}(t) \le \frac{S(t)}{k(t)} sf[k(t)].$$

Therefore, if we consider the minimum time to create $L(t_0)$ jobs of intensity greater than k_{max}, where the rule of motion of the system is that

$$\dot{S}(t) = \frac{S(t)}{k(t)} sf[k(t)],$$

and where $S(t_0) = sf(k_{max})L(t_0)$, again we would find a lower bound for $\overline{\Delta t}$.

More formally, given

$$\dot{S}(t) = \frac{S(t)}{k(t)} sf[k(t)], \qquad S(t_0) = sf(k_{max})L(t_0),$$

we minimize $\widetilde{\Delta t}$ such that

$$\int_{t_0}^{t_0 + \widetilde{\Delta t}} \frac{S(t)}{k(t)} \, dt \geq L(t_0) \qquad \text{provided } k(t) \geq k_{\max}.$$

Here $\widetilde{\Delta t}$ will be a function of $k_{\max}$ alone. Thus we write $\widetilde{\Delta t}(k_{\max})$.

Building machines of type $k_{\max}$ increases $S(t)$ by the maximal rate in this system. At the same time it creates the maximum possible number of new jobs, given $k(t) \geq k_{\max}$.

Hence, $k(t) = k_{\max}$ is the optimal control, and

$$S(t) = S(t_0)sf(k_{\max}) \exp \left(\frac{sf(k_{\max})}{k_{\max}} t \right).$$

We see that $\widetilde{\Delta t}(k_{\max})$ is a rising function of $k_{\max}$, since $sf(k_{\max})/k_{\max}$ is a decreasing function of $k_{\max}$. But $k_{\max} \geq k_{\bar{w}}$. Therefore, $\widetilde{\Delta t}(k_{\max}) \geq \widetilde{\Delta t}(k_{\bar{w}})$. Therefore, there is a nonzero lower bound for $\overline{\Delta t}$.

References

1. Inada, K., "Economic Growth and Factor Substitution," *International Economic Review*, Vol. 5, No. 3 (September 1964), pp. 318–327.
2. Johansen, L., "Substitution Versus Fixed Production Coefficients in the Theory of Economic Growth: A Synthesis," *Econometrica*, Vol. 27, No. 2 (April 1959), pp. 157–176.
3. Phelps, E. S., "Substitution, Fixed Proportions, Growth and Distribution," *International Economic Review*, Vol. 4, No. 3 (September 1963), pp. 265–288.
4. Solow, R. M., "Substitution and Fixed Proportions in the Theory of Capital," *Review of Economic Studies*, Vol. 29, No. 3 (June 1962), pp. 207–218.

Selected Bibliography

Allais, M., "The Influence of the Capital-Output Ratio on Real National Income," *Econometrica*, Vol. 30 (October 1962), pp. 700–728.

Arrow, K. J., "Discounting and Public Investment Criteria," 1965 Western Resources Conference, Seminar in Water Resources Research, July 6, 1965.

Atsumi, H., "Neoclassical Growth and the Efficient Program of Capital Accumulation," *Review of Economic Studies*, Vol. 32, No. 2 (1965), pp. 127–136.

Bardhan, P. K., "Optimum Accumulation and International Trade," *Review of Economic Studies*, Vol. 32, No. 3 (July 1965), pp. 241–244.

Black, J., "Optimum Savings Reconsidered, or Ramsey without Tears," *Economic Journal*, Vol. 72 (1962), pp. 360–366.

Cass, D., "Studies in the Theory of Optimal Economic Growth," unpublished dissertation, Stanford University, Stanford, Calif., June 1965.

Cass, D., "Optimum Growth in an Aggregative Model of Capital Accumulation," *Review of Economic Studies*, Vol. 32, No. 3 (July 1965), pp. 233–240.

Cass, D., "Optimum Growth in an Aggregative Model of Capital Accumulation: A Turnpike Theorem," *Econometrica* (forthcoming).

Chakravarty, S., "The Existence of an Optimum Savings Programme," *Econometrica*, Vol. 30, No. 1 (January 1962), pp. 178–187.

Chakravarty, S., "Optimal Savings with Finite Planning Horizon," *International Economic Review*, Vol. 3, No. 1 (September 1962), pp. 338–355.

Chakravarty, S., "Optimal Investment and Technical Progress," *Review of Economic Studies*, Vol. 31, No. 3 (1964), pp. 203–206.

Chakravarty, S., "Optimal Programme of Capital Accumulation in a Multi-Sector Economy," *Econometrica*, Vol. 33, No. 3 (July 1965), pp. 557–570.

Chakravarty, S., "Optimal Savings with Finite Planning Horizon: A Reply," *International Economic Review*, Vol. 7, No. 1 (January 1966), pp. 119–123.

Chenery, H. B., and A. MacEwan, "Optimal Patterns of Growth and Aid: The Case of Pakistan," in I. Adelman and E. Thorbecke (eds.), *The Theory and Design of Economic Development*, Baltimore, Md.: The Johns Hopkins Press, 1966.

Dasgupta, A., "A Note on Optimum Savings," *Econometrica*, Vol. 32, No. 3 (July 1964), pp. 431–432.

Desrousseaux, J., "Expansion stable et taux d'intérêt optimal," *Annales de Mines* (novembre, 1961), pp. 31–46.

295

Diamond, P. A., "The Evaluation of Infinite Utility Streams," *Econometrica*, Vol. 33, No. 1 (January 1965), pp. 170–177.

Diamond, P. A., "Optimal Paths of Capital Accumulation under the Minimum Time Objective: A Comment," Institute of Business and Economic Research, University of California at Berkeley, April 1965.

Eckaus, R. S., and K. S. Parikh, "Planning for Growth: Multisectoral, Intertemporal Models Applied to India," Center for International Studies, Massachusetts Institute of Technology, Cambridge, Mass., April 1966.

Gale, D., "On Optimal Development in a Multisector Economy," Operations Research Center, University of California at Berkeley, April 1966.

Goldman, S. M., "Economic Growth and International Trade: A Study in the Theory of Economic Development," Working Paper No. 90, University of California at Berkeley, May 1966.

Goldman, S. M., H. E. Ryder, and H. Uzawa, "Optimum Patterns of Trade and Investment in a Two-Sector Model of International Trade," Technical Report No. 7, NSF: GS-420, Department of Economics, University of Chicago, Chicago, Ill., January 1965.

Goodwin, R. M., "The Optimal Growth Path for an Underdeveloped Economy," *Economic Journal*, Vol. 71 (1961), pp. 756–774.

Graaff, J. V. D., *Theoretical Welfare Economics*, Cambridge, England: Cambridge University Press, 1957, Chapter VI.

Hamada, K., "Economic Growth and Long-Term International Capital Movement," unpublished dissertation, Yale University, New Haven, Conn., 1965.

Hicks, J. R., *Capital and Growth*, Oxford, England: Oxford University Press, 1965, Chapters 17 and 21.

Inagaki, M., "The Golden Utility Path," memorandum, Netherlands Economic Institute, Rotterdam, November 1963.

Inagaki, M., "Utility Maximization over Infinite Time: A General Existence Theorem," memorandum, Netherlands Economic Institute, Rotterdam, February 1966.

Intrilligator, M. D., "Regional Allocation of Investment: Comment," *Quarterly Journal of Economics*, Vol. 78, No. 4 (November 1964), pp. 659–662.

Johansen, L., "Some Theoretical Properties of a Two-Sector Model of Optimal Growth," memorandum of the Institute of Economics, University of Oslo, Norway, 1965.

Koopmans, T. C., "Stationary Ordinal Utility and Impatience," *Econometrica*, Vol. 28, No. 2 (April 1960), pp. 287–309.

Koopmans, T. C., "On the Concept of Optimal Economic Growth," in *Semaine d'Etude sur le Rôle de l'Analyse Econométrique dans la Formulation de Plans de Développement*, Vatican City: Pontifical Academy of Sciences, 1965, Vol. I, pp. 225–287.

Koopmans, T. C., P. A. Diamond, and R. E. Williamson, "Stationary Utility and Time Perspective," *Econometrica*, Vol. 32, No. 1–2 (January–April 1964), pp. 82–100.

Kurz, M., "Optimal Paths of Capital Accumulation under the Minimum Time Objective," *Econometrica*, Vol. 33, No. 1 (January 1965), pp. 42–66.

Kurz, M., "Optimal Economic Growth and Wealth Effects," Technical Report No. 136, Institute for Mathematical Studies in the Social Sciences, Stanford University, Stanford, Calif., 1965.

Levhari, D., "Essays on Optimal Economic Growth," unpublished dissertation, Massachusetts Institute of Technology, Cambridge, Mass., June 1964.

Malinvaud, E., "Capital Accumulation and Efficient Allocation of Resources," *Econometrica*, Vol. 21, No. 2 (April 1953), pp. 233–268.

Maneschi, A., "Optimal Savings with Finite Planning Horizon: A Note," *International Economic Review*, Vol. 7, No. 1 (January 1966), pp. 109–118.

Maneschi, A., "Optimal Savings with Finite Planning Horizon: A Rejoinder," *International Economic Review*, Vol. 7, No. 1 (January 1966), pp. 124–126.

McFadden, D., "On Malinvaud Prices," Working Paper No. 123, Center for Research in Management Science, University of California at Berkeley, 1965.

McFadden, D., "Evaluation of Development Programs in a General Linear Model," Part I: "A One-Sector Model," Part II: "The Multi-Sector Model," Working Papers Nos. 124 and 126, Center for Research in Management Science, University of California at Berkeley, 1965.

Mirrlees, J., "Optimal Planning for a Dynamic Economy," unpublished dissertation, University of Cambridge, Cambridge, England, 1963.

Pearce, I., "The End of the Golden Age in Solovia," *American Economic Review*, Vol. 52, No. 5 (December 1962), pp. 1088–1097.

Phelps, E. S., "The Golden Rule of Accumulation: A Fable for Growthmen," *American Economic Review*, Vol. 51, No. 4 (September 1961), pp. 638–643.

Phelps, E. S., "A Comment," *American Economic Review*, Vol. 52, No. 5 (December 1962), pp. 1097–1099.

Phelps, E. S., "The Ramsey Problem and the Golden Rule of Accumulation," Cowles Foundation Discussion Paper No. 194, Yale University, New Haven, Conn., 1965.

Phelps, E. S., "Second Essay on the Golden Rule of Accumulation," *American Economic Review*, Vol. 55, No. 4 (September 1965), pp. 793–814.

Phelps, E. S., *Golden Rules of Economic Growth, Studies of Efficient and Optimal Investment*, New York: W. W. Norton & Company, Inc., 1966.

Radner, R., *Notes on the Theory of Economic Planning*, Center of Economic Research, Athens, Greece, 1963.

Radner, R., "Optimal Growth in a Linear-Logarithmic Economy," *International Economic Review*, Vol. 7, No. 1 (January 1966), pp. 1–33.

Rahman, Md. A., "Regional Allocation of Investment," *Quarterly Journal of Economics*, Vol. 77, No. 1 (February 1963), pp. 26–39.

Ramsey, F. P., "A Mathematical Theory of Saving," *Economic Journal*, Vol. 38 (1928), pp. 543–559.

Robinson, J., "A Neoclassical Theorem," *Review of Economic Studies*, Vol. 29, No. 3 (June 1962), pp. 219–226.

Samuelson, P. A., "Comment," *Review of Economic Studies*, Vol. 29, No. 3 (June 1962), pp. 251–254.

Samuelson, P. A., "A Catenary Turnpike Theorem Involving Consumption and the Golden Rule," *American Economic Review*, Vol. 55, No. 3 (June 1965), pp. 486–496.

Samuelson, P. A., and R. M. Solow, "A Complete Capital Model Involving Heterogeneous Capital Goods," *Quarterly Journal of Economics*, Vol. 70 (November 1956), pp. 537–562. Reproduced in J. Stiglitz (ed.), *The Collected Scientific Papers of Paul A. Samuelson*, Cambridge, Mass.: The M.I.T. Press, 1966, Vol. I, pp. 261–286.

Sen, A. K., "On Optimizing the Rate of Savings," *Economic Journal*, Vol. 71 (September 1961), pp. 479–496.

Sengupta, J. K., "On the Relative Stability and Optimality of Consumption in Aggregative Growth Models," *Economica*, N.S. Vol. 31, No. 121 (February 1964), pp. 33–50.

Shell, K., "Patterns of Technical Change and Capital Accumulation," unpublished dissertation, Stanford University, Stanford, Calif., April 1965.

Shell, K., "Toward a Theory of Inventive Activity and Capital Accumulation," *American Economic Review*, Vol. 56, No. 2 (May 1966), pp. 62–68.

Solow, R. M., "Comments," *Review of Economic Studies*, Vol. 29, No. 3 (June 1962), pp. 255–257.

Srinivasan, T. N., "Investment Criteria and the Choice of Techniques of Production," *Yale Economic Essays*, Vol. 2, No. 1 (Spring 1962), pp. 59–115.

Srinivasan, T. N., "Optimal Savings in a Two-Sector Model of Growth," *Econometrica*, Vol. 32, No. 3 (July 1964), pp. 358–373.

Stoleru, L. G., "A Quantitative Model of Growth of the Algerian Economy," technical report, Institute for Mathematical Studies in the Social Sciences, Stanford University, Stanford, Calif., June 1963.

Stoleru, L. G., "An Optimal Policy for Economic Growth," *Econometrica*, Vol. 33, No. 2 (April 1965), pp. 321–348.

Stone, R., "Three Models of Economic Growth," in *Logic, Methodology, and Philosophy of Science: Proceedings of the 1960 International Congress*, Stanford, Calif., 1962, pp. 494–506.

Strotz, R. H., "Myopia and Inconsistency in Dynamic Utility Maximization," *Review of Economic Studies*, Vol. 23, No. 3 (June 1956), pp. 165–180.

Tinbergen, J., *On the Theory of Economic Policy*, Amsterdam, Netherlands: North-Holland Publishing Company, 1952.

Tinbergen, J., "The Optimum Rate of Saving," *Economic Journal*, Vol. 66 (December 1956), pp. 603–609.

Tinbergen, J., "Optimum Savings and Utility Maximization over Time," *Econometrica*, Vol. 28, No. 2 (April 1960), pp. 481–489.

Uzawa, H., "Optimal Growth in a Two-Sector Model of Capital Accumulation," *Review of Economic Studies*, Vol. 31, No. 1 (January 1964), pp. 1–24.

Uzawa, H., "Optimum Technical Change in an Aggregative Model of Economic Growth," *International Economic Review*, Vol. 6, No. 1 (January 1965), pp. 18–31.

Uzawa, H., "An Optimum Fiscal Policy in an Aggregative Model of Capital Accumulation," Center for Mathematical Studies in Business and Economics, The University of Chicago, Chicago, Ill., 1966.

von Weizsäcker, C. C., *Wachstum, Zins, und optimale Investitionsquote*, University of Basel, Switzerland, 1961.

von Weizsäcker, C. C., "Existence of Optimal Programs of Capital Accumulation for an Infinite Time Horizon," *Review of Economic Studies*, Vol. 32, No. 2 (April 1965), pp. 85–104.

Vosgerau, H. J., *Über optimales wirtschaftliches Wachstum*, Basel, Switzerland: Kyklos Verlag, 1965.

Yaari, M. E., "On the Existence of an Optimal Plan in a Continuous-Time Allocation Process," *Econometrica*, Vol. 32, No. 4 (October 1964), pp. 576–590.

Index

Adelman, I., 217
Akerlof, G., ix
Allen, R. G. D., 82
Arrow, K. J., vi, 1, 31, 33, 35, 67–68, 87, 159, 231
Asimakopulos, A., ix, 269–270
Attiyeh, R., 233

Bardhan, P. K., vii, 87
Bator, F., 143, 227
Bellman, R., vi
Bendixon, I. (Poincaré-Bendixon theorem), 77
Bentham, J. (Benthamite criterion), ix, 269–271, 275–277, 279
Berrill, K., 280
Bliss, G. A., vi, 184, 186
Böhm-Bawerk, E., 276
Boltyanskii, V. G., vi, 3, 56
Bolzano, B. (Bolzano-Weierstrass theorem), 76
Bose, S., 117
Brumberg, R., 233–234
Bruno, M., viii, 165
Burmeister, E., 217, 219

Canitrot, A. M., 88
Carter, N., viii
Cass, D., ix, 1, 8, 67, 125, 175, 177–179, 184, 206
Chakravarty, S., 141, 146, 182, 184
Chamberlin, E. H., 228
Chase, E. S., viii
Chenery, H. B., 147, 165, 216
Cobb, H. S. (Cobb-Douglas utility function), 9–11, 33, 43, 83, 115, 152, 226

Dantzig, G. B., 165
Datta-Chaudhuri, M., vii
Delhi School of Economics, 141

Diamond, P. A., ix, 91, 233, 253, 255, 261, 269–270, 275–277, 279–280
Dobb, M., 148
Domar, E. D., 219
Dorfman, R., 182, 192, 224
Douglas, P. H. (Cobb-Douglas utility function), 9–11, 33, 43, 83, 115, 152, 226
Drandakis, E. M., 53–54, 64, 219

Eckaus, R. S. (Eckaus model), 165–166, 172, 216
Eckstein, O., 148
Engel curves, 168, 170
Erdmann(Erdmann-Weierstrass condition), 186
Euler, L., v, 74, 132, 222, 225, 272, 274
Euler-Lagrange equation, 145, 150, 184, 186

Findlay, R., 219
Fisher, F. M., 1, 181
Fisher, I., 145–146, 160, 235, 275
Fomin, S. V., v
Friedman, M., 237
Furuya, H., 228

Gale, D., 182
Galenson, W., 147, 149, 151
Gamkrelidze, R. V., vi, 3, 56
Gelfand, I. M., v
Goldman, S. M., 88, 90
Goldman model, 88

Hadley, G. F., 170
Hague, D. C., 84
Hahn, F., viii, 219–220, 223, 226, 228–229
Hamada, K., 117

301

Hamilton, Sir William R. (Hamiltonian form), 3, 17, 56, 60, 63–64, 120, 132, 205
Harrod, R. F. (Harrod equilibrium model), vii, 53, 56, 59–61, 63–64, 87, 111, 115, 219, 221, 234
Hawkins, D., 206
Hicks, J. R., 14, 53, 82
Hicks-neutral technical change, vi, 28–29, 61
Hurwicz, L., 67, 159

Inada, K-I., 219, 228, 281, 289
Intrilligator, M., 129

Johansen, L., x, 281
Jorgenson, D. W., 196, 206, 211

Kahn, A. E., 147
Kaldor, N., 67–68
Kaplan, W., 209
Karlin, S., 231
Kemp, M. C., 117, 289
Kennedy, C. (Kennedy model), 53–57, 64
Keynes, J. M., 145, 230
Koopmans, T. C., ix, 6, 91, 119, 181, 233, 242, 246–248, 271–272, 278–279
Kuhn, H. W., vi
Kurihara, K. K., 268

Lagrange, J. L. (Euler-Lagrange equations), 145, 150, 184, 186, 225, 272
Lagrange multiplier, 71, 185–186
Lagrange variables, 56
Lange, O., 158, 163
Legendre condition, 61
Leibenstein, H., 147, 149, 151
Leitmann, G., 184, 186
Leontief, W., 165, 191, 194, 196, 206, 211, 216, 288
Lerner, A. P., ix, 158, 163, 269–272, 275–277, 279–280
Levhari, D., 32
Lewis, W. A., 141
Lipschitz system, 6
Lutz, F. A., 84

MacDougall, C. D. A., 117
MacEwan, A., 216
McKenzie, L., 117
Malinvaud, E., 297
Malthusian trap, 111
Manne, A. S., 165

Marglin, S., vii–viii
Markowitz, H. M., 173
Marshallian offer curve, vii, 90, 109, 111
Maruyama, M., 78
Marx, K., 141
Marxian model, 259
Meade, J. E., 13, 234
Mishchenko, E. F., vi, 3, 56
Modigliani, F., 233–234
Morishima, M., 182, 196, 206

Neumann, J. von, ix, x, 182, 195, 211, 226–228, 289
Nordhaus, W. D., vii

Ohlin, B., 130
Oniki, H., 73

Pajestka, J., 143
Pareto, V., ix, 234, 246–249, 257–258
Parikh, K. S., 216
Pearce, I. F., 117
Phelps, E. S., ix, 6, 53–54, 64, 119, 222, 242, 246, 248, 269–272, 274, 277–281
Poincaré, J. H. (Poincaré-Bendixon theorem), 77
Pontryagin, L. S., vi., 3, 7–8, 10–11, 17–18, 32, 38, 47, 56, 73, 92, 106, 112, 120, 181, 184–185
Ponzi-game, 270

Rahman, A., 129
Ramsey, F. P., vi, vii–viii, x, 8, 117, 119, 143, 145, 148, 175, 179, 181, 204, 212, 215, 222–223, 226, 271, 273–275, 277–278
Ramsey-Keynes rule, 145, 179
Ramsey-Koopmans-Weizäcker "trick," 119
Ramsey model, 117, 212
Robinson, J., 6, 194, 223
Rosenstein-Rodan, P. N., 79
Rowan, D. C., 117
Rybczynski, T. N., 79–80
Ryder, H. E., Jr., vii, 47, 181, 184

Samuelson, P. A., viii–x, 1, 8–9, 53–54, 64, 79, 181–182, 192, 198, 212, 233, 253, 255, 261
Sandee model, viii, 165–172
Scarf, H., 233
Schumpeter, J., 67, 271, 273, 275, 278
Sen, A. K., 141, 148
Shell, K., vi–vii, x, 31, 53, 56, 158, 165, 181–182, 184, 196, 200, 206, 230

Sheshinski, E., vi, x, 182, 217, 281, 289
Silverman, R. A., v
Simon, H. A., 206
Skidmore, F., 219
Solow, R. M., x, 1, 31, 141, 181–182,
    192, 196, 206, 211, 219–224,
    281–282
Srinivasan, T. N., 87, 90
Stiglitz, J., 230–231, 268, 280
Stoleru, L. G., 216
Stolper, W., 79
Strotz, R. H., 91
Swan, T. W., 1, 222, 269–270, 274, 278

Thorbecke, E., 217
Tilak, V. R. K., 142
Tinbergen, J., 146
Titchmarsh, E. C., 244
Trirogoff, K. W., vi
Tucker, A. W., vi

United Nations, Center for Industrial
    Development, 141

Interregional Symposium on Industrial
    Project Evaluation, 141
U.S. Department of Agriculture, 70
U.S. Department of Commerce, 70
U.S. Department of Defense, 70
Uzawa, H., 1, 8, 13, 62–63, 67, 72–73,
    80, 87, 90, 159, 182, 219

Valentine, F. A., vi, 181–182, 184
Von Neumann model, 211, 226–228
    see also Neumann, J. von

Walrasian equilibrium, 79
Weierstrass, K. T., 76, 186
Weizsäcker, C. C., von, 66, 119
Wicksell effect, 194, 204, 212
Williamson, R. E., 91
Wise, J., 79
Working, H., 230

Yaari, M., ix